JOHN

ABINGDON NEW TESTAMENT COMMENTARIES

JOHN

D. MOODY SMITH

Abingdon Press
Nashville

ABINGDON NEW TESTAMENT COMMENTARIES:
JOHN

Copyright © 1999 by Abingdon Press

This book is printed on recycled, acid-free, elemental-chlorine–free paper.

Library of Congress Cataloging-in-Publication Data

Smith, D. Moody (Dwight Moody)
    John / D. Moody Smith.
       p.   cm. — (Abingdon New Testament commentaries)
    Includes bibliographical references (p.   ) and index.
    ISBN (0-687-05812-0 (pbk.: alk. paper)
       1. Bible.   N.T.   John Commentaries.   I. Title.   II. Series.
    BS2615.3.S66   1999
    226.5'07—dc21   99-31075
                                                                                 CIP

Scripture quotations, unless otherwise indicated, are from the New Revised Standard Version Bible, copyright © 1989, by the Division of Christian Education of the National Council of the Churches of Christ in the United States of America.

Scripture quotations noted AT are the author's translation.

Scripture quotations noted KJV are from the King James Version of the Bible.

Scripture quotations noted RSV are from the Revised Standard Version of the Bible, copyright 1946, 1952, 1971 by the Division of Christian Education of the National Council of Churches of Christ in the USA. Used by permission.

99 00 01 02 03 04 05 06 07 08—10 9 8 7 6 5 4 3 2 1

MANUFACTURED IN THE UNITED STATES OF AMERICA

To W. D. Davies
and
Paul S. Minear

My first teachers of New Testament

CONTENTS

FOREWORD

The *Abingdon New Testament Commentaries* series provides compact, critical commentaries on the writings of the New Testament. These commentaries are written with special attention to the needs and interests of theological students, but they will also be useful for students in upper-level college or university settings, as well as for pastors and other church leaders. In addition to providing basic information about the New Testament texts and insights into their meanings, these commentaries are intended to exemplify the tasks and procedures of careful, critical biblical exegesis.

The authors who have contributed to this series come from a wide range of ecclesiastical affiliations and confessional stances. All are seasoned, respected scholars and experienced classroom teachers. They take full account of the most important current scholarship and secondary literature, but do not attempt to summarize that literature or to engage in technical academic debate. Their fundamental concern is to analyze the literary, socio-historical, theological, and ethical dimensions of the biblical texts themselves. Although all of the commentaries in this series have been written on the basis of the Greek texts, the authors do not presuppose any knowledge of the biblical languages on the part of the reader. When some awareness of a grammatical, syntactical, or philological issue is necessary for an adequate understanding of a particular text, they explain the matter clearly and concisely.

The introduction of each volume ordinarily includes subdivisions dealing with the *key issues* addressed and/or raised by the New Testament writing under consideration; its *literary genre, structure, and character;* its *occasion and situational context,* including its wider social, historical, and religious contexts; and its *theological and ethical significance* within these several contexts.

In each volume, the *commentary* is organized according to literary units rather than verse by verse. Generally, each of these units is the subject of three types of analysis. First, the *literary analysis* attends to the unit's genre, most important stylistic features, and overall structure. Second, the *exegetical analysis* considers the aim and leading ideas of the unit, deals with any especially important textual variants, and discusses the meanings of important words, phrases, and images. It also takes note of the particular historical and social situations of the writer and original readers, and of the wider cultural and religious contexts of the book as a whole. Finally, the *theological and ethical analysis* discusses the theological and ethical matters with which the unit deals or to which it points, focusing on the theological and ethical significance of the text within its original setting.

Each volume also includes a *select bibliography,* thereby providing guidance to other major commentaries and important scholarly works, and a brief *subject index.* The New Revised Standard Version of the Bible is the principal translation of reference for the series, but the authors draw on all of the major modern English versions, and when necessary provide their own original translations of difficult terms or phrases.

The fundamental aim of this series will have been attained if readers are assisted, not only to understand more about the origins, character, and meaning of the New Testament writings, but also to enter into their own informed and critical engagement with the texts themselves.

Victor Paul Furnish
General Editor

PREFACE

A commentary should inform and assist the reading and understanding of the text. The kind of understanding we seek will be advanced by situating the Gospel of John in a historical setting, or settings, and asking how it would have been read and heard there. The question of what the author intended to say to his readers is not a bad or misleading one, although it may be too simple. For example, there may have been more than one author, or the author may have worked over his text more than once as his goals shifted. Moreover, the meaning of a text cannot be confined to what an author intended.

Commentaries offer background information relevant to the reading of a text as well as a coherent interpretation of the text. Obviously, for a commentary of limited scope such as this, the latter is a more feasible goal, but this does not obviate the necessity of conveying essential information. Thus, "word" *(logos)* must be shown to be a term with a significant background and range of meaning in ancient Greek philosophical and religious circles, as well as in biblical and later Jewish texts. Background or milieu is thus crucial for interpretation. Of first importance, however, for the interpretation of the Gospel of John, or almost any document, is the shape, character, and content of the document itself. Then one must consider the closely related Letters of John, and sometimes the book of Revelation. The events, themes, and data that John shares with other NT or early Christian writings will likely prove relevant. John also frequently quotes, or alludes to, Scripture, and the Gospel's use of Scripture is also important for our understanding. Finally, as in the case of *logos,* the broader Jewish and hellenistic culture must be taken into account.

Any commentary stands on the shoulders of its predecessors and takes as well established certain positions or perspectives set out in groundbreaking works. My purpose is not to enter into dialogue with scholarly forebears and contemporaries, but to make their achievements accessible to the serious reader and student. Several established commentators have continued to be most helpful to me: Rudolf Bultmann (1971); Raymond E. Brown (1966, 1970); and C. K. Barrett (1978). For his careful exegesis as well as astute articulation of more conservative positions, I have also found D. A. Carson (1991) quite valuable. Rudolf Schnackenburg (1968–1982) I have usually turned to later, but often. Among recent commentaries I find Gail R. O'Day's (1995) most congenial. The scope of her commentary is similar to this one, although her purpose and focus are somewhat different.

J. Louis Martyn's groundbreaking work, *History and Theology in the Fourth Gospel* (1979), has been of fundamental importance to my understanding of John. Both his work and Raymond E. Brown's (*Community of the Beloved Disciple*, 1979, and *The Epistles of John*, 1982; in addition to his commentary on the Gospel) have changed and shaped the direction of Johannine studies in our generation. John Ashton's *Understanding the Fourth Gospel* (1991), which brings together in an imaginative and fruitful way the work of Bultmann and Martyn, did for this generation what C. H. Dodd's *The Interpretation of the Fourth Gospel* (1953) had done for an earlier one. R. Alan Culpepper's *Anatomy of the Fourth Gospel* (1983) introduced us to new perspectives on reading and interpretation that New Testament exegetes cannot ignore. While I continue to believe, along with Percival Gardner-Smith (1938), Dodd (1963), and Robert Thomson Fortna (1970, 1988), that John knew and used important traditions or sources independent of the other canonical Gospels, Frans Neirynck (1992) and his Louvain colleagues have made us again take seriously the question of John and the Synoptics, as I believe this commentary will show. Naturally, I have also relied on such tools as the twenty-seventh edition of *Nestle-Aland* (1993), Walter Bauer's lexicon (1979), Robert Kysar's summaries of Johannine scholarship (1975, 1985), as well as those of John Ashton (1991, 3-117) and Paul N.

Anderson (1996, 17-69), and the bibliographies of Edward Malatesta (1967) and Gilbert Van Belle (1988).

My colleagues on the ANTC Editorial Board, presided over by Victor Furnish, invited me to participate in the series as the author of this volume. Victor has continued to make his good judgments and advice available to me, as he did when we were graduate students together decades ago. I am grateful to him and to other members of the ANTC board, as well as to other ANTC authors from whom I have learned.

For the most part this commentary was written while I was teaching the Gospel of John to theological students at Duke Divinity School. Their thoughtful responses have been encouraging and stimulating. Throughout the process of writing I was greatly helped by my graduate assistant, Diana M. Swancutt, a Ph.D. candidate in New Testament at Duke. She made helpful suggestions and saved me from some embarrassing omissions or errors. Not least, she made the index. At points Jane Allen Smith ably represented the intelligent and informed but nonprofessional reader for whom this series is intended, as I tested out what I had written on her. She is responsible for some significant changes. The dedication expresses my long-standing and profound gratitude to professors W. D. Davies and Paul S. Minear, who were my first teachers of New Testament at Duke and Yale respectively. Scholars of outstanding accomplishment, if differing approaches and methods, they are both great teachers who have always possessed a common commitment to the importance of the theological subject matter of the New Testament.

Inasmuch as I continue to write mostly in the old-fashioned way, Mrs. Gail Chappell assisted me enormously in keying this commentary into the word processor and then making numerous changes as I marked them on hard copy.

Finally, a sabbatical leave from the University, recommended by Dean L. Gregory Jones and approved by Provost John Strohbehn, made the completion of this project possible. I am also grateful to them.

D. Moody Smith

LIST OF ABBREVIATIONS

1 Enoch	Ethiopic *Book of Enoch*
1QH	*Thanksgiving Hymns* (Qumran Cave 1)
1QM	*War Scroll* (Qumran Cave 1)
1QS	*Rule of the Community* (Qumran Cave 1)
CD	Cairo text of the *Damascus Document*
4Q246	*Aramaic Apocalypse*
1 [2] Apol.	Justin Martyr, *First [Second] Apology*
1 [2] Clem.	*First [Second] Clement*
2 Apoc. Bar.	*Syriac Apocalypse of Baruch*
AB	Anchor Bible
'Abot	*Abot*
Adv. Haer.	Irenaeus, *Against Heresies*
AnBib	Analecta biblica
ANF	The Ante-Nicene Fathers
ANRW	*Aufstieg und Niedergang der römischen Welt*
Ant.	Josephus, *The Antiquities of the Jews*
ANTC	Abingdon New Testament Commentaries
Barn.	*Barnabas*
BBET	Beiträge zur biblischen Exegese und Theologie
BETL	Bibliotheca ephemeridum theologicarum lovaniensium
CBQ	*Catholic Biblical Quarterly*
Conf. Ling.	Philo, *On the Confusion of Tongues*
Dial. Sav.	*Dialogue of the Savior*
Dial. Trypho	Justin Martyr, *Dialogue with Trypho*
Did.	*Didache*

EGJ	*Exploring the Gospel of John in Honor of D. Moody Smith.* Edited by R. Alan Culpepper and C. Clifton Black. Louisville: Westminster John Knox, 1996.
Gaium	Philo, *The Embassy to Gaius*
Gen. Rab.	*Genesis Rabbah*
Gos. Pet.	*Gospel of Peter*
Gos. Thom.	*Gospel of Thomas*
Hist. Eccl.	Eusebius, *The History of the Church*
HTCNT	Herder's Theological Commentary on the New Testament
IBC	Interpretation: A Bible Commentary for Teaching and Preaching
IDB	G.A. Buttrick (ed.), *Interpreter's Dictionary of the Bible*
IDBSup	Supplementary volume to *IDB*
Ign. *Rom.*	Ignatius, *Letter to the Romans*
Ign. *Smyrn.*	Ignatius, *Letter to the Smyrnaeans*
Int	*Interpretation*
IRT	Issues in Religion and Theology
JBL	*Journal of Biblical Literature*
JSNTSup	Journal for the Study of the New Testament—Supplement Series
JTC	*Journal for Theology and the Church*
J.W.	Josephus, *The Jewish War*
Ker.	*Keritot*
Ketub.	*Ketubbot*
KJV	King James Version
LCL	Loeb Classical Library
LXX	Septuagint
m.	*Mishnah*
MeyerK	H. A. W. Meyer, Kritisch-exegetischer Kommentar über das Neue Testament
NCB	New Century Bible
Ned.	*Nedarim*
NIB	*New Interpreter's Bible*

NICNT	New International Commentary on the New Testament
NIV	*The Holy Bible, New International Version*
NovTSup	Novum Testamentum, Supplements
NRSV	New Revised Standard Version
NTL	New Testament Library
NTS	*New Testament Studies*
Odes Sol.	*Odes of Solomon*
OTP	J. H. Charlesworth (ed.), *The Old Testament Pseudepigrapha*
Pol. Phil.	Polycarp, *Letter to the Philippians*
Post. Cain	Philo, *On the Posterity and Exile of Cain*
Pss. Sol.	*Psalms of Solomon*
REB	*The Revised English Bible*
Rosh HaSh.	*Rosh Hashanah*
Sanh.	*Sanhedrin*
Shab.	*Shabbat*
SBLTT	SBL Texts and Translations
SJT	*Scottish Journal of Theology*
SNTSMS	Society for New Testament Studies Monograph Series
Somn.	Philo, *On Dreams*
TBü	Theologische Bücherei
TDNT	G. Kittel and G. Friedrich (eds.), *Theological Dictionary of the New Testament*
WBC	Word Biblical Commentary
WUNT	Wissenschaftliche Untersuchungen zum Neuen Testament
ZNW	*Zeitschrift für die neutestamentliche Wissenschaft*

INTRODUCTION

STRUCTURE, GENRE, AND STYLE

L ike the other canonical Gospels, the Gospel of John is a narrative of Jesus' ministry. The others coincide so closely in outline, content, and wording, that they are known as the synoptic Gospels. They see the ministry of Jesus together, as the Greek-based term "synoptic" implies. John, *The Maverick Gospel* (Kysar 1993), differs, as we shall see, in all those respects. Yet the common factors are sufficient to ensure most readers that the narrative concerns the same Jesus, a Jewish teacher who performed amazing deeds, encountered opposition from other religious leaders, and was eventually put to death with the cooperation of Roman and Jewish authorities at a Passover in Jerusalem when Pontius Pilate was governor of Judea.

All the canonical Gospels divide the story of Jesus into a public ministry and a passion week. In the Synoptics the public ministry takes place in Galilee and seems to last for a year or less. Jesus then goes to Jerusalem for the one annual Passover Feast, at which he is arrested, tried, and executed. In John, however, there are three different Passovers (2:13; 6:4; 11:55), indicating a ministry of between two and three years. Other Jewish feasts that Jesus attended are also mentioned (5:1; 10:22), and Jesus spends much time in Jerusalem before the final Passover. Yet the division between public ministry and passion is still observed, and the latter becomes the occasion of Jesus' long conversations with his disciples, which are without close precedent in the other Gospels.

Accordingly, the Gospel of John falls into two major parts, preceded by an introduction and followed by an epilogue. The first part (chaps. 2–12), the public ministry, is variously called the Book of Signs (Dodd 1953, 290-91, 297-389), because the account seems to center on Jesus' deeds, or the Revelation of the Glory before the World (Bultmann 1971, 111-454). The second part (chaps. 13-20) is then the Book of the Passion (Dodd 1953, 290-91, 390-443) or the Revelation of the Glory before the Community (Bultmann 1971, 457-699; cf. Bultmann 1955, 49-69). The introduction (chap. 1), consisting of the prologue (1:1-18) and the several episodes of the calling of the disciples (1:19-51), is integral to the Gospel, although some commentators have suggested that the prologue may have been added after the Gospel was basically written, rather than having been composed first. The epilogue (chap. 21) is pretty clearly a later addition to the Gospel, although no existing manuscript omits it.

Although the presentation of Jesus in John differs from the Synoptics much more than they differ among themselves, the Gospels, taken together display a notable general similarity and distinctiveness. Interpreters have, however, wrestled with the question of their literary genre or form. Are the Gospels to be placed in the genre ancient *lives (bioi)* or are they sufficiently distinctive so as to constitute a separate genre? Early in this century, and with the rise of form criticism, the latter view became dominant, typified in the influential article of K. L. Schmidt (1923) on the place of the Gospels in the general history of literature. Schmidt argued that the Gospels were not literature at all properly speaking. (They are *Kleinliteratur* not *Hochliteratur,* he wrote, in a distinction that became famous.) Their authors were not literary personalities *(Schriftstellerpersönlichkeiten).*

Obviously, Schmidt's position needed qualification, particularly insofar as Luke and John are concerned (cf. Luke 1:1-3; John 21:24-25). Indeed, John fell outside his purview. Moreover, genre is a matter of reader perception as well as authorial attention or lack of it. Most contemporaries probably would have read the Gospels thinking that they were reading ancient *lives,* despite their many distinctive features. Yet the form-critical movement, which Schmidt represents, rightly emphasized the importance of the Gospels' distinctively religious, cultic function, which to a considerable extent determined their shape and content. (On the recognition of the Gospels as *lives, bioi,* see Talbert 1977, and more recently Burridge 1992.)

It is perhaps worth noting that when they were composed the Gospels were not called by that name. Ancient manuscripts had the title "the Gospel" at the head of all four, and then "According to Matthew," and so forth. "The Gospel" obviously meant "the good news" (as the NRSV translates), that is, the Christian message, and was not the designation of a literary genre. Indeed, at mid–second century Justin Martyr characteristically refers to the synoptic Gospels as the "memoirs" *(apomnēmoneumata)* of the apostles; only three times does he call them Gospels (Koester 1990, 37-41). Only in the latter part of the second century did the traditional usage, "Gospels," become common (Koester 1990, 24).

The Gospel of John is written in an elevated but simple koine (common or popular) Greek, with the smallest vocabulary of any canonical Gospel. Yet its style is impressive; with reason Clifton Black has spoken of its "grandeur" (Black 1996, 220-239). John is somewhat longer than the Gospel of Mark, but shorter than either Matthew or Luke. In vocabulary and style it manifests a strong relationship to the three Epistles or Letters of John, especially 1 John. The Jesus of John sounds less like the Jesus of the synoptic tradition than like the author(s) of these letters. The Greek of this Gospel has sometimes been described as semitizing, that is, similar to a Semitic language, especially Hebrew, the language of scripture, or Aramaic, the spoken language of Jesus. Yet the characteristic features of John's style can also be found in common Greek letters and similar documents dating from the same period (Colwell 1931).

Because of the elevated style, the philosophical tone of parts like the prologue, the profound differences from the synoptic Gospels, and especially the fact that Jesus is set apart from "the Jews" as if he were not Jewish, John was once thought the most hellenistic or Greek of the Gospels. More recent discoveries have, however, shown that John's contacts and involvement with Judaism are deep and essential to its full and proper understanding (see below, pp. 34-38).

INTRODUCTION

AUTHORSHIP

As in the Gospel of Luke (1:1-4), the question of authorship is raised in the text of the Gospel of John itself, quite clearly in 21:24, probably in 19:35, and possibly even in 1:14. Perhaps because John is so different from the other Gospels, it became widely accepted as a part of Christian Scripture only in the belief that it was written by an authoritative figure, one of the twelve disciples of Jesus, namely John the son of Zebedee, whom tradition holds to be the author also of the three letters of John as well as the book of Revelation (see Culpepper 1994). Thus the Gospel's authority has from very early times been related to the question of its authorship.

As we see, tradition has long supplied the answer that gives this Gospel its name. Ancient manuscripts bear the title "According to John" *(KATA IŌANNĒN)*. As far as we know, this John has always been taken to be the disciple of Jesus, the Son of Zebedee. Yet in the late–second century, Irenaeus of Lyons, one of the earliest Christian authors to name him as author refers to John only as "the disciple of the Lord." By the time of Irenaeus, Tatian, who made a no longer extant harmony of the Gospels called the *Diatessaron*, had just incorporated the Gospel of John into his work.

When the Fourth Gospel, as it is often called, is clearly cited as authoritative, that is, from the time of Irenaeus on down, it is called the Gospel of John. Yet in the early and mid–second century there are traces of this Gospel, or allusions to it, in other writers, although it is not named. For example, Justin Martyr, at mid–second century seems to quote John 3:5 (*1 Apol.* 61), but does not cite his source, nor apply to it the term *memoirs (apomnēmoneu-mata)* of the apostles, which he uses when referring to the synoptic Gospels. In the early second century writings of Ignatius of Antioch, there are also apparent allusions to Johannine themes. For example, in Ign. *Rom.* 7:1-3 we find water (John 4:10; 7:38), Jesus as bread (John 6:33), and Jesus' blood (John 6:53), as well as love and the world, which are pervasive themes in John. Later than Ignatius, but earlier than Justin, one finds an apparent reference to the Johannine Epistles (either 1 John 4:2-3 or 2 John 7) in Polycarp's *Letter to the Philippians* (7:1). The *Odes of Solomon* (for example, 7:6-7; 8:8, 12) seem to presuppose John's idea of the incarnation of God in Jesus or at least use theological terms familiar to us from this Gospel. Yet the Gospel is never cited in the *Odes,* and the date of these early Jewish-Christian hymns is uncertain. It is even conceivable that they are not later than the Gospel (Charlesworth 1990, 107-36, especially 124-25).

Yet we know that the Gospel of John existed before the mid-point of the second century. An early fragment of chapter 18 (designated P[52]) is dated by paleographers to the second quarter of the second century (125–150). Moreover, the Gnostic *Gospel of Truth* (ca. 150) seems to presume knowledge of John, and Irenaeus himself disputed earlier Valentinian Gnostic interpretations of John's prologue in his treatise *Against Heresies* (3.11.1-6). A few decades later, the learned theologian and exegete Origen in his commentary debated the interpretation of the Fourth Gospel with an earlier, Gnostic commentator named Heracleon, who wrote at mid–second century or a little after. Interestingly, although Origen disagrees with Heracleon and corrects or refutes him on points of interpretation, he apparently does not disagree on the question of authorship. Presumably, Heracleon, like Origen, accepted this Gospel as the work of John.

It is sometimes suggested (e.g., J. N. Sanders 1943) that John did not emerge in the favor of orthodox Christians until about the end of the second century, when interpreters like Irenaeus and Origen wrested it from the hands of heterodox Christians. There may be an element of truth in this, although some early Christians seem to have had doubts about the Fourth Gospel just because it was so different from the Synoptics, which were already well established (see Joseph D. Smith 1979). Only under the patronage of the apostle John did this rather different Gospel gain widespread, and eventually universal, acceptance among Christians.

When one examines the Fourth Gospel itself, however, it becomes apparent that although the question of authorship is raised, and at least a close relationship to an eyewitness is claimed, the name of that author or eyewitness is never given. We may conclude that he is John, but that is because of the strength of the synoptic, not Johannine, tradition. By a process of elimination (not Peter, not James) one arrives at John as the most likely source of this Gospel. John the son of Zebedee does indeed play a prominent role in the synoptic Gospels, as well as in the early chapters of Acts, but he is never named in John (cf. however, John 21:2, where the sons of Zebedee are mentioned without being named). Of course, the Beloved Disciple appears at crucial points in the Fourth Gospel, and is named as the authorizing witness, if not the author, in 21:24. Yet if we assume that he is John, that again is because of the strength of the synoptic, and church, tradition. He is never named as such in the Fourth Gospel.

In fact, exactly those episodes in which John the son of Zebedee is present in Mark, or the Synoptics generally, from the healing of Peter's mother-in-law to the Garden of Gethsemane, are absent from the Gospel of John (see Mark 1:16-20, 29-31; 3:13-19; 5:35-43; 9:2-8; 10:35-41; 13:3; 14:32-42; also Luke 22:7-13, where uniquely Peter and John are mentioned, is missing from the Fourth Gospel). Strangely, John would have omitted the accounts involving himself but could nevertheless refer to himself as the Beloved Disciple. This is possible, but a little hard to imagine. Once the long-dominant church tradition that identifies John the son of Zebedee with the Beloved Disciple, and hence with the author of the Fourth Gospel, is bracketed out of consideration, it becomes apparent that there are at least as many reasons for doubting Johannine authorship as for embracing it.

Not surprisingly, scholars sometimes ask whether the tradition of authorship by John the son of Zebedee is a case of mistaken identity. Was the Beloved Disciple, who appears only in Jerusalem and not at all in Galilee (obviously the home region of John the son of Zebedee whom Jesus found working as a fisherman on the Sea of Galilee), a Judean disciple or associate of Jesus? The fourth-century church historian Eusebius of Caesarea quotes an earlier Christian author, Papias (fl. 125–150?) to the effect that there was another John, John the Elder, who had known and heard Jesus (*Hist. Eccl.* 3.39.3-7). (Interestingly, the author of 2 and 3 John identifies himself as "the Elder.") Apparently the graves of two Johns were known to exist at Ephesus. Was the Elder John (or some other Jerusalem disciple) the Beloved Disciple and the author or authority of the Johannine witness and tradition? This intriguing possibility has been embraced by more than one modern scholar (most recently Hengel 1989, 1993; cf. also Cullmann 1979, 63-85), but it is at best a reasonable conjecture based on bits and pieces of evidence. In the nature of the case the connections have to be supplied.

This commentary will not be predicated on the traditional ascription of authorship to John the apostle or to any John. On the other hand, the ascription of the Gospel to some authoritative witness is clearly a part of the document as we have received it, and must be dealt with seriously. John is certainly not history or biography in the modern sense of those terms. Yet John may contain historical information, even at those points where it departs from the other Gospels. When all is said and done, however, it must be remembered that John's references to history and the work of an eyewitness serve a theological purpose. On the one hand, this does not mean that they are historically baseless. On the other, they cannot be taken as a general confirmation of what we would call the historicity of this Gospel.

COMPOSITION AND SOURCES

There are reasons for thinking that the Gospel of John once existed in an earlier, probably briefer, form and has been edited, augmented, and perhaps rearranged. Moreover, its obvious similarities to the Synoptics, as well as differences, raise the question of whether John knew and used them. If not, what were his sources?

Evidence of a literary process of development is plentiful. Chapter 21 is apparently a later addition, for with the colophon of 20:30-31 the Gospel would seem to come to an end. Yet here is an additional chapter, an epilogue, with a quite similar colophon (21:24-25). By the same token, 14:31 seems to end the farewell discourse of Jesus and prepare for his imminent arrest. If chapters 15 through 17 were missing we would never suspect they existed, so nicely does 14:31 lead into 18:1. Were these chapters inserted into the Gospel so as to disturb an otherwise perfect connection? A positive answer is altogether plausible. Chapter 6 suddenly transports Jesus back to Galilee after he has just been active in Jerusalem (chap. 5). If the order of these chapters is reversed, the connection is better. In chapter 4 Jesus is found in Samaria. Then toward the end he moves to Cana of Galilee. If chapter 6 followed he would next appear by the Sea of Galilee. If we drop 5:1, a transitional statement necessitated by the presence of chapter 4 immediately preceding, 5:2-47 would then follow chapter 6, continued by chapter 7, which contains references to the healing of chapter 5 and its aftermath (7:19-24, 25).

While the overall structure of the Fourth Gospel is quite clear, and individual episodes are carefully crafted, connections between episodes are sometimes lacking at best or problematic at worst. There is reason to suspect that an earlier form of the Gospel was augmented and rearranged, even if in the nature of the case it is impossible to prove it.

Perhaps it will be useful to indicate in a preliminary way at least three, and possibly four, stages and settings embedded in the canonical text of the Gospel of John. There may well be a correlation between the stages of composition and these settings. There was, first of all, the stage of Jesus' historic ministry, represented by the accounts of Jesus' miracles and his death. Certainly Jesus was a healer, a miracle worker, who died at the hands of the Roman authorities, probably with the complicity of certain chief priests. John takes quite seriously the earthly ministry of Jesus, culminating in his death. A collection of miracle stories and a narrative of Jesus' passion may point back to this stage. Second, there was apparently a stage of conflict within the synagogue between Jesus' followers and those who rejected his claims, which would be represented by the arguments between Jesus and "the Jews," particularly during his public ministry (see below, pp. 35-38). As comparison with the synoptic tradition also shows, these discussions probably represent a stage and setting after the historic ministry of Jesus itself. Third, there was a stage, after a split from the synagogue and Judaism, during which distinctly Christian theological issues arose. This stage is represented in the farewell discourses, Jesus' departing prayer, as well as the resurrection scenes. This leads to the question of whether one may identify a fourth stage, which would be a further Christian stage, reflected in the epilogue (John 21), the Johannine Epistles, perhaps in part of the farewell discourses and the prayer (chaps. 15–17), and even in the prologue. The problem in identifying such a stage and setting lies in finding adequate criteria to distinguish it from the third stage. Yet the theological interests of these last-named sections or items do not entirely coincide, although they are not contradictory.

John and the Synoptic Gospels

Obviously the evangelist had access to knowledge that we draw from the synoptic Gospels. (On the question of John and the Synoptics, see Smith 1992; cf. Neirynck 1992.) In fact, the Gospel as it stands seems to presuppose that the reader is not ignorant of who Jesus is. When he is first mentioned, alongside Moses, he is called Jesus Christ (1:17) as if the proper name, Jesus, conjoined with the title, Christ, needed no explanation. When Jesus appears in the narrative (1:29) he is not really introduced to the reader, although John the Baptist introduces him to his disciples. In Mark, Jesus, who has been named in the introduction (1:1) is described in terms of his origin in Galilee and journey to the Jordan (1:9). Of course, by means of their infancy narratives both Matthew and Luke introduce Jesus in a quite thorough and distinctive way. Moreover, the Gospel of John presupposes that the reader will know that Jesus has been raised from the dead (2:22), that the Spirit has come after the resurrection (death/glorification; cf. 7:39), and that Jesus had chosen an inner circle of twelve disciples, whose appointment is referred to, but not narrated (6:70). Nor is there a list of their names (cf. Mark 3:16-19). Christians have long read the Gospel of John as if it were intended to be studied alongside or after the other three. When Clement of Alexandria at the end of the second century spoke of John's intention of writing a spiritual Gospel in full cognizance of its difference from the other three (cf. Eusebius *Hist. Eccl.* 6. 14.7), he was in all probability expressing the consensus of the early church that enabled this quite different Gospel to be accepted as canonical alongside the others.

Despite this consensus there were, and are, real problems in reconciling John and the Synoptics that were already recognized in the early church (Joseph Daniel Smith 1979; see D. Moody Smith 1992, 5). John records a three-year ministry, mostly in Jerusalem or Judea, whereas the Synoptics seem to assume a one-year ministry in Galilee culminating in Jesus' one visit to Jerusalem for the fateful Passover at which he was executed. Whereas in the Synoptics Jesus eats the Passover meal with his disciples the evening before he is executed, in John he is executed on the afternoon before the Passover. The Last Supper in John, in distinction from the Synoptics, is then not a Passover meal. John apparently also differs from Mark at least on the hour of Jesus' crucifixion (cf. John 19:14; Mark 15:25). As Jesus dies John, unlike the Synoptics, reports no darkness at noon, no rending of the temple veil, no confession of a centurion, each of which would have suited his theological purpose. That he omits Jesus' cry of dereliction (Mark 15:34; cf. Ps 22:2) is not surprising, however, since it otherwise does not fit his portrayal of Jesus.

Indeed, John's portrayal of Jesus, particularly his teaching and self-presentation, differs sharply from the Synoptics. There Jesus debates with opponents about practical issues involving the law, speaks in parables, and in Mark particularly seems reluctant to discuss his own status and role. In John, on the other hand, Jesus expounds and defends his own status and role against "the Jews," who contest his claims. There is scarcely a true parable in John, and Jesus speaks in extended discourses and arguments rather than short, epigrammatic sayings. Typical of John is the fact that Jesus' extraordinary deeds, miracles, are called "signs," that is, they signify who he is. (In the Synoptics they are called "mighty works" or "deeds of power.") In John, Jesus' self-consciousness comes to expression in "I am" sayings, in which Jesus declares himself to be "the bread of heaven," "the light of the world," "the good shepherd," and "the resurrection and the life." He seems to be a different Jesus. And yet, in a curious way, the Johannine Jesus has provided for many Christians a deeply satisfying answer to the synoptic Jesus' question: "Who do people say that I am?" (Mark 8:27). When John Calvin, the great sixteenth-century Reformer, said that he saw in the Fourth Gospel the (christological) key to the other three, he was speaking for millions of Christians (Calvin 1959, 6). John taken as a whole seems to be a significant commentary on the synoptic Gospels, or the synoptic tradition. But when compared more closely with these other Gospels, the differences, and even contradictions, are striking, as we have seen. Not surprisingly, the possibility that John did not know and use the synoptic Gospels in writing his own has been raised by twentieth-century critical scholarship (Gardner-Smith), and a number of modern commentaries have proceeded on the assumption of John's independence (e.g., Bultmann, Brown, Schnackenburg, Haenchen).

Yet interpreters have long noted general similarities between Mark and John particularly (Dodd 1936, especially 69-75). As we observed at the outset, Mark and John are the shorter of the four Gospels. Moreover, most of the additional material in the longer Synoptics consists of Jesus' teaching, as if the reader will acknowledge Jesus' messianic role and will want to be instructed (as a disciple, that is, student) about his teaching. In quite different ways, Mark and John concentrate on that messianic role, as they emphasize Jesus' deeds during the public ministry. In John, Jesus' teaching about his own role follows upon and develops out of his deeds. Indeed, the question of Jesus' messiahship dominates discussion, as Jesus seems to proclaim openly who he is. In Mark, the deeds raise the question that hangs over the narrative: "Who then is this, that even the wind and the sea obey him?" (Mark 4:41). Of course, both emphasize the crucial role of Jesus' approaching death. The motif or theme of the disciples' lack of understanding prior to Jesus' death pervades the Gospel of Mark, and is an aspect of that Gospel's messianic secret, which is commonly said not to exist in John, where Jesus talks openly of himself. Yet even in John the disciples display a similar ignorance, which does not dissipate until Jesus is raised from the dead. What is remarkable about Mark and John is that, despite similarities of purpose and theme, with the notable exception of the passion narrative they draw mostly on different material or traditions.

Other Sources

If John did not use or even know the synoptic Gospels, what were his sources of information about Jesus' ministry? Various proposals have been made. In the nature of the case, all remain hypothetical, whether invoking oral tradition (Gardner-Smith, Dodd) or written sources (Bultmann, Fortna, Boismard). The fact that there are some verbatim agreements between John and the Synoptics suggests that we are dealing with well-established traditions, if not the Synoptics or other written sources. Quite possibly the author drew upon an earlier collection of miracle stories already joined to a passion narrative (Fortna 1970, 1988).

Paul alludes to the institution of the Lord's Supper as having occurred "on the night on which he was betrayed" (1 Cor 11:23), implying that he and his readers share some sense of the order of events of Jesus' passion. The death of Jesus was extremely important, as well as traumatic, for the earliest followers of Jesus. They had to explain, in the light of Scripture and their resurrection faith, how and why the execution of Jesus did not disprove, but rather confirmed, his messianic status and role. To this end, a narration of his passion, with appropriate references to the Scriptures, would have played an essential part. Therefore, it is understandable that although John differs widely from the other Gospels throughout most of the narrative, it comes back very close to the others in the passion narrative. Yet there are even here unaccountable differences. Mark and John could well represent two separate, if not unrelated, responses to the need for such a narration.

Remarkably, no extant Gospel narrative is significantly earlier than the period of the Roman-Jewish war of 66–70. Mark is sometimes dated just before, sometimes a bit after that period. This means there is a gap of thirty to forty years between Jesus and the first Gospel. We have little literary evidence to fill that gap. There are, of course, the letters of Paul, who manifests some knowledge of what Jesus said and did (e.g., 1 Cor 11:23-26; 7:10-12; 9:14), although he does not intend to give an account of Jesus' ministry. Did he have some general conception of it? It is often assumed that Mark, the earliest extant Gospel, was the first Gospel ever written and that Mark invented the Gospel or Gospel genre. This is possible, but not necessarily the case. The assumption begs the question of whether the Jesus story was remembered, as sayings and individual narratives of Jesus' deeds surely were. To entertain the possibility that it was remembered lessens the achievement of Mark, perhaps, while it enhances the possibility that two such obviously independent Gospel narratives as Mark and John could have arisen without one evangelist's necessarily having known or been dependent upon the other.

SETTING AND AUDIENCE

The interpretation of John has naturally been influenced by the fact that it stands alongside three other Gospels in the Christian canon of Scripture. This fact invites and compels the interpreter to inquire about their relationship. Yet even if John the evangelist knew Mark, or the Synoptics generally, his purpose in composing a Gospel may not be deducible from a comparison with them, because he need not have written with them primarily in view. Quite possibly he knew these or other Gospels, but such knowledge was not determinative. Certainly he did not have in view the Christian canon of Scripture, which only began to emerge a century later. We have, however, at our disposal other means of interpreting the Gospel of John in relation to its original setting, and of inferring from that setting its probable purpose or purposes. John's distinctive character and relationships are more likely grounded in circumstances that the parallels or differences from the Synoptics do not entirely explain.

To begin with, the New Testament contains three smaller documents, the Johannine letters, traditionally considered the work of the same author. Although there are reasons for doubting identity of authorship (see, for example, Brown 1982, 14-35; Rensberger 1997, 17-20), their close relationship in style, vocabulary, and theology cannot be denied. As we have already observed, the style and vocabulary of even the words of Jesus in John are closer to the Johannine letters than to the words of Jesus in the Synoptics. Probably the letters of John presuppose the Gospel of John or some earlier version of it. The Revelation of John, for all its differences, also contains some remarkable points of contact or similarities: Jesus is called the word *(logos)* of God (Rev 19:13); Zech 12:10 is applied to the crucifixion of Jesus (Rev 1:7; John 19:37); witnessing and conquering are important themes; Jesus speaks through the Spirit to his churches (Rev 1–3; cf. the Paraclete sayings of the Gospels' farewell discourses); opposition from Jews is suggested, although not so strongly as in the Gospel (Rev 2:9; 3:9; cf. 11:1-14). So, in addition to the synoptic Gospels, the Gospel of John has relations with other New Testament documents in the so-called Johannine corpus. Moreover, some relationship to the writings of Paul cannot be excluded. Not only is there a deep theological affinity (Bultmann 1955, 6-10, 12), but both deal fundamentally with the relationship of Christianity to Judaism, albeit with different issues in view.

There is then evidence of a Johannine community or school.

John and Judaism

The relationship to Judaism is an important and constitutive aspect of the Gospel of John (as distinguished from the Johnannine letters). Jesus goes at least twice to Jerusalem at Passover (2:13; 11:55) and a third Passover is mentioned (6:4). He is also present in Jerusalem for an unnamed festival (5:1), for Booths (7:2), and for Dedication or Hanukkah (10:22). Thus major Jewish festivals and the Jerusalem temple loom large in John and are obviously more important than in the other Gospels (see Yee 1989). Moreover, the discovery of the Dead Sea Scrolls revealed some remarkable similarities in theological language and conceptuality to the Essene sect of Qumran. The *Community Rule* (esp. cols. 3 and 4) manifests a theological terminology identical to John's: *world, spirit, life,* as well as such pairs as *truth* and *falsehood* or *light* and *darkness,* which reflect a dualism similar to John's. The conceptual framework of John's theology thus finds a place in first-century Palestinian Judaism (see Charlesworth 1990, especially his own article on 1QS and John, 76-106, as well as Charlesworth 1996).

Throughout the Gospel one is struck by the omnipresence of Jesus' opponents, usually called "the Jews," although sometimes "the Pharisees." They oppose him and challenge his claims concerning his role, authority, and mission. The fact that they are called "Jews" seems strange. Jesus himself is clearly a Jew (4:9), as are his disciples, not to mention John the Baptist, who appears in an entirely positive light. It has, moreover, been observed that in the synoptic Gospels almost everyone can be assumed to be Jewish, except Pilate and the Roman soldiers, and parties or types within Judaism are named: not only Pharisees, but Sadducees, the disciples of John the Baptist (who also appear in John), scribes, Herodians, and even Zealots. (In John Sadducees, scribes, Herodians and Zealots are not mentioned.) In other words, "the Jews" do not present a solid front against Jesus, as is the case in the Gospel of John. In Luke some Pharisees even warn Jesus that he is in danger from Herod Antipas (13:31)! Moreover, Jesus can say to a scribe, an official interpreter of the law, that he is not far from the Kingdom (or rule) of God (Mark 12:34).

That the Johannine Jews are primarily concerned to oppose Jesus' claims concerning himself is also somewhat at odds with the synoptic portrayal, as well as Paul. The synoptic Jesus does not often make claims for himself. In fact, his self-estimate has to be, so to speak, wrung from him (see Mark 8:27-30; cf. Matt 16:13-20; Luke 9:18-21; 14:61-62). Only toward the end of the synoptic account (e.g., Mark 14:62-64) do we learn that Jesus' claim to be the Messiah or Christ is mortally offensive to the Jewish authorities, something that becomes apparent early on in the Johannine account. Furthermore, simply the claim to be the Messiah, that is the anointed descendant of David, destined to assume his throne, was not offensive to other Jews, even if, as in the case of Bar Kokhba a century later, it was proven false by history. Indeed, Paul's controversies with Jewish believers concerned the status of the Jewish law, not claims of Jesus' messiahship.

Obviously, in John something is going on between Jesus' followers and his opponents that is distinctive and different from what we find either in the Synoptics or Paul. Probably this offers some clue to the circumstances of John's origin and thus of its meaning. The fact that there seem no longer to be parties among the Jews, but only the Pharisees, suggests a time after the disastrous Roman war and the destruction of the Jerusalem temple. The Sadducean high priesthood had lost the temple over which they presided. The Essenes of Qumran had lost their monastery on the Dead Sea to Roman attack. The Zealots, who had advocated resistance to Rome, had been discredited if not killed. Judaism was being reconfigured as even more the religion of the book (Scripture or the Christian Old Testament) and of the law. Sectarians, such as those who believed that the crucified Jesus was somehow nevertheless the Messiah, were not in good odor. "Jews" and "Pharisees" could be virtually equated, and set over against Jesus' followers.

At a couple of points in John (9:22; 12:42) Jewish people are said to fear expulsion from the synagogue (that they will become *aposynagōgoi*, "people separated from the synagogue") if they confessed their belief that Jesus was the Messiah. (Greek here is *christos*.) According to 9:22 the Jews had decided to expel such Christ-confessors (see below, pp. 194-96). Moreover, Jesus finally predicts to his disciples that this will happen to them (16:2). In no other Gospel does this threat appear (but cf. Luke 21:12), which would be strange if it had originated during the time of Jesus' ministry. More likely, it reflects the time and setting of the Johannine community after Jesus' death and after the Roman war, that is, nearer the end of the first century, at the time Judaism was engaged in a process of self-definition and retrenchment.

Given the general situation, are there Jewish texts that reveal measures taken against the early Christians, who were in their own eyes still Jews? (For a Christian to also be a Jew seems anomalous today. But we must remember that the apostle Paul considered himself to be Jewish, as Galatians 2:14-15 shows, and was searching for ways in which Jewish and Gentile Christians could coexist within one church.) With reason an earlier version of an ancient Jewish liturgical text has been thought to speak to the question (Martyn 1979, esp. 50-62; Brown 1966, lxx-lxxv). One form of the Twelfth Benediction (called the *birkat ha-minim*, "Blessing of the Heretics") of the so-called Eighteen Benedictions of the Jewish synagogue liturgy reads:

> For the apostates let there be no hope
> And let the arrogant government
> be speedily uprooted in our days.
> Let the Nazarenes (Christians) and the Minim
>   (heretics) be destroyed in a moment
> And let them be blotted out of the Book of Life and
>   not be inscribed together with the righteous.
> Blessed art thou, O Lord, who humblest the proud!

This form of the ancient text may date from the eighties of the first century (cf. Davies 1966, 275-86, as well as Martyn), although this date is not certain. All extant versions of this text are centuries later, but talmudic evidence (Berakoth 28) suggests the Benediction goes back to the first century (see below on John 9:22). The identity of the parties mentioned is not entirely clear either, but reasonable surmises may be made. "Apostates" are those who have left Judaism, but perhaps not Christians (i.e., Jews who believe in Jesus). The latter are described as Nazarenes and Minim, who according to the concluding prayer (above), are to be excluded from the company of those accepted by God. Presumably this means they are to be excluded from Judaism. ("The arrogant government" is pretty clearly a reference to the Romans.) Quite possibly this text is related to the fear, or the reality, of being put out of the synagogue (and presumably out of Judaism) that is expressed or reflected in John 9:22; 12:48 and 16:2. Whether and how this was the case continues to be a matter of scholarly debate. Exclusion from the synagogue per se is not mentioned in the Twelfth Benediction or *birkat ha-minim* and the date of its relevant form remains uncertain. Yet at mid–second century Justin

Martyr refers to Jews cursing Christians in their synagogues (*Dial. Trypho* 16.4; 95.4; 110.5; 133.6), which may be a reference to practices intended or reflected in the *birkat ha-minim.*

Clearly much of the Gospel arose out of a situation in which Jews and Christians—or better Jews who believed Jesus was the Christ and those who rejected this claim—were at loggerheads. John would seem to assume as a matter of course that Jews who believed in Jesus and confessed him to be the Messiah were being put out of synagogues by order of Jewish authorities. The obvious hostility toward Judaism in John is then not a function of their remoteness from one another but of a one-time close relationship gone sour. (For a good example of the influence of this position in subsequent research, see Neyrey 1988.)

Church and Spirit

Yet important parts of the Gospel of John, especially the last meal, farewell discourses, and departing prayer of chapters 13–17, deal with distinctly Christian, or inner Christian, issues (as do the Johannine letters).

As the conflict with Judaism has receded into the background, the dominant question of these discourses is, How is the now departed Jesus accessible, available, to his followers who have, so to speak, been left behind? Jesus speaks directly to that question at the beginning of the farewell discourses (14:1-4), but there he seems to refer to the eschatological future, or so it seems. Not surprisingly, these words are frequently read at funerals. Yet the focus is really on the present, postresurrection situation of the disciple that is future from the standpoint of Jesus' ministry. How will Jesus be present among his disciples as they continue to live in this world, which hates them, as it hated Jesus himself (15:18–16:4)? Jesus speaks of his coming again (16:16-19; cf. 14:3, 18) and of sending the Holy Spirit, called here the Advocate (NRSV) or Counselor (RSV). (The Greek *paraklētos* means one called to the side of.) In several passages (14:15-17, 26; 15:26; 16:7-15) Jesus spells out the work of the Spirit-Advocate, which is essentially to continue and interpret his own revelatory mission.

In an important sense the Gospel of John itself is a fulfillment of the promise of the Spirit as an active, life-giving, and guiding power in the community, that is, the church. As we shall see, the story of Jesus' ministry is now told from the perspective of his glorification (that is, crucifixion and resurrection). This is true of all the Gospels, but only in John is this fact made explicit, and indeed highlighted (2:22; 12:16; 13:7; 16:4). The disciples do not understand Jesus during his earthly ministry, but they could not have. The Spirit had not yet been given, and he had not been glorified (7:39). Only Jesus' glorification and the coming of the Spirit will create conditions under which understanding will be possible.

John's expressly different perspective and interests, as well as the interpretative work of the Spirit, account for the quite different portrait of Jesus in the Fourth Gospel. It has been said that there is no story of Jesus' transfiguration (see Mark 9:2-8) in John because the Johannine Jesus is transfigured throughout the Gospel. Moreover, the work of the Spirit that is promised in the Gospel may account for the radically different rendering of Jesus' teaching in John as compared with the Synoptics. We no longer hear the words of the earthly Jesus, but those of the exalted Jesus, perhaps delivered by prophets in the Johannine community. (See Smith 1995, esp. 79 and the works cited there, particularly Boring 1978/79.) There are, of course, a number of synoptic-like words of Jesus in the Fourth Gospel, but they are usually clothed in Johannine language (e.g., 12:25). The words of Jesus, like the general portrayal of him, are given anew in light of new situations and problems and under the inspiration of the Spirit. It is because the Gospel focuses on the question of how the departed Jesus is going to return and abide with his disciples that it emphasizes the crucially important work of the Spirit in the church.

Place and Date of Origin

Ephesus as the Traditional Site

According to traditions conveyed through Irenaeus, the Gospel was written in Ephesus, apparently rather late in the first century

(Irenaeus *Adv. Haer.,* 2. 22.5; 3. 3.4; see also Eusebius *Hist. Eccl.* 3.23.3-4). That view accords rather well with what became a traditional position on the relation of John to the synoptic Gospels, namely, that the Fourth Evangelist knew them and wrote in full cognizance and basic agreement with them (see above, pp. 29-30). Ephesus was a major Christian center, even in Paul's day (Acts 19:1; 1 Cor 16:8). Whether John was written in Ephesus is then not irrelevant to that issue.

Yet the New Testament and Christian documents of the early second century mention no Ephesian residence of the apostle John. Bishop Ignatius of Antioch, who wrote to the church of Ephesus between 115–120 makes a great deal of the apostle Paul's residence there, but, strangely, does not mention John. The book of Acts last mentions John in Jerusalem and Samaria (for Jerusalem, 4:13, 19; cf. 12:2; for Samaria, 8:14). When in the late forties Paul visited Jerusalem he found John there, and he links him with Peter and Jesus' brother James as one of the pillars of the church (Gal 2:9). The author of the book of Revelation, who wrote on the island of Patmos, not far from Ephesus, was named John (1:1, 4, 9; 22:8), although he does not call himself the son of Zebedee or claim to be an apostle (cf. Rev 21:14, where the twelve apostles would seem not to include the author). Was this John nevertheless the evangelist? Revelation differs so much from the Gospel in style and vocabulary that this hardly seems possible, as Bishop Dionysius of Alexandria pointed out at mid–third century (See Eusebius *Hist. Eccl.* 7.25.1-27).

The situation with respect to place of origin is similar to that with authorship. Toward the end of the second century there is ample testimony, but earlier our sources are silent.

Yet the account of Christianity in Ephesus found in Acts 18 and 19 corresponds in some important respects with what we might expect in the environment of the Gospel of John. For example, John (the Baptist) figures more prominently in the Gospel of John than in any other Gospel, as he points away from himself to Jesus (1:15, 30). Acts tells us of disciples of John, who were converted to Christianity and baptized in Ephesus (18:25; 19:1-7) after Paul told them that John had told people to believe in the one who was to come after him. There Paul carries on discussions about Jesus with Jews (18:19; 19:8-10), until a rupture occurs, and he departs from their synagogue (19:8-9). As we have observed, in the Gospel of John (alone among the canonical Gospels) the opponents of Jesus are characteristically called Jews, and believers fear expulsion from the synagogue (cf. 9:22; 12:48; 16:2). In Ephesus Paul performs impressive miracles (Acts 19:11), as Jesus did in the Fourth Gospel. Despite the hostility, the close contact between Christians and Jews in Ephesus is reminiscent of the Gospel of John, where Jesus and his Jewish opponents, as well as his disciples, are in close contact with one another. Thus Jewish exorcists there invoke the name of Jesus (19:13-16). Although no exorcisms of any sort are performed by Jesus or his Jewish opponents in the Fourth Gospel, the practice of exorcism may lurk in the background, for Jesus himself is accused by some Jews of having a demon (cf. 8:48-49, 52). The Gospel of John strongly suggests a background or milieu that in significant ways fits what Acts describes as happening in Ephesus. Although certainty is obviously impossible, this traditional site remains a viable candidate. (On John and Ephesus see Van Tilborg 1996.)

Date of Origin

The statement of Irenaeus that John the disciple lived in Ephesus until the time of Trajan (see above references, pp. 39-40) implies that he wrote his Gospel relatively late in the first century, and this is the traditional, ancient Christian position. It comports well with the view generally accepted in the ancient church, that John wrote last, with knowledge of the other synoptic Gospels. While something may be said for the possibility that John's Gospel is actually much earlier (Goodenough 1945; Lamar Cribbs 1970), that is a view of modern criticism rather than Christian antiquity.

For a time, particularly in the early part of the twentieth century, the possibility that John was not written, or at least not published, until mid–second century was a viable one (cf. Bacon 1910, 224). At that time Justin Martyr espoused a *logos* ("word")

Christology, without citing the Fourth Gospel explicitly. Such an omission by Justin would seem strange if the Gospel of John had already been written and was in circulation.

Then the discovery and publication in the 1930s of two papyrus fragments made such a late dating difficult, if not impossible, to sustain. The first and most important is the fragment of John chapter 18 noted already (P^{52}), dated by paleographers to the second quarter of the second century (125–150); the other is a fragment of a hitherto unknown gospel called Egerton Papyrus 2 from the same period, which obviously reflects knowledge of the Gospel of John, if not of its sources. (See Metzger 1992, 38-39, on P^{52} and Schneemelcher 1991, 96-99, on the fragment of an Unknown Gospel.) For the Gospel of John to have been written and circulated in Egypt, where these fragments were found, a date no later than the first decade of the second century must be presumed. Such a dating is also supported by the discovery (in 1947) of the Dead Sea Scrolls, particularly the *Community Rule* (1QS), whose language and conceptuality show remarkable similarities to the Gospel of John. This ancient evidence implied—although it did not prove—that the Gospel's origin could have lain in first-century Palestinian Judaism. No longer was it obviously the product of a later hellenistic Christianity that had long since transcended its Jewish origins.

If a date of origin well into the second century can no longer be sustained, how early could the Gospel of John be? Here the matter of John's knowledge and use of the Synoptics comes into play. If John presupposes the other canonical Gospels, it could hardly have been written before the last decade of the first century, by which time all the Synoptics were probably circulating. Whether John does continues to be a matter of disagreement, however.

We have observed that the Gospel of John reflects a fear, and probably the historic reality, of expulsion from synagogues of Jews who accepted Jesus as the Messiah (see 9:22; 12:42; 16:2; above, pp. 35-38). If such expulsion occurred with the promulgation of the Blessing of (against) Heretics, and if that event can be dated in the eighties, then we have established the earliest possible date *(terminus post quem)* for the Gospel of John. Given 110 as the latest possible date *(terminus ante quem)*, we would then have a range of a couple of decades (90–110), within which John was likely written (see Brown 1966, lxxx). That John was written later than this is scarcely possible. That in its present form it was published earlier is not impossible, but is unlikely.

THEOLOGY AND ETHICS

John the evangelist came to be known as the theologian, an appropriate title (D. Moody Smith 1995, 1-2). John is the most explicitly theological of the Gospels, and in a quite specific sense, for in this Gospel, Jesus himself sets out a distinctly Christian, Johannine theological position. Although each canonical Gospel is written from a Christian point of view, in the others the theology lies mainly in the presuppositions, the framework, and the editorial interstices rather than in the preaching and teaching of Jesus himself.

Basic to John's thought is a bipolarity or dualism in which God and the estranged would seem to stand at opposite poles. Beyond this, perhaps the most characteristic aspect of Johannine theology is its distinctive Christology, according to which Jesus appears as the Son of God who descends from heaven into this estranged world to make God known (1:18) and then ascends on high (3:13; 6:33, 38, passim). While in the synoptic Gospels Jesus speaks of the Son of Man's rising from the dead (8:31; 9:31; 10:34), he never speaks of his descent from heaven. Among the Gospels this is a distinctly Johannine theme, although it may be suggested also by Paul (Phil 2:6-11; Gal 4:4).

The Johannine doctrine that Jesus was the incarnation, enfleshing, of the Word who was God (1:1-2, 14) logically requires the idea of the descent of God the Word to take up dwelling in him. (On the development of this doctrine, see Dunn 1980, especially 248-50.) When did this happen? The Nicene Creed, based upon the New Testament canon of the four Gospels, brings in the concept of the virginal conception from Matthew and Luke to identify the onset of the incarnation with precisely that point ("incarnate of the Holy Spirit and the Virgin Mary"), at the outset of the story of Jesus. This is a logical move, but whether John even knows the birth narratives is a good question (cf. 7:42). He does not appropriate them explicitly. In John's thought the descent must be prior to the revelation of God in the earthly Jesus and, of course, prior to his ascension. In the historical process, however, the exaltation/ascension of Jesus was the given from which the truth of the descent and incarnation was inferred. Probably John was not unaware of this reverse progression. We have observed that in John the Holy Spirit functions in an indispensable way to bring to light the reality of the revelation of God, which has in the historical Jesus already occurred, but is not understood as such until afterward. (On Johannine Christology and theology generally, see Bultmann 1955, 3-93; Loader 1989; Anderson 1996; as well as D. Moody Smith 1995.)

Johannine ethics is constituted by obedience to God as manifested in the actions and words of Jesus. One must do what Jesus commands (13:34), and he commands love "of one another," that is, among the fellowship of his disciples, the church. Yet Jesus does not command disciples to do more than he has done for them. He has loved them and laid down his life for them, and they must be willing to do as much for each other (15:12-14 for Johannine ethics in a nutshell). With good reason John's ethical perspective, based on his understanding of the mission, message, and ministry of Jesus, is sectarian. Jesus loves his own and they love one another. The division between Jesus and the world characterizes Johannine dualism, which sees the world sharply divided between good and evil. One must belong to the strictly defined circle of Jesus' disciples over against the world for the love command to be significant. Yet it embodies a profound understanding of the distinctive character of Christian existence (see Meeks 1996, 317-26).

Probably the sharp Johannine dualism, with its dangerous potentialities, is itself a product of a situation of the earliest circle of Jesus followers who produced this Gospel. Living under stress and persecution, or the threat of persecution, they saw their lives and the world defined by the necessity of sharp choices that excluded compromise or tentativeness. Thus their life situation deeply informed their view of God and the alienated world as fundamentally (although finally not irrevocably) opposed to one another (see Meeks 1972; Peterson 1993).

Unfortunately, this conflicted setting in which the Gospel arose had led the author to refer to his own opponents, those of the disciples, and those of Jesus as "the Jews." Doubtless they were, but Jesus (cf. John 4:9), John the Baptist, and the earliest circle of disciples were also Jews. It is a mistake, but a not unnatural one, to assume that all Jews, then and now, are characterized as enemies of Jesus in the Gospel of John. The depth of John's indebtedness to Judaism, or Jewish tradition is, however, shown by the Gospel's use of Scripture (which Christians call the Old Testament). As we shall see in the course of exegesis, much of the Gospel of John cannot be understood, at least not understood fully, apart from its references or allusions to Scripture. Yet belief in Jesus produces a sharply different view of what Scripture means (John 5:39, 45-57; cf. the similar view of Paul in 2 Cor 3:14-16). The incipient conflict with Judaism is in a profound sense a conflict about biblical interpretation.

COMMENTARY

THE PROLOGUE OF THE GOSPEL (1:1-18)

The first task of exegesis is to delimit a text to be studied, and here the prologue presents no problem. It clearly delimits itself. The simple, elegant, almost poetic style that is set out in verse 1 continues, with a few interruptions and shifts through verse 18, where the prologue ends. In verse 19 the mention of the testimony of John marks a turning point, as the narrative of the Gospel proper begins. Yet the prologue is a narrative too, the narrative of the Word, which began in creation (1:1-3), became flesh (v. 14), and is finally named Jesus Christ (v. 17). After the prologue the Word in this sense disappears, for Jesus in whom the Word is present or may be encountered, is now the center of attention.

The prologue's elevated, hymnic style is at two points (1:6-8; 1:15) interrupted by rather prosaic references to John the Baptist, which set off the basic quasi-poetic pattern even more. Within the hymnic portion there are differences: 1:1-5 and 1:9-11 fall into doublets of fairly brief strophes, while the periods or sentences are longer in the latter portion of the prologue (vv. 12-14, 16-18). In 1:1-5 and 1:9-11 there is a remarkable chainlike sequence of terms in which the last word of one strophe becomes the first word of the next. Translating literally:

> In the beginning was the *word*
> and the *word* was with *God*
> and *God* was the *word*. (v. 1)

. . . .

> In him was *life*
> and *life* was the *light* of human beings; (v. 4)

47

And the *light* shines in *darkness,*
and the *darkness* has not overcome it. (v. 5)

Such a pattern, called a sorites, is found also in the Wisdom of Solomon (6:17-20). Its appearance there is doubly significant in view of the apparent conceptual relationship between the role of the Word in John's prologue and that of wisdom in the Wisdom of Solomon and similar Jewish wisdom writings (see below, pp. 51-52). Yet despite this distinction, the basic hymnic portions seem similar vis-à-vis verses 6-8, 15, not to mention the rest of the Gospel. Are they portions of, or derived from, an ancient Christian hymn? It is worth noting that there are hymnic passages in other New Testament books that deal with Christology and particularly Christ's preexistence. In fact, Col 1:15-20 and Phil 2:6-11 are set out in strophic form in the latest (*Nestle-Aland* 1993) edition of the Greek New Testament (although John 1:1-18 is not).

The prologue falls into three parts, divided roughly by the statements about John the Baptist (who is never called "the Baptist" in John) in 1:6-8 and 1:15. The first part presents the role of the Word in creation (1:1-5); the second the appearance of the Word in history (1:9-13); the third part the Incarnation and its benefits (1:14-18). The last part differs decisively in that the author and those who are united with him speak in the first-person plural, adding a note of personal confession to what has been said. As commentators have long noted, verse 14 is central theologically, in that it summarizes what is said in verses 9-13, but it also lays the basis for the statements about Jesus Christ in the remainder of the prologue. Yet verses 12-13 are pivotal (see Culpepper 1980), because they state, albeit still in the third person, the effect of the Word's appearance on the historical plane, and thus they prepare for the confessional statement of verse 14. That statement is then elaborated with respect to the effect of Christ upon the Christian community (v. 16), his relation to Moses and the law, (v. 17) and finally his relationship to God the Father (v. 18).

The Word in Creation (1:1-5)

The opening phrase, "in the beginning," is reminiscent of Gen 1:1, where God speaks, creating a world out of the formless chaos. That light and darkness figure prominently (vv. 4-5) also recalls the creation scene of Genesis, where God creates light over against the darkness (Gen 1:3-5). Moreover, the Gospel of Mark begins similarly: "The beginning of the good news of Jesus Christ . . ." (1:1). But John is actually much closer to Genesis, in that both John and Genesis are giving a narration about creation (Borgen 1983, 13-20, 95-110). Although in Genesis God speaks, while, in John, Jesus is his Word, there is an ancient Targum (translation of the Hebrew Bible into Aramaic) in which God's speaking is personified, or reified, as his *Memra* or Word (Gen 1:13): "From the beginning with wisdom the Word of the Lord created and perfected the skies and the earth. . . . And the Word of the Lord said: "Let there be light and there was light according to the decree of his Word." (The translation of the Targum Neofiti is helpfully given by Malina and Rohrbaugh [1998, 36], who draw upon the work of McNamara [1992, 56].) Interestingly enough, in the closely similar prologue of 1 John 1:1-3, "the beginning" is no longer the primordial beginning, but pretty clearly the beginning of the Christian story (cf. 2:7; 3:11).

Interpreters of John have exhausted every conceivable possibility in an effort to understand the background, meaning, and implications of the Greek word *logos*. "Word" is the most obvious and safest translation, but *logos* has numerous other meanings. In the Greek philosophical tradition *logos* had a long history already, beginning with Heraclitus in the late–sixth century BCE and coming to a head with the Stoics, who saw in the *logos* the principle of intelligent order governing the universe. The ideas of reason as well as communication are therefore basic. In Scripture one thinks immediately of the word (Heb. *dabar*; LXX *logos*) that moves the prophet to speak and is the content of his message (Jer 1:2, 4; Ezek 13:1; Hos 1:1; Zech 1:1). Clearly in the prophets, as in John, the *word* is a revelatory concept: it has to do with God's revelation. Thus in the New Testament, apart from John, the word can be the equivalent of the good news, the gospel. (See Acts 4:4; Rom 9:6; 1 Thess 1:6, 8, where *logos* is used. In 1 Pet 1:25 exactly this equation with the gospel is made, although there one sees not *logos* but the synonym *rhēma*, following LXX of Isa 40:8.) That John was aware of such biblical usage, whether rooted in Israel's prophetic tradition or earliest Christianity is altogether probable. Yet the meanings found there do not make the point that is essential to John: the Word's participation in God as the extension of God's creativity and revelation into the universe (or world; Gk. *kosmos*). There are other, and closer, parallels to John's usage.

That the Word was, and is, closely related to God is not only stated (v. 1), but reiterated (v. 2). Even God does not antedate the Word. Indeed, "the Word was God." It immediately becomes clear that the Word has played a key role in creation (v. 3). The Word's coexistence with God at the beginning affords a contrast with the Baptist's clear statement that Jesus (the Word) was before him (1:15, 30), a significant indication of the latter's superiority. Thus the Word's being present with God in the beginning betokens his equality with God.

At this point first-time readers would not know that the Word was to be identified with the Incarnate One (v. 14), Jesus Christ (v. 17). The evangelist slowly opens the curtain onto who this person is. One could read through verse 11 or even 13 or the assumption that the Word was not identical with a single person, but was perhaps personified by the prophets. But by verse 14 it becomes clear that the Word has become flesh in a single individual, to whom John the Baptist has testified (v. 15). Probably most readers or hearers would have known the gospel, or at least the Jesus story, and would have recognized the allusion to Jesus, at least as early as verse 5 or 10. If, in fact, the prologue was based on an early Christian hymn, recited or sung by congregations, this would have been all the more likely. That the reader would not have found the idea of the preexistence of Christ, and even his role in creation, strange or unfamiliar is proven by the existence of similar hymns or hymnlike passages (Phil 2:6-11; Col 1:15-20) already cited. Early Christianity did not begin with a low

Christology and move by degrees to a higher one. Within the first generation the apostle Paul writes that through Jesus Christ we and all things exist (cf. also 1 Cor 8:6), even as he identifies Jesus Christ with the wisdom of God (1 Cor 1:24).

Although Paul does not spin out a theory of Christ as the wisdom of God, his use of the term is quite suggestive and may help explain the ease with which John so quickly assigns to the Word a role in creation. In the wisdom tradition of Scripture and ancient Jewish literature there is precedent for the Johannine conception of the Word's playing such a role.

In Prov 8:22 wisdom speaks and describes herself (*sophia* is feminine) as the Lord's first creation, "at the beginning of his work" (v. 23). When God created the earth in all its parts she was beside him "like a master worker" (v. 30), presumably assisting him in his work. In Wisdom of Solomon wisdom is said to be "the fashioner of all things" (7:22). Moreover:

> she is a breath of the power of God,
> and a pure emanation of the glory of the Almighty...

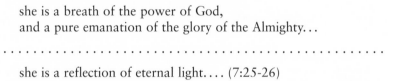

> she is a reflection of eternal light.... (7:25-26)

Of course, the terms *glory, eternal,* and *light* are also important in the Gospel of John, and *glory* and *light* appear in the prologue. Indeed, *wisdom* and *word* are found in synonymous parallelism in Wis 9:1-2:

> O God of my ancestors and Lord of mercy,
> who has made all things by your word,
> and by your wisdom has formed humankind.... (AT)

Obviously wisdom and word can be used interchangeably, and the Word is God's agent in creation. (Wisdom and law are also closely related, as in Wis 6:18 and Sir 19:20.) At this point the writings of Philo, the late-first-century Jewish philosopher of Alexandria, Egypt, also become relevant (see Borgen 1983, 15). In a discussion of "Sons of God" (Deut 14:1), who are "they who live in the knowledge of the One," Philo writes:

God's First-born [is] the Word *(logos)*, who holds the eldership among the angels.... And many names are his, for he is called "the Beginning," and the Name of God, and His Word, and the Man after his image and "he that sees," that is Israel.... For if we have not yet become fit to be thought sons of God yet we may be sons of His invisible image, the most holy Word. For the Word is the eldest-born image of God. (*Conf. Ling.* 146-47)

Borgen also cites other examples of ancient Jewish exegesis, for example, *Gen. Rab.* III, 1-3, on Gen 1:3. That God created "all things" through the agency of the Word, an idea set forth and reiterated (v. 3), is therefore rooted in biblical ideas of word and wisdom and Jewish exegetical traditions. In view of the similar roles of word and wisdom in Jewish sources of the period, where wisdom is often more prominent than word, why does John use "Word" rather than "wisdom"? For one thing "word" has connotations from its use in Scripture and early Christian tradition that "wisdom" lacks (see above, pp. 49-50). Moreover, *logos* is a masculine noun and the Greek (as well as the Hebrew) word for wisdom *(sophia)* is feminine. Jesus was, of course, a male, as most prophetic figures were, and the use of the masculine pronoun would have already conveyed to the knowledgeable reader the reference to Jesus.

There is a question about how to punctuate verse 3. (Punctuation in printed texts, whether Greek or English, is a modern device.) Does the full stop come at the end of the verse (RSV) or in the middle, before the final clause (NRSV)? This is not just a question of punctuation, but of how the statement should be understood, and commentators ancient and modern differ. (Contrast Barrett 1978, 156-57; and Schnackenburg 1968, 236-41; who agree with the RSV, with Bultmann 1971, 36-40; and Brown 1966, 3, 6; who agree with the NRSV.) Either way, the indispensable role of the Word in creation is stated unequivocally. In the RSV it is simply reiterated; in the NRSV life is said to have come into being in the word. In favor of the RSV's punctuation and reading is the fact that "all things" have just been said to have come into being through the Word. It is not clear how this squares with the statement that life came to being in him. The RSV's reading may cause an imbalance in the rhythm of the prologue, but there is precedent in verses 1-2, where verse 2, while also creating an imbalance, similarly reiterates what has just been clearly stated in verse 1. Again, in either case the Word mediates life and light to all people (v. 4; cf. 1 John 1:1-2), as the two are virtually equated. At this point light receives the greater emphasis, doubtless because the point is the revelation that Christ the true light (v. 9) brings into a darkened world (v. 5).

The contrast of light and darkness is typical of the Johannine dualism and is reminiscent of the similar phenomenon in the *Rule of the Community* of the Dead Sea Scrolls (1QS3:17-24; cf. Charlesworth 1990, 76-106):

> He has created man to govern the *world,* and has appointed for him *two spirits* in which to *walk* until the time of his visitation: the *spirits of truth* and *falsehood* [Vermes 1962; Vermes 1995 has "injustice"]. Those *born* of *truth* spring from a fountain of *light,* but those *born* of *falsehood* spring from a source of *darkness.* All the *children* of righteousness are ruled by the *Prince of Light* and walk in the ways of *light,* but all the children of *falsehood* are ruled by the *Angel of Darkness* and *walk* in the ways of *darkness.* (emphasis added)

Obviously John's language and conceptuality were not foreign to first-century Palestinian Judaism, as the Scrolls now demonstrate. But again, Philo, the Alexandrian Jew, also comes close to John's language in his commentary on Gen 1:3 (*Somn.* 1.75):

> God is light. . . . And he is not only light, but the archetype of every other light, nay, prior to and high above every archetype, holding the position of the model of a model. For the model or pattern was the Word which contained all His fullness—light, in fact, for as the lawgiver tells us, "God said, 'let light come into being' " (Gen 1:3), whereas He Himself resembles none of the things which have come into being. (See Borgen 1983, 15.)

That the light shines in darkness (v. 5) could, outside of this context or up to this point, be taken in a general sense of God's revelation to the world. Probably John means it in that sense, although he has something more specific in view, as we immediately learn (cf. also Jesus' proclamation of himself as the light of the world, e.g., 8:12; 12:35). That the darkness did not overcome the light is probably an allusion to Jesus' death and resurrection. If so, that allusion is better conveyed by the NRSV's "did not overcome it" (reflecting the Greek aorist tense), than by the RSV's "has not overcome it" (which implies a continuing state consequent upon a past event). The old KJV reads, "the darkness comprehended it not," which is a perfectly legitimate translation of the Greek verb *(katalambanō)*. John delights in using words with double meaning when, as in this case, both are appropriate. Probably "overcome" is the primary meaning, but "comprehend" lurks in the background. The darkness has no more understood the light than it has overthrown it.

The Word Enters History (1:6-13)

Suddenly the scene shifts to early-first-century Jewish Palestine and the appearance of John (1:6-8). If, however, one reckons with what is suggested in verse 5, the shift is not as abrupt as might otherwise appear. The introduction of John is cast so as to evoke Old Testament language and scenes (e.g., Judg 13:2; 1 Sam 1:1). John is sent from God, like the ancient prophets (cf. Isa 6:8; Jer 14:14). He is a prophetic figure whose sole mission is to bear witness or testimony (the Greek stem is the same for either English word) to the light, that is, to Jesus (v. 7). Unlike the others (cf. Mark 1:6), this Gospel gives no preparatory explanation of who John was or what he did. That all are to believe through John clearly implies that his witness is full, complete, and true. It will later be said that John has been sent to reveal Jesus to Israel through his baptism (v. 31). Probably because John's function was simply to testify he is not called "the Baptist."

John himself was not the light (v. 8). Whether John is simply used as a literary or theological foil or whether the Gospel here drops a hint as to its actual historical setting is a good question. It is probably the latter, given that John's appearances are carefully crafted so that the reader will understand that whoever, or whatever, he may be, he is clearly subordinate to Jesus (1:15, 30; 3:25-30); as well as a witness to him (1:8, 19, 29, 35; 5:33). We know from Acts 19:1-7 (cf. 18:25) that there were disciples of John in Ephesus (the traditional place of origin of the Gospel of John). Were there such disciples in John's close environment? Quite possibly, and if so they would seem to have embraced John as the Messiah, a circumstance that would explain his denials (1:20; cf. 1:15; 30; 3:28-30; cf. Luke 3:15). More than in any other Gospel the Baptist here goes out of his way to define his role, as witness, in relation to Jesus. He is not the light, but came to bear testimony to the light.

The true light, which enlightens every human being, was coming into the world (v. 9; cf. 8:12; 12:35). (*Anthropos* here as in v. 4 means "human being" not "man" in the sense of a male.) "True light" implies that there were false claimants, as does Jesus' announcement that he is the Good Shepherd or the True Vine. The dualism of truth and lie, known from the Scrolls (see above, p. 53), seems to be in the background. That the light already enlightens every person who comes into the world is a possible translation (cf. KJV), but would not seem to be what is meant, inasmuch as only those who receive Jesus are truly enlightened. Yet the light shines on all, showing or exposing people for who and what they really are (3:19-21). The NRSV takes verse 9 as the conclusion of the preceding paragraph, while the RSV and *Nestle-Aland* (1993 edition) take it with the following. The fact that verse 9 lacks the rhythmic scheme of the following verses favors the NRSV. Moreover, the Greek relative pronoun is still neuter, agreeing with "light" *(phōs)*, while the pronouns in verse 10 are masculine, agreeing with Word *(logos)* and, of course, with Jesus *(Iēsous)*. But the substance of verse 9 is perhaps more closely related to verses 10-14, which expound the nature and consequences of Jesus' advent. In fact, verse 9 is a transitional statement, which leads from the Baptist's denial into the subsequent exposition. The imperfect tense ("was coming") dramatizes the moment of Jesus' coming, as the Baptist testifies to him.

Next, what has already been said about the Word is summarized and in one brief clause the reception accorded Jesus, who is of course not yet named, is anticipated (v. 10): "The world knew him not" (KJV). This not knowing cannot, in view of the concept of knowledge in John, be an innocent ignorance. Three things are here said about the world (Gk. *kosmos*), each of which puts it in a somewhat different light. That the Word (Jesus) was in the world is simply a statement of fact, in which "the world" appears in an entirely neutral sense. That the world came into being through the Word means that whatever else may be said about it, the world is not intrinsically evil. Rather, it is the creation of God through the Word. Yet the world did not know the Word of God when he appeared, and thus it will stand condemned. These three aspects, or evaluations, of the world are altogether characteristic of the Fourth Gospel. The world is the locus of God's revelation; it is created by God and is not intrinsically evil; yet it turns away from God, and God's revelation, and rightly therefore incurs wrath and judgment.

The following assertion (v. 11) is more specific. Not only did the world in general not receive the Word, but neither did his own people. In both verses 10 and 11 the crucial Greek verbs ("did not know," "came," and "did not accept") are in the aorist tense, indicating a specific, punctiliar event in the past. Probably Jesus' crucifixion and death are in view, and verse 11 narrows the world's rejection of Jesus (v. 10) down to his not being accepted by his own people, Israel, or the Jews (so also Calvin 1959, 16, who judiciously decides against its applicability to all people). The Gospel will tell that story. Perhaps verse 11 is deliberately left somewhat vague awaiting the reader's encounter with the events themselves.

But then we read of those who do receive or accept the Word and what happens to them, or what they are given (vv. 12-13). Jesus' rejection by his own people will turn out to be largely a rejection by their religious leaders or authorities. Those who receive Jesus are those who believe in his name. This use of *name*, signifying the reality of the person or of God is common in the Old Testament (see especially Deut 18:18-22). "*Believing* in the name" seems, however, to be a distinctly Christian, even

Johannine, way of speaking. The name, of course, is the name of Jesus, which has not yet been mentioned (cf. v. 17), but is clearly already in view. The power that believers receive to become children of God (the Greek specifies children, not sons) will be given by the risen Christ, who will bestow the Spirit upon his followers (20:22). In the closely related Johannine letters, believers are frequently called children (cf. also John 11:52; 21:5). The mention of children leads naturally to the idea of birth, which is also important in John (v. 13; 3:3, 5; 1 John 4:7). Only those who believe in Jesus are born from above (3:3).

Quite naturally there follows then a description of believers as those born of God (v. 13). The contrast with natural birth is drawn as sharply as possible by the process of negative reiteration: "not of blood, or of the will of the flesh or of the will of man, but of God." Here the Greek word means "a man" or "a male" *(anēr),* as the act of human procreation may be in view. ("Blood" is actually plural and could allude to the union of man and woman in the act of conception, but the language already indicates the natural, human sphere and probably should not be pressed.) In saying that the mention of children leads to the idea of birth (above), perhaps we assume a modern perspective. For John the idea of birth from above, or from God, may actually lead to the designation of believers as children. The question of which comes first, belief or birth from above, may not have occurred to John, but it has occurred to commentators since. Modern Christians would likely assume that belief precedes, and is the prerequisite of, birth from above. For John they are more likely coincident, obverse sides of the same coin. (This question will be discussed further in the commentary on 3:1-21.)

The Word Is Seen and Received in the Community
(1:14-18)

With verse 14 we reach the culmination of the narrative of the Word, although this is certainly not the first hint of his presence on the historical plane, among other human beings. Nor is Jesus even yet specifically named. Of course, the knowledgeable

Christian reader would have known from early on (v. 5) that Jesus was in view already. John 1:14 is often regarded as the classical statement of the Christian doctrine of the Incarnation, as 3:16 aptly states the doctrine of salvation. The Gospel of John has fundamentally influenced the way Christians have thought about, and articulated, basic beliefs. John now states what has been foreshadowed from the beginning, and especially since verse 5. Significantly, the narrator at this point begins to speak in the first-person plural, "we." A community now speaks and bears witness (cf. 1 John 1:1-4). The entire prologue is full of terms and concepts that will be unpacked in the course of the Gospel, but in this sentence about every other word is crucial: Word, flesh, lived, we, glory, son, father, grace, truth.

The idea, presented here as historical fact or event, that the Word became flesh underscores the humanity of Jesus uniquely (cf. 1 John 1:1-3), perhaps even more than would the assertion that God had become a human being *(anthrōpos)* or a man *(anēr)*. The idea that gods came to earth or took human form was not unknown in pagan antiquity, and John's language differentiates this event from such manifestations. Philo *(Gaium* 16.118) wrote that "God would sooner change into a man than man into a god" in denouncing emperor worship. In saying this he assumes the extreme unlikelihood of God's becoming human. (On v. 14 and the prologue generally see the relevant sources assembled by Boring, Berger, and Colpe 1995, 238-46.)

Because the Word is from this point on incarnate (enfleshed), the term itself now disappears, and we read of the Son, or of Jesus Christ. That the Word lived among us is a very suggestive statement. The NRSV has "lived" where the RSV had "dwelt" (v. 14). "Dwelt" may be preferable because the Greek verb *(skenoō)* used here means to take up residence as in a tent. The noun form *(skēnē)* means tent or tabernacle. It is the word used in Scripture of the tabernacle or tent of meeting where the Lord's presence dwelt in the wilderness (Exod 27:21; Lev 1:1; Num 1:1) and the people encountered him. "The LORD summoned Moses and spoke to him from the tent of meeting... " (Lev 1:1). The very word suggests a subtle but important theme of the prologue and of the Gospel, namely, that Jesus will become the place where the people will meet God, displacing the tent and its successor, the Jerusalem temple (cf. 2:19-21; 4:20-24). Like the temple and the tent, Jesus was a visible presence: "We have seen his glory."

That the incarnate Word lived or dwelt among us could be taken to mean "us human beings," and that would be true. Yet the following "we have seen his glory" can scarcely mean all people, but his earthly followers and disciples. To see the glory is to see Jesus for who he truly is, God's emissary, God's Son. Again, the tent or temple imagery is evoked, for the Lord God dwells in glory (cf. Isa 6:1-5; Ezek 3:12). In fact, John explicitly interprets the Isa 6 temple scene as the prophet's vision of God's glory (John 12:41). That God the Father's only Son is full of grace and truth is another way of asserting his close relationship to God. For God is ultimately the source of grace, as outgoing beneficent love, and the ground of truth, as what is real and reliable as opposed to all that is false (Bultmann 1971, especially 434-36). Truth is God's saving, life-giving reality. "Truth" is a characteristically Johannine term. "Grace" is more characteristic of Paul and New Testament writings influenced by him. Yet of all the Gospels "grace" in the theological sense occurs only in John, indeed, only in the prologue. It is as if the evangelist wants to make contact with a broader spectrum of early Christianity.

Although John 1:14 is considered the classic statement of the doctrine of the Incarnation, and it seems so when read in light of other similar passages in the New Testament such as 1 John 1:1-4; 4:2-3; 2 John 7; Phil 2:5-11; and Heb 2:14-18; it actually says little about the nature of incarnation, but states the fact boldly and briefly. Quite possibly readers supply meaning from these other texts, especially from the passages in the Johannine letters, which emphasize the tangibility of the Revealer or denounce those who deny his fleshly reality. How much is to be understood as said or implied in John's brief statement that the Word became flesh? Among recent exegetes opposing poles are represented by Bultmann (1971), who understands John to emphasize uniquely the humanity of the Revealer, albeit in a paradoxical way, and his onetime student Ernst Käsemann (1968, 9, 66), who holds that John does no more than say that Jesus appeared in human form, but in other respects negates his real humanity in presenting Jesus as a quasi-divine being. The essential point of Bultmann's contention that John intends to present Jesus as truly human is confirmed in the way Jesus' opponents and others know all too well his human origins and connections and assume that he can be explained solely with reference to them. He is really a human being, but he is also at once more than that, and this is what his opponents should see but do not (see Thompson 1993, especially 33-52, "Incarnation and Flesh").

John testifies, or bears witness, again (v. 15; on "crying out" cf. 12:44, where Jesus "cries out"). John's reference to what he has already said is a bit puzzling. Apparently the evangelist can have John speak in this way because the saying is well known, perhaps from the synoptic Gospels or tradition (cf. John 1:30, as well as Mark 1:7 par.). But the Johannine form is quite different. The saying is puzzling. Obviously, Jesus' preexistence is in view. The "insider" (to John's theological knowledge) would recognize this, but the "outsider" would be puzzled. The point is clearly once again the superiority of Jesus to John.

If the saying of verse 15 fell out of the picture, the reader would never miss it, as verse 16 follows quite well after verse 14. "Of his fullness" picks up on *"full* of grace and truth" (v. 14, emphasis added) as the narrator now resumes the first-person plural. What has occurred in the Incarnation overflows, so to speak, to the benefit of those who follow Jesus. The final phrase *(charis anti charitos)* is translated "grace upon grace" (NRSV, RSV) as if it means "grace abounding." Yet *anti* also has the meaning "opposite" or "instead of" and the phrase could be rendered "grace instead of grace." It might then point forward to the law and Moses as preceeding grace and Jesus Christ in verse 17. Nevertheless, to link the phrase to verse 17 appears questionable, because the latter is readily understood as presenting a contrast between law and grace (and truth) rather than continuity between one grace and another. Therefore the NRSV's "grace upon grace," indicating that every moment of the believer's life is determined by grace, seems quite appropriate. (A similar formulation is found in Philo, *Post. Cain* 43.145, and is usually taken to support this sense.)

Yet the seeming contrast between Moses and Jesus Christ (v. 17), now finally named, raises an important issue, which will reappear through the Fourth Gospel: What is the status of the revelation that was given through Moses? The grace and truth that have come through Jesus are clearly the salvation that he brings from God. Do they simply displace and negate the Mosaic law so that it no longer has any validity or force?

Paul, of course, faced this question, and while he clearly believed that God's graciousness, and righteousness, had been manifested apart from the law (Rom 3:21; cf. 10:4), he did not maintain that the law was wrong or had been invalid all along, or that it had not come from God (see Rom 7). Indeed, he was reluctant to say that the law is now, after Christ's coming, null and void.

In fact, John seems to occupy a similar position, even though he can call the law "your [the Jews'] law" (John 8:17). The law was given *through* Moses (v. 17), but the presumption that it is from God is never denied. Moreover, verse 17 begins with the conjunction *hoti* ("for" or "because"; omitted in the NRSV), which apparently links verse 17, as the causal explanation, to verse 16. There is no question that the grace and truth of Jesus Christ are the surpassing gifts. To read 1:16-17 as the supersession of law by gospel is natural, particularly given John's treatment of "the Jews," not to mention the development of Christian thought. Moses (i.e., the law), as read before Jesus' advent and as read by the contemporary Jews, has been superseded, but that does not call into question what God really did through Moses in John's view (see also Carson 1991, 131-34). We shall see the question of the status of the law reemerge later in this Gospel (5:39-46; 8:17; 9:28; 10:35).

The prologue concludes with a statement about Jesus that forms an appropriate closure or *inclusio* with what is said about the Word in the prologue (v. 18). As the Word *(logos)* is said to be God *(theos)* in the beginning (1:1) so now Jesus is declared God *(theos)* at the end. Perhaps understandably, there are various readings in different manuscripts, but the major alternative is between Son *(huios)* and God *(theos)*. The oldest manuscripts read *theos* (P^{66} P^{75} B and others). It is also the more difficult reading in that one would expect *huios,* since Jesus is repeatedly referred to as God's Son in the Fourth Gospel and elsewhere in the New Testament. (Moreover, *monogenēs,* "only" or "only begotten," is more compatible with "Son" than with "God." Bultmann [1971, 81] insists on similar grounds that *huios* must be original. If *monogenēs* means "only," then "God" makes little sense; if it is understood literally as "only begotten," it becomes possible, if unusual.) Yet at the end of the Jerusalem resurrection scenes, when Thomas has been shown the wounds in Jesus' hands and side and is invited to touch them he exclaims "My Lord and my God *(theos)*!" (20:28). This confession again forms a closure or *inclusio* with the prologue (1:18 as well as 1:1), and supports the more strongly attested reading "God" as the original. Furthermore, in the farewell discourses, Jesus says simply to Philip, "Whoever has seen me has seen the Father" (14:9). The NRSV's "God the only Son" (1:18) is therefore not a bad translation. It is faithful to the best manuscript readings and does justice to the adjective *monogenēs* (literally "only begotten") as well as to John's belief that Jesus is indeed *theos.* "Close to the Father's heart" *(kolpos;* NRSV) stretches the meaning of *kolpos* ("breast," "bosom"), however, and loses the important connection with 13:23, where the Beloved Disciple is said to recline in the bosom *(kolpos)* of Jesus. (Certainly "heart" will not do in 13:23, so the NRSV says simply "next to him [Jesus]." The RSV has "bosom" in 1:18 and "breast" in 13:23—better, although the same English word might have been used both places.)

Much of the discussion of whether Jesus can be called *theos* assumes a knowledge of what is meant by God. John's view, however, is that apart from Jesus God is not known, or in the coming of Jesus knowledge of God is now given in a definitive way, and is available from no other source.

The verse begins with the assertion that no one has seen God, an assumption that is apparently based on Scripture (Barrett 1978, 169; cf. Deut 4:12; Ps 97:2; but cf. Matt 5:8). God is not seen by mortals. The prologue concludes with the affirmation that Jesus (God the only Son) has made him known. Of course, Jesus has been seen by his disciples and others, so he has made the Father known, indeed, seeable (14:9). It is interesting, and perhaps significant, that the Greek verb translated "to make known" *(exēgeomai)* means to explain or interpret. The nominal form is literally *exēgesis*, what we do when we interpret texts!

◊   ◊   ◊   ◊

The prologue is a summation of the gospel message as well as of this Gospel's narrative. A person reading it for the first time, however, might partly understand or agree with it even down through verse 13 without knowing what its culmination will be. The distinctly Christian belief in the incarnation of God's Word in Jesus is not explicitly announced until verse 14. Until then what is said about God's activity through the Word might have been agreed to by Jewish or other readers of monotheistic faith. The knowledgeable reader, particularly the Johannine insider, would have seen what was coming early on and would have been well prepared for the announcement of the Incarnation in verse 14.

In fact, themes of the Gospel are suggested from the beginning of the prologue: light and life (in contrast with darkness and, although not yet mentioned, death); the role of John as witness; Jesus' rejection by the world and by his own; faith and the begetting of children of God; the incarnation and glory of the Word; grace and truth; Jesus' relation to Moses; his relation to the Father. At the beginning, the groundwork is laid for the prologue and the Gospel as a whole, as the positive role of the Word in creation is set out. The world that rejects God's Word was nevertheless created, along with everything else that exists, by God through him. At the outset of the Gospel any thoroughgoing, ontological dualism, which equates this world with evil or sees it as the product of evil forces, is rejected. The world is creation from God through the Word.

The prologue is just that. It is a prelude or overture to the Gospel, in which the major themes of the Gospel are struck. The evangelist will return to them in the course of the longer narrative. The prologue prepares the reader for that narrative, and particularly for the Jesus who is its protagonist. Insofar as the Jesus of John differs from the Jesus of the synoptic Gospels or synoptic tradition, John's prologue prepares the way for his appearance, so that the reader will be informed and impressed in the way the author intended, but will not be confused.

This language or vocabulary of the prologue, like the language of the Gospel generally, is quite simple. The principal theological terms, such as word, light, life, and truth, are common terms, known to everyone, but capable of a variety and depth of meaning. They have a history in ancient religion and philosophy. This is an aspect of the genius of John. More than halfway through the prologue the language and conceptuality are not specifically Christian. The religious or theological terms that seem most specifically Christian are "glory" and "grace." In Scripture and ancient Judaism glory is, of course, characteristically associated with the presence and manifestation of God. So its presence in verse 14 is telling. The glory of Jesus signifies his manifestation of God (cf. 12:42-43; 17:4-5, 22, 24). The grace that comes into being for believers through Jesus Christ is finally mentioned in verses 16-17. Grace is a predominantly Christian theological term and concept, although not without precedent in Jewish Scriptures and tradition. In fact, it is characteristically Pauline. God's grace betokens his goodness and initiative in inaugurating the salvation of all people. The reader of the New Testament will not be surprised to find that grace figures prominently, and appropriately, as Jesus Christ is named at the conclusion and culmination of the prologue.

The announcement of the Incarnation (v. 14) is cast in confessional form, as suddenly the author speaks in the first-person plural, "we." The existence of a community of Jesus' followers who have seen and borne witness or testified (19:35) is thus implied (cf. also 1 John 1:1-3). The Beloved Disciple is finally cast in the role of the one who authorizes this witness (21:24). Are we to infer that he is the leader of this community (cf. the title of Brown's *The Community of the Beloved Disciple* [1979])?

Probably. Yet efforts to press behind his seemingly intentional anonymity usually fall short of conviction. In any event, it becomes clear as we read John, and particularly in the farewell discourses (chaps. 14–16/17), that we are hearing the testimony of a group of believers who have reflected deeply, at some length and under the aegis of the Spirit (which is not yet mentioned), on the significance and role of Jesus as the revelation of God. Obviously such reflection has taken place in light of his death and their experience and belief in him as the Risen One.

INTRODUCTION TO JESUS (1:19-51)

As the prologue quite clearly delimits itself, so does the introduction of the Gospel narrative proper. After the prologue there is a fresh beginning (v. 19) as John reappears to give his testimony to Jesus. With Jesus' enigmatic word about the revelation of God in him the climactic moment of this entire episode is attained (v. 51). A new chapter begins a new episode (2:1). (The chapter-and-verse markers were inserted many centuries after the biblical books were written, and although they are often accurate indicators of textual divisions, they should not be taken as givens determining the analysis of the text.) Throughout this section there are at least two narrative threads: Jesus is revealed for who he is and his disciples are being gathered about him. In both, John plays a key role. While each Gospel has an account of the calling of the disciples, the Fourth Gospel's is quite different from the others, in which the disciples' work as fishermen figures prominently. This is true even of Luke's story (5:1-11), in other respects different from Matthew and Mark and similar to the resurrection appearance by the sea in John 21:1-14. The Johannine call stories neither mention the disciples' vocation nor place the scene by the sea. Instead John the Baptist appears and leads his disciples to Jesus.

The Fourth Gospel omits two very important episodes or items that intervene between the encounter with John the Baptist and the call of the disciples in the Synoptics. First, while Mark reports Jesus' temptation (1:12-13) and Matthew (4:1-11) and

Luke (4:1-13) give lengthy and quite similar accounts of it, John does not mention it at all. (Perhaps significantly there is a hint of the temptation in Heb 2:18; 4:15; as there is a suggestion of Jesus' fervent prayer in Gethsemane in 5:7.) Second, in Mark (1:14-15) and Matthew (4:17) Jesus announces at the beginning of his ministry that the kingdom of God has come near. This announcement is more strongly set apart and emphasized in Mark than in Matthew, but in Luke it is missing (but see 10:9, 11), as it is in John.

Whether or not John wrote with Mark or the Synoptics before him, it is not difficult to understand why he makes no mention of either episode. The temptation does not fit the portrayal of Jesus for which the prologue has prepared the reader. The announcement of the approach of the kingdom of God does not properly introduce the message of Jesus, which is about Christology, not the coming rule of God. What is more, John does not speak the language of apocalyptic, in which such talk of the kingdom is often cast. There is evidence, however, that John is not unfamiliar with such language (3:3, 5; 14:22; 21:22) or expectation. Rather, the focus is shifted to the present and to what has already occurred (11:23-25).

The Witness of John (1:19-28)

Priests and Levites (v. 19) represent the functionaries of the Jerusalem temple. (On "priests and Levites" see 1QS1-2.) They are sent by "the Jews," to whom they are apparently responsible. The identification of "the Jews" (Gk. *Ioudaioi*) in John is an important, and difficult, matter. The obvious fact that they are Jews does not warrant the assumption that they are the Jewish people generally. (*Ioudaioi* can also be translated "Judeans," as is appropriate in 11:1-44. Jesus' opposition is centered, significantly, in Judea. Yet that translation does not do justice to all the theological implications of the term.) Obviously, these Jews who send priests and Levites are persons of authority. They will appear throughout the Gospel of John as the opponents of Jesus, and they frequently seem identical with the Pharisees as is the case here (v. 24; cf. chap. 9; see above, pp. 35-36). Other people who are undoubtedly Jewish stand in fear of them (9:22; 12:42). Moreover, Jesus himself is clearly a Jew, as John knows (4:9, 22; cf. 1:45). So are his disciples, and so is John the Baptist. John, whose knowledge of Jesus and witness to him is entirely accurate, is never, however, called a Jew. Because "Jew" and "Christian" have long ago become mutually exclusive categories, and because in John the Jews seem unalterably opposed to Jesus, it is natural, although mistaken, to identify "the Jews" in John with the Jewish people. We should be aware that the situation within the Gospel itself is more complex.

The priests' and Levites' question to John is typical of this Gospel. They and the Jewish authorities want to know who John is, as they will be vitally interested in who Jesus claims to be. At the same time, their question allows the reader to once again hear John assert his subordination to Jesus. The motif of John's subordination appears in all the Gospels (Matt 3:11; Mark 1:7-8; Luke 3:16), but is more emphatic in the Fourth Gospel, whose interest in putting John in his place is apparently related to its setting and purpose. John denies he is the Messiah or either of the other eschatological figures, Elijah and the prophet (see Bultmann 1971, 90). Although John himself is identified with Elijah, the herald of the day of the Lord (Mal 4:5; cf. 3:1-2, which is quoted in Mark 1:2) in Matthew (17:11-13) and probably Mark (9:11-13; cf. 1:6), here he explicitly denies that he is Elijah or the prophet (probably the Mosaic prophet of Deut 18:15-22). Jesus himself is said to be that prophet in John 6:14 and 7:40, and this designation, while not adequate or complete in the evangelist's view, is not wrong (Meeks 1967). Although it is obvious why John denies he is the Messiah or even the prophet, since those titles are reserved for Jesus, it is less clear why he should not be identified as Elijah. Unless Jesus himself was in some circles identified with Elijah, the reason is apparently that the evangelist wishes to limit his role to that of witness to Jesus. John has no independent status in the plan of salvation, but is Isaiah's "voice of one crying out in the wilderness" (v. 23; see Isa 40:3). (Isaiah 40:3 is quoted in connection with John's appearance in all the Gospels; it also appears in 1QS8:15 justifying the community's retreat to the desert.) As the prophetic voice John may also represent the voice of Scripture, which he here quotes.

The statement that the questioners had been sent from the Pharisees (v. 24) serves to identify the latter with the Jews of Jerusalem (v. 19) as authority figures of the religious establishment. John is then asked about his baptizing activity in view of the fact that he accepts none of the roles or titles suggested (v. 25). Actually, baptism was expected of none of these figures, but all the evangelists as well as the Jewish historian Josephus (*Ant.* 18.116-19) knew that John baptized. John's answer is similar to his statement in Mark 1:7-8, and although he does not follow the other Gospels in immediately mentioning Jesus' baptism with the Holy Spirit, he will later on (v. 33). The conclusion of this day's activity is marked with a brief statement of place (v. 28). Bethany across the Jordan (that is, on the eastern side of the river) has never been satisfactorily identified. It is plainly not the Bethany Jesus will later visit on the outskirts of Jerusalem (11:1-44; 12:1-8; cf. Mark 11:1, 11-12). Interestingly enough, the first and last scenes of Jesus' public ministry occur in a place called Bethany.

As the narrative of John the Baptist moves forward, the similarities to the synoptic accounts grow more and more apparent, while at the same time there are noteworthy differences. An important difference is the way in which these events are told. In the Fourth Gospel uniquely, John himself is the narrator, as he looks back on events that have already occurred. This retrospective attitude is typical of the Fourth Gospel, which in large part reads well as a retrospective look at Jesus' ministry and seems to presuppose some knowledge of it on the part of readers.

John's Acclamation of Jesus (1:29-34)

John's appearance covers several days (vv. 29, 35). Jesus now comes to John (cf. Mark 1:9) and is hailed by John as the Lamb of God who takes away the sin of the world (v. 29). "Lamb" is capitalized in the NRSV as if it were a title, and that is not misleading. That Jesus as Lamb of God takes away the sin (note singular) of the world means that John here evokes the language and imagery of Scripture and specifically the temple cult, where the lamb appears as a sacrificial animal. Perhaps the Paschal (Passover) Lamb is in view, although that lamb is not actually a sin offering. Paul, however, speaks of Christ the paschal lamb as having been sacrificed (1 Cor 5:7), and for him Christ's death was quite clearly for sin (Rom 3:25). In the Synoptics, Jesus' last supper with his disciples is a Passover meal, and there in the words of institution of the Lord's Supper he speaks of his coming death as a sacrifice (Mark 14:22-25; Matt 22:14-23; 26:26-30). (Of course, in John the Last Supper is not a Passover meal, and there are no words of institution.)

In connection with the Lamb of God one also thinks of the Suffering Servant of Isaiah, who "like a lamb . . . is led to the slaughter" (Isa 53:7), in whose fate early Christians saw the prototype of Christ's suffering and death (cf. 1 Pet 2:18-25, which contains several references to Isa 53). Moreover, in the story of Abraham's obeying God's command to sacrifice his son Isaac, we read that at the last moment God stepped in to provide an animal (a ram) to die in Isaac's place. Just previously Isaac has asked Abraham "Where is the lamb?" and Abraham has replied that God will provide the lamb (Gen 22:7, 8). Although the imagery of the binding (Heb. *akedah*) of Isaac is reminiscent of the sacrificial death of Christ, it is not explicitly cited in the New Testament. On the other hand, Isaiah is cited or alluded to many times, particularly in the Gospel of John, and a background in Isaiah is more likely.

The theme of Jesus as the sacrificial Lamb of God pervades the book of Revelation, and is used in such a way that the readers' familiarity with it as a description of Jesus is presumed. In fact, however, two different Greek words are consistently used: in John *amnos* (1:29, 36), in Revelation *arnion* (5:6, 8, 12, 13 and *passim*). Yet since they clearly designate the same animal, some connection between the Gospel and Apocalypse remains quite likely.

The idea of Christ's death as cultic sacrificial, and vicarious atonement for sin is, of course, quite prominent in the New Testament from an early point in time and was sometimes based explicitly on Scripture (Mark 14:24; 1 Cor 15:3; 1 John 1:7; 2:2). Yet beyond this point the Gospel drops the language and conceptuality of bloody sacrifice, but retains and emphasizes the belief that Jesus died on behalf of his followers (10:15; 15:13-14; 18:8-9). Apparently the evangelist here appropriates a traditional and central idea, widely known and accepted among Christians, upon which he develops his own thought about Jesus' self-sacrificial death using somewhat different terms. (On the background of the Lamb of God see the excellent and succinct discussions of both Barrett 1978 and Schnackenburg 1968 on 1:29.)

John (v. 30) then repeats the statement attributed to him in verse 15, which is already a reference to something said earlier. That John did not know Jesus (v. 31) clearly contradicts Matt 3:13, which may be only the obvious inference from Mark 1:7-8 (but cf. Luke 1:36-56, according to which Jesus and John were related). Possibly John denies knowledge of Jesus because in this Gospel knowledge of Jesus, that is, of who he really is in relation to the Father, can only come by revelation (cf. v. 33). John links his baptizing with water to the revelation of Jesus to Israel: that is its purpose. The reader is not told whether John's baptism of Jesus—never explicitly mentioned—or his baptizing activity generally is meant. Either is possible. Probably the evangelist knows Jesus was baptized by John and omits mentioning it both because it can be assumed and because he wants to emphasize the subordination of John to Jesus.

John's testimony (vv. 32-34) echoes the synoptic account (cf. Mark 1:9-11 par.), except that again John is the narrator as he looks back retrospectively on what has happened. By John's telling it, however, he becomes a believing, confessing witness to the descent of the Spirit upon Jesus (cf. v. 34). The contrast between water baptism by John and Spirit baptism by Jesus is common to all the Gospels, but only John speaks of the Spirit's remaining upon him. The Greek verb for "remain" *(menō)* occurs in important theological contexts in John, as we shall frequently observe, where it is usually translated "abide" (e.g., John 15:4-16; 2 John 2:6-28).

The climax of John's narrative is the designation of Jesus as Son of God (v. 34). Again, it is John who has seen and testified to this. The testimony is doubtless based on what has been revealed to John by God. John's role in this respect is unique to the Fourth Gospel. "The one who sent me" (v. 33) is clearly God (cf. v. 6). While the evangelist is on the one hand careful to subordinate John to Jesus (on the implications for the Gospel's setting see above, pp. 54-55), on the other he accords to John a status above and beyond any other human witness, including Jesus' disciples. His voice (v. 23) and baptizing (v. 31) reveal to Israel who Jesus is. Even the Beloved Disciple does not attain a level of understanding above John's. John's knowledge corresponds roughly to what we have learned from the prologue: he knows about Jesus' preexistence (1:15, 30) and he knows that Jesus is the Son of God. Indeed, at this stage of the narrative his knowledge is unique.

The Gathering of Disciples (1:35-42)

As another day dawns (v. 35), John is now accompanied by two of his disciples, and he again designates Jesus the Lamb of God. Previously Jesus was coming to John (v. 29); now he is walking by. The disciples apparently understand that John is directing them to follow Jesus (v. 37) although he does not say as much. Of course, until now we have not known that John had disciples, a fact that we also learn from Acts (18:25) and the Synoptics (Mark 2:18; Luke 11:1).

That John is portrayed as sending disciples to Jesus may reflect the fact, "that there were erstwhile disciples of the Baptist among Jesus' first disciples, who perhaps joined him when he broke away from the Baptist" (Bultmann 1971, 108). However that may be, some important relationship between John the evangelist and John the Baptist is altogether likely. One can imagine that the disciples of John literally began to follow Jesus (v. 38), but the idea of following in the sense of discipleship is obviously near at hand (Mark 2:14-15; 8:34). Perhaps even John's description of Jesus as coming after him—verses 15, 30—has the sense of discipleship. For as Bultmann suggests, Jesus also may have once been a follower of the Baptist. If so, there would be all the more reason for the evangelist to explain and insist on the real theological order of precedence.

When Jesus turns and asks the disciples what they are looking for, the important quest motif of the Fourth Gospel appears for the first time (Painter 1993). That they respond with a question, "Where are you staying?" (Gk. *menō*), implies they are seeking something or someone in Jesus. The translation of "Rabbi" as teacher is functional rather than literal, and tells us something about the regard for teachers in ancient Judaism. The Hebrew word (*Rab;* Rabbi) means "great one," (cf. Mark 9:5, "Master" in the RSV). Of course, the translation also implies that the intended reader, or hearer, might not understand Hebrew (cf. also vv. 41-42). (*Rabbi* is used of Jesus again in v. 49; 4:31; 11:8; also of John by his disciples in 3:26.) Jesus' invitation to them to come and see (v. 39) is a response to their quest, so it is not surprising that they accept and remain *(menō)* with him that day. The time of day, the tenth hour (4:00 P.M. according to the NRSV, which in biblical, Semitic fashion reckons from 6:00 A.M. or sunrise) is a superficial explanation of their reason for staying, but probably not the real and profound one. They want to abide with Jesus (cf. 15:1-11). Their abiding will be the fulfillment of their quest, but not, ultimately, until Jesus is glorified.

One of the two disciples of John is now identified (vv. 40-41): he is Andrew, the brother of Simon Peter, who is spoken of as if he were already known (v. 40). Of course, they are otherwise known from the synoptic Gospels, where they are frequently mentioned. Although they figure as brothers in the Markan–Matthean call story (e.g., Mark 1:16), that story bears little resemblance to the Johannine account, and their identification here is somewhat belated. One now expects to have James and John, the sons of Zebedee and the other pair of brothers in that call story, similarly identified, but they are not. At least there is no explicit mention of James and John, and to expect them implies that John is to be read in light of the Synoptics—a reading that sometimes fits but just as often jars.

As Peter is found, Jesus is identified as the Messiah by Andrew (v. 41). This Semitic term, "Messiah," is then also translated into Greek. The NRSV renders the translation, "Anointed," which is literally correct, but conceals the fact that the Greek is *christos,* a word that is, of course, the technical theological title "Christ," and has usually been translated as such in the New Testament. The RSV translates "Messiah (which means Christ)" and there is no problem.

The problem is rooted in the NRSV's practice of translating *christos* as "Messiah" in the Gospels and usually also in Acts, although it is translated "Christ" in the Epistles. Actually, the Hebrew term transliterated into Greek as *messias,* appears *only* in the Gospel of John, and nowhere else in the New Testament. The NRSV's translation practice uses the Hebrew-based word in Jewish contexts, but thereby obscures the fact that the first-century New Testament *readers* saw only the Greek *christos,* or Christ, except here in John, where *messias,* Messiah, is actually found. Two significant issues are thus highlighted. One is the inevitable intertwining of translation and interpretation. Translation is already interpretation. The other is the relationship between Jewish messianic concepts and Christology as a distinctly Christian enterprise. The NRSV is trying to do justice to Jewish messianism. Jesus was the Messiah of Israel, or claimed to be, before he was acknowledged as the (Christian) Christ. The two are of course related, but are not the same, and the relationship is complex. Certainly in early Christianity and the New Testament the meaning of Jesus' being the Christ was different from what Judaism ascribed to, or anticipated in a Messiah, and there were different forms of messianic expectation (see below, pp. 74, 78-79, 175-76).

The Gospel of John seems deliberately to use the term *messias* here so as to emphasize that Jesus fulfills Jewish messianic expectation (cf. 1:45). Similarly, when the same term is used by the Samaritan woman in 4:25 it is intended to evoke the Jewish-Samaritan context. (In both cases *messias* is translated in the Gospel itself as *christos* ["Christ"].) In fact, in John *christos* (Christ) is otherwise used, even in contexts where "Messiah" might seem appropriate (e.g., 7:41-42).

When Simon is brought to Jesus and Jesus bestows the name Peter upon him (v. 42), it too is given first in the Semitic tongue (Aramaic), "Cephas" (used also by Paul of Peter, for example in

Gal 1:18), and then translated. Here affinities with the Synoptics, and especially Matthew, are striking. First of all, Peter is present at the announcement that Jesus is the Messiah, even though he himself does not make it (cf. Matt 16:13-20; Mark 8:27-30; Luke 9:18-20). Then in Matthew and John alone Jesus bestows on Simon the name Peter (in Mark and Luke he is called Peter from the outset). Moreover, he describes him as "son of...": in Matthew "son of Jonah" (16:17); in John "son of John." In Matthew, of course, Jesus also bestows upon Peter the power of the keys, of binding and loosing. Without mentioning the keys, the risen Jesus in John also gives to the disciples the power of binding and loosing (John 20:23; cf. also Matt 18:18). What is united in at least one of the Synoptics (Matthew) is scattered in John (see Brown 1961).

The climactic moment of the synoptic narratives, the identification of Jesus as the Messiah or Christ, is attained already at the beginning of the Fourth Gospel. The contrast with Mark, where the question of Jesus' identity has been building, is particularly noteworthy. The identification of Jesus as the Messiah is not the culmination, but a beginning point. Nevertheless, it is an important, indeed indispensable beginning point (cf. 20:31, where the NRSV translates *christos* "Messiah"). Jesus is the fulfillment of historic expectations even as he transforms them.

Messianic Fulfillment and Coming Revelation (1:43-51)

The question of Jesus' origins and relation to Jewish expectations is now spun out in such a way as to suggest that those expectations will be fulfilled, but transcended (cf. 1:49 and 1:51). Verse 43, probably correctly, gives Jesus as the subject of the initial sentence, although the subject is actually not named. (Peter, last named, would be the alternative.) In that case, the subject of "found" would also be Jesus. Of course, no one else in the Gospels commands "follow me," as Jesus does to Philip. That Bethsaida, Philip's city (v. 44), is also the home of Andrew and Peter seems to contradict Mark 1:29, where they have a house in Capernaum. (Capernaum is in Galilee on the northwestern shore of the Sea, whereas Bethsaida is on the northern shore, actually just east of the mouth of the Jordan as it empties into the Sea.) Archaeologists have uncovered foundations of a house in the ruins of Capernaum that is traditionally identified as Peter's.

Just as Andrew found Simon (v. 41) and Jesus (if not Peter) found Philip (v. 43), so now Philip finds Nathanael (v. 45), whose name means in Hebrew "God has given." To this point the disciples named are all known from the Synoptics; Nathanael is not, although he appears again in 21:2, where he is said to be from Cana (a place in Galilee mentioned only in John). Efforts to identify him with one of the twelve named elsewhere (e.g., Mark 3:13-19) prove fruitless, although John may consider him one of their number. John mentions the choice of the twelve (6:70), but never gives a list of them, as the other Gospels do. Most modern commentators (e.g., Barrett, Brown, and Schnackenburg) reject as groundless the identification of Nathanael with Bartholomew, which has often been suggested (apparently because Bartholomew's name follows Philip's in the Gospels' lists of the twelve).

The brief exchange between Philip and Nathanael (vv. 45-46) brings out major theological themes of the Gospel. Philip, in saying Jesus is the one about whom Moses and the prophets wrote, affirms him as the fulfillment of scriptural expectation (cf. 5:39, 45-47; 2 Cor 3:12-16). At the same time he describes Jesus in human terms; he is from Nazareth, the son of Joseph. One would scarcely expect the Messiah to emerge from the obscure village of Nazareth, the son of a humble Galilean. Nazareth is not mentioned in the Old Testament, or in other ancient sources antecedent to Jesus' birth. In 7:41-42, where the tradition that the Davidic Messiah will come from Bethlehem—David's city—is cited, John does not claim Jesus fulfills this prophecy. Moreover, John, like Mark and Paul, does not mention the Virgin Birth, associated with this tradition in Matthew and Luke. Both Jesus' humble origin and his humanity are affirmed, along with his messianic role. Nathanael's question (v. 46) is a perfectly natural one, but the note of irony will scarcely be missed by the knowledgeable reader.

This irony lies at the heart of the Johannine concept of revelation (see O'Day 1986; Culpepper 1983; Duke 1985). God speaks and reveals himself, improbably, in a man whose earthly origins are known, and who can be explained in terms of those origins (6:42). Such explanations may be true, but miss the essential point. Jesus is not only the Messiah, but the incarnate Word who comes from God. God is so present in him that he can say, "The Father and I are one" (10:30). To believe in Jesus is to see in this human being God revealing himself: "God's action is surprising and incredible; and the offence of the Messiah's coming from Nazareth belongs, as the Evangelist understands it, to the offence of the incarnation of the Logos" (Bultmann 1971, 103-4).

Jesus sees in Nathanael one whose skepticism is innocent and "guileless" (see v. 47 RSV) (cf. the translation of Brown 1966, 80; he links, and compares, Nathanael's guilelessness to Jacob's guile or deceit in Gen 27:35; see Brown 1966, 87). To be an Israelite in John's Gospel is a good thing, although "the Jews" characteristically appear as enemies of Jesus. Nathanael's response (v. 48) confirms Jesus' judgment about his innocence; his ignorance is not culpable. Those who pretend to know, and do not, are the really guilty (cf. 9:40-41). Jesus' enigmatic response to Nathanael is surprising, but not atypical. We have not previously heard that Nathanael was under a fig tree, and what that might mean goes unexplained. Perhaps Jesus assumes the scriptural, and proverbial "under his vine and under his fig tree" (see 1 Kgs 4:25; Mic 4:4) and simply means "while you were still at home." In any event, Nathanael rightly perceives that Jesus has uncanny supernatural knowledge of him (v. 49). That Jesus' knowledge of individuals precedes their knowledge of him fits the Johannine understanding of Jesus and of revelation.

In addressing Jesus as Rabbi, Nathanael speaks accurately, but not fully, about who Jesus is, as he goes on to affirm that he is Son of God and King of Israel. One might think Nathanael bestows on Jesus the most exalted titles of Greek and Jewish religion respectively. Yet matters are more complex than that. Judaism does come to a sharp rejection of the notion that Jesus is Son of God, and the roots of this rejection can be seen in the Fourth

Gospel. (Interestingly, Islam traditionally honors Jesus as a prophet, but the Koran sharply rejects the idea that God has a Son.) Yet Ps 2:7 has the Lord (God) say to the Davidic king, "You are my son; today I have begotten (LXX: *gegennēka*) you," language that may well lie behind the reference to Jesus as "only begotten" *(monogenēs)* in the prologue. Moreover, Jesus keenly observes that the people are called gods in Scripture (10:34, obviously citing Ps 82:6). So the claim that Jesus is God's Son has basis in Scripture and in specifically messianic tradition. Apparently, that the Messiah was known as God's Son is attested in the Dead Sea Scrolls. Thus in one fragment (4Q246ii1-3) the Messiah is to be called "Son of God" and "Son of the Most High." Yet while the divine sonship of the Messiah is not a purely Greek, or pagan, idea, it cannot be said to be prominent in Judaism, as it became in early Christianity.

The King of Israel is the Messiah, the Anointed, the Christ, who may be called also God's Son (Ps 2:7), as we have just seen. In him traditional hopes and aspirations for Israel will be fulfilled, but not in ways that could have been anticipated. One recalls certain statements and questions in Luke (24:21): "We had hoped that he was the one to redeem Israel"; or Acts (1:6): "Lord, is this the time when you will restore the kingdom to Israel?" They seem also to presuppose a traditional, unrevised, set of expectations. The extent to which Jesus will depart from traditional expectations is, however, yet to be seen, even in this Gospel.

Jesus' response (v. 50) suggests a certain inadequacy or incompleteness in Nathanael's confession, fulsome as it seems. Obviously Nathanael has believed because of Jesus' impressive demonstration of foreknowledge. Jesus' response sounds like "you haven't seen anything yet!" Then his further statement is again enigmatic and mysterious (v. 51). Interestingly enough, the verb in verse 51 now becomes plural as Jesus describes what you (plural) will see. Jesus is not just addressing Nathanael, but apparently the community of his own disciples in general (cf. 1:14; 16-18). Of course, exactly what he then describes is literally never seen by anyone in the course of the Gospel's narrative.

Scripture explains what is meant. In Gen 28:12 Jacob's dream at the place he called Bethel (28:19; in Hebrew *beth el* means "house of God") is described. In fact, this is the "Jacob's Ladder" passage, in which the angels of God are seen ascending and descending on it (that is, the ladder). How can this scene be applied instead to Jesus? In Greek, it scarcely could be, for the word for ladder *(klimax)* is feminine. But in Hebrew "ladder" *(sulam)* is masculine, so the Hebrew, which the evangelist must have either known or presumed, could be read "upon him," that is, upon the Son of Man, Jesus. (For a full discussion see Barrett 1978, 186-87.) Behind this use of the Genesis text is the belief that a new place of revelation has superseded the old. In Genesis (28:10-22), Jacob, who is called Israel (Gen 32:28; 35:10), sees in his dream a defining revelation of the God of Abraham and Isaac who promises to be with him and to bestow upon him and his offspring the land on which he is lying. After the dream, Jacob exclaims that the place of this revelation is the house of God and the gate of heaven (28:17). John the evangelist either knows that the reader believes, or wishes the reader to believe, that there is now this new place of revelation, the Son of Man, who is Jesus (John 1:51). Bethel (Gen 28:19) is no longer old Luz or even the Jerusalem temple, but Jesus. Jesus is the place of revelation, and thus the house of God and the gate of heaven. Inasmuch as John writes that "the Word became flesh and tabernacled among us" (AT) he appropriates for Jesus this whole ideology or theology of the place of revelation (see above on 1:14).

◊ ◊ ◊ ◊

This opening narrative (1:19-51) introduces Jesus and establishes that whatever or whoever else he may be, he is the Expected One, the fulfillment of Israel's messianic hopes. Thus it has somewhat the same function as the infancy narratives of Matthew and Luke. Yet the anticipation and hopes that were stirred were not fulfilled, at least not in the manner most Jews expected. Naturally, the evangelists are convinced that the failure was not Jesus'. But whose was it?

One traditional, Christian way of viewing the matter is that

Jesus was rejected when he came to fulfill those hopes and expectations because he redefined them in some spiritual sense that disappointed nationalistic aspirations. In fact, however, there was no single set of Jewish messianic hopes, but several. The picture was more complex than any simplistic characterization allows. Nevertheless, the Jesus-movement, and early Christianity, presented a revision of those hopes that Judaism was to find intolerable. The Gospel of John, as a historical document, is then an important witness to the process that produced ancient Judaism and early Christianity as rivals.

If as a historical document John testifies to the consolidation of Judaism and Christianity as closely related, but at some points tensely antagonistic communities, it also has a more irenic message and function. It expresses the faith and ethos of a closely knit community of people for whom the reality and love of Jesus were taken to be basic to their existence, life, and mutual support. Therefore, Christian readers have with good reason seen in it a valid distillation of what they believe and hope for, as well as how they ought to live with one another (13:34; 15:12-13; cf. 1 John 4:7-12, 16-21). A less fortunate legacy of the Fourth Gospel, however, has been the dismal view of Judaism it has begotten. But even on this point John's portrayal may be more complex, or ambiguous, than at first appears (D. Moody Smith 1996a).

By the end of the prologue the reader has been prepared to encounter the Johannine Jesus, who is obviously the same person described in the synoptic Gospels, but with dimensions the Synoptics may suggest, but do not fill out. He is the Word of God incarnate. By the end of this narrative we have seen this Jesus as he has encountered John the Baptist and acquired disciples. Even at that point, however, we do not yet know this Jesus fully, but we do learn what traditional Jewish titles or roles rightly apply to him. He is a rabbi or teacher, the Messiah, the King of Israel, and the Son of God. Because John denies that he himself is Elijah or the prophet, as well as the Messiah, the question must also arise of whether or not Jesus fulfills these roles. Although there are connections with the biblical pictures of Elijah and Elisha who raise the dead or feed people with barley loaves (1 Kgs

17:17-24; 2 Kgs 4:32-37, 42-44), Jesus is never identified with Elijah (or Elisha), but he is called prophet (4:19; 6:14; 7:40) and that perception of him is not contradicted. Of course, John introduces him as the Lamb of God, a figure who evokes powerful memories and images in Jewish tradition: the sacrificial cult generally, the Passover, Abraham and Isaac, and the Isaianic servant of the Lord. Finally, Jesus draws on the language of Gen 28:12 to suggest that he may be Bethel (House of God), the place of revelation.

Several elements of this episode contribute to, or form an indispensable background of, the introduction and presentation of Jesus the Messiah. John, whose witness has already been noted (1:6-8, 15), now appears to testify to Jesus, first before Jesus' potential opponents (1:19-28) then to his own disciples (1:29-42). Those disciples who hear him and follow Jesus will become the nucleus of Jesus' own community, the church. Although the term "church" is never used in John, the conception of a community of Jesus' followers is clearly present and indispensable to Johannine theology. There can be no Messiah apart from a messianic community, as the apostle Paul makes clear in Rom 9–11. Further, the community of Jesus' disciples will witness the revelation of God that Jesus brings (1:14) and will testify to others about it (17:20; 20:29). This revelation justifies the claim of those who hail him as the Messiah, but at the same time what Jesus says, does, and is goes beyond and even against traditional messianic expectation. After all, Jesus is condemned by the authorities of his own people and crucified by the Roman authorities.

THE REVELATION OF THE GLORY BEFORE THE WORLD (2:1–12:50)

Jesus' mysterious statement in 1:51 should lead the reader to anticipate the revelatory deeds that he will perform. Thus the wine miracle at Cana, his first sign, is the manifestation of his glory, and his disciples believe in him (2:11; cf. 1:14: "we have seen his glory..."). Immediately thereafter Jesus appears at

Passover in Jerusalem and encounters "the Jews" in the temple (2:13-22). It is the first of a series of encounters with Jewish authorities who will become his mortal opponents as the story progresses through chapter 12. Viewed from the perspective of the disciples, chapters 2–12 contain an account of the continuing and growing manifestation of Jesus' glory in deed and word. From the perspective of his opponents it is an account of the increasing manifestation of Jesus' offensiveness and even blasphemy (5:18; 10:33). There is a crescendo of conflict that reflects the setting of the Johannine church more directly than that of Jesus himself.

Jesus' ministry culminates in chapter 11, where after he raises Lazarus from the dead (11:1-44), the highest Jewish authorities, the council (or Sanhedrin), plot to put him out of the way. The anointing of Jesus (12:1-8) and his so-called triumphal entry into Jerusalem (12:12-19) are the concluding episodes of the first half of the Gospel. It now becomes clear from Jesus' own statements (12:23-26, 30-36, 44-50) that he has completed his ministry and will not emerge into the public eye again until his arrest (18:1-12). Jesus' manifestation of his glory in deed and word will now culminate in his death, which he often refers to as his glorification (12:23). Indeed, only from the perspective of his death would the disciples be able fully to perceive his incarnate glory.

The general function of the signs and discourses of chapters 2–12, as well as their relations to one another, is not difficult to discern, and there is a perceptible progress in the development of the narrative. Yet there are breaks and anomalies as well. For example, chapter 5 seems to interrupt a more obvious geographical connection between chapters 4 and 6. Moreover, as the many different suggestions of commentators indicate, there are few if any subgroups of episodes within the first half of the Gospel that are entirely obvious. In any event, there does seem to be a major watershed at chapter 5, where the hostility between Jesus and his interlocutors becomes more heated, and their opposition to him takes an ominous turn. If the Jews in the temple-cleansing scene (2:13-22) are perplexed by Jesus, those who challenge him after the healing at the pool (chap. 5) are out to do him in. Moreover, within this first part of the public ministry there seems to be a natural division between the two epiphany stories of chapter 2 and the series of encounters between Jesus and representative individuals (chaps. 3–4).

Jesus' Epiphany (2:1-22)

As different as the two episodes of chapter 2 may seem, they have a common purpose or effect. They show Jesus as he makes his first appearances: on the one hand, at a marriage, a family and community celebration in Cana of Galilee; on the other, at the center of Jewish worship and identity in the Jerusalem temple. In the first instance Jesus' disciples see his glory and believe. In the second his potential opponents are perplexed by his actions and words.

The Replacement of the Water with Wine (2:1-12)

As a major installment of the Gospel ends with 1:51, there is now a change of time and place (2:1). Cana is found only in the Fourth Gospel (cf. 4:46; 21:2); apparently the town was some miles northwest of Nazareth, although the exact location is disputed. The third day does not tally with the preceding enumeration of days (1:29, 35, 43). One thinks of Jesus' resurrection on the third day (1 Cor 15:4), although nothing in the context directly supports that interpretation. Possibly the expression means simply "the day after the morrow" (Barrett 1978, 190). This episode clearly concludes with the summary statement of verse 11 and the interlude of verse 12. The pericope is thus bounded on either side, and, as we shall see, has internal integrity.

There are unusual aspects of this story. Jesus' mother is present. His brothers are also mentioned in the aftermath (v. 12), and one wonders whether they belong in verse 1 or 2, since in some ancient manuscripts (notably Sinaiticus) the disciples, but not the brothers, are missing from verse 12. The second-century *Epistula Apostolorum* 5 (see Schneemelcher 1991, 253) mentions this wedding and says that Jesus was invited with his mother and brothers. Jesus rebuffs his mother, but nevertheless does what she apparently wanted him to do and provides wine to keep the wedding festivities going. In other Gospel miracle stories Jesus overcomes illness and demons, or in the feeding stories fills more pressing human needs. In an odd way, we recognize here the synoptic Jesus who came eating and drinking and was disparaged as "a glutton and a drunkard, a friend of tax collectors and sinners" (Matt 11:19; Luke 7:34). With some reason this story has been compared with tales of the youthful Jesus' miraculous deeds as recounted in the *Infancy Gospel of Thomas* (see Lindars 1972, 127). But this story is told with much greater subtlety, and when it is over the reader may even wonder what exactly happened. Jesus apparently performs a miracle, but the reader does not know exactly when or how he did it.

As puzzling as this story may be to modern readers, it is obviously important in this Gospel, in which it is Jesus' first public act. In Mark, Jesus' first public act is an exorcism in the synagogue at Capernaum; in Matthew it is the Sermon on the Mount; in Luke it is the programmatic sermon in the synagogue at Nazareth on the sabbath. Each of these events is typical and paradigmatic of the portrayals of Jesus in its respective Gospel. Something significant about Jesus and his ministry is evidently being said by means of John's rather unusual story. It is not just an odd and amusing tale.

The fact that this sign is numbered (v. 11) along with the next Cana sign (4:54) has led some exegetes to suggest they were both derived from a sign source the evangelist used (see below, p. 124).

◊   ◊   ◊   ◊

Jesus' mother's informing Jesus that the wine has run out (v. 3) contains an implicit appeal that he do something. Only in John's Gospel is Jesus' mother (never called Mary in John) present at the beginning of his ministry, and also at his death (19:25-27). (On Jesus' familial relationships in John, see van Tilborg 1993, *passim*.) Although there is no story of Jesus' birth, the mother of Jesus plays an important role in John. Here she evidently knows that he can take care of the situation. That Jesus then seems to rebuff her (v. 4) is on the face of it incomprehensible, but fits a picture that will develop through this Gospel: Jesus' interlocutors do not understand him, not even his family (cf. Jesus' response to his brothers in 7:1-10). Yet despite Jesus' apparent rudeness, his mother knowingly instructs the servants that they should obey him.

What Jesus has said to his mother (v. 4) merits closer examination, for it has to do with John's view of revelation. This is why Jesus puts distance between himself and his mother: "Woman, what concern is that to you and to me?" (cf. a demon's use of the same expression in addressing Jesus in Mark 1:24). Only on a superficial reading is Jesus being discourteous to a parent. He is equally brusque in rejecting his brothers' helpful suggestion about how he should carry forward his ministry, and for basically the same reason: his hour, or time, has not yet come. To his unbelieving (7:5) brothers Jesus says in effect, "Any old time is your time." He does not, however, say this to his mother, who also is not described as unbelieving. (Of course, Jesus' brothers would believe after his resurrection; cf. 1 Cor 15:7. According to Acts 1:14 Jesus' mother and his brothers are among the postresurrection believers.) Nevertheless, both episodes make clear that Jesus' agenda is not set by human considerations or prompting. As he will say repeatedly, he takes his direction only from God, and God sets the hour. Jesus' whole ministry looks forward to a denouement, in which he will be revealed in a full and final way. This *hour* (Gk. *hōra*) is the moment of his glorification, which encompasses his death and resurrection (cf. 12:23-25). It is significant that Jesus, in the presence of his mother, looks forward to the coming of the hour, even at this early point of the Gospel.

We are now told that six stone water jars used in Jewish purificatory rites are standing nearby (v. 6; the NRSV gives their capacity in gallons for the benefit of English readers, rather than saying two or three measures). It is very important for the progress of the story that these jars are nearby. They are, as one would expect, stone, because stone does not transmit impurity. That they are used "for the Jewish rites of purification" becomes important as things develop. Jesus is the new revelation that supersedes the old.

Nevertheless, he knows that salvation is of the Jews (4:22), as he himself is a Jew (4:9).

Jesus gives instructions to the servants, and they perform what he commands (vv. 7-8). At some point, as we can later surmise, the Jewish purificatory water has become wine. The chief steward is apparently a kind of headwaiter or caterer in charge (v. 9). In a long period, or sentence (vv. 9-10), we first learn of the steward's ignorance of the wine's origin (to be contrasted with the servants' knowledge of it). The steward is an "outsider" and the servants somehow are "insiders," but beyond that it is difficult to determine whom they may represent. That the steward is ignorant of the wine's origin recalls the motif of Jesus' origin, of which outsiders are ignorant. The steward wrongly, but naturally, assumes that the bridegroom (v. 9) is responsible for providing the wine. (Jesus appears as the bridegroom in 3:29 [cf. Mark 2:19-20] but does not play that role here.) The steward's word to him (v. 10) is complimentary and presumes a general practice, although efforts to document it in antiquity apparently have come up short (Bultmann 1971, 118, n. 4). That the bridegroom has kept the best for last would seem to make a theological point. If Jesus, or the salvation he brings, is symbolized by the wine, then the story says that, miraculously, out of the water of the (Jewish) rites of purification comes wine of Jesus (and the gospel). The defining revelation of God comes not at the beginning of salvation history, but at the end (Meyer 1967). What the steward has said is profoundly true, but his own understanding remains at the everyday level (cf. 11:50).

One can ask who the—presumably drunk—guests symbolize or represent as one can ask about the chief steward or the servants. Yet there is no easy answer. The whole episode is a kind of parable of the meaning of Jesus' appearance that should not be allegorized. If it were actually, originally, a parable, it would be comparable to the parable of the vineyard (Mark 12:1-12 par.) as applied to Jesus' ministry. One might in this connection ask whether John constructs a historical event from the parable of Lazarus (Luke 16:19-31; cf. John 11:1-44). John does not give us parables so much as parabolic episodes.

Jesus' deed is the first installment, so to speak, of the revelation promised in 1:51. Signs become quite important in the Fourth Gospel, and this is the first time they are mentioned. That they reveal Jesus' glory means they reveal God present and at work in him (cf. 1:14). The disciples believe (v. 11), as is appropriate after what Jesus has said just previously (1:51). Incidentally, we are not told how many disciples are with Jesus, but perhaps the twelve are meant, who appear without introduction in 6:67, as if they could be presumed in the narrative.

This simple concluding statement suggests a couple of major tensions that will be worked through in the Gospel. There is first of all a tension between faith elicited by signs and a deeper, more profound faith. Such a tension is already suggested by Jesus' statement in 1:50. There is also a tension between the revelation of Jesus' glory now, in signs, and his glorification in the Cross and Resurrection. The two tensions are not unrelated, because faith can advance beyond sign faith only in light of Jesus' glorification at the end of his ministry. Yet the fact that the disciples believe or trust in him now is not insignificant, even if their understanding is necessarily incomplete.

Between the wine miracle and the immediately following episode in Jerusalem there is a brief notice of the whereabouts of Jesus, his family, and his disciples (v. 12). Its connection with the preceding episode is curious, in that the same people are involved, with the exception of Jesus' brothers, who, as we have observed (v. 2), may have been present in Cana. Capernaum is, of course, the site of much of Jesus' Galilean ministry in the synoptic Gospels. Perhaps here John indirectly acknowledges the synoptic Gospels or tradition (cf. 6:59; Matt 4:13; Mark 1:21-34; etc.). As it stands, 2:12 simply sets the stage for Jesus' move to Jerusalem.

◊   ◊   ◊   ◊

Two issues concerning the origin and meaning of this story should be mentioned. First, there are parallels between the miraculous gift of wine here and pagan legends about miraculous gifts of wine for the feast of Dionysus (Bultmann 1971, 118-19). Has

John adapted such a legend? One also finds that in scriptural and other Jewish sources wine symbolizes God's eschatological salvation. (Schnackenburg 1968, 338, cites Hos 2:22; Joel 3:18; Amos 9:13; *1 Enoch* 10:19; *2 Apoc. Bar.* 29:5, as well as Jacob's promise to Judah in Gen 49:10-11.) The strangeness of this story in the gospel tradition justifies looking farther afield for its origin, but the fact that wine can symbolize salvation in Scripture and Judaism makes it reasonable to look there first, given what we know of this Gospel's milieu.

The second issue is whether in the wine symbolism there is also a deliberate allusion to the wine of the Eucharist. Also at the end of the ministry of Jesus, as the body of the crucified Jesus is pierced and blood and water flow out (19:31-37), the reader may again be reminded of the sacraments of the Lord's Supper and Baptism. At many points in this Gospel the Christian reader may be reminded of one or the other of these sacraments. Yet John is tantalizingly vague, in the sense that the Gospel usually does not drive such allusions home or make them explicit. We shall necessarily return to the question of sacramental symbolism at 6:52-58 and in chapter 13.

Despite the mysterious character of this story, with its complexities and difficulties, its purpose and effect are not hard to grasp. In the midst of a joyous celebration of life Jesus appears and, at a superficial level, seems to keep the party alive by producing the best wine when the host's supply had run out. The wine symbolizes the salvation that Jesus brings now, in the latter days of God's dealing with his people. The way in which Jesus does this also symbolizes his miraculous, but subtle, power. Jesus is able to effect salvation, to bring the new out of the old.

Although the Gospel arises from a Christian community under duress, the salvation Jesus brings is defined as joy (15:11). Indeed, the disciples' sorrow after Jesus' death and departure will be turned into joy (16:20). In the fulfillment of their prayers to Jesus their joy will be complete (16:24). Salvation is not a wedding party, but this almost universal form of human celebration symbolizes the joy that Jesus is said to bring and provides an analogy that makes that joy comprehensible.

The Displacement of the Temple (2:13-22)

So far, the Gospel of John has shown obvious similarities to, as well as striking differences from, the synoptic Gospels. Jesus' ministry begins in both with the appearance of John, his announcement of the advent of "he who comes after me" (1:27 RSV), and his encounter with Jesus. There is following the Baptist scene, however, no mention of Jesus' temptation (mentioned in Mark, narrated in Matthew and Luke), nor of his announcement of the nearness of the kingdom of God (omitted also in Luke). The Fourth Gospel then narrates the calling of disciples, but in a scene quite different from the Synoptics. Although there are hints of Jesus' ministry in Galilee (1:43; 2:12), Jesus' first public act, the miracle of the wine (2:1-11), is without parallel in the other Gospels and occurs in the town of Cana, which they never mention.

After a brief respite in Capernaum (2:12), Jesus goes up to Jerusalem for the first of three Passovers mentioned in the Gospel (v. 13). (The tradition of Jesus' three-year ministry is based entirely on the Gospel of John, in which it must last from two to three years.) He now cleanses the temple (to use the traditional language) while at the same time hinting at its destruction or supersession. This episode, found in all the Gospels, occurs in the Synoptics (Matt 21:12-13; Mark 11:15-17; Luke 19:45-46) on Jesus' one visit to Jerusalem, at Passover, just before his death. That it occurs at the beginning in John is a remarkable and significant difference. The explanations for it range from John's having it right historically to his having deliberately altered the synoptic chronology for his own theological purposes. The latter is much more likely the case. Clearly John's theological agenda is served by placing the temple cleansing here. Moreover, Jesus' arrest was likely triggered by this action against the temple. It may well be, however, that Jesus' activity lasted more than one year and that he therefore attended more than one Passover.

◊ ◊ ◊ ◊

Although the event itself is obviously the same one recounted in the Synoptics, there are many differences of detail. For example, nothing is said about sheep and cattle (v. 14) or a whip of cords (v. 15) in the other Gospels. More important, the words of Jesus are different. In the Synoptics, Jesus quotes Isa 56:7 and Jer 7:11; in John his disciples remember Ps 69:9 (v. 17), and in his previous saying (v. 16) Jesus probably alludes to Zech 14:21. In all the accounts Jesus drives out the money changers and turns over their tables (vv. 15-16). So far, there is nothing distinctly Johannine in the differences, except that the disciples remembered the word of Scripture. One might assume that they remembered it at the very moment (Barrett 1978, 198), but in verse 22 they remember only after Jesus has been raised from the dead. That is likely the case here as well (Bultmann 1971, 124; cf. 12:16 also), for John emphasizes the retrospective insight of the disciples, and the quotation itself seems to presuppose, and interpret, Jesus' own death.

Immediately there is another Johannine touch, as the Jews ask Jesus to produce a sign as authorization for what he has just done (v. 18). Jesus has just previously performed his first sign in Cana; we have not yet been told of signs in Jerusalem (but cf. v. 23). This demand is the Johannine counterpart of the question of authority posed by the chief priests, scribes, and elders in the Synoptics (Mark 11:27-33 par.). Possibly John has simply transposed the synoptic accounts into another key, although the many differences of detail suggest that John is relying upon another, closely related, tradition about this same event (cf. already Dibelius 1935, 45: "two different Paradigms"). Jesus' response to the demand for a sign (v. 19) is typically mysterious, in that there is no way those who are not in on the secret of his death and resurrection will get it. This saying about the temple is reminiscent of a number of references in the other Gospels and even Acts (cf. Mark 13:2; 14:58; 15:29; Acts 6:14). Aside from Mark 13:2 (followed by Matt 24:2 and Luke 21:6) only in Acts and John is a saying about the destruction of the temple attributed directly to Jesus. Otherwise, he is accused by enemies of prophesying the destruction of the temple made with hands and the restoration in three days of a temple not made with hands—seemingly a veiled allusion to his resurrection. There is then a remarkable similarity between what Jesus is there accused of and what he actually says in John.

Predictably, the Jews, who could not understand Jesus' reference to his death and resurrection—indeed, his disciples probably could not at this point (v. 17)—object to this seeming impossibility (v. 20). The forty-six years presumably date from the beginning of Herod's reconstruction in the eighteenth year of his reign (Josephus *Ant.* 15.380), that is, 19 or 20 BCE, which would put this Passover in 26 or 27 (not an impossible date on other grounds). Most important, however, is the Jews' misunderstanding of Jesus, so typical in John. Nicodemus will, of course, fail to understand (3:4), as will the Samaritan woman (4:15), and even Jesus' disciples (13:9). Their misunderstanding stems from their failure to comprehend his meaning, whether his role or his destiny. It is a function of their unbelief or, in the case of the disciples, their standing this side of the Crucifixion and Resurrection. Misunderstanding, like irony, is an implicate of John's conception of revelation. Until you understand who Jesus is and what he must undergo, the meaning of what he says is frustratingly hidden from you. Thus the believing, or informed, reader may know, but the participant, even the disciple, may not. Although the disciples' failure to understand in John is similar to a related motif in Mark, it is handled very differently.

The reader is told what Jesus was really talking about (v. 21). Then the postresurrection perspective is invoked (v. 22). In no other Gospel are we so clearly informed that only from this perspective did even the disciples understand (see also 7:39; 13:7, 19; as well as 2:17 and 12:16). This should not surprise us. All along Jesus points ahead to the arrival of his hour (2:4), which is his glorification (7:39; 12:23), at the same time indicating to the reader that lack of comprehension, even on the part of his disciples, is temporally conditioned. They had not reached the moment or gained the perspective from which Jesus might be perceived as glorified. Only with glorification comes adequate remembering and knowing, whether of Jesus' word *(logos)* or Scripture. The Jews on the other hand do not believe and cannot understand, although they are not yet hostile.

◊   ◊   ◊   ◊

That the temple cleansing follows the wine miracle makes narrative and theological sense. Jesus appears at the joyful human celebration that betokens the creation of new life, marriage, and out of the purificatory water of Judaism mysteriously creates the wine of salvation. Then Jesus appears at the central focus of his ancestral religion, the temple, in order to present himself as the new site of God's revelation (cf. 1:51 and Gen 28:12). The theme of Jesus' replacing the temple has already been suggested (1:14) and will recur (4:19-24). These two stories hang together as epiphany stories; Jesus presents himself through symbolic acts, one a miracle, the other a dramatic, prophetic deed. It is highly significant that both narratives portray Jesus as bringing or embodying what is new, displacing the old. (On the relation of the two, see C. Koester 1995, 77-85.)

Jesus Encounters Representatives of Israel (2:23–4:54)

This section is held together by a common motif: Jesus' encounters with representative individuals. But should they be called Israelites? Jesus calls Nicodemus "a teacher of Israel" (3:10). John is the quintessential gospel witness to Israel (1:31). The woman of Samaria is not even an Israelite according to the Jewish standards. Yet she belongs to a people who claim direct descent from the Northern Kingdom of Israel, even though that claim is rejected by Judeans. (Note that the Greek *Ioudaios* can be translated either "Jew" or "Judean.") In the fourth encounter the man who seeks Jesus out is not identified as a Jew. Is he a Gentile? Perhaps, but in the parallel account of the centurion's servant (Matt 8:5-13; Luke 7:1-10), the centurion is obviously a Roman soldier and therefore a Gentile. Indeed, his not being Jewish is intrinsic to the point of the story. Here John deliberately avoids saying or implying that he is a Gentile. This is particularly significant if the evangelist knows the Synoptic (apparently Q) version of the story.

The Reception of Jesus (2:23-25)

This is again a transitional passage, like 2:12, but one in which Jesus remains in Jerusalem. The general character and purpose of this passage is clear enough, although its precise meaning may be elusive. In fact, the Fourth Gospel often presents beautifully constructed and subtly crafted episodes linked by rather awkward transitions, or no transitions at all. (For example, the transitions between chapters or episodes are poor to nonexistent from chapters 5 through 10.)

◊ ◊ ◊ ◊

The opening statement is clear and straightforward (v. 23). Jesus is still at the same Passover. Already Jesus has performed a sign in Galilee (2:11); the Jews in the temple have asked for a sign (v. 18); indeed he has raised the anticipation that he will perform such signs in his subtle word to Nathanael (1:51). Nevertheless, to this point there has been no narrative of a sign performed at Passover or in Jerusalem. The presumption must be that such signs have, however, taken place (cf. 20:30; 21:25; on such "gaps" in the narrative, see Culpepper 1983, 74-75). That people believe on the basis of Jesus' signs exactly fulfills their purpose, and yet, as we next see, sign faith per se is not adequate (vv. 24-25; 3:2-3). (On believing on Jesus' name, see 1:12).

The next statement (vv. 24-25) is rather long and complex. Occasionally John constructs such a long, involved sentence, especially in a transition (cf. 4:1-3; 13:1, 2-5). Its clear implication is that Jesus does not accept such sign faith at face value. The common Johannine and New Testament verb usually translated "believe" *(pisteuō)* is here properly rendered "entrust." Jesus does not entrust himself to these people because he knows them. Jesus' uncanny knowledge of Nathanael led to the latter's confession (1:47-49), as the Samaritan woman will recognize Jesus as a prophet because of his knowledge of her past (4:16-19). So what is here said by way of explaining why Jesus does not entrust himself is not problematic. It is, however, stated in a mysterious way, but, again, mysterious speech is, as we have seen (e.g., 1:51), not uncommon in this Gospel. The NRSV translation renders the Greek superbly, and, indeed, clarifies it. As the use of *pisteuō* ("believe," "entrust") was somewhat unusual, so the use of "testify" *(martyreō)* is unique in John as applied to knowledge about something or someone other than Jesus.

That we have understood the meaning of this initially mysterious statement will become clear as we read the story of Jesus' encounter with Nicodemus, who exemplifies what is here said. A number of Johannine themes surface in this brief transition: belief in Jesus' name; the effect of signs; Jesus' omniscience and his superiority to ordinary human consciousness.

Nicodemus, a Leader of the Jews (3:1-21)

The appearance of Nicodemus obviously introduces a new episode, which runs through verse 21. Verse 22 is similar to 2:12; it is a brief statement that locates Jesus and his disciples geographically and affords a kind of transition to the next episode. While 3:1-21 clearly constitutes a unit, it is not easy to determine where the conversation with Nicodemus actually ends. After Nicodemus asks his perplexed question in verse 9 he does not speak again in this episode. Jesus responds to him directly in verse 10, and seems to refer to him in the second person in verses 11-12. Yet there the "you" is plural, a fact that the English translation cannot reveal, and Jesus, who is still speaking, seems to include others among his audience. In verses 13-15 Jesus may still be speaking, although he now refers to himself in the third person ("Son of Man"). From verse 16 onward Jesus, if he is still speaking, refers to himself as God's Son, but verses 16-21 are best read as John's theological affirmations rather than as words of Jesus.

Nicodemus is introduced as a man of the Pharisees (RSV; cf. 1:6). He is obviously a prominent Jew (NRSV: "leader"; RSV: "ruler"; Brown 1966, 128 elaborates: "member of the Jewish Sanhedrin"). His name is the Greek version of the Hebrew Naqdimon (see Barrett 1978, 204; Lindars 1972, 149). Although a person (or persons) of that name is known from Jewish sources, his exact identity will likely always elude us.

That Nicodemus comes to Jesus "by night" (v. 2) is suggestive, particularly in view of the role of darkness and light at the conclusion of this pericope (vv. 19-21; see C. Koester 1995, 5, 9). At the end of the Last Supper, moreover, Judas departs into the night (13:30). Night may have also been a time when rabbis studied and discussed the law, so there could be more than one level of significance in this simple statement. Nicodemus addresses Jesus as "Rabbi," as do Jesus' disciples-to-be when they first encounter him (1:38). Furthermore, Nicodemus acknowledges Jesus' authority and role on the basis of his signs (cf. Egerton Papyrus 2 3:44-45), seemingly exemplifying those who believed on the basis of signs (2:23). (The NRSV's "apart from the presence of God" in v. 2 represents an effort to avoid sexist language or presuppositions: The RSV translates literally, and more accurately, "unless God is with him.") "Nicodemus and Joseph of Arimathea represent those who believe but refuse to confess lest they be put out of the synagogue (12:42)" (Culpepper 1983, 136). Although belief in signs is not adequate for faith in Jesus as the Christ (cf. 20:30-31), it is the gateway to such faith. Thus Nicodemus returns to defend (7:50-52) and finally to bury Jesus (19:39). Those who reject or dispute Jesus' signs seemingly have no possibility of coming to faith. Signs function as proof of divine authorization in Scripture, especially the Exodus narratives (e.g., Exod 4:1-9, 17, 30). Here the figure of Moses looms large. The expectation to which the signs of Jesus correspond may have more to do with the prophet like Moses (Deut 18:15-22) than the Davidic Messiah, who was not expected to perform such deeds (see Martyn 1979, 93-100).

After Nicodemus' respectful approach, Jesus' response (v. 3) seems abrupt, if not rude. That response nevertheless affords a crucial insight into what is going on: Nicodemus and Jesus cannot converse meaningfully because Nicodemus has not yet been born from above (cf. 1:13; also 1 Pet 1:3), as Jesus is from above (v. 13). Jesus and Nicodemus inhabit two different realms of discourse, so to speak, as will become increasingly evident; their conversation is like ships passing in the night! Jesus' reference to the kingdom of God is a rarity in the Fourth Gospel (also in v. 5; cf. the references to Jesus' kingdom in 18:36 and to Jesus as king in 1:49; 6:15; 12:13, 15). Yet John knows this early Christian language and rightly puts it on the lips of Jesus. Probably as in Acts the kingdom of God signals the realm of gospel truth (cf. Acts 8:12; 28:23, 31). The apocalyptic eschatology, associated with the kingdom of God in the synoptic words of Jesus, is reinterpreted in John in favor of an emphasis on present, individual salvation (*life* or *eternal life*). Thus "unless you (sing.) are born from above.... " The Greek word *anōthen* means either "from above" or "again." The NRSV's choice is good, in that "from above" is the more relevant meaning. Nicodemus will hear Jesus say "again," which is not incorrect, although it is not the main point. Rebirth must be birth from above, that is, from God (1:12-13).

Nicodemus' rejoinder is quite natural and, one might say, that is precisely the point. He misunderstands the otherworldly word of Jesus in terms of this world (v. 4). Obviously, Nicodemus's questions pose an absurdity, as Nicodemus himself would know. Jesus' answer (vv. 5-8) is a reiteration of, but a considerable expansion upon, his initial response. Birth from above is now further described as "being born of water and Spirit." Birth by water is almost certainly a reference to Christian baptism, which would be accompanied by the gift of the Spirit. Moreover, being born of water *and* Spirit is obviously the equivalent of being born from above (v. 3).

The fundamental distinction of flesh and spirit, which reflects the Johannine dualism, is now drawn out (vv. 6-7; cf. 6:63). Flesh-spirit dualism is found also in Paul (Rom 8:3-14). On the other hand, *flesh* in John may also have a neutral or more positive sense (1:14; 6:52-58). It is worth observing (see the NRSV note) that the same Greek word *(pneuma)* means both wind and spirit (e.g., pneumatic tires and pneumatic people). The same is true of the Hebrew *ruaḥ* John plays on this double meaning, emphasizing this distinction and the dualism that goes with it as he equates birth from above with birth by the Spirit (vv. 7-8). That water is not again mentioned led Bultmann to suggest that it was added by the later, churchly redactor in verse 5 in order to introduce a reference to the sacrament of Baptism (1971, 138, n. 3), but ancient manuscript evidence does not strongly support this omission.

The point of the play on wind/Spirit (v. 8) is the unpredictability of the Spirit's activity. That, unaccountably, some are born of the Spirit while others are not must be the meaning of the concluding statement of this verse—not that such people are themselves unpredictable! Humanly speaking, it is impossible to account for the Spirit's work. But, at best, Jesus' words are mysterious and enigmatic, particularly if Nicodemus naturally understands *pneuma* as "wind." Thus his question is again "natural" and understandable (v. 9). Nevertheless, Jesus sharply chides him (v. 10). Nicodemus, who at the beginning of the conversation called Jesus "Rabbi" and a teacher come from God is now called the teacher of Israel, as Jesus feigns astonishment at his ignorance. So this is a conversation between two rabbis, two teachers, as Jesus also has been sent to Israel (1:11; cf. 1:31).

That Nicodemus, who has been introduced as a prominent and fully credentialed Jew, is now called "*the* teacher of Israel" is worth pondering. (The Greek definite article is not translated as such in either the NRSV or RSV.) "The article emphasizes the status of Nicodemus: the great, universally recognized, teacher" (Barrett 1978, 211). Obviously, as the teacher of Israel Nicodemus should understand about Jesus, but he does not. While "the Jews" are pretty consistently presented as the opponents of Jesus, "Israel" and "Israelite" are used in a positive sense. Israel is still viewed as the people of God, even if her teachers no longer understand the Word of God, as Jesus presents it—and himself. Still, Nicodemus is not simply consigned to the realm of darkness and unbelief as verses 11 and 12 might imply. He returns to defend Jesus and to give him honorable burial (7:50-52; 19:39). At this point, however, he represents Jewish officialdom's incomprehension of Jesus. Nicodemus assumes that he and Jesus can carry on a conversation on equal terms, so to speak (v. 2). After all, are they not both teachers of Israel? But Nicodemus does not, or does not yet, understand that he and Jesus do not stand on the same level.

When Jesus begins to answer Nicodemus's question (v. 9), with a somewhat off-putting response (vv. 11-12), he does not seem to expect Nicodemus, who has behaved as a perfectly reasonable man, to understand. A subtle shift, not even discernible in English, has, however, taken place. The NRSV footnote indicates that Jesus addresses Nicodemus in the plural, even as he himself speaks in the plural ("we"). It is as if Jesus and Nicodemus are no longer speaking as individuals, but Jesus is addressing Nicodemus as the representative of a community. Indeed, they are: Nicodemus of the Jewish synagogue generally and Jesus of the disciples who testify to him. (Even when Jesus switches back to the first-person singular in v. 12, he continues to use the plural of Nicodemus or whomever he is addressing.) From this point on, Nicodemus does not speak. In fact, the question of verse 9 is his departing word in this episode.

Verse 11 is quite intelligible as a statement of Jesus, or on behalf of Jesus by his followers, to those Jews—or better, other Jews— who do not believe. (On Jesus' followers' knowledge cf. 9:24-34, especially v. 25; on "What we have seen" see 1:14 as well as 1:34 and 1 John 1:1, 3.) On the other hand, Jesus' next statement (v. 12) is tantalizingly mysterious and even vague. Can what Jesus has just said about birth from above be regarded as "earthly things"? Perhaps, since they have to do with the anthropology of salvation rather than the mysteries of God, or the kingdom of God per se. The latter are suggested by Jesus' words about his ascent to, and descent from, heaven that immediately follow (v. 13). Or is this simply a form of the ancient topos by which a slow learner's aspirations for higher knowledge are cut down to size (see Meeks 1972, 53-54)? In that case, our search for the antecedents of "earthly things" and "heavenly things" may be misdirected.

After this rather disparaging aside to Nicodemus and his fellow unbelievers ("you" plural), Jesus begins to unfold the gospel, at first in terms that are rather veiled (vv. 13-15), but then more explicitly. Quite conceivably the ascent and descent of the Son of Man, as well as his being lifted up in order to bestow eternal life, qualify as "heavenly things." The Son of Man who ascends and descends, who is lifted up, is of course the same Jesus who is speaking—from this point on in the third person. The NRSV puts the rest of the discourse—through verse 21—in quotes, but the RSV ends the quotation at verse 15; in fact, the original Greek had no such punctuation. Conceivably, it is the evangelist who speaks from verse 13 on, although what the evangelist says and what Jesus says are one and the same. Our quandary about punctuation may therefore be irrelevant to the ancient author.

The apparently polemical statement of verse 13 ("No one has ascended into heaven . . . ") may have in view claims of (or for) those other than Jesus who were said to have ascended into heaven, perhaps Moses (Meeks 1967, 299, 301; cf. Deut 34:5-6) or even Enoch (Gen 5:24) or Elijah (2 Kgs 2:1-12). The ascent of a human being to heaven was uncommon, but not unknown, in Judaism (cf. also 2 Cor 12:2-4). The claim that Jesus has descended from heaven (cf. Phil 2:6-11) is more likely unique. (Yet in Isa 55:10-11 God's word's departure from his mouth is likened to the descent of rain, and it is said to return, i.e., ascend, to him). Certainly Moses figures fundamentally in the typology that follows (v. 14). Moses in his saving work is a type of the Son of Man, even the crucified Jesus. The biblical scene in view here is Num 21:8-9, where the Lord instructs Moses to make an image of a serpent and elevate it on a pole, so that the rebellious Israelites, against whom the Lord had actually sent serpents in the first place, might, if snakebitten, look on it and live. The analogy with the work of the crucified Jesus, the Son of Man who is lifted up, is very striking indeed. It is a classic typology. The element that is new in John, and characteristically Christian, is the emphasis on belief, which is absent from the story in Numbers. (Of course, comparisons of Jesus with the serpent are misplaced; the analogy applies only to being lifted up.)

In any event, the language of verses 13-14 is mysterious and veiled, although the statement of verses 14-15, when applied to Jesus, is plain enough. It is as if Jesus, as long as he is speaking directly to Nicodemus, or Nicodemus and company, uses veiled and mysterious language. If so, the RSV does well to close the direct quotation with the statement ending at verse 15. These then may be the heavenly things just alluded to (v. 12). From verse 16 onward we read an open and explicit statement of the Christian message, cast in Johannine terms.

For good reason John 3:16 is widely viewed as a classic summation of that message. That God gave his Son because of his love for the world, or for us human beings, is said by Paul (Rom

5:8), with particular emphasis on the saving work of Christ's death, which is surely implicit in "God gave" in 3:16 (Bultmann 1971, 153-54, n. 3). "Son of Man" here gives way to "Son," and there is little reason for seeing a significant difference in this context. "Son of Man" is the title used in the synoptic Passion predictions (cf. Mark 8:31; 9:31; 10:33), which find in 3:14 a Johannine parallel. "Only" in "only Son" (3:16) again translates the Greek *monogenēs*, literally "only begotten," which becomes important in the later creedal formula "begotten, not made" (which is actually a reasonable interpretation of John's statement, 1:1-2, that the Word was in the beginning with God).

The alternative of perishing or having eternal life is obvious enough, but fits the Johannine dualism: light or darkness (vv. 19-21); life or death. "Eternal life" rather than "kingdom of God" is the typically Johannine term for the blessing of salvation. Eternal life is fundamentally a gift of God, through the Son, available to all who believe. It is perhaps noteworthy that the language of new birth is replaced by the language of believing or faith, obviously understood as an option the individual may choose to exercise. (Throughout the Gospel the language of faith and decision is paralleled with that of new birth and election. The two are not mutually exclusive modes of appropriating salvation through Jesus. Rather, they are different sides of the same coin.)

God's purpose in sending the Son, as well as its actual effect as people encounter him, next becomes the subject of reflection (vv. 17-21). The purpose of Jesus' coming as God's Son was salvation rather than judgment. That seems clear enough, and is said again at the end of Jesus' public ministry (12:47). But the opposite can also be said (9:39), and apparently with equal seriousness: "I came into this world for judgment.... " Can both statements be true? "Unbelief, by shutting the door on God's love, turns his love into judgement" (Bultmann 1971, 154). That is about right, although it flies in the face of some of John's statements. The Johannine dualism accommodates the view that God's will is salvation, but rejection of that salvation incurs judgment. Statements that make judgment Jesus' purpose in coming into the world are usually made in conflictual situations, where Jesus is opposed or opposition is in view (5:22-30; 9:39; 12:31). The tension between Jesus' judging and not judging is manifest in 8:15-16, where he says that he judges no one, but then seems to concede that he does.

This tension between salvation and judgment is worked out in the subsequent discussion (vv. 18-21), in which Bultmann's assessment (above) is corroborated. The alternatives are set out clearly (v. 18). "Condemned" translates the same verb *(krinō)* that is elsewhere rendered "judge" (e.g., 5:30). Clearly it means "judge" in the sense of condemn in verse 18, but to translate "judge" would make the connection with "judgment" in verse 19 even stronger and would agree with 5:24: the believer does not come under judgment. To disbelieve is to incur judgment. Characteristically, John speaks of believing in the name of the only—or only begotten—Son of God (cf. 1:12). The nature of, or reason for, the judgment is now described (vv. 19-20), as is the destiny of those who do not come into judgment or condemnation (v. 21).

These statements (vv. 19-21) are plain enough. The light is, as the reader by now knows well, Jesus the Son of God. The world, although the object of God's salvation, is otherwise in darkness, in which people whose deeds are evil can—or so they imagine—hide from the light. On the other hand, there are "those who do what is true" (v. 21), a phrase that is found also in the Qumran Community Rule ("practice truth"; 1QS1:5; 5:3; 8:2; cf. Tob 4:6; 13:6). To see such a phrase in the context of this light/darkness dualism, also found in the Qumran Community Rule, is not at all surprising. Nor is the fact that the context is decidedly eschatological. "The light shines in the darkness, and the darkness did not overcome it" (1:5). The coming of the light reveals darkness for what it is, and the division between light and darkness is the eschatological judgment. Jesus brings it with himself, and those who believe in him do not come under judgment, but have passed from death to life (5:24). They are not condemned, or judged (3:18). As those who do evil flee the light (v. 20), those who do what is true come to it (v. 21), so that the source of their deeds may be seen.

One asks, however, what does the coming of Jesus as the light effect? Does it effect anything—that is, does it make any difference—or does it simply reveal what people already are? The dualism that we have observed might suggest that the coming of the light shows what is already the case. It has a revelatory function, so to speak, but does not change anything. (See Haenchen 1984, 207; cf. 82; who assigns the passage for that reason to later redaction.) This is one way of reading this description of the effect of the coming of the light. But does the Gospel not allow an alternative reading? "Rather what is meant is that in the decision of faith or unbelief it becomes apparent what man really is and what he always was.... His decision as to his destination at the same time settles his decision on his origin" (Bultmann 1971, 159). Believing carries with it a kind of double determinism: who I shall be and who I was all along can only be known from the standpoint of my reaction to the light, so that everything is at stake in that decision.

The conversation with Nicodemus begins with his acclaiming Jesus as a teacher sent from God. But Jesus' reply indicates that Nicodemus, even though a teacher of Israel, is not yet in a position to converse with Jesus, because he has not attained knowledge of who Jesus really is. Jesus cannot be understood by old standards, even those of the traditional Judaism represented by Nicodemus. He is God's new and final revelation to Israel, but also humankind generally (1:10, 11). At the same time, he is sent by the same God who has created and will redeem Israel. For John the (Old Testament) Scriptures are still valid, but they must now be properly understood as bearing witness to Jesus (1:45; 5:39-47). Jesus came after John, but was before him (1:15, 30), even as, indeed, he was before Abraham (8:58). Jesus is the fresh and final revelation of God, who sets all that came before in a new light. Thus the teacher of Israel cannot judge Jesus by old standards, valid as they once may have been. Rather, Jesus himself becomes the standard of judgment, because he is the self-authenticating Word of God.

Prerequisite to such knowledge of Jesus is birth from above, of water and Spirit (vv. 3-7). Because he cannot comprehend these necessities (earthly things?), Nicodemus will scarcely be able to grasp Jesus' veiled speech about who he is and what he has accomplished (vv. 13-15; heavenly things?). Then the evangelist openly declares (v. 16) the basic Christian proclamation about who Jesus is, where he comes from, and the salvation he brings (whether or not presented as words of Jesus is not clear and perhaps not so important). The episode concludes with a reiteration of God's purpose in sending the Son (v. 17), an affirmation about its immediate effect (v. 18), and a description of how this effect may be recognized (vv. 19-21). In effect, it begins with Jesus laying out the anthropology of salvation, the regeneration of persons, and ends with the explanation of how that regeneration is manifest in their actual living: they do what is true and come to the light. At both ends emphasis falls on practical, human experience and effects, without any suggestion that such effects are self-generated. They depend fundamentally on the sending of the Son and the gift of the Spirit.

John the Baptist (3:22-36)

At first glance this section may seem less clearly defined than the one just preceding, but in fact they are remarkably similar in that each begins with a conversation, in the one case between Jesus and Nicodemus (3:1-10/15) in the other between John and his disciples (3:22-30), and concludes with a series of assertions that brings out the theological dimensions of the conversations. This episode differs from the ones that precede and follow in that there is no direct encounter between Jesus and John, but of course they have already met (1:29-42). It is strikingly significant that between Jesus' encounter with Nicodemus, who does not understand at all, and the woman of Samaria, who understands imperfectly, there comes John, who understands completely and testifies unhesitantly, although seemingly to his own detriment. Clearly a new episode begins at 4:1-2 as Jesus leaves Jerusalem and heads for Galilee.

Because the statements of verses 31-36 seem inappropriate as words of or about the Baptist, some commentators have suggested moving them to a point earlier in the chapter (after v. 12 or v. 21). We shall argue below that the section can be read intelligibly where it now stands. Such an appearance of John during Jesus' ministry is unparalleled in Mark, but is found in Matthew (11:2-19) and Luke (7:18-35), where John sends emissaries to Jesus from prison to inquire about his status and role. Once again the Johannine narrative has a point of contact with the Synoptics, although in substance the accounts are quite different.

◊ ◊ ◊ ◊

3:22-30: Jesus withdraws into Judea (v. 22). Since Jesus is already in Jerusalem and Jerusalem is in Judea, John doubtless means the Judean countryside as the NRSV translates (RSV: "land of Judea"). Obviously this is a transitional moment in the narrative (cf. 2:12 especially; also 5:1; 6:59; 10:40). Jesus is accompanied by his disciples (cf. 2:2, 12), although we have not yet been told they are twelve in number, and will not be until 6:67 and 70. (The twelve are never listed in John. Readers of the Synoptics will likely assume that the twelve are meant, but this is not necessarily the case; Jesus has other disciples, as 6:66 shows.) Surprisingly, Jesus is said to baptize, something he never does in the other Gospels. Moreover, John's disciples refer to Jesus' baptizing (v. 26), but the evangelist or an editor takes exception to, and corrects these statements (4:2). If, in fact, Jesus had been a follower of John (cf. 1:15, 30) he would seem to be expanding the latter's own ministry. It is noteworthy that the baptizing activity of Jesus is set in the period before John's imprisonment (3:24), while Jesus' own ministry does not begin until after John's arrest according to the synoptic account (Matt 4:12; Mark 1:14). The view that John reports Jesus' earlier activity is at least as early as Eusebius (*Hist. Eccl.* 3.24.7-13). Obviously the context requires us to think of baptism with water, so this is not the baptism with the Spirit that Jesus will administer (1:33).

The location of John's baptizing is given precisely (v. 23), and there is little reason to think the author, or his source, is not confident of his information. Aenon may be based on a Hebrew word for spring, while Salim is the name of a town near ancient Bethshan or Scythopolis, probably six or eight miles south of it near the border of Samaria (Schnackenburg 1968, 412-13). The evangelist's, or an editor's, note in verse 24 presumes knowledge of John's imprisonment, which is recounted in the Synoptics (cf. Mark 1:14), but not in this Gospel. Yet, John's imprisonment and execution were widely known facts (Josephus *Ant.* 118.116-19).

The stage is now set for some further description and assessment of the relation between John and Jesus, but it is introduced in a puzzling way. The Jew who discusses purification with John's disciple (v. 25) disappears from the scene as quickly as he has entered. In some ancient manuscripts (including P[66] and the original reading of Sinaiticus) one finds "Jews," doubtless an accommodation to the fact that "the Jews" appear frequently in John's narrative, while this single Jew is mysterious and unexplained.

Nevertheless, a discussion about purification makes sense in the setting, which deals with baptism, for baptism would have been considered a rite of purification, exceptional though it may have been. Not coincidentally, the water Jesus transformed into wine was "for the Jewish rites of purification" (2:6). That this story follows upon the long episode of Jesus' encounter with John is understandable. Although John does not baptize Jesus in the Fourth Gospel, his role as one who baptizes is nevertheless prominent (1:25, 31).

John's disciples now turn to him, as might be expected (v. 26), and what they say gives the reader further information, namely, that Jesus is obviously baptizing more people than John. Surprisingly, the discussion with "a Jew" just mentioned does not figure in what they report, as they refer back to John's earlier witness to Jesus. They call John "Rabbi," agreeing exactly with what Jesus' disciples initially called him (1:38). (The Fourth Gospel consistently puts John's activity across the Jordan [cf. 1:28], on the eastern side, while the Synoptics place him in the Judean wilderness, which is along the Jordan, as in Matt 3:1.)

This second appearance of John in the narrative corresponds in a general way to Matthew (11:2-19) and Luke (7:18-35), where John from prison sends word to Jesus by his disciples. Here John's disciples go to him to ask about Jesus. (This second appearance of John is not found in Mark and presumably represents a remote agreement of John and Q, that is, material common to Matthew and Luke; cf. also Matt 8:5-13; Luke 7:1-10; John 4:46-54). In the Synoptics John asks, through his disciples, whether Jesus is the one to come; in the Fourth Gospel he tells his disciples that Jesus is. The difference is, of course, typical of John in comparison with the Synoptics. That all are going to Jesus is a bit of hyperbole (which contrasts with the statement of v. 32).

John's response to his disciples' seemingly alarmed report is calm and factually theological (v. 27). The clear import of his next statement (v. 28) is that although he himself is not the Christ but his forerunner, Jesus is. Thus each, John and Jesus, fulfills the role given him by God. The fact that John's disciples are said to have been witnesses to his testimony about Jesus is something of a surprise. Presumably the narrator's assumption is that John's disciples were already with him when he denied that he was the Christ (1:20) and pointed ahead to Jesus (1:26-34). Again John says "Messiah" in the NRSV, but here the Greek is *christos* (Christ), which in effect becomes a technical Christian theological term or title.

John now speaks of Jesus and himself metaphorically as the bridegroom and the friend of the bridegroom the "best man" (Heb. *shoshbin*). We have here a brief Johannine parable, albeit uttered by John rather than Jesus (Dodd *Tradition*, 282-85; 385-86), whose details should not be pressed (e.g., Who is the bride?). It makes one point quite clearly: the joy of the friend (John) comes entirely from the bridegroom's (Jesus') joy. The friend knows his place. His assessment of their prospects (v. 30) applies not to stature, but to the importance of their roles. John's concluding word is well crafted to ensure that his disciples, and the reader, are left with no doubt about who is more prominent in their relationship. Again there is a relation to the Synoptics (Mark 2:18-20), where Jesus refers to himself as the bridegroom.

3:31-36: The NRSV (as well as the RSV) ends the quotation with verse 30. The Baptist ceases speaking at that point, so verses 31-36 are presented as the words of the evangelist. (There would be no quotation marks in the ancient mss.) Some commentators propose moving verses 31-36 to an earlier position in the chapter (Schnackenburg 1968, 361, 380-92, places it immediately after v. 12, while Bultmann 1971, 131-33, 160-69, places it after v. 21), mainly because if left here it seems to contradict the generally positive role assigned John in the Gospel. He is then apparently called the one who "belongs to the earth and speaks about earthly things" (v. 31). Moreover, the assertion that no one accepts the testimony of the one who comes from heaven, obviously Jesus (v. 32), seems to contradict what John's disciples say in verse 26 ("all are going to him"). (Yet v. 33*a* also seems to contradict v. 32.)

In favor of the present position, however, is the pattern of the earlier conversation with Nicodemus, which similarly ends with a meditation best ascribed to the evangelist rather than Jesus (vv. 16-21, following the RSV's punctuation rather than the NRSV's; D. A. Carson [1991, 212]: "Like vv. 16-21...these verses appear to be the reflective explanation of the Evangelist himself."). The evangelist knows better than the disciples of John the shallowness of those who flock to Jesus (v. 32*b*; cf. 2:23-25). The difficulty about applying these words to John the Baptist, however, remains. One could perhaps see here a kind of Johannine analogy to what is found in Matthew and Luke. John is praised, but is clearly placed in the old age rather than the new, that is, the kingdom (Matt 11:11; Luke 7:28; cf. Luke 16:16). There the comparison is, so to speak, temporal and eschatological. Here, in the Fourth Gospel, it would be spatial (from above and from below; cf. Isa 55:9-11)—again a typically Johannine transposition of a synoptic perspective.

Yet even if the statements of verses 31-36 are read in their present position, and there is no manuscript evidence for transposing them, they can be understood as a kind of commentary on the entire Judean episode rather than upon the Baptist specifically. The whole section would thus function in somewhat the same way as if it had intervened between 3:12 and 13 (Schnackenburg's proposal). It would apply to Nicodemus as well as to all who are of the earth, even John. (Precisely in this context one should bear in mind that this Gospel reflects a rivalry with the claims of the Baptist's followers.) At best, however, we are confronted with a characteristic anomaly of the Fourth Gospel, which we shall see again (cf. 4:1-3; chaps. 5 and 6). Alongside skillfully composed episodes there are abrupt or awkward transitions or juxtapositions that create exegetical problems.

Given the extant textual order, the evangelist's typical dualism appears as a kind of screen on which the preceding Judean episode is projected. It is finally Jesus who is sent by God from heaven, from above; and only those who accept his testimony (v. 33) are on his, and God's side. They can "certify" (or, literally, "set the seal"; cf. the same expression in 6:27) that God is true in the sense of real, or "for real," while every other—particularly every opposed—claim on reality or truth is false. What Jesus has seen and heard and speaks are the words of God (v. 34). After the prologue Jesus is no longer called the Word of God, but as the Son he speaks God's words. At the conclusion of his final public proclamation (12:48-50), Jesus claims to have spoken only what the Father has given him. Thus he is, in effect, as the prologue claims, God's word (Miller 1993).

The meaning of the giving of the Spirit (v. 34) is problematic: Is it God who gives it to the Son or the (glorified) Son who gives it to believers (cf. 7:39; 20:22)? In the Fourth Gospel emphasis later falls upon God's giving the Spirit to believers at the behest of Jesus (14:16, 26). Yet in this context God gives to the Son without measure; that is, he places all things in his hands (v. 35). Moreover, John the Baptist has seen the Spirit descend and remain upon Jesus (1:33). So, given the continuation in verse 35, we should here understand that it is God who gives the Spirit to Jesus (as most commentators agree).

The eschatological alternatives are finally set forth (v. 36), as at the end of the evangelist's previous meditation (vv. 18-21). The first, positive alternative (v. 36a) is clear enough (cf. v. 18), and it is noteworthy that those who believe have (present tense) eternal life already. This present possession of life conforms to the eschatology of the Gospel of John. Eternal life is not just a future hope but a present gift for those who believe. (See Jesus' explicit correction of Martha in 11:25.)

The obverse, negative side (v. 36b) requires closer analysis and explanation. First of all, we now read "disobey" rather than "disbelieve," but certainly unbelief is implied (cf. v. 18). Yet unbelief is manifest in behavior (vv. 19-20) even more than in words, as belief becomes manifest in "doing the truth" (see v. 21; cf. 6:29, where doing the works of God is believing; also 1 John 3:17; 4:20), so the evangelist has apparently here chosen his words carefully. That those who are disobedient to the Son do not see life is then obvious enough; but the NRSV's rendering of the final clause, "must endure God's wrath," seems to threaten God's wrath as a future consequence, and is less felicitous than the RSV's "but the wrath of God rests upon him [or her]." It is important to let John say clearly that this wrath exists for such persons already (v. 18). Present eschatology means on the one hand the presence of external life, on the other the presence of judgment and wrath. Already Paul had seen in the cross of Jesus Christ the eschatological event, in that through his death God pronounced sinful humans righteous already, but he characteristically viewed salvation itself as still principally in the future (cf. Rom 13:11). Apparently John in this respect advances a step beyond Paul.

The reappearance of John after the Nicodemus episode affords the reader a sharp contrast between the well-meaning but uncomprehending teacher and the unerring witness. It is tempting to suggest Nicodemus represents the old law that is being displaced, while John represents prophecy of the new age that is dawning. Although the law is not simply displaced, older ways of understanding it, as embodied by Nicodemus, certainly are. Meanwhile John as the witness par excellence embodies the true meaning and bearing of Scripture, which testifies to Jesus as it points forward to him—even as John does.

It is noteworthy that at the conclusion of this discourse (vv. 35-

36) God is called Father and Jesus Son. This is typical Johannine usage. Of course, the two are correlatives. It is not coincidence that in the Gospel in which Jesus is most frequently called Son, God is so often called Father. This is clearly a way of speaking that has roots in the synoptic Gospels and tradition, and in all probability in the language of Jesus. Yet the concept of God as Father certainly has scriptural—Old Testament—roots, so it is not merely a corollary of Jesus' sonship, and maleness. It should also be observed that the point is clearly the intimate union of Jesus and God, which is expounded in the farewell discourses and final prayer (chaps. 14–17), rather than their gender.

The Woman of Samaria (4:1-45)

The length of this episode bespeaks its importance as well as the significant role of women in the Fourth Gospel (cf. 2:1-11; 12:1-8; 19:25-27; 20:1-18; cf. 4:27). Moreover, this narrative plays a large role in the series of Jesus' encounters with individuals and raises significant issues related to his role and the scope of his mission: to Samaritans; to women. In obvious respects it is parallel to the description of the Samaritan mission in Acts 8, which is an important transitional moment in the movement of the gospel preaching from Judaism (and Judea) to the broader, Gentile world. This narrative, coming as it does immediately after the John the Baptist episode, shows the woman as a perceptive, if also tentative, witness to Jesus. Yet in comparison to Nicodemus she makes a major breakthrough in understanding Jesus. Without full or proper perception, she nevertheless wants what Jesus can give her and asks him relevant questions. The irony of an outcast, a Samaritan woman, coming to some understanding while the learned teacher of Israel was clueless is not lost on the author of this Gospel, nor should it be on the reader.

The lengthy episode is framed by two transitional passages, which describe Jesus as arriving in Samaria on the way to Galilee (4:1-6) and then moving on from Samaria to Galilee (4:43-45). Toward the end Jesus speaks about the Samaritan mission (vv. 31-38) as the Samaritans themselves return to affirm Jesus as Savior of the world (vv. 39-42).

4:1-6: The next main episode will be set at Jacob's well in Samaria, and the reader is here prepared for it as Jesus' arrival in Samaria is described (4:1-6). Again we have a long transitional sentence, as Jesus heads from Judea back to Galilee (vv. 1-3), a journey that must take him through Samaria (v. 4). The sentence is quite awkward, but actually not unclear. Part of the awkwardness stems from Jesus' being called by his name twice in quick succession (v. 1), when the reader expects a pronoun in the second reference. Important witnesses (P^{66} P^{75} A B) read "the Lord" and then "Jesus," but this scarcely improves matters.

We learn for the first time of the Pharisees' hearing of Jesus' making and baptizing more disciples than John. These Pharisees will prove to be Jesus' enemies soon enough (7:32). So far they have appeared as authorities responsible for the rather hostile questioning of John (1:19), and one of them, Nicodemus, has shown himself unable to comprehend Jesus (3:1-21). Enough has been said about Pharisees that the careful reader will understand why Jesus leaves Judea for Galilee (v. 3), when he gets this word. The Pharisees are based in Jerusalem (1:19, 24) and Jesus wants to avoid them.

That Jesus was baptizing has been indicated in 3:23 and the word of John's disciples to their teacher (v. 26) has already informed us that at least a majority of those who have come out to be baptized are going to Jesus. Now, however, we are suddenly informed that not Jesus, but his disciples, were baptizing (v. 2). This rather awkward interjection looks like an effort to square John's account with the Synoptics (cf. 3:24). Yet even there we do not read that Jesus' disciples baptized. The distinctively Johannine notion that Jesus (or his disciples) baptized more than John proves Jesus is the superior of John. On the other hand, it puts him in the same category as John. One suspects this is an ancient tradition, if not a historical fact, that the Synoptics have suppressed or ignored.

John has the geography straight (vv. 3-4), as he has Jesus arrive at the Samaritan city (or village) of Sychar (v. 5). Many commentators have identified Sychar as modern Askar, although two ancient Syrian manuscripts read "Shechem," a nearby ancient city, which had been destroyed over a century and a half before by the Hasmonean John Hyrcanus. Both were in Samaria near Jacob's well, Shechem even closer to it than Askar. The plot of ground Jacob gave his son Joseph seems to be mentioned in Gen 48:22 (cf. 33:18-20), but there is no mention of Jacob's well specifically in the Old Testament. A Jacob's well still exists near Askar today (see Schnackenburg 1968, 424, for a description). The scene is set with Jesus at the well, tired from his journey, at midday (v. 6). (The text actually says "the sixth hour," which by ancient Jewish reckoning would be noon.) Although John does not say it, the reader of Scripture would know that Jacob was named Israel by God (Gen 35:10), so Jacob's well is Israel's well, and "Israel" is still a good name in John, even if "Jew" is not.

4:7-30: As Jesus rests at the well, the Samaritan woman arrives and Jesus accosts her (v. 7). The long conversation (vv. 7-30) then begins. The theme of an encounter of a man with a woman at a well has deep roots in Scripture (Gen 24; 1 Sam 9:11; 1 Kgs 17:10). In a scene of which Jesus' encounter with the Samaritan woman is reminiscent, the servant of Abraham finds a wife for his son Isaac at a well (Gen 24). The servant opens the conversation with Rebekah by asking her for a drink. Likewise the prophet Elijah opens a conversation with the widow of Zarephath by asking for a drink (1 Kgs 17:10). The setting marks the encounter as biblical, and the theme of water, which symbolizes Jesus and the salvation he brings, already enters the picture.

The absence of Jesus' disciples is quickly noted and accounted for (v. 8). They will, however, return, seemingly to interrupt the conversation (v. 27). Jesus' request strikes the woman as surprising, because she is a Samaritan and he a Jew (v. 9). Later the disciples will be surprised because Jesus is conversing with a woman (v. 27). After the woman expresses her surprise, the narrator interjects a note explaining why the Samaritan woman, who has recognized Jesus as a Jew, is surprised that he should make such a request of her. (Here as elsewhere in the Gospels, the parentheses are supplied by the modern translator.) How she recognizes him as such is not said. It is important for the Gospel that Jesus is a Jew (cf. 1:11), and this may simply be presumed in the narrative. Interestingly enough, the Samaritan here calls Jesus a Jew, while the Jews will later call him a Samaritan (8:48). Jesus is in a sense a stranger to both (Barrett 1978, 232; cf. also the apt title of de Jonge's book *Jesus: Stranger from Heaven,* 1977). Yet the Jews ("his own"; 1:11) will reject him, while the Samaritans, the outsiders, receive him.

What exactly the Samaritan woman said (v. 9) in response to Jesus presents a problem of translation. The NRSV gives a more accurate translation of the verb ("share things in common") and reflects more precisely actual practice. There is, however, no direct object in the Greek ("things"), and the older translation (cf. the RSV: "Jews have no dealings with Samaritans") is still possible. Either way the point is clear enough. A gulf separates Jews and Samaritans. The alienation has its roots in the fact that large numbers of the Samaritans (the ten tribes of the Northern Kingdom of Israel) were deported after the Assyrian conquest of 721 BCE. Moreover, according to 2 Kgs 17:24-41, they were replaced by foreigners. Judeans (= "the Jews"; Greek *Ioudaioi* can be translated either "Judeans" or "Jews") were deported after the Babylonian conquest of 586. The Jews returned from exile in 537 BCE, although many remained in Babylonia. The returned Jews regarded the Samaritans, who had presumably intermingled with foreigners, as corrupt and apostate. Yet the Samaritans understood themselves to be worshipers of the same God, although they recognized only the Pentateuch as Scripture. After the return of the Jews from exile, the Samaritans attempted to assist them in the rebuilding of the Jerusalem temple but were rebuffed, so they opposed and for a time delayed the reconstruction of the temple (Ezra 4). Later, the Samaritans built their own temple on Mount Gerizim, the site of which would have been clearly visible to Jesus and the woman as they conversed (John 4:20). (The Samaritan temple itself had been destroyed by John Hyrcanus in 128 BCE.)

Jesus' openness to Samaria and Samaritans is clearly implied by John and Luke (cf. 10:30-37; 17:16). Acts reports the conversion of Samaritans (8:4-8, 25; cf. also 1:8), a fact that is probably reflected later in this epidode (4:31-42). Mark does not mention

Samaria or Samaritans, and Matthew's one reference to Samaritans seems negative (10:5). John and Luke's portrayal of Jesus' attitude fits a general gospel picture of Jesus' openness toward outcasts. Certainly that is true of this episode, in which Jesus initiates a conversation with a Samaritan woman, who may also, as it turns out, be a notorious sinner (4:17-18).

For the woman at least, Jesus' response is enigmatic (vv. 10-11). To the "insider," however, its meaning would be perfectly clear (cf. 2:19; 3:3; see Meeks 1972, 57, 70). Jesus' statement is expressed in a Greek contrary-to-fact conditional sentence. The woman does not know Jesus' meaning, but could scarcely be expected to. "The gift of God" is an unusual expression in John. Probably the phrase picks up the statement about God's giving the Son in 3:16. The woman will eventually come to some recognition, tentative though it may be, of who Jesus really is (4:19, 29). Jesus speaks of "living water" (Gk. *hydōr zōē*) with a phrase that could also mean "running water," in effect playing to her lack of understanding. Jesus means the water of life, not natural, running water, but the woman, in using the same phrase, does not yet know this.

Water, particularly running or flowing water, symbolizes God's gift of salvation in Scripture (Jer 2:13; Ezek 47:1-8; Zech 14:8; cf. Rev 22:1-2, as well as John 7:38-39), and this symbolism appears also in later Jewish writings (cf. CD3:16-17, 6:4-11, where the well of water is the law; also 1QS4:20-22, where the purifying waters represent the Holy Spirit; 1QH8:1-21; also *1 Enoch* 48:1; 49:1, where the water is wisdom). There is a striking similarity to John's usage in a passage about the drinking of living water in Odes of Solomon 11:6-8. Of course, in John the purificatory waters of Judaism (2:6) become the wine of Jesus Christ (2:9-10); water is displaced by wine. This shows simply that water symbolism cannot be pressed, although it is quite prominent and significant (C. Koester 1995, 155-84, especially 167-72). John is rich in symbols, but has no rigid symbolic system.

The Samaritan woman's question (v. 11), like Nicodemus's (3:4), reflects common sense and natural understanding, which are, of course, inadequate for comprehending who Jesus is or what he is talking about. And that is just the point. In a manner reminiscent of the conversation with Nicodemus, she and Jesus are like ships passing in the night. Nevertheless, her questions (vv. 11-12) advance the conversation, as Nicodemus's do not. She asks about the source of the water, and she asks about Jesus and Jacob. Underlying her questions is a growing awareness that Jesus can supply her need. As the reader has already seen, the question of source or origin is significant. (It is raised in a somewhat different way by Nathanael in 1:46, and it will be raised again by the Jews in 7:40-42, 52). The question about Jacob concerns the Fathers of Israel (cf. Abraham in 8:53). Jesus is being compared with them, and a significant parallelism or comparison with Moses seems also to lie behind the text (cf. 6:32; 9:28-29). The woman's naive question of verse 12 is constructed in Greek so that the reader will expect a negative answer: "You are not greater than our ancestor (literally "father" as in the RSV) Jacob, are you?" The description of Jacob's giving the well and drinking from it with his sons and flocks affords a parallel to the work of Jesus, which has not yet been explained to the woman (but cf. v. 14). Jacob is, of course, Israel (Gen 35:10), so this is the well from which the children of Israel drink. Although it is the well of Israel, it does not permanently relieve thirst (cf. 6:32-35).

Thus Jesus makes a comparison between the water Jacob gives and the water he himself will supply (vv. 13-14). The former is still natural, everyday water; the latter is different. Jesus first states what is obvious about the water of Jacob's well or any water (v. 13) before going on to speak of "the water that I will give" (v. 14), which is internal and eternal. It "gushes up," which is surprising in a well. It is running, that is, living water. Yet two different Greek words for "well" have been used, "well" *(phrear)* and "spring" *(pēgē)*. "Well" is used of the well of Jacob, which was (and is) dug deep into the earth (v. 14). (John's choice of terms is significant, although *pēgē* is used of Jacob's "well" in v. 6.) "Spring" is used of the source of the water that Jesus gives. The woman now catches on; there is an alternative source of water (v. 15), but she is apparently still thinking in this-worldly terms. How nice never to be thirsty or to have to draw water!

Jesus now seems abruptly to change the subject (v. 16), as the woman has asked him for this water. He tells her to call her husband, and the ensuing interchange obviously affords him the occasion to demonstrate his uncanny knowledge of her; he promptly does so (vv. 17-18). Unlike the Greek *anēr*, the English noun "man" does not also mean "husband." So when Jesus says, literally, "Well do you say that you have no man, for you have had five men and the one you now have is not your man," emphasis naturally falls on the "your." The implication is that she is living with someone else's man. (Also Hebrew and Aramaic, as well as German and French, do not distinguish between "man" and "husband.") Moreover, five husbands, or men, would have been considered excessive, even in succession (Barrett 1978, 235). The woman's statement (v. 17) is true as far as it goes, but not very revealing. Jesus reveals that he knows her, and knows her past, quite fully. He expands upon the truth she has spoken. Although her past is apparently unsavory, nothing more is made of it explicitly. Yet to such people Jesus comes, a point made in other Gospels (cf. Mark 2:17).

The woman in effect acknowledges the truth of what Jesus has said as she recognizes him as a prophet (v. 19; possibly *the* prophet of Deut 18:15, although the noun is anarthrous; cf. also John 6:15). Is the expected Samaritan redeemer figure *(Taheb)* in view? We shall discuss this question below (vv. 25-29). Perhaps the woman means no more by "prophet" than a spokesman for God (cf. 9:17). The question she poses (v. 20), asking him to arbitrate between Samaritan and Jewish claims as to the proper place for (sacrificial) worship (Mount Gerizim or Jerusalem) does not take for granted he is a figure expected by Samaritans per se, for if so the answer would be a foregone conclusion. Jesus gives an extended response (vv. 21-24). By "this mountain," Mount Gerizim, the site of the Samaritan temple, is surely meant. "Ancestors" (literally "fathers") and the past tense ("worshiped") suggest that this cultic site is now gone, while by the same token Jerusalem temple worship is still in progress ("...must worship is...Jerusalem"). In all probability the Jerusalem temple had also been destroyed by the time this Gospel was written, although at the (narrative) time of Jesus' ministry it was of course still standing.

Jesus' response does not initially decide the question the woman asked, except to deny its future relevance: "neither on this mountain nor in Jerusalem" (v. 21). But then Jesus does come down on the side of Jewish rather than Samaritan worship (v. 22), in a statement which, if deleted, would not be missed. Moreover, the assertion that salvation is from the Jews (KJV: "of the Jews") is hard to square with the frequent Johannine portrayal of the Jews as Jesus' mortal enemies (5:18). "We" here would seem to mean "we Jews," while "you" (plural in Greek) refers to Samaritans generally. (Bultmann 1971, 190, n. 6, excises v. 22 in whole or in part, because it is extraneous and incompatible with the Gospel's negative view of the Jews, even though in v. 9 Jesus is recognized as a Jew.) Yet the Gospel appeals not only to Moses as a witness to Jesus, but to the prophets (1:45), especially Isaiah (1:23; 12:38-39, 41) and the Psalms, in other words, to the Scriptures of Israel (that is, of the Judeans, "Jews," rather than the Samaritans, who recognize only the Pentateuch). Moreover, Jesus is presented as the rightful King of Israel, the Messiah (1:41, 49; 20:31), who is expected by the Jews (again Judeans rather than Samaritans).

Jesus expands now upon the nature of this coming true worship of God (vv. 23-24). The *hour* is, of course, the hour of Jesus' glorification and death (cf. 2:4; 12:23). For Jesus to say that it is coming and now is (cf. 5:25) probably reflects both the eschatology and the perspective of this Gospel. By this curious and seemingly contradictory expression John implies that what might be expected in the future is now somehow present. With Jesus the long-awaited deliverance of God is now here. From the standpoint of Jesus' historic ministry it was, however, still coming, that is, in the future. Only from the postresurrection standpoint of the Gospel is it present. So this brief expression encapsulates both John's realized eschatology and the Gospel's postresurrection perspective. Thus, from the Gospel's perspective, the true worship of God the Father is already taking place.

Worship in spirit probably implies an end of animal sacrifice, inasmuch as certainly the Samaritan temple, and probably the

Jerusalem temple, were destroyed when the Gospel was written. Yet God is spirit, and worship in spirit (specifically the Spirit the Father sends at the behest of Jesus—14:16), while not sacrificial worship, is most important, worship in the name of Jesus and under the aegis of the Spirit, who continues his ministry (14:28; 16:12-13). Similarly, truth is not simply correspondence to reality generally conceived or the absence of falsehood. Truth is the reality that is God, and nothing else, made known in Jesus Christ. Thus it was said in the prologue that "grace and truth came through Jesus Christ" (1:17; cf. 1:14).

The idea that God is *seeking* people who will worship in spirit and truth may sound incongruous in a Gospel that emphasizes so strongly God's power and initiative. Yet the God whose being is defined by the historic ministry and death of Jesus, who gives himself for his followers, is a God who seeks, or requires, those who will respond to his love in worship. God is spirit (v. 24), and God is also love, as the author of 1 John quite logically—within the context of Johannine theology—infers and affirms (1 John 4:8). Thus to say that God seeks those who will worship him in spirit and truth is not out of keeping with the theology of this Gospel. God *seeks* true worshipers, but God's reality and revelation (spirit and truth) define the nature of that worship.

The woman's response (v. 25) seems to be something of a non sequitur, for she appears to change the subject. Yet in reality her statement picks up the eschatological note in what Jesus has just said about future worship. The Messiah is the eschatological deliverer. (The NRSV here rightly differentiates between the Jewish and Semitic term, represented by *Messiah,* and the Greek and Christian term *Christ.*) The basic sense and thrust of this statement are clear enough. Yet it raises a couple of problems.

First, the Samaritans expected no Davidic Messiah. As heirs of the Northern Kingdom the restoration of the *Judean* monarchy was emphatically not a part of their future hope. They did, however expect one who returns as a restorer *(Taheb),* who would be the prophet like Moses predicted in Deut 18:15. Probably the woman simply adopts Jewish messianic terminology, which Jesus fulfills (cf. 4:22), and one should not attempt to relate her statement specifically to Samaritan expectations, although such expectations contributed to the development of John's Christology (see Martyn 1979, 108; Meeks [1967, 31, n. 1] speaks of the "leveling of different terminologies"). Second, that Jesus would proclaim all things may correspond to Samaritan expectations (cf. Barrett 1978, 239), but the woman's statement here clearly functions to indicate her perplexity at what Jesus has just told her. She looks forward to a future revelation, as indeed everyone must, even Jesus' disciples, who will not understand who Jesus really is until he is glorified.

Jesus then reveals himself to the woman (v. 26). He is the Messiah, the Christ, the one who will proclaim all things. This is the first occurrence of "I am" or "I am he" (Gk. *egō eimi*) on Jesus' lips. Jesus' "I am" sayings are both distinctive and typical of the Fourth Gospel. Sometimes they occur without a predicate, as here, in which case they are reminiscent of the "I am" sayings attributed to God in Exodus (3:14) or Isaiah (41:4). Often, and somewhat more characteristically, they take a predicate, for example "I am the bread of life" (6:35), or "I am the light of the world" (8:12), as Jesus describes himself in familiar terms that designate basic and universal human needs or desires. While Jesus is the fulfillment of traditional messianic hopes in John, he is also the fulfillment of universal human necessities and longings. Emphasis upon the latter is typical of Johannine Christology.

The return of Jesus' disciples (cf. v. 8) interrupts the conversation (v. 27), as we are told of their astonishment. Perhaps surprisingly, they are astonished because Jesus is talking with a woman, while the fact that she is a Samaritan is not mentioned. (Although *m. Abot* 1.5 strongly discourages conversation with women, rabbinic thought is actually more diverse; cf. Barrett 1978, 240.) But the reader has already learned how surprising it is that Jesus should initiate a conversation with a Samaritan by asking for a drink (v. 9). The disciples do not question Jesus, but we are not told why. "It is not for disciples to question the actions of their Master" (Barrett 1978, 240). "The awe of his friends makes the mystery of the revealer stand out more strongly" (Schnackenburg 1968, 443). Probably both observations are correct, but the latter comes closer to the distinctively Johannine theme and interest.

The woman's departure for the city (v. 28) allows Jesus to be left alone with his disciples for the conversation that will ensue (vv. 31-38), while she bears witness to her fellow Samaritans. That she leaves her water jar implies that she goes with a sense of urgency and purpose. Her word of witness (v. 29) appears quite uncertain, but indicates she has heard Jesus' claim (v. 26). The question expects a negative answer, as the Greek construction indicates, but the negativity is obviously tentative and open-ended. Later the Samaritans will be described as believing because of her testimony (vv. 39, 42); the implication is that her question was taken in a positive sense or led to their belief. In any event, on the basis of this testimony they start out to see Jesus (v. 30).

Obviously the basis of the woman's witness is Jesus' revelation to her of her own past (vv. 17-18; cf. 1:48). "Everything I have ever done" may be something of an exaggeration for effect, but it is understandable: Jesus has known the relationships that have defined her life and his knowledge is perceived by her as miraculous or God-given. Thus she has already called him a prophet (v. 19).

4:31-42: Between the woman's departure and her return with the other Samaritans who have believed, there is a conversation between Jesus and his disciples (vv. 31-38), in which the disciples are solicitous of Jesus' welfare (v. 31), but cannot yet understand what he means (v. 33). Jesus' statement (v. 32) is as mysterious to them as to outsiders.

Their lack of understanding is of a piece with their hesitancy to question Jesus (v. 27). Jesus' further explanation is straightforward (v. 34), and expresses a theme central to John's narrative and Christology. Jesus will say this, or something quite similar, repeatedly (i.e., 5:36; 10:37-38; 17:4). He does all, but nothing other than, the work God sent him to do. By the same token, Jesus speaks what God has given him to say (as in 12:49). Jesus can claim to be fully the revelation of God and nothing other than the revelation of God. His uniqueness lies in his complete devotion and obedience to the Father's will. In claiming nothing for himself Jesus becomes transparent to the Father, so that it can be said of him that he is *theos* ("God"). This is the paradox of the revelation of God in a human being who does not cease to be a human being throughout his life. The relationship of food to doing God's will recalls Deut 8:3 (cf. Isa 55:2), which is cited in the narratives of the temptation of Jesus (Matt 4:4; Luke 4:4). The Matthean version of the Deuteronomy quotation that gives the contrast between living by bread alone or "by every word that comes from the mouth of God" (4:4) is reminiscent of the statement of Jesus in John. It is conceivable that John knows and reflects the Matthean account, or an earlier tradition of it, but it is equally possible that John is influenced more directly by Deuteronomy, a book with which the Gospel shows familiarity (e.g., Deut 8:15-22).

Even to the knowledgeable reader, the remainder of the conversation between Jesus and his disciples (vv. 35-38) is possibly as obscure as the preceding has been clear. Jesus' quotation of the saying about the coming harvest makes a new departure, as he seems to allude to a familiar saying ("Do you not say… "). There is a Matthean and Lukan saying of Jesus about the harvest and the workers (Matt 9:37-38; Luke 10:2; probably Q) that reflects a similar urgency. Although there is no known proverb that corresponds to Jesus' saying, it may refer to a commonly accepted interval of four months between sowing and harvest. In any event, Jesus sharply qualifies the expectation of a future harvest as he declares that the harvest is at hand (Barrett 1978, 241). This, of course, suggests the Johannine-realized eschatology. Yet the Matthean and Lukan saying also indicates that harvest is at hand. Probably we are dealing with independently transmitted versions of the same or related sayings. As the Synoptics speak of laborers, John has sowers and reapers who labor (vv. 36-38).

An eschatological harvest is evidently in view, in Matthew and Luke as in John. But in both cases, Jesus seems to have in mind specifically a harvest of followers, adherents, or believers, and that fits this scene exactly. Here the harvest would seem to be the Samaritan believers. The problem is how to apportion Jesus, his disciples, and the Samaritan woman in relation to sower, reaper, those who have labored, and "you [who] have entered into their labor" (4:38). In fact there are real difficulties in construing these sayings allegorically; perhaps the difficulty stems from the fact that John has brought together traditional sayings materials, beyond what we have been able to identify in verse 35. What Jesus says is reminiscent of such scriptural sayings as Deut 20:6; 28:30; Mic 6:15; and Job 31:8 that could be presumed to be known to Jesus and his disciples. The reaper is not of course gathering fruit for eternal life as a reward for himself, rather his harvest is people being gathered as fruit to be given eternal life.

Clearly the disciples reap a harvest where others (the Samaritan woman and Jesus?) have labored. One thinks also of the description of a mission to the Samaritans in Acts 8. There the deacon Philip (Acts 6:5) preaches in a city of Samaria (8:5) and wins converts. Subsequently, the Jerusalem apostles send Peter and John to confirm their work (8:14, 25). Again, the disciples enter into the labor of someone else, in this case Philip the deacon. Doubtless in John 4:35-38 events of a Samaritan mission provide the background for what is written, but exactly what these events were, as well as how they related to what is said in the text, remains somewhat unclear.

The woman's testimony (cf. vv. 17-18, 29) leads many Samaritans to faith (v. 39). Because of its basis, this seems to be sign faith, indeed, sign faith at second hand; they have believed the woman's testimony. Yet this is just the beginning.

The Samaritans come to Jesus (vv. 39-40), who is presumably still at the well (v. 30). All this is portrayed as occurring in a matter of hours at most. When the Samaritans reach Jesus and ask him to remain with them the action slows down. Jesus remains with them two days, presumably in the Samaritan city where many more believe because of his word (v. 41). But even those who believe are changed by hearing Jesus (v. 42). Their address to the woman whose word occasioned their belief in the first place should not be construed as a put-down. Rather it emphasizes the importance of communion with Jesus. In the nature of the case, nothing can be as assuring as the word of Jesus himself. They have advanced from sign faith to believing because of firsthand knowledge; they have heard for themselves.

Yet elsewhere those who have not seen and yet believe are called blessed (20:29), and Jesus will pray for those who believe because of the word of the disciples (17:20). The Samaritans believe because they have heard Jesus, and therefore their faith is deepened: it is no longer based on miraculous signs described at second hand. They know that Jesus is the Savior of the world. The same title, "Savior of the world," is applied to Jesus in 1 John 4:14. (In the Pastorals and 2 Peter the title "Savior" is rather frequently used of Jesus; in the uncontested Pauline letters it is applied to him only in Phil 3:20.)

4:43-45: Jesus now continues his journey from Sychar (never named after 4:5) to Galilee (v. 43; cf. v. 3). Next we hear of Jesus' statement that a prophet has no honor in his own country (v. 44), a version of which is found in every canonical Gospel, as well as the *Gospel of Thomas* (Matt 13:57; Mark 6:4; Luke 4:24; Thomas 31). Except in a few cases where they are integral to a narrative, Johannine sayings of Jesus with synoptic parallels are never found in the same context in John, probably an indication of their separate traditional origins. In all the canonical Gospels the saying is set in Galilee, in the Synoptics probably in Nazareth (although Nazareth is mentioned by name only in Luke). In each, as well as Thomas, the saying is differently formulated, although it is recognizably the same saying.

The Johannine version raises the question of what is Jesus' own country. While in the Synoptics it is clearly the town or region of his origin (Mark 6:1-6a; Luke 4:16), here that is not so clear. In the Johannine narrative Jesus is leaving Judea, where he has not received a good reception, for Galilee, and one might well infer that Judea is his own country. It is so theologically, because it is the site of the Jerusalem temple, where Jesus should be accepted, but he is not. Moreover, in John most of Jesus' activity seems to take place there. By contrast the Galileans will welcome Jesus (v. 45). The festival mentioned is apparently the Passover of 2:13, and the reaction of the Galileans is similar to that of the

Jerusalemites described in 2:23-25, except that a negative assessment on the part of Jesus himself is not mentioned, and in the next incident recounted (4:46-54) Jesus finds acceptance and faith in Galilee.

◊ ◊ ◊ ◊

The artfully constructed episode of the woman of Samaria advances the narrative of Jesus' ministry and mission. Having asked Jesus relevant questions and expressed her need of what he can give her—even though she misunderstands the living water as natural running water—she ultimately testifies, if somewhat tentatively, about who Jesus is (v. 25). She has advanced in her perception beyond Nicodemus. Subsequently, Jesus, in response to his disciples' questions, endorses a mission to Samaria and Samaritans (vv. 31-38). Although his words are enigmatic, their puzzling, veiled character is partly the product of John's style, and perhaps partly the result of the use of traditional words of Jesus in this discourse. After Jesus endorses this mission the Samaritans respond to him with an invitation and firsthand faith (vv. 39-42). Their intention (v. 42) is not to devalue the woman's witness, but rather to underscore the importance of firsthand communication and communion with Jesus himself. Of course, the fact that Jesus here encounters a female who is a foreigner and deals with her on the same basis as everyone else is fundamental to the role and importance of this episode. In fact, its unique character lays the basis for the Samaritans' climactic affirmation that Jesus is the Savior of the world (v. 42).

The Healing of the Official's Son (4:46-54)

This is the second miracle story narrated in the Fourth Gospel, although other signs are mentioned (2:23-25; 4:45). It is typical of this Gospel to mention signs that have happened offstage (2:23; 3:2), and to make clear that it is intended to deliver only a partial and representative account of what Jesus did (20:30-31; cf. 21:25). This account has a distant, but recognizable, parallel in the Synoptics (Matt 8:5-13; Luke 7:1-10). It is scarcely a typical miracle story, in that Jesus performs the healing at a distance, without ever seeing the victim. Yet it is told with the characteristic economy of style and brevity that we associate with such stories in the Synoptics. The statement of verse 53 rounds off the story and effects closure. The sign is then enumerated as the second in verse 54. The wine miracle (2:1-11), also at Cana, is the first (v. 11).

The statement that this is the second sign is curiously qualified: "after coming from Judea to Galilee" (v. 54). Are we to think that Jesus had done a previous sign just now in Galilee that is not recounted? Moreover, why are these signs numbered, while others in the Gospel are not? Has the evangelist perhaps incorporated these signs from a sign source (Bultmann 1971, 113-14) or Sign Gospel (Fortna 1970, 1988)? If so, this would explain the source of John's miracle tradition without recourse to the other Gospels. Also, at two crucial points, the end of Jesus' public ministry (12:37; cf. also 11:47) and the end of the Gospel proper (20:30), the ministry is described simply as the performance of signs, as would befit the conclusion of a Sign Gospel or sign source, but seems odd as a characterization of Jesus' ministry in the Fourth Gospel as we have it. On the one hand, it is quite difficult to imagine that these and other Johannine miracle stories were constructed on the basis of synoptic narratives. On the other, the search for a source within a single document, with few if any certain external points of comparison is bound to be frustrating and to invite the construction of various theories, some more probable than others, but none capable of eliciting the kind of following that Markan priority (and use by Matthew and Luke) commands.

The source-critical task is daunting. Less difficult and obscure, however, is the role of this sign story in the development of the narrative of the Gospel and its theology.

◊ ◊ ◊ ◊

Cana (v. 46) is mentioned only in the Gospel of John (cf. 2:1; 21:2, where Nathanael is said to be from Cana of Galilee). There are several modern candidates for Cana, as there are for Sychar. (Brown 1966, 98, believes Khirbet Qana, a ruin about nine miles north of Nazareth is the site of ancient Cana, as does Schnackenburg 1968, 326.) That John refers back to a previous event, the wedding at Cana, is not unusual in this Gospel, although such an analepsis (Culpepper 1983, 56-61) is found rarely, if at all, in the Synoptics. The official's son is not in Cana, however, but in Capernaum, the site of a similar healing narrative in Matthew (8:5-13) and Luke (7:1-10) in which Jesus heals a sick lad at some distance.

Probably the same episode or tradition lies at the root of the two stories; the synoptic accounts are obviously very closely related in wording and content and can scarcely represent different incidents. The Johannine version is quite different. According to the most widely accepted account of synoptic relationships, the Matthean–Lukan version comes from the Q source, since it is found in Matthew (8:5-13) and Luke (7:1-10), but not in Mark. (For a succinct discussion of the relationship of the Johannine and synoptic versions of the story, see Brown 1966, 192-94.) In John the principal character aside from Jesus is a "royal official" (Gk. *basilikos;* v. 46), probably to be understood as a member of the court retinue of Herod Antipas, tetrarch of Galilee. (Josephus refers to relatives and officials of the Herods as *basilikoi,* the term used here.) In the Synoptics he is a Roman centurion, and the ill lad is not his son, but his servant (Matthew) or slave (Luke). In the synoptic version the point of the story hinges upon the fact that the man is a Gentile. Whether or not John knows that version, his point is different.

The Herodians' position vis-à-vis Judaism was ambiguous. They presented themselves as Jews, but were not universally accepted as such. (Bultmann 1971, 206, n. 7: "It is evident that he is a Jew, since nothing is said to the contrary.") The common factors in all three accounts are that Jesus is approached by this principal character or his emissaries (Luke), the question of faith is raised, Jesus pronounces a word of healing at a distance, and the lad is healed. It is perhaps characteristic of the Fourth Gospel that in its account Jesus and the lad to be healed are in separate towns, Cana and Capernaum (the site of the synoptic story), a number of miles apart.

Again there is an analepsis (v. 47): the official knows Jesus' itinerary, which is familiar to the reader (4:43-45; cf. vv. 1-3 and 54). The son's desperate condition leads the father to beg Jesus to come down to Capernaum. Jesus appears to question the official's faith in that he says, apparently without reason or motivation, that unless the man sees signs and wonders he will not believe (v. 48). (Signs and wonders are mentioned in Acts 4:30; 5:12; 15:12; the connection with Moses and the Exodus tradition is made in Acts 7:36. "Signs and wonders" are associated with the Exodus and Moses in Deuteronomy particularly; e.g., 4:34; 6:22.) Commentators often take verse 48 to be a disparaging comment about the official, since Jesus' saying seems to mirror Jesus' negative attitude toward the desire for signs in the Synoptics (Matt 12:38-42; 16:1-4; Mark 8:11-12; see Bultmann 1971, 206; also Fortna 1970, 41). Interestingly, "you" becomes plural at this point in the narrative as in 3:11-12, so more people than the official are in view (cf. Paul's statement that "Jews demand signs" in 1 Cor 1:22). Yet verse 48 can also be interpreted as simply stating the necessity for signs. According to John, signs precede faith. One can see the significance of signs and fail to attain the knowledge of faith, as the Jerusalem crowd (2:23-25) and Nicodemus (3:2) did. Yet in John no one who rejects Jesus' signs ever comes to faith in him. Nicodemus, on the other hand, returns to the narrative to defend Jesus (7:50-52) and to help Joseph of Arimathea bury him (19:39). In fact, the official will see a sign and will believe, come to faith, in Jesus. He is not the least deterred by Jesus' statement, but continues to urge him to heal his son (v. 49).

The question of faith is raised here, as in the synoptic accounts, but in a different and typically Johannine way. In the synoptic version the centurion's faith is never in question. Here the official's faith is the question. Yet in neither synoptic Gospel do we hear the healing word of Jesus as we do in John. In John Jesus' word is given so the man can affirm his belief in it. (At this point in the Greek sentence, "believe" need mean no more than that the official believed what Jesus said would actually happen.) In the

Synoptics, the result—the lad's healing—is very briefly recounted; in John it is told in considerable detail (vv. 51-53), with particular attention to the time at which Jesus had spoken and the time the boy began to recover. The father then realizes that the recovery came at the exact time when Jesus spoke (v. 53). In the case of both Cana signs the crucial, miraculous event occurs offstage, so to speak, and one is left to infer that Jesus did it, as the father here does. That is, of course, the correct inference, and the father and his household now believe; clearly they come to faith in Jesus. The language used is remarkably similar to that found in Paul's writings and Acts where the conversion of households (slaves as well as wife and children) is sometimes in view (Acts 16:33-34; 1 Cor 1:16).

The final, closing statement (v. 54) apparently links this sign to the previous Cana episode (2:1-11), although quite awkwardly. It is less clearly the second narrated sign Jesus did "after coming from Judea to Galilee" in the present order of things than it is the second narrated sign in Cana. As we noted above (p. 124), exegetes have detected in this awkward statement traces of an earlier sign source that the evangelist used. The "after" clause (in Greek an aorist participle) introduces confusion and has to be understood to mean "When Jesus had come from Judea to Galilee, he (again) performed this second sign." Actually, such a translation is possible, if not obvious.

This story is like the typical miracle story of the synoptic Gospels in that it is rounded off neatly and briefly. Instead of a demonstration of the healing (Mark 1:31) or a general statement of wonder (e.g., Mark 2:12), it concludes with the father and his family's believing, that is, coming to faith in Jesus (cf. Acts 18:8; cf. also Acts 11:14; 16:15, 31). Later on we shall see the miracle story develop into a discussion and controversy that will center on Jesus himself, his meaning and claims.

It is perhaps noteworthy that the two Cana miracles are not followed by such debate, but simply by faith: in the one case

Jesus' disciples believe (2:11); in this case the man who has besought Jesus to heal his son (4:47). In each case Jesus' deed is accepted as a benefaction, and no one questions it or disputes about what Jesus has done. But in the next and subsequent episodes such dispute will not only arise but become ominous.

The fact that there is no ensuing discourse or dialogue that makes explicit theological points does not mean the story has no further implications. It is a sign that manifests the power, authority, and role of Jesus. Beyond that, Jesus encounters a man in desperate need who believes that he will be able to save his son, to give him life. There is a sense in which his faith is tested, and his belief in Jesus' word is confirmed as his son is saved from life-threatening illness. Like the woman of Samaria, the official's status as an Israelite is at best suspect. But even better than the Samaritan woman he understands that Jesus can bring the life-saving help he and his son need.

◊ ◊ ◊ ◊

After this series of encounters with Jesus (3:1–4:54), the course and tone of the narrative will take a sharp turn. To this point Jesus has met people who respond with perplexity, and perhaps obtuseness, but not overt hostility. (This is true even in the story of the temple cleansing, which immediately precedes the present section.) They are representative of Judaism, but at the same time adumbrate the broader world he has come to save (4:42). The true Israel, its scriptural and prophetic traditions, is represented by John the Baptist (3:22-36). The contemporary magisterium, or teaching office, of the Judaism that confronted Jesus (and confronts the evangelist) is embodied in Nicodemus, who on the basis of his learning cannot comprehend Jesus. Yet even Nicodemus does not reject Jesus or turn against him. Rather, he returns to defend him (7:50-52) and finally to help bury him (19:39). It is probably significant that in the course of the narrative Nicodemus's incomprehension is followed immediately by John's truthful and theologically accurate witness.

The meetings with the Samaritan woman and the (presumably Herodian) official foreshadow Jesus' mission to the wider world as they portray him encountering figures who stand at the periphery of Judaism. From the standpoint of a Nicodemus they may stand outside Judaism altogether. Yet, surprisingly, the woman of Samaria understands Jesus better than Nicodemus, as she perceives that he can supply her need and that, in ways she cannot yet understand, he is the fulfillment of the hope of Israel. Something of the same is true of the official, whose appeal to Jesus arises from his desperate hope in the face of illness and death. In the way such desperation incites hope and incipient faith, this story is reminiscent of the synoptic tradition of Jesus' healings, to which it is related. Of course, this story in itself has nothing explicit to say about Jesus' relation to Israel or Judaism.

As to that relation and the fulfillment of traditional expectations and hopes, the Gospel narrative is pointedly open-ended. There have been hints of the coming hostility (1:11; 2:17, 19-21; 3:14), but little more. That will now change, as resistance and rejection of Jesus emerge and become the central themes of the narrative as he moves to Jerusalem and to his death.

Increasing Opposition to Jesus (5:1–12:50)

Jesus Heals a Man as Opposition Mounts (5:1-47)

Chapter 5 is a distinct unit, and marks a clearly perceptible stage in the deterioration of Jesus' relationship with people called "the Jews." In chapter 1 the Jews or Pharisees initiate a skeptical, but not overtly hostile, interrogation of John, who has already appeared as a witness for Jesus (1:6-8, 15). When Jesus cleanses the temple (2:13-22), the Jews question him about his authority to do this: "What sign can you show us for doing this?" (v. 18). Yet many of the Jerusalemites believe because of Jesus' signs, including, apparently, Nicodemus. Although Nicodemus cannot understand Jesus, he is not portrayed as hostile (3:1-10). Significantly, the Samaritan woman (4:1-42), who is actually approached by Jesus—Nicodemus had approached Jesus—comes much closer to appreciating who Jesus is.

This episode also marks a sharp break in the continuity of the narrative, inasmuch as Jesus again goes up to Jerusalem for a Jewish festival (5:1; cf. 2:13). If chapters 5 and 6 were transposed, the sequence would be better, for Jesus is again in Galilee in chapter 6. So the present order of the text suggests the possibility of its disruption or rearrangement.

The healing story that begins the episode and gives rise to the theological controversy that develops is reminiscent of stories found in the Synoptics, particularly those that create controversy, whether over Jesus' authority (Mark 2:1-12) or, as here, over his failure to observe the sabbath properly (Mark 3:1-6). In fact, Jesus' command to the healed man (5:8) replicates his command to the paralytic in Mark 2:9, 11. That John's story is a rewriting of Mark's seems on the face of it unlikely. They evince similarities, but in different narrative contexts. (By contrast, John 4:46-54 is arguably a different version of the same narrative found in Matt 8:5-13; Luke 7:10.) Presumably there were more stories circulating about Jesus than were incorporated into Mark or any of the canonical Gospels (20:30; cf. 8:1-11). This is likely one of these. (None of the Johannine healing stories exactly matches a synoptic narrative, and most are quite different.) Possibly it belonged to an earlier sign source or Gospel of Signs, although unlike its predecessors, it is not numbered (cf. 2:11; 4:54).

This episode's most striking, and typically Johannine, feature is the controversy that erupts out of the healing itself. In fact, from this point in the Gospel Jesus' deeds, as well as his words, lead to sharp controversy. The signs signify who Jesus is, but not everyone accepts their testimony. Yet the theological, specifically christological issues they raise become the center of discussion.

◊ ◊ ◊ ◊

5:1-9: Jesus goes back to Jerusalem for a feast or festival (v. 1). The festival is not named. As things now stand it is evidently not Passover (see 6:4), but likely would be construed as such if chapter 6 had originally preceded chapter 5.

Although the healing narrative of the man at the pool bears some similarity to the synoptic healing stories, there are important, characteristically Johannine, differences. To begin with, the scene is Jerusalem, and no healing in Jerusalem is recounted in the synoptic Gospels (cf. mention of them in Matt 21:14). The site is near the present Church of St. Anne, where the ancient pool has been discovered and excavated (see Brown 1966, 207; Barrett 1978, 251-53; Carson 1991, 241-42; Charlesworth 1995, 67). There are problems of text and translation (v. 2), but the NRSV's reading and translation is possible and makes the best of the rather obscure Greek. ("There is by the Sheep Pool a place.... ") Probably the roughness and difficulties arise from the fact that the narrative is here based on a more ancient tradition; perhaps the author himself was not fully conversant with the material he was using. Since the ancient pool is a double pool with a divider, the five porticoes can easily be accounted for. The name of the place is given differently in various manuscripts: Bethesda, Bethsaida (actually the village at the northeastern end of the Sea of Galilee), and Bethzatha, which most translators and commentators now accept. Exactly what Bethzatha meant is a matter of some debate. "Beth" is, however, clearly the transliteration of the Hebrew (or Aramaic) word for house. ("House of Olives" is perhaps the best possibility.) There is no reason to doubt that John sets this scene at a real place in Jerusalem. It may have been a kind of healing spa, where people with infirmities sought comfort, if not healing (v. 3). At this point in many manuscripts—but not the most ancient ones—there is the description of the angel's periodically stirring up the pool (v. 4). In all probability it was added to explain the urgency of getting into the water (v. 7).

Only now is the ill man whom Jesus will heal mentioned (v. 5). Although nothing is explicitly made of this, the fact that he had been ill for thirty-eight years recalls Israel's thirty-eight years of wandering in the wilderness (Deut 2:14). This is hardly coincidental. With the scene now set, Jesus approaches the man who has been ill for a long time. That Jesus already has knowledge of his lengthy illness is a distinctly Johannine trait (cf. 1:48; 4:17-18, 29), as is the fact that Jesus approaches the man, rather than vice versa. Jesus' question to the man (v. 6) functions as a conversation opener; at least we should not too quickly assume that the desire for healing is a prerequisite for the healing itself. Obviously the man wants to be healed, or he would not be at this pool. Yet, in John, it is understood that seeking Jesus, or desiring the life he brings, is a good and even necessary thing (see Painter 1993, *passim;* 1996, 354-64).

His answer to Jesus (v. 7) is curious, and doubtless has given rise to the later addition of verse 4, which explains the urgency of getting into the water. Jesus then cuts the scene short by giving the command that already implies the healing (v. 8), and the sick man obeys (v. 9). He gave the same command to the paralytic in Mark 2:9 with the same result (cf. v. 11). This similarity, together with the fact that both episodes raise the question of the relation of sin and sickness (Mark 2:5-7; John 5:14), has led some commentators to see a relation between them. If so, John is thought to have used, or at least known, the Markan account, and would have picked up from it the easily remembered word of Jesus and the theological motif of sin and sickness. Whether the man in John is also paralyzed is a good question. This is not said, but his inability to get into the pool could mean this. Otherwise, the stories differ widely. (Of course, in both cases the man also does what Jesus has commanded, but that might have been expected in any miracle story as a proof of the healing.) Only at the end of the story do we learn that the healing has taken place on the sabbath (v. 9*b*). This is, of course, a common motif in the synoptic Gospels (e.g., Mark 3:1-6), and it will recur in John (9:14). Interestingly, the Jews at first attack Jesus only indirectly by accosting the man carrying his mat (v. 10), and therefore working (cf. Mark 2:24).

5:10-18: A sabbath controversy now breaks out. God commands the keeping of the sabbath day in the Ten Commandments (Exod 20:8-11; Deut 5:12-15). To violate the sabbath commandment by working on the sabbath was no small infringement of the law of God, and profanation of the sabbath by working on it was to be punished by death (Exod 31:14-15). According to the Old Testament, such death penalties were actually carried out (Num 15:32-36). Later, Jews died rather than fight in battle on the sabbath (1 Macc 2:29-41; cf. E. P. Sanders 1992, 209). Yet in Jesus' day the sabbath commandment could scarcely be enforced by the death penalty. Even if the Johannine Jews seek to kill Jesus (7:19, 25), their intent is not specifically linked to the breaking of the sabbath commandment. Although it has often been thought that the Pharisees sought Jesus' death because he defied their legalism, it is remarkable that in the Gospels they play little or no role in the trial and execution of Jesus. Moreover, in the Gospels generally, and particularly in John, Jesus is not portrayed as wantonly violating the sabbath commandment. Rather, he justifies his behavior by referring to Scripture and traditional practice (cf. Mark 2:26-27; 3:4; Luke 13:14-16; 14:5; John 7:23).

After the healed man is accused of violating the sabbath (v. 10), however, he shifts the responsibility for his action to the man (Jesus) who has commanded him to do so (v. 11). Naturally, the Jews ask about the identity of that figure, whom they do not yet know (v. 12). Neither does the healed man, apparently (v. 13)! Jesus has now disappeared or withdrawn (or "slipped away," Brown 1966, 205). That the healed man does not yet know Jesus parallels the similar ignorance of the man born blind (chap. 9), who at first does not have theological knowledge of Jesus, nor does he know Jesus' name. The similarities and differences between the two stories, and the individuals involved are striking (Culpepper 1983, 139).

When Jesus finds the healed man in the temple, he again takes the initiative (v. 14). The scene has shifted but slightly; the temple area is only a few hundred yards south of the pool. Jesus' warning raises the question of the relation of sin and sickness, or incapacity, that will recur in 9:2-3 (cf. Mark 2:5; also Luke 13:1-5 on sin and misfortune). That misfortune is punishment for sin was a common view, which has not died out in modernity. Although Jesus does not accept this simple equation in John 9:2-3 or Luke 13:1-5, here he seems to (v. 14). But his warning functions to anticipate the man's returning to the Jews (v. 15). Now the man knows who Jesus is, and he "reports" on Jesus to the Jews. If one judges by the Jews' response of persecuting Jesus (v. 16), the healed man's action is a betrayal, whatever he may be thought to have intended. (The NRSV's "started persecuting" is not justified by the Greek imperfect, which is better translated "were persecuting.") In fact, it is not Jesus who has been caught violating the sabbath law, but the healed man. This statement is therefore best understood as a general characterization of what Jesus was doing, and causing others to do, and the Jews' reaction.

Jesus' response (v. 17) seems innocent enough, for God can be presumed to be the Father of all, as well as the Creator who continues his work, even on the sabbath (despite Gen 2:2). (On God's working, see Barrett 1978, 256; and Borgen 1983, 100; both of whom appeal to Philo as well as to rabbinic exegesis.) That verse 16 presumes things going on offstage, so to speak, which have not been fully narrated, seems to be confirmed by the Jews' response to Jesus (v. 18). In what he does and encourages others to do Jesus represents a threat to traditional theology. The Jews' persecution is, literally, deadly, and has obviously already been going on, for they seek "all the more" to kill Jesus.

Does calling God "Father" constitute a claim to be equal to God? The Lord's Prayer, composed and taught by Jesus himself (Matt 6:9-13; Luke 11:2-4), makes such an inference quite dubious (cf. also Mark 14:36, where Jesus' original Aramaic for "Father" is given; also Paul's adoption of the same expression in Rom 8:15 shows it was generally used by Christians). God is, of course, known as Father in the Old Testament (e.g., Isa 63:16; 64:8; Jer 3:19; Ps 68:5). Nevertheless, Jesus' calling God his own Father makes a great difference. It signals that Jesus makes a unique claim of sonship for himself. Again, it would seem that developments offstage must account for the sudden appearance of such hostility toward Jesus, for what has so far happened in this episode scarcely suffices to explain it. The Gospel of John presupposes a conflict and struggle between Jesus and his opponents, probably between his followers and those who reject him, ultimately between church and synagogue. (On this passage see especially Martyn 1979, especially 68-72; on "God" and "Father" see Meyer 1996, 255-73.)

5:19-47: Jesus now responds. At this point one might expect him to deny the charge that he is making himself equal to God.

But the reader should recall that such equality with God is exactly the claim that this Gospel makes for Jesus (1:1, 18; 10:30; 14:9; 20:29). For Jesus to deny it in the face of these accusations would be disingenuous, to say the least.

Thus when Jesus begins to speak (v. 19), it is not to deny this claim but rather to explain it. The paradox of this Gospel now finds expression. Jesus' equality with God consists of his being totally transparent to his Father's will, word, and work. In a variety of ways Jesus says that the Father has sent him, and this sending is always for the sake of manifesting and revealing God's will to human beings. Such language is not intended as cosmological, christological speculation. It is the language of mission, revelation, and redemption. (Bultmann 1971, 249: "All this is said not in order to provide the basis for a speculative Christology, but because his origin is grounded in what he means for us.") The basis for the Father's showing the Son "all that he himself is doing" is his own love for the Son, which through him will be extended to the world (v. 20). "Greater works than these" doubtless alludes to the healing just performed, but means more than that. In view of the reference to the Son's giving life (v. 21), one thinks ahead to the raising of Lazarus (11:1-44). The future holds more than the past, or even the present. The crux of the matter is that the Son will execute God's work (v. 21), not only the raising of the dead and giving life, but judgment (v. 22). Raising the dead, giving life, and holding eschatological judgment are the distinctive works of God, that is, works that belong to God and not to human beings (see Ezek 37:11-14; Rom 4:17; 2 Cor 1:9). So if Jesus, or John, had an opportunity to allay fears by denying any claim to equality with God, he not only misses it, but moves decisively in the opposite direction: What God does, Jesus does, because God has given him it to do.

That the Son gives life to whom he wishes (v. 21) does not signify arbitrariness, nor does the Father's having given all judgment to the Son mean that he has abdicated his role (v. 22). In both cases we are dealing with seemingly extreme statements, which are intended to emphasize how completely the revelatory and eschatological work of God is now vested in Jesus. If the statement that all judgment has been given to the Son seems to contradict 3:17 and 12:47, we must remember John's emphasis on Jesus as the revelation of God. Rejection of God's intention to reveal and save inevitably implies judgment. Just this unity of the Father and Son in revelation now becomes entirely explicit in verse 23. The honoring of the Son signifies recognition of who he is, particularly in relation to the Father. In the Bible honor, of course, belongs to God as God (cf. Mark 7:6, quoting the Greek version of Isa 29:13; also Rom 1:21), so in John's view Jesus is to be honored as God, because he is the defining revelation of God, and accordingly this statement is put on Jesus' own lips.

Such claims by Jesus himself are uniquely Johannine. Yet they are not unprecedented in the New Testament, or even in the other Gospels. Matthew (1:23), quoting Isa 7:14 in the Septuagint says that Jesus shall be called "Emmanuel," and correctly renders the Hebrew "God with us." How seriously this assessment is to be taken is underscored at the very end of the Gospel, where Jesus promises to remain with his followers always, "to the end of the age" (Matt 28:20). This promise obviously forms an inclusion with Emmanuel in 1:23 and is extremely important for Matthew's Christology. Yet John clearly goes beyond other New Testament witnesses, even Paul, who regards Jesus Christ as a preexistent divine being, through whom God created the world (1 Cor 8:6; Phil 2:5-11), but does not call him *theos,* God. Yet for Paul, as for John, Jesus is the definitive and final revelation of God.

The final statement of this paragraph sums up the effect of Jesus' appearance on people generally (v. 24). First of all, it creates division. What is now said is entirely compatible with 3:17-21, the previous summation of the revelatory and salvific work of Jesus. Yet there is also something distinctive here. One who hears Jesus' word should believe the God who sent him. It would seem natural for Jesus to say "anyone who hears my word and believes me (or it)." But to hear and believe Jesus is to believe God, to trust God. The person who does so already has eternal life (cf. 3:16, 18). The eschatological event has already taken place, and this again invites a comparison with Paul, for whom the eschatological judgment, God's pronouncing the believer righteous, that is, justification, has occurred already (Rom 3:21, 24-26; 4:24–5:2), but salvation (life) remains in the future (Rom 13:11). John declares that the person who hears and accepts the word of Jesus believes *God* and already has attained salvation or life. If so, it is inconceivable that such a person would come under judgment, having already "passed from death to life" (v. 24). John is now engaged in the reinterpretation of traditional (apocalyptic) eschatological hopes.

The pattern of an encounter or healing leading into a relatively long conversation or discourse is typical of the Gospel of John (cf. chaps. 3, 4) and distinguishes it from the Synoptics. Also characteristic of John is the subject matter: Jesus himself, his dignity, role, and saving work. The Johannine Jesus talks at length about such christological matters, which are at most touched upon, suggested, or hinted at in Mark and the other Synoptics, but are not the subject of Jesus' own discourse.

In verses 25-29, Jesus continues to speak of resurrection and life. What is said in verses 25-27 fits with verse 24 and the present, or realized, eschatology of the Fourth Gospel: With Jesus' advent, life and light, the symbols of eschatological salvation, are already present for those who believe. That the Son executes the eschatological work of the Father, to give life and hold judgment (vv. 26-27), agrees with verses 19-24 (especially vv. 21-22). The reference to the dead in verse 25 takes up, or presumes, the Father's raising the dead (v. 21)—resurrection—and thus makes vivid the fact that by the Father's delegation Jesus does the same. Here "the dead" would seem to mean those who are physically alive, but dead to God, destined for death, for when they believe they pass from death to life (v. 24).

That the Son of Man is to execute judgment (v. 27), agrees with what is said of him in the synoptic Gospels (cf. Matt 28:31-46; Mark 8:38), where he is presented as the regent of God who holds judgment. In numerous synoptic sayings the Son of Man is a figure that apocalyptic eschatology associated with the cataclysmic end of this world or this age (Mark 13:24-27). In John (e.g., 11:23-26; cf. 14:18-24), such an apocalyptic eschatology is reinterpreted. What some ancient Jews and Christians believed was coming soon has in effect already transpired with the appearance of Jesus.

Yet a more primitive view now seems to reemerge in what is said about resurrection and judgment in 5:28-29. In fact, the view of resurrection presented here, in which both those who have done good and those who have done evil participate, recalls Dan 12:2, where both the just and the unjust are raised. That is, resurrection per se is not necessarily a good thing, not salvation or eternal life, but a necessary prelude to judgment. Elsewhere, and even in this chapter, however, the equation of resurrection and eschatological life is simply presumed (vv. 21, 25). Not surprisingly, the passage has been attributed to a later editor. Rudolf Bultmann (1971, 261) proposed that such an editor added these and other verses that introduce an apocalyptic eschatology into the Gospel (e.g., 6:39, 44, 54).

There may, however, be a simple solution to the problem, and seeming contradiction, posed by this statement. We are told only that "the hour is coming," not that "the hour is coming, and now is here" (as, for example, in v. 25). If this difference is taken at face value, then what is said applies to the future, not to the present (whether of Jesus or of the postresurrection church). Thus Jesus seems to anticipate a future resurrection at which as judge (cf. Matt 25:31-46) he will decide between people who have died *before his advent* on the basis of their deeds, whether they have done good or evil (v. 29). Of course, unlike Matt 25:31-46, John gives no picture of such a judgment scene, but Jesus has just said that the Son of Man will be the (eschatological) judge. Something like the Matthean scene seems to be in view, as Matthew is presumably depicting a last judgment of all people. If this interpretation is correct, it accords with 1 Pet 3:19-20, although there the disobedient are given a second chance, and perhaps also with the *Gospel of Peter* (10:41), where a voice from heaven asks the risen Jesus whether he has "preached to those that sleep." At many crucial points Jesus espouses the present, or realized, eschatology, which is John's dominant position. Yet the fact that John reinterprets traditional Jewish and Christian eschatology does not necessarily mean that he totally rejects it.

The astounding claim that Jesus raises the dead and holds judgment is not an assertion of his own authority but of God's (v. 30). What he carries out is not his own will but God's; thus his judgment is just, righteous, or simply right (Gk. *dikaios*). Jesus reiterates what he has already said in verse 19, and thus repeats the paradoxical claim of the Incarnation. Not because he claims anything for himself, but because he is completely obedient, and transparent to God's will for him, his word and deed carry absolute authority (see 12:49; 17:4; 19:30; cf. Phil 2:6-8, especially v. 6).

The remainder of this episode (vv. 31-47) has to do with testimony or witness (Greek stem: *martyr-*); the word is the same in Greek. Why Jesus' testimony or witness for himself should not be true is a good question. But in 8:13 his opponents, the Pharisees, say that Jesus testifies on his own behalf and his testimony is not valid. In 5:31 they have not yet said that he proposes to testify on his own behalf, but he himself contemplates such testimony as problematic. Why so? According to Pentateuchal law one tried in a capital case cannot be put to death on the strength of one witness's testimony (Num 35:30; Deut 17:6). In the Mishnah this principle is extended: a person is not to be believed when he testifies about himself (*m. Rosh HaSh.* 3.1; *m. Ketub.* 2.9; cited by Barrett 1978, 338). Obviously, such scriptural and traditional stipulations are in view. At least two witnesses are needed. So Jesus claims that he has another witness (v. 32), whose testimony he knows is true. That witness could be John (v. 33), but probably Jesus here alludes to the Father (cf. v. 37), although his statement is typically mysterious. One thinks also of the true witness of 19:35, who in 21:24 is identified as the author of this Gospel. In the Old Testament God is called upon as a witness, for example, between Laban and Jacob (Gen 31:50; cf. 1 Sam 12:5-6; Jer 42:5; Mic 1:2), and the apostle Paul more than once calls upon God as his witness (Rom 1:9; 2 Cor 1:23; Phil 1:8). In all probability Jesus' statement belongs in this tradition too, even though he does not name God the Father as witness until later on (v. 37). (On the juridical elements of the Fourth Gospel see Harvey 1976.)

The preeminent earthly witness to Jesus is John (the Baptist), whose testimony is also true (v. 33). Already priests and Levites

(1:19) had been sent to John by Jews and Pharisees (v. 24). That John "testified to the truth" (v. 33) is everywhere evident, as Jesus certifies the validity of his testimony. What Jesus next says (v. 34) does not invalidate John's testimony, which is true, despite the fact that Jesus does not need it. This rather negative view actually corresponds with the previous scene in which John appeared (3:22-36). Although John's witness continues to be true, he himself is being demoted. What Jesus says about John's testimony even suggests that 3:31-36 may also apply to John. John is, seemingly, once more praised by Jesus (v. 35), if in a qualified way. But who are those who were willing to rejoice for a while in his light? Probably Jews generally (v. 18), whom Jesus has been addressing all along in chapter 5. If so, to what episode does Jesus' statement refer? In the Gospels we read only of John's baptizing activity and his witness to Jesus. Josephus, however, describes the great popularity of John among the people (cf. Mark 11:30-32) and suggests that just that popularity was the factor that made Herod Antipas decide to put him out of the way (*Ant.* 18.3.116-19). Perhaps the Fourth Gospel here confirms this assessment, for it implies more than that many people were moved to repentance.

John's testimony is true, but Jesus has a greater witness, his works (v. 36). The Gospel speaks of Jesus' works as well as his signs. His signs are his miraculous deeds that signify who he is. His works (Gk. *erga*) include signs, but refer "to the whole of Jesus' activity as the Revealer" (Bultmann 1971, 265; cf. also von Wahlde 1989, who locates "signs" and works in different literary strata); in particular his works of giving life and judging are here in view. Jesus at the end of his ministry prays to God, saying that he has accomplished the work (singular) that God gave him to do (17:4). Like the signs (2:23; 3:2), the works testify to who Jesus is. Finally, the Father also testifies to Jesus (v. 37). Exactly how is not said. But undoubtedly the works, which God has given Jesus to do (cf. 10:32, 37-38; 14:10-12), are God's testimony to Jesus. (Moreover, Jesus has just said that his works are God's [vv. 19-24]). Of course, in the next paragraph (vv. 39-46) Jesus will discuss the witness of Moses, which is the witness of Scripture and the God of Scripture (cf. 1:45), if only it is rightly understood.

Verses 37*b*-38 form a transition to the subject of Scripture (vv. 39-47), and in a way are well calculated to strike his hearers as offensive. That the Jews have not seen God's form (Gk. *eidos*) actually agrees with Scripture (Deut 4:12, 15-18; cf. John 1:18), although the assertion that they have not heard God's voice and do not have God's word abiding in them, would seem to contradict the Sinai theophany (Exod 20:1; Deut 5:4-5; 30:11-14; see the discussion of Meeks 1967, 298-301). As we shall see, the Jews' claims, here implied and denied, are deemed invalid because of their unbelief. Does failure to believe in Jesus now also mean that the Father's historic revelation to Israel was not received and understood? That should not be inferred, because John consistently focuses on his contemporaries and the new situation created by the sending of the Son. The old interpretation of what happened was not invalid back then, but now must be reconsidered, as everything must be, in light of the sending of the Son.

The practice of the opponents of Jesus and their expectations are succinctly described (v. 39). The Scriptures are read, but not really understood, because apart from belief in Jesus their hermeneutical key is missing (v. 40; cf. 2 Cor 3:14-15). Now the polemical volume of Jesus' discourse is turned up (vv. 40-44). The harsh tone doubtless does not reflect Jesus' own time so much as the intensity of the conflict going on behind the text. Quite basic is the fact that these Jews do not accept the claims made for Jesus (v. 40). What is first said in verse 40 is reiterated in verse 43, but now the contrast is made between the one who comes in his own name and Jesus, who comes in God's name. The reader is not told the identity of the one who comes in his own name, or whether anyone specifically is in view. Quite possibly this figure is posed hypothetically, to afford a contrast with Jesus and to draw out the irony of the Jews' rejection of him. The point is that Jesus makes no claim whatever for himself—except to speak for God, but that is God's claim for him. In verse 41 Jesus seems to forestall an objection (cf. 2:23-25; 3:2), and in verse 42 he hurls invective at his opponents. "Love of God" probably means "love for God" rather than "God's love." (As the NRSV note indicates, "in you" could mean "among you" or "among yourselves.") To love Jesus is to obey his word (14:21, 23), which is God's word. Consequently, those who disobey God's Word cannot claim to love him. They do not love God, even as they do not seek the glory that comes from the one who alone is God (v. 44). Jesus' refusal to accept glory from other people (v. 41) contrasts with the behavior of his opponents, who seek glory from each other and do not seek God's glory. Not seeking God's glory means they do not honor God as God (cf. Rom 1:21, where the same Greek stem *doxa* is used for honoring God). Thus the love of (or for) God is not in (or among) them. No one who refuses to honor the Son can honor the Father or love God.

Finally, Jesus comes back to the initial point of the paragraph. Although he seems to have been accusing his opponents, their accuser is really Moses, the author of the Scriptures they are searching (v. 45; cf. v. 39). They have set their hope on Moses in that they search the Scriptures, which Moses wrote, thinking that in them they will find eternal life. But they lack the hermeneutical key that opens them (cf. 2 Cor 3:14-15). The fundamental hermeneutical insight is then made explicit (v. 46). Moses becomes their accuser because they do not believe Moses who wrote about Jesus. They cannot believe Moses because they have not acknowledged Jesus, who is Moses' actual subject (v. 46). The Johannine Christians take possession of the Hebrew Bible in the name of Jesus. No wonder there is such strife. What could be more precious to the ancient Jew than the Bible, and here the Johannine Christians claim it for Jesus through the lips of Jesus himself. The final statement (v. 47) parallels the preceding one and, in effect, reiterates it, playing upon the difference between Moses' writing and Jesus' speaking. Of course, in Jewish and Christian tradition Moses wrote the Pentateuch. Jesus, however, only spoke; he did not write. John is in this respect right on target.

◊ ◊ ◊ ◊

Chapter 5 is a complete, discrete unit. The healing of the ill or lame man at the pool of Bethzatha (vv. 1-9) leads to a controversy with Jesus' opponents (vv. 10-18) as the man carries away his mat on the sabbath. As the Jews then persecute Jesus for sabbath breaking, he announces, in order to justify himself, "My Father is still working, and I also am working" (v. 17). This announcement then becomes the thematic key to Jesus' following discourse (vv. 19-47), as it is immediately interpreted as a claim to equality with God (v. 18). Although Jesus could have easily claimed he did not mean equality, what he then says actually confirms his opponents' worst suspicions and fears. By the commission of God, Jesus does the eschatological work of God: he raises the dead and holds judgment (vv. 19-30).

Having made these astounding, and to his opponents offensive, claims, Jesus then issues a disclaimer. He does not testify on his own behalf, but others testify for him (v. 31). Ultimately the Father testifies for him. Thus God is his witness, although Jesus does not put it quite that way. This claim then leads to the question about Scripture, for both John and his opponents believe that Scripture is the Word of God. The question, however, now becomes a hermeneutical one. How is Scripture to be read?

The level of christological confession that John here attains is remarkable and distinct, if not entirely unique, in New Testament, or early Christian writings. In popular theological discussion and debate, the question of whether Jesus is God frequently comes up, and the basis for such discussion is the claims the Johannine Jesus makes for himself, or are made for him (e.g., 1:1; 5:19; 10:30; 14:9; 20:28). An affirmative answer to the question of whether Jesus is God can adduce the Fourth Gospel's seemingly unequivocal testimony. Actually, John's claims are rather finely nuanced, but they lend themselves to interpretation in this direction. Jesus is the Christ, the Son of God, indeed, God.

Yet in Jewish Scripture and traditions there is no thought of the Messiah's being God. It is rare enough for the Messiah, the expected ruler, to be called Son of God (see above, pp. 76-77). In the synoptic Gospels there is little if any basis for thinking Jesus made such a claim. He is, however, a prophetic figure, and the ancient prophets boldly proclaimed God's word. Clearly, Jesus understood his own role within that prophetic tradition and viewed himself as the bearer of a crucial message from God for his own time (Sanders 1993, 238). The view that Jesus is in some significant sense God *(theos)* would seem to be peculiarly Johannine. As such it is retrojected even into the words of Jesus as the only adequate expression of who he is, the definitive and final revelation of God to humanity.

The Bread of Life (6:1-71)

Although it contains several distinct events or segments, this chapter is a discrete literary unit. The beginning is marked by a sudden change of locale (6:1), for Jesus has been in Jerusalem, and the feeding of a multitude (6:1-15). It ends with Jesus' conversation with his disciples (6:60-71), which follows upon the bread discourse (6:25-59). The next episode clearly begins afresh with a narrative about Jesus' brothers urging him to go to Jerusalem (7:1-8).

The events of chapter 6 all occur in Galilee. (Chapter 5 was set in Jerusalem, and in chapter 7 Jesus will eventually return there.) We begin with Jesus on, or in the vicinity of, the Sea of Galilee. At the end of the long conversation or discourse on the bread of heaven we learn that it has taken place in Capernaum (v. 59), and presumably the subsequent conversation with the disciples takes place there as well.

Chapter 6 is one of three places in the Gospel where its narrative runs close to the Synoptics. The first and briefest is the encounter with John the Baptist (especially 1:24-34); the last and longest is the Passion narrative (chaps. 18–19). In fact, chapter 6 contains all the Johannine parallels to Jesus' Galilean ministry as narrated in Mark. And, aside from 4:46-54 (cf. Matt 8:5-13; Luke 7:1-10), it contains all the parallels with the synoptic Galilean ministry. (The two Cana miracles lack Markan parallels, and the wine miracle lacks any synoptic parallel.) Definitely parallel with Mark are the stories of the feeding (vv. 1-15; cf. Mark 6:30-44 and 8:1-10) and Jesus' walking on the water of the Sea of Galilee (vv. 16-21; cf. Mark 6:45-52), as well as Peter's confession (vv. 66-71; cf. Mark 8:27-30). More remotely parallel are the discourse on bread (vv. 25-58; cf. Mark 8:14-21) and the mention of signs (v. 26; Mark 8:11-12). Moreover, all the parallels occur within Mark's central section, either in Mark 8 or the similar feeding cycle of Mark 6:30-52, where Jesus walks on the water, as he does in John 6:16-21. It is worth noting that after the second feeding in Mark, Jesus embarks on a boat with his disciples (8:13-14), although there is no sea-walking, and at the end of the boat trip in 6:52 the loaves of bread are mentioned, although there is no discussion about bread. Obviously, there is some substantial relation between John 6 and the similar accounts of Mark 6 and 8. (As Brown [1961] has observed, what is scattered in the Synoptics—here in Mark 6 and 8—is often consolidated in John—as here in John 6.) Although there are verbatim parallels between John 6:1-21 and Mark 6:30-44; 8:1-30, especially in the feeding stories, they mainly involve essential elements of the basic story, such as the numbers of loaves, fish, and people. We shall look closely at the points of similarity or contact as we read John's account closely.

The principal questions about this chapter have to do with its source(s), its literary integrity, and its position. (Bultmann 1971, 209-37, 443-51, rearranges material within the discourses, but Anderson [1996], who sees the tensions in the chapter as understandable expressions of faith, proposes different solutions.) The narrative portions, as distinguished from the discourse, could be based on Mark, although that premise presents some difficulties. The problem of literary integrity is obvious, although not insurmountable, and there is a correlation with the source question: 6:1-21 is synoptic or synoptic-like; 6:26-59 is Johannine basically, with at most a few synoptic-like traces. In the case of 6:22-25 and 6:60-71 there is a kind of mixture: 6:22-25 seems to be concerned about getting everyone to the proper side of the sea, so that the feeding can take place there; 6:60-71 marks a watershed in the narrative, somewhat like Mark's confession of Peter (Mark 8:27-30; cf. John 6:66-71), but contains material distinctive to John as well (vv. 60-65). Whether John brought these materials together (following Mark) or worked with a traditional complex has been difficult for exegetes to decide.

In addition, we have already noted (see above, p. 130) that chapter 6 brings Jesus suddenly back to the Sea of Galilee, although he has just previously been in Judea (chap. 5), and the transition is abrupt and somewhat awkward. Conceivably, chapter 6 once followed, or was intended to follow, immediately after chapter 4. With chapter 5 following 6 Jesus would go to Jerusalem or Judea only once after his stay in Galilee (chaps. 4, 6) and actually remain there, with perhaps one interlude (10:40-42). He is then no more in Galilee.

Yet the present order, the only one found in extant manuscripts, makes sense in terms of the development of plot, even though it creates a problem in narrative continuity. The mortal hostility between Jesus and his Jewish opponents (chap. 5) lays the basis for Jesus' negative response to the Jews (6:36) who seemingly in all innocence have asked Jesus for the bread from heaven.

6:1-15: Jesus will now feed a multitude of five thousand people. There is no preparation for his going to the other side of the Sea of Galilee (v. 1), for in the episode just previous he was in Jerusalem and no journey to Galilee is mentioned or contemplated. Thus it is frequently noted that at least as far as geography is concerned, chapters 5 and 6 may have been transposed (see above, and pp. 28, 130). The Sea of Galilee is called Tiberias (only here in the New Testament) after the city of Tiberias, founded on the southwestern shore by Herod Antipas in honor of Tiberius Caesar in the early 20s CE. That Jesus goes to the other side apparently means that he goes to the eastern, pagan shore. In Mark (6:32, 45) Jesus is presumed to be on the Galilean side (in "a deserted place") for the feeding and then goes across to Bethsaida, which is at the top of the sea, just east of the point where the Jordan empties into the sea. (Luke 9:10 has the whole scene in Bethsaida, and thus represents a kind of compromise between John and Mark.) John's statement that a large crowd followed Jesus basically agrees with the Synoptics (although Matthew and Luke speak of crowds and Mark has simply "many"), but only John gives the reason that they saw the signs he was doing for the sick—a typically Johannine explanation

(v. 2). Also, only John portrays Jesus going up on a mountain with his disciples (v. 3; cf. Mark 6:46) and refers to the nearness of Passover (v. 4; cf. 5:1). At the end, Jesus retires to the same mountain (v. 15), even as he retires to a mountain, presumably near Bethsaida, in Mark (6:46).

The feeding of five thousand is the only miracle story found in all four Gospels. In the Synoptics the disciples express concern over how so many people can find food so late in the day (Mark 6:35-36), but in John Jesus himself raises the question with Philip of finding food for the people, apparently in some perplexity as he sees them approaching (v. 5). Then in typical Johannine fashion the reader is told that it is only a test question to Philip; Jesus knows what he will do (cf. 12:30). The Johannine version calls for such an explanation, as the synoptic would not. Philip's amazed response (v. 7) underscores the size of the crowd. In the synoptic accounts the disciples are present, but no individual is named. But now Andrew, again identified as Simon Peter's brother (cf. 1:40), intervenes to point out the boy with five barley loaves and two fish, but also to express the futility he senses in the face of so many people. It is noteworthy that Andrew and Philip appear together, as they do in 1:43-45 and 12:22; all of these instances are unique to John. Moreover, only John mentions the boy and the fact that loaves were barley, traditionally the bread of the poor, although that motif is not explicit here. The barley loaves recall the scene in 2 Kgs 4:42-44, where similarly Elisha, despite his servant's despair, feeds a hundred people with only some fresh ears of grain and twenty loaves of barley. The parallel is almost too striking to be coincidental. The Elisha story may explain the departure from the Synoptics, although likely at the level of prior tradition, for the evangelist makes nothing further of this. Moreover, the boy with the loaves and fish plays no further part in the story, again suggesting he belongs to an independent tradition. That seems more likely than that John derived the story solely from Mark (or any one of the Synoptics) and embellished it with these details.

The number of loaves and fish is the same in each Gospel. The difference is that only John specifies their source. In John, as in the Synoptics, Jesus tells the disciples to have the people sit down (v. 10); we are also told there was grass there. John gives the number fed as five thousand, which agrees with Matthew and Mark. Luke cites no figure, and the others give it only at the end of the story. (In fact, all the numbers referred to in this story are the same in the various Gospels.)

Jesus then gives thanks and distributes the loaves directly to the people, but the fish appear only as an afterthought (v. 11). The language of the Synoptics more than John echoes that of the Lord's Supper (Mark 14:22-25 par.). The blessing and breaking of the loaves is in the Synoptics exactly the same wording as in the Lord's Supper. Interestingly, however, John here (v. 11) and Luke in the Lord's Supper (22:17, 19) say that Jesus gave thanks *(eucharisteō),* employing the Greek word that produced the term *Eucharist,* traditionally used by Christians of the celebration of the Lord's Supper. Perhaps it should not be surprising if in other respects John's version of the feeding has fewer connections with the Eucharist, for, unlike the Synoptics, John does not narrate the institution of the Lord's Supper at the Last Supper. Yet at the end of Jesus' discourse (6:52-58) he commands his disciples to eat his flesh and drink his blood in language usually taken to be eucharistic.

In different words, John and the Synoptics make clear that the disciples ate their fill (vv. 11-12, 26; cf. Mark 6:42). In John only does Jesus command the disciples to take up the leftover fragments (v. 12), "so that nothing may be lost." The distinctive Johannine emphasis on Jesus' not losing what has been given to him (cf. 6:39; 18:9) appears here, although it is not yet clear that the leftovers represent people, that is, believers. As in the Synoptics, twelve baskets of fragments are gathered (v. 13; cf. Mark 6:43). The loaves are referred to later in Mark (6:52), as well as the number of baskets taken up (Mark 8:19-21). In John in a different context Jesus refers back to the loaves (6:26), but not to their number. With the gathering of the fragments, the Synoptic version of the story ends, but not the Johannine.

John's ending is quite different and distinctive: as the people recognize in the miraculous feeding a sign they hail Jesus as *the* prophet, probably the prophet like Moses of Deut 18:15, "who is to come into the world" (v. 14). In Greek the phrase is the same as the description of the as yet unnamed Jesus in the prologue (1:9): "The true light...was coming into the world" *(erchomenos[n] eis ton kosmon)*. It is John's way of speaking of the advent of Jesus. The feeding leads the people to recognize Jesus as the prophet, and when Jesus anticipates they will seize him and make him king as well (i.e., Messiah) he withdraws into the mountain from which he had fed the multitude in the first place (v. 3). The feeding thus suggests that Jesus is the expected prophet-king (see Meeks 1967), but obviously these perceptions of him, while not entirely off base, are not yet full or adequate. Jesus avoids accepting this acclaim of the people. Yet they will follow him, and the discussion of what has happened, and who Jesus is, will go on (vv. 25-59). Here, as in chapter 5, and indeed chapter 4, Jesus' miraculous deed leads to recognition of him, but recognition that is at best partial or inadequate. As in chapter 5, the clarification of who he claims to be will result finally in rejection, but not until the crowd has crossed the lake in pursuit of Jesus. (This is, incidentally, the only point in any of the Gospels where Jesus is said to fear a popular misinterpretation of his mission or messiahship.)

6:16-24: After the feeding there is a scene in which the disciples and Jesus encounter each other on the sea (cf. Matt 14:22-33; Mark 6:45-52). In John they are coming back from the Transjordan where the feeding has obviously occurred, toward Capernaum, on the northwestern shore. (Tabgha, the traditional site of the feeding and of the ruin of a church commemorating it, is a few miles south of Capernaum, on the western shore, agreeing with the synoptic version of the feeding account.) According to Mark (6:46) and Matthew (14:23), Jesus goes up on the mountain to pray, as in John he withdraws to the mountain to escape the crowd (6:15; cf. v. 3). As the disciples set out by boat there is already a hint that Jesus is going to come to them (v. 17). With great economy of style in comparison with the Synoptics John describes the storm at sea and Jesus' approaching the disciples' boat walking on the sea (vv. 18-19). As in the Matthew and Mark accounts, the disciples are frightened, and Jesus addresses their fear (v. 20), identifying himself, "It is I," even as he calms their fears. The NRSV note indicates that one could read "I am" (Gk. *egō eimi*). If so, this becomes one of the typical "I am" sayings of this Gospel (cf. 4:26; 6:35). On the other hand, the other Gospels have the same expression, and it is the typical identification formula in Greek (cf. the French *C'est moi*). Yet given the importance of the expression in John, it is probably justifiable to see a deeper meaning here.

The conclusion of John's version of the episode is curious. As in the other Gospels, Jesus gets into the boat with the disciples, but the statement about the boat's being near the land is unique to John. John could be saying that with Jesus' arrival they got to land with unusual speed. On the other hand, rationalist critics once saw here the key to the "miracle": Jesus was actually walking in the shallows. Whatever may have been the case in the history or tradition of this story, John scarcely would have espoused such a rationalistic explanation. Again, the story as a whole bears few distinctively Johannine theological traits. At this point Matthew has added to Mark the narrative of Peter's abortive attempt to walk on the water (Matt 14:28-33), of which there is no trace in John.

If John knows the synoptic version, he presumably knows Mark. (Luke omits the episode entirely.) In favor of John's knowledge of Mark is the fact that the story immediately follows the feeding. (In fact, most of what John shares with Mark he has in the same order.) On the other hand, the difficulty of deriving the details of the Johannine version from Mark suggests that at best the latter was known only at a distance. Moreover, the juxtaposition of the episodes may, as we have noted above, bespeak a traditional origin.

The crowd left on the transjordanian side after the departure of Jesus and the disciples must now get back across if they are to participate in the conversation about bread, as they clearly do (6:26). These people belong on the western shore because they are Jews (or "Judeans"; *Ioudaios* can mean either; see v. 41). The observation about who actually departed in the one boat (vv. 22, 24) confirms Jesus' miraculous crossing. He did not embark with them. Boats now conveniently arrive near the place where the feeding occurred (v. 23) to take the crowd across. Tiberias, the new city on the southwestern shore of the Sea of Galilee, would have been built only a decade or so before by Herod Antipas as his capital (cf. v. 1).

Because John has placed the feeding across the Sea of Galilee he must devise ways of getting the crowd back across to Capernaum, on the side for which they now depart, apparently confident that they will find Jesus there (v. 24), as indeed they do (vv. 25, 59). Probably the effort to construct a historical sequence will prove fruitless. It is, however, worth observing that unless the evangelist found these episodes in this order with the geographical places as given, he certainly made a great deal of trouble for himself and his narrative, particularly with respect to the synoptic narratives. More likely, he is working with a given tradition.

6:25-59: Jesus now engages the group that has followed him to Capernaum in a long discourse and discussion about the bread that they have eaten. The crowd's question to Jesus (v. 25) underscores the mysterious, miraculous nature of Jesus' crossing. Jesus seems immediately to change the subject, as he refers back to the feeding (vv. 26-27).

Jesus' statement (v. 26) immediately raises the question of whether it is a good thing that the crowd is seeking Jesus because they ate their fill of the loaves. Would it not have been better had they seen signs? Probably. Apparently they did see a sign (v. 14); yet their reaction was not on target, although not entirely wrong. Their initial reaction (v. 15) misfired. Now again they seem to be seeking Jesus for the wrong reason. They have indeed eaten their fill of the loaves that Jesus has miraculously provided (v. 26), but they have scarcely partaken of Jesus himself who is the bread of life (v. 35). Seemingly, they have not understood the sign character of the loaves Jesus provided them, that is, they have not understood that they signify his role as the bringer of salvation, indeed as salvation itself. The food (Gk. *brōsis*) that perishes (v. 27) they have already eaten; now Jesus will speak to them of the food that endures to eternal life. The Son of Man is, of course, Jesus himself. That God the Father has set his seal on him is an unusual way of speaking, but actually has appeared already in 3:33 ("certified," but see the NRSV note) in a similar sense. God attests something or someone is true. (The same verb, *sphragizō,* or noun, *sphragis,* occurs with some frequency in Revelation, perhaps a subtle link between these two documents.)

The crowd, not yet called "the Jews," responds to Jesus' claim and command with a reasonable question (v. 28), which is not badly put, even as it betrays their own perplexity. Presumably the Jew would want to do the works of God (although this is not a typical or biblical expression). Of course, Jesus' answer (v. 29) is not unexpected, at least not in this Gospel. Work is defined as belief, faith. What must one do, accomplish? One must believe, have faith. Does the Pauline dialectic of faith and works—one is justified not through works but through faith—lurk in the background here? For both Paul and John to obey God—and that is, after all, what is at stake here—is to believe, put one's faith or trust in Jesus (John 3:36; Rom 10:16). Because Paul has a great deal to say about human works, as well as faith, his thought affords an appropriate background to this question, whether or not John knows and deliberately presupposes his work.

The question about a sign (v. 30) is perfectly straightforward and biblical. Signs are intended to lead to faith (Gen 9:12-17; Exod 4:8-9, 17; Isa 7:11, 14), even though the synoptic Jesus seems loath to perform them on demand (Mark 8:11-12). Again, Paul says "Jews demand signs" (1 Cor 1:22), seemingly in a negative sense, but he can also speak of having performed signs of an apostle among his followers (2 Cor 12:12), that is, signs that should be credited. Here sign *(sēmeion)* and work *(ergon)* seem to be equated, although this is not always the case. The people then challenge Jesus to perform a sign equivalent to the manna miracle of the Exodus, although the manna is not specifically a sign in the Old Testament. (Manna is mentioned nowhere else in the Gospels.) In so challenging Jesus they quote Scripture. The passage (v. 31) is actually no single Old Testament quotation, but seems to mirror or reflect several similar statements: Exod 16:4, 15; Neh 9:15; Pss 78:24; 105:40—perhaps others. Probably John is aware that he brings together several scriptural texts. The giving of bread from heaven is something God was known to have done. Not insignificantly Jesus' questioners refer to their ancestors' eating manna in the wilderness; they are, or believe themselves to be, Israel. The discussion will become a kind of exegesis or midrash upon this scriptural statement (Borgen 1965; Swancutt 1997, especially 219-20, argues that John here interprets Ps 78 [LXX 70] in light of Isa 54–55).

Jesus' response contradicts not what they have said, but what is assumed. As often, he introduces a solemn saying with "very truly" (literally "truly, truly," translating the Greek, ultimately the Hebrew, *amēn, amēn*). There is now an exegetical, midrashic discussion (Borgen 1965), and the point of contention is the true meaning of this biblical word. Jesus says it was not Moses but "my Father who gives . . . the true bread" (v. 32). The crowd might have here countered, "Of course, it was not Moses but God who gave the manna, or bread from heaven." At most, Moses gave directions, and his role was important. The crucial point, however, is that wilderness manna is not the true bread from heaven. It is at most a type of the true bread that God, who is in a unique sense Jesus' Father, now gives. Jesus' statement in verse 33 admits of two translations; the NRSV can give only one, but alternatively the statement can also be read as referring to Jesus (because "bread" or "loaf"—*artos*—is masculine in Greek and therefore takes the masculine participle): "The bread of God is he who comes down from heaven and gives life to the world." That is, of course, Jesus himself, but his interlocutors do not suspect this (v. 34). Like the woman of Samaria (cf. 4:15) they want a permanent supply of this, presumably earthly, bread. Once again we see the typical Johannine misunderstanding, which embodies the irony of revelation. The double meaning of Jesus' statement in verse 34 enhances this irony.

In response Jesus utters a solemn revelatory formula (v. 35; see Bultmann 1971, 225). The crowd wants the bread of heaven, and Jesus reveals himself as that bread in a typical Johannine formu-

lation, an "I am" saying: "I am the bread of life." With the revelation comes a word of promise and assurance to the one who
comes to Jesus and trusts him. The term "believe," *pisteuō,* con-
notes trusting in, as well as believing affirmations about, Jesus.
Those who come to Jesus and believe are seeking sustenance for
life. Somewhat strangely, Jesus then denounces his conversation
partners as unbelievers (v. 36), seemingly knowing the judgment
they have rendered or will render before it is spoken. Something
similar happens in 5:17-18 where hostility to Jesus suddenly
emerges without what would seem a natural, or even requisite,
development in the narrative. Such phenomena bespeak the controversy between Christ-confessors and deniers that lies behind
such texts. Chapter 5 in its present position (especially 5:16-18),
however, makes Jesus' response here more intelligible.

Bultmann regards the Johannine "I am" saying in 6:35 and in
many other passages as a "recognition formula" (see 6:41, 48, 51;
8:12; 10:7, 9, 11, 14; 15:1, 5). That is, it answers to the question
"Who is the one who is expected, asked for, spoken to?"
(Bultmann 1971, 225-26, n. 3). In each case it is assumed that
there is more than one claimant to the title or role of bread, light,
shepherd, and so forth, so that Jesus is asking his hearers to recognize him as the true bread, shepherd, or light. Certainly Jesus'
claim to be the bread of life fits this formula exactly, for the
exegetical discussion has to do precisely with the question of what
(or who) is this bread. (See the illuminating discussion of Eduard
Schweizer 1996, 208-19, where he refers to his 1939 dissertation
inspired by Bultmann, who first recognized and classified such
sayings. Scriptural parallels to this form of divine speech are
found, for example, in Exod 3:14; Isa 41:4. Boring, Berger, and
Colpe 1995, 272-73, give the text of the *Hymn of Isis,* which consists solely of several dozen such self-predications.)

Jesus' next statement (v. 37), another word of promise and
assurance, fits well after verse 35 and leads to a succinct expression of the typically Johannine Christology (v. 38). John's
Christology is "high" in the sense that Jesus presents himself
unequivocally as the revelation of God, but he is that revelation
only as he is completely transparent to the Father's will. Jesus

then reiterates in verse 39 what he has said in verse 37, a familiar theme that he actually takes up again at the moment of his
arrest (18:8-9; cf. also 6:12). The paragraph and this phase of the
discourse end with a summary statement (v. 40) that picks up elements from the immediately preceding sentences, concluding
with a reference to resurrection at the last day (v. 40; cf. vv. 39,
44, 54).

Here eternal life and resurrection appear to be in synonymous
parallelism (that is, they mean the same thing), but perhaps not
exactly, for eternal life, as we have learned (5:24) is already a present possession, while resurrection at the last day or end time, a
concept taken from apocalyptic literature (Isa 26:1, 19; Dan 12:2;
cf. John 11:24), is obviously future. Although his eschatological
project involves the reinterpretation of apocalyptic language and
concepts, John can nevertheless use that language and those concepts (see 5:27-29 and our discussion above). The concluding
statement of the paragraph then reiterates what has been said.
Indeed, it encapsulates the message of this Gospel (cf. 3:16).

The Jews' complaint (v. 41) accurately summarizes what Jesus
has just noted (v. 36). Clearly the complaining evokes the memory of Israel's complaining (RSV: "murmured") against Moses in
the wilderness (cf. Exod 16:2-12; Num 14:2-29). The Greek verb
stem *(gongyzō)* is the same in John and in the Septuagint. Of
course, the grounds for complaint are different, for here they
have to do with Jesus' christological claims. The refutation of
those claims seems obvious: the Jews know his parents (v. 42).
Here we encounter once again the motif of Jesus' origin (cf.
1:46): Jesus' earthly origins are thought to explain him. He is a
human being, whose village and family are known (cf. 1:45,
where Jesus is first called the son of Joseph). Moreover, he will
not measure up to traditional messianic standards (7:41-42).
John is, of course, quite aware of those humble origins and never
corrects or contradicts the statements that refer to them. Yet it is
precisely the point that such statements—while true in themselves—do not explain Jesus. That Jesus is the Man from Heaven
is the premise of Johannine Christology (Meeks 1972; de Jonge,
Jesus: Stranger from Heaven). Yet he is not an angel, nor some

other heavenly or divine figure, but a man, that is, a human being. The classical paradox of the claim of incarnation, that a human being fully reveals God, so that he himself can be called *theos* (God) is rooted in the Fourth Gospel. Moreover, it is quite clear that the claim that he has come down from heaven is in John an assertion about his origin and mission, not about any literal descent. Thus it is reasonable to ask how Jesus can possibly say that he has come down from heaven. But to make that protest reveals that the Jews have not understood the character of the claim.

Jesus, in response to the not unreasonable complaint of the Jews, at first seems simply to shut them up (v. 43), but then he goes on to explain that anyone's coming to him (in faith) is the work of God the Father; apart from this divine initiative it cannot happen (v. 44; cf. 3:8). John does not hesitate to state bold paradoxes, as we have just seen. Jesus is God and a human being. One is invited to come to Jesus and believe, seemingly an act of the human will (6:35, 40). At the same time the initiative finally belongs to God. If one asks about the resolution of the seeming contradiction with respect to the freedom of the human will, an answer is hard to come by. Yet the assertion of the initiative of God, that is, the priority of grace, is an important aspect of the consciousness of faith, whether in early Christianity (Paul as well as John) or ancient Judaism (e.g., Qumran; cf. E. P. Sanders 1977, 261-68). It is also clear, however, that John insists upon the cruciality of human decision (see Keck 1996, 274-88). The promise of resurrection at the last day does seem to be something of an afterthought here, but it has a certain logic nevertheless. God has the last word as well as the first (cf. Rev 1:8; 21:6; 22:13).

Jesus makes his point about the Father's crucial role by a testimony or proof from Scripture (v. 45), referring to Isa 54:13 (cf. Jer 31:33-34) with the explicit notation, "It is written in the prophets." Scripture is still valid, if rightly understood, and particularly for Jews. Again Jesus underscores the priority of God in people's coming to him. The believer's learning from the Father is not, however, to be confused with Jesus' distinctive relationship to him (v. 46). Only Jesus has seen the Father (cf. 1:18; cf. 14:8-10); his relation to God is primary and unique.

Jesus now summarizes and states the other side of the paradox (vv. 47-48): "whoever believes...." Eternal life is a gift already in the present. The reiterated "I am" saying (cf. v. 35) signals that the discourse is coming to a climax and conclusion, as does Jesus' repeated reference to the gift of manna in the wilderness (v. 49; cf. v. 31). That Israelites ate the manna is neither denied nor disparaged. Significantly, however, they are called "your ancestors" rather than "our ancestors," which seems to set Jesus apart from the Jews. This is, in fact, the case, but in a variety of ways Jesus is also set apart from all other human beings (cf. v. 46). Moreover, he can scarcely concede that even the Patriarchs, the Fathers of Israel, are his ancestors: "before Abraham was, I am" (8:58; cf. 4:12). Useful as the gift of manna may have been—and Jesus does not deny its reality—it was not the bread from heaven of which Jesus is now speaking. That bread obviously did not give eternal life (v. 49); this bread does (vv. 50-51). Those who ate of the manna died; those who eat of the true bread from heaven do not die (v. 50). There is, obviously, a fundamental distinction. The bread that Jesus brings, and is, sets him apart.

Another "I am" saying underscores this point (v. 51). Jesus as the living bread (the literal translation could be "the loaf who lives"; cf. "living water" in 4:10) is both the one who is alive and who gives life. John delights in dual meanings. Jesus now summarizes and reiterates his essential message once more, but goes beyond what has been previously said in that he identifies the living bread with his flesh that he gives for the life of the world. This is a veiled allusion to his own death. In 3:16 God gives his only Son; here Jesus gives his flesh; in either case the goal and end is salvation as the gift of life through Jesus' death.

After Jesus' summation, the Jews disputing (or even fighting) among themselves ask the natural and obvious question (v. 52), but Jesus does not give a direct answer. Yet the wilderness manna was eaten, and the text that has been under discussion from the beginning of this discourse (v. 31) reads: "He gave them bread from heaven *to eat*." The phrase "to eat" has so far not been discussed, but now it must be. Otherwise its exegesis is not complete (Borgen 1965, especially 28-38; also Dwight Moody Smith 1965, 144-52).

Now Jesus insists not only that his flesh (the living bread) must be eaten, but that his blood must be drunk if life is to be gained (v. 53). The consuming of blood is strictly forbidden in the law (Lev 17:10-14), so Jesus' requirement would be offensive to Jews. Moreover, the flesh and blood of Jesus recalls the body and blood of the Eucharist (cf. Mark 14:22-25 par.; 1 Cor 11:23-28). That John writes "flesh" rather than "body" is perhaps not surprising, because of his affirmation that the Word became flesh (1:14; but cf. also Ps 78:27, where God is said to rain flesh, as well as bread, upon the people). Also, "flesh and blood" may be a common way of referring to humanity, a mortal, human being (cf. 1 Cor 15:50, where Paul uses the expression; so also Matt 16:17; Sir 14:18; 17:31), although in the Old Testament "flesh" alone usually suffices (e.g., Joel 2:28 cited in Acts 2:17). Jesus therefore requires those who come to him desiring eternal life to consume his humanity; to them alone the promise of eternal life and resurrection is given (v. 54).

Historically, there have been two ways of construing these startling words of Jesus, the eucharistic and the incarnational, and the two may be related. Ignatius seems to know of docetic Christians who both deny Jesus' humanity and neglect the Eucharist (Ign. *Smyrn.* chaps. 5, 7; cf. Barrett 1975, 53-55). There is then precedent for a relationship between Eucharist and Incarnation in this Johannine passage. That this whole section has been deeply involved in Christian discussions about the role of the Eucharist in the economy of salvation is not surprising. Does the Johannine Jesus here make participation in the Eucharist indispensable for attaining the eternal life that Jesus brings? That the sacrament should become the *sine qua non* of salvation seems to clash with other passages in John that speak of the attaining of eternal life as contingent upon belief or election without mentioning Baptism or the Lord's Supper (1:13; 3:3, 16; 5:24). (Bultmann 1971, 218-22, thinks that the ecclesiastical redactor has brought in references to both, the Eucharist here and baptism at 3:5; while Carson 1991, 294-99, denies that the burden of 6:52-58 is fundamentally sacramental.) In a church in which the Lord's Supper was widely, if not universally, celebrated, however, it is difficult to imagine that John could be read without his words being interpreted with the sacrament in view (as Carson concedes, 1991, 295; cf. H. Koester 1965, 116-22).

Jesus continues, implicitly contrasting the reality of his flesh and blood with all inauthentic food and drink (v. 55), and then offering assurance to those who eat and drink of their mutual indwelling. (The Greek verb used here, *menō*, "to dwell" or "abide," occurs frequently in this pregnant sense in John, beginning with 1:39, where the first disciples abide with Jesus.) This mutual indwelling actually begins with the Father himself (v. 57). Jesus underscores once again the source of his commission and says, in effect, that God is the source of life ("the living Father," an unusual expression in John) for himself, as he is for those who "eat me." (The Greek verb, *trōgō*, means "to munch" or eat audibly as animals do, and some commentators have suggested this denotes a kind of earthiness and crudity. On the other hand, John does not elsewhere use the present form of the stem *phag*—to eat, which is *esthiō*—and he may simply be substituting *trōgō* without intending any special connotation [see Barrett 1978, 299].) The construction John uses here would be awkward in English, but the NRSV's smoother translation does not catch the emphasis of the original Greek: "whoever eats me *that one* will live because of me."

Again, and finally, Jesus contrasts his heavenly bread with the wilderness manna, as well as with the wilderness generation and their fate (v. 58). It is significant that all the important elements of the text of verse 31 are taken up here: "He gave them bread from heaven to eat." In the discourse, verses 32-51 deal with the giving of the bread from heaven and its true identity, and verses 52-58 with eating it. Thus the exegesis of the text is incomplete without verses 52-58.

Although it is necessary and proper to seek the meaning of this pericope in issues of theology and liturgy that have been important from the beginning of the Christian movement, its antecedents must not be lost from view. God's salvation is often described in Scripture in terms of eating and drinking (see Morris 1995, 301; also Swancutt 1997, 218-51), nowhere more impressively than in Isa 55, where the descent of the word from God's mouth is likened to that of rain and snow, which water the earth and make possible its production of bread (v. 10). This after the opening (of Third Isaiah) invitation:

> Ho, everyone who thirsts,
> come to the waters;
> and you that have no money,
> come, buy and eat!
> Come, buy wine and milk
> without money and without price. (Isa 55:1)

With good reason it has been observed that wisdom is associated with eating and drinking. For example, wisdom invites the reader or hearer: "Come, eat of my bread and drink of the wine I have mixed" (Prov 9:5). Or again: "Come to me, you who desire me, and eat your fill of my fruits.... Those who eat of me will hunger for more, and those who drink of me will thirst for more" (Sir 24:19, 21; cf. John 4:13-14). The significance of wisdom in the background of the prologue suggests its presence at other important points (Witherington 1995, 148-63, especially 149-50).

Because wisdom motifs are so closely associated with incarnation in Johannine theology, and because wisdom supplies food and drink—indeed, is to be consumed—there is here a natural or logical link between incarnation and sacrament. Wisdom is the key. Yet in the words about flesh and blood, Jesus offers himself to those who desire life. Indeed, he offers himself in such terms as to indicate clearly that unless he is accepted, that is, eaten and drunk, one can have no part in him. This is why interpreters have seen in his words the presentation, indeed enforcement, of a sacramental view of salvation through Christ.

But do these words have to do primarily with the Eucharist, and if so, why? This is a pressing question in view of John's presentation of salvation elsewhere. Such emphasis on the sacrament becomes intelligible in view of the Gospel's insistence on the importance of confessing Jesus at the cost of being expelled from, or coming out of, the synagogue. It may be that participation in the eating and drinking of the flesh and blood of the Eucharist is the dividing point, in worship, between those who do not believe in Jesus, or, indeed, believe but do not confess Jesus publicly for fear of being put out of the synagogue, and those who have believed, confessed, come out of the synagogue, and now meet for worship as Jesus' disciples. Their defining act of worship is the eating and drinking of the meal that is his sacrifice and himself (see Rensberger 1988, 70-80, especially 77-80). John then becomes a kind of *magna carta* of distinctly Christian worship. The eating and drinking of Jesus defines Christian worship as such in John, as it has ever since.

The discourse then concludes with the statement of place (v. 59; cf. v. 24; 1:28; 2:12; 10:40; 11:54), itself a kind of concluding formulation. Capernaum was a central site of Jesus' public ministry in the Synoptics (cf. Mark 1:21). It actually figures less, or less centrally, in John, but here John seems to recognize its historic and traditional importance (cf. 2:12).

6:60-71: Heretofore Jesus' conversation partners have been "the Jews." Now we hear his disciples reactions to Jesus' statements. First, they react to the discourse specifically, then to Jesus and their own calling as disciples more generally. We thus begin a new episode or section of the narrative, but one with obvious connections with what precedes.

Many of his disciples react negatively (v. 60), as moments later many will draw back from him (v. 66). The characterization of Jesus' word, presumably about eating and drinking his flesh and blood, as a hard one may reflect the fact that participation in the distinctively Christian rite would constitute a public confession that would take one out of the synagogue (cf. 9:22; 12:48). Perhaps many would prefer to avoid such a sharp break. Jesus characteristically knows that his disciples are "complaining" (v. 61) and addresses them with another challenge (v. 62). ("Complaining" again represents the disciples as being like the complaining or murmuring wilderness generation of Israel [cf. v. 41].) Jesus' knowledge may be supernatural or miraculous, although the synoptic Jesus is also represented as having a kind of sixth sense of what people are thinking (cf. Mark 2:8). The claim of (or about) Jesus that he is the one who has descended from God and will return thence is, indeed, the supreme and crucial offense. Even the demand to eat flesh and drink blood pales before the vision of the descending and ascending Son of Man. Conceivably John expresses a "high" Christology of preexistence, which is foreign to some who believe Jesus is the Messiah, but stay within traditional Jewish categories—and within the synagogue.

Then Jesus suddenly returns to the problem at hand and addresses what would seem to be the basis of the disciples' complaint by a statement that could be taken to undercut everything that he has just said about the necessity of eating the bread from heaven, which is his own flesh (v. 63). This statement is sometimes cited as grounds for regarding 6:52-58 as a later addition, since it seems so obviously to contradict what has just been said about the efficacy of Jesus' flesh. The problem may, however, be less frustrating than at first appears. We have observed that John uses "world" in several different senses (1:10). The same is true of "flesh." Obviously, the flesh of Jesus Christ (1:14) has a positive theological significance, which is an aspect of the background of the term's use in 6:52-58. Yet John can also employ the dualism of flesh and spirit (cf. 3:6), as does Paul (Rom 8:1-17). (See Krodel 1983, 283-88, who traces the perception of two meanings of "flesh" back to Luther's exegesis of 6:63.)

The following statements (vv. 64-65; cf. vv. 70-71) have in view Judas, who betrayed Jesus in the strict sense of handing him over *(paradidōmi)*, and possibly also believers whose faith is inadequate. (On the meaning of *paradidōmi* and the history of Judas scholarship, see Klassen 1996.) It is as if Jesus has been faulted for not knowing that some of his disciples were not true believers and one of the twelve whom he had chosen (v. 70) would hand him over to the authorities. Now he meets that charge (v. 64). Moreover, Judas is linked with others who do not remain faithful to Jesus. All of them are comprehended under the general state-ment about election that Jesus has already made (v. 65; cf. 6:37; 17:6; 18:9). If John is answering such a charge about Jesus, the charge itself has been made offstage, so to speak; we do not hear it explicitly, or from the Jews. The calling of the twelve, narrated in the other Gospels (Matt 10:1-4; Mark 3:13-19; Luke 6:12-16; cf. 1 Cor 15:5), is here presumed. It too has happened offstage. If the Gospel of John does not presuppose the Synoptics, it at least presupposes the readers' knowledge of matters we know from those other Gospels.

Because it was not granted (or given) them by the Father to stay, many of Jesus' disciples now turn away (v. 66). Such defec-tions probably did occur in the postresurrection period. Yet, if these only were in view, Jesus might well have predicted them dur-ing his farewell discourse (chaps. 13–17). Perhaps John here recalls defections that actually occurred during Jesus' ministry. We do not learn of these from the other Gospels, but it would not be surprising if they had actually taken place. This possibility is supported by the way such defections are described: "[they] no longer went about with him." Apparently they just went home (cf. Matt 8:18-21; Mark 4:1-20; Luke 9:57-62).

Jesus then puts a challenging question to the twelve (v. 67), and Peter responds on their behalf. We now have the Johannine ver-sion of Peter's confession (see Mark 8:27-30 par., where Peter also responds on behalf of the other disciples). Peter's answer is for-mulated in Johannine terms after Jesus is addressed as Lord *(Kyrie)*, apparently here the christological title (cf. the use of the same term in 4:11 by the Samaritan woman, where it can hardly mean more than "Sir"). He has the words of eternal life, and this is now the reason why the disciples have believed, a better basis than the sign of 2:1-11 that first elicited their faith. For Peter to confess Jesus as Messiah or Christ would be redundant at this point, since that has already happened in John 1:41, again in Peter's presence. They now have not only belief but knowledge that he is the Holy One of God (exactly what the demon of Mark 1:24 has, correctly, called Jesus). One who is holy is also, in a tech-nical, theological sense, set apart for God (see *hagios* in *TDNT*), and this is certainly true of Jesus, and eventually of his disciples (see 17:17-19, where sanctify, *hagiazō,* means "make holy").

Finally, there is again a reference to Judas (vv. 70-71), which confirms the claim of Jesus' foreknowledge that has just been made (vv. 64-65). The naming of Judas as one of the twelve tends to confirm them as a group chosen by Jesus during his earthly ministry. Moreover, Judas was not only a disciple, but apparently a member of the inner circle (cf. 12:6; 13:29). The synoptic account of Peter's confession leads immediately to Jesus' first Passion prediction (8:31; cf. 9:31; 10:33). Although such predictions are missing from John, the reference to Jesus' betrayal is an allusion to his death. The common connection is evident. Yet had John been writing with Mark specifically in view, it is difficult to understand why he would not have explicitly reported such predictions, which fit so nicely his concept of Jesus' foreknowledge.

◊ ◊ ◊ ◊

In chapter 6, as now increasingly in John's narrative, theological themes are explicit in the text. Jesus proclaims himself the bread of life, as his interlocutors, first the Jews, then his disciples, are perplexed. Already in chapter 5 Jesus had forthrightly announced that as the Son he would perform the Father's eschatological work: raising the dead, giving life, holding judgment (5:21-22, 27). There he does the work of God, here is the gift of God: "I am the bread of life" (v. 35). The long discourse on bread follows upon the story of Jesus' multiplying the five loaves of bread and two fish for the assembled multitude of five thousand. Here again we have a deed of Jesus, like one otherwise known from the Synoptics, from which develops a discourse that draws out the relevant theological themes.

The intervening story of the crossing of the sea is given by tradition, either from Mark or a parallel source. Although it is an interruption of the bread theme, it also enhances the portrait of Jesus, the one who comes to the terrified disciples walking across the sea and announces "It is I" *(egō eimi).* Although no scripture is cited, one thinks of Ps 107:23-30, where the Lord saves those in distress at sea. Clearly the coming of Jesus is like the appearance of God (as it is also in Matthew and Mark). The *egō eimi* is reminiscent of God's announcement of himself in Exodus (3:14) and Second Isaiah (41:4). The incident of the crossing of the sea, including the crowd's observation that Jesus did not cross the sea with his disciples in the boat (6:22), serves to enhance Jesus' mysterious, numinous character beyond what is found in the synoptic parallels.

Jesus' presentation of himself as the true bread from heaven is developed out of the exegesis of the scriptural word, "He gave them bread from heaven to eat" (v. 31), which looks like a reflection of several scriptural texts (e.g., Exod 16:4; Ps 78:23-25). This midrashic development nicely illustrates John's use of Scripture. Such texts, which speak of the manna miracle in the wilderness following the Exodus, attest to its presumed historical factuality (v. 49); yet it is without power to save the people from death. The true bread from heaven, Jesus, has precisely this power to save people from death.

Jesus makes clear that those who want to receive such power must eat and drink his flesh and blood (vv. 52-58). While eating and drinking are biblical images of receiving salvation, drinking blood is expressly forbidden in Scripture (Lev 17:10-14) and would be abhorrent to the Torah-abiding Jew. Of course, in the synoptic and Pauline account of the institution of the Lord's Supper, Jesus offers to his disciples his body and blood (Mark 14:22-25 par.; 1 Cor 11:23-26). Not surprisingly, many interpreters see here a reference to the sacrament of the Eucharist, and probably correctly so. But why this almost strident emphasis? To see John advocating the position that the sacrament itself effects salvation *(ex opere operato)* is probably anachronistic, although such a view has been attributed to the evangelist or to a later redactor. Quite possibly, however, the sacrament of the Lord's Supper or the Eucharist is actually in view, and it has become a hallmark of discipleship for those who confess Jesus as Lord. They gather now outside the synagogue as their worship of the Father centers on the Son, whose life, his flesh and blood, has been given for them (cf. 3:16).

Jesus at the Festival of Booths (7:1-52)

The beginning of a fresh episode is marked by the vague transition "after this" (7:1). It comprises the entire chapter, which is set at the festival of Booths or Tabernacles, and the dialogue and events of this episode are related to the place and themes of that festival. The following chapter presumably continues the discussion (see 8:12), but, as we shall see, the connection is tenuous, so that another episode (7:53–8:11) has in many manuscripts been inserted between these chapters. Among the Gospels, only John mentions a visit by Jesus to Jerusalem at a time other than Passover.

As we have observed, chapter 6 follows poorly upon chapter 5, so that it is sometimes proposed that their order has been reversed (see above, p. 146). In that case, chapter 7 would follow rather well directly after chapter 5. In the latter, Jesus is in Jerusalem; then the statement that Jesus no longer wished to go about in Judea because of the Jews' intention to kill him (7:1; cf. 5:18) would be entirely appropriate. As matters now stand, that intention reaches back over chapter 6 to 5:18. Yet the present connection is after all not intolerable, because in the section immediately preceding, Jesus is in Galilee, which is obviously where he is placed at the beginning of chapter 7.

Jesus goes up to Jerusalem, despite, rather than because of, the urging of his brothers (7:1-10). At first he encounters people called "the Jews" (v. 15), with whom he has a rather sharp exchange (vv. 14-24). Then the people of Jerusalem appear open to the possibility that Jesus is the Messiah (vv. 25-31) against the background of an attempt to arrest him (v. 30), the first of a number of such attempts (see vv. 32, 45; 8:59; 10:39; cf. 11:45-53). The chief priests and Pharisees then mobilize police officers to arrest Jesus (vv. 32-43), who are, however, unsuccessful (v. 43). Their failure leads to a concluding discussion and dispute about Jesus' identity, in which Nicodemus again appears on the scene (vv. 50-52) and becomes involved in a controversy that seemingly ends with Jesus' opponents having the last word.

This story continues an emphasis that recurs in John, uniquely among the Gospels. Jesus appears in Jerusalem for Jewish festivals, mostly at Passover (2:13; 11:55; cf. 6:4), but on other occasions as well: an unnamed feast (5:1); Hanukkah (10:22); and here Booths or Tabernacles. Of course, it is only in John that Jesus goes to Jerusalem at any time other than the final Passover at which he dies. Yet these festival appearances at least dramatize Jesus' position as an alternative center of authority and worship in Judaism.

The question of John's relation to other Christian sources is raised by the discussion of traditional messianic expectation (vv. 40-44), which seems to reflect knowledge of traditions found in the Matthean and Lukan birth narratives, if not of those Gospels themselves. Also, as happens more than once in this Gospel, a specific personage reappears in the narrative. Nicodemus, who wholly failed to understand Jesus earlier, now returns to defend him, as he will later come with Joseph of Arimathea to help bury him (19:39).

7:1-9: Jesus' brothers will now appear in order to give him advice, or so they think. The threat to kill Jesus (5:18) now hangs over the narrative and understandably influences his itinerary (v. 1), for his hour has not yet come (v. 6). The festival of Booths (v. 2) was the autumnal harvest festival celebrated for eight days (cf. v. 37) from Tishri 15, which would fall in late September or early October. (On Booths, see Exod 23:16; 34:22; Deut 16:13-15.) Booths, with Passover and Weeks, was one of the three annual festivals at which Israelite males were commanded to appear before the Lord at the Jerusalem temple (see Exod 23:17; 34:23). According to 1 Kgs 8, Solomon dedicated the temple at this festival, and at it every seventh year the Torah, or law, was to be read (Deut 31:10-11). Zechariah looks toward the time when all nations will go up to Jerusalem at Booths to worship the Lord (Zech 14:16; cf. use of Zech 14:21 in John 2:16). The terms "Booths" or "Tabernacles" (Gk. *skēnopēgia*) connote dwelling, and as we have observed at 1:14, Jesus is said to have dwelt *(skēnoō)* among human beings. During the festival, the Israelites dwelt in booths (Lev 23:42-43).

Jesus' brothers give him gratuitous advice about going to Judea (vv. 3-4). Strikingly, the assumption is that Jesus' disciples are in Judea, or at least that some disciples are there. In either case John differs from the Synoptics, in which the disciples are Galileans. The brothers refer to works rather than signs, although one infers that they have Jesus' astounding deeds in mind. But Jesus refuses his brothers' well-intended advice (vv. 6-8); his time (Gr. *kairos*) has not yet come. Also, in 2:4 Jesus tells his mother that his hour *(hōra)* has not yet come. In both cases the knowledgeable reader detects an allusion to Jesus' death. Jesus did not, however, say to his mother that her time was any time (cf. 7:6). Not surprisingly, the fact that the world does not hate Jesus' brothers implies they are of the world; Jesus, however, opposes the world (v. 7). The description of the world's work as evil recalls 3:20. There is a subtle but significant difference between the treatment of Jesus' mother and his brothers. Over against both Jesus asserts his independence. Yet his mother seems to know what Jesus will do and instructs the servants (2:5). Later she will appear with the Beloved Disciple at the foot of the cross (19:25-27) as Jesus entrusts her to his care. (In Acts 1:13 after Jesus' ascension, Mary, the mother of Jesus, as well as his brothers were staying together in "the room upstairs.")

That Jesus' brothers were not followers during his historic ministry is implied also by the synoptic account (see Mark 3:21, 31-35; 6:1-6). In Mark (6:4), Jesus implies that he is without respect among his own kin and in his own house. Only Mark has Jesus refer to his kinfolk. Indeed, insofar as Mark suggests anything about Mary, she is not favorable to Jesus' ministry (cf. Mark 3:31-35). As far as we can tell, only after the Resurrection did Mary (Acts 1:14), James (1 Cor 15:7), and others of Jesus' brothers (1 Cor 9:5) become believers.

The distance between Jesus and his brothers is underscored by the report that he stays in Galilee (v. 9), while the brothers go up (to Jerusalem) for the festival (v. 10). Nevertheless, there is no polemic against Jesus' brothers, as against Judas (e.g., 6:70-71), nor are they called "Jews," although they certainly were Jewish. They simply fail to comprehend Jesus; but until his glorification no one, with the exception of John the Baptist and the Beloved Disciple, fully understands Jesus—not even his own disciples.

7:10-24: Jesus goes to Jerusalem (v. 10), doing what his brothers have advised, but doing so independently, and secretly, rather than openly, as they suggested (v. 4). In the Gospel of John, Jesus acts at the behest of no one. There is an attitude of expectancy at his arrival, even among the Jews (v. 11). The attitude of the Jews is probably to be distinguished from that of the crowds (vv. 12-13); the Jews are presumably looking for Jesus in order to do him harm (cf. 7:1). The NRSV's translation, which has the crowds "complaining" is less apt than the RSV's "muttering," for those who thought Jesus a good man were scarcely complaining about him. (The NRSV has attempted to translate the Greek *gongysmos* consistently as "complaining"; see instances in chap. 6 above.) The view that Jesus is a deceiver (v. 12) may have deep roots (cf. 7:47; Luke 23:2; see Martyn 1979, 64-81: "beguiler"). In any event, what is said now is reiterated later on in the same episode (7:46-48). Through this episode the role of the crowd is ambivalent. Some think Jesus a good man, but others suspect he has a demon (v. 20). The relative silence of those who think well of Jesus is explained by their fear of the Jews, apparently their fear of certain religious authorities (v. 13; cf. 12:42; 20:19).

Jesus goes up to the temple to teach (v. 14), which is what one might expect of him (cf. 18:20; Mark 12:35). The Jews' reaction to him (v. 15) might have been expected, but it is particularly interesting for what it says about Jesus. The Jews are astonished because Jesus "[knows] his letters, when he has never been taught" (NRSV note). (Note that in Acts 4:13 Jesus' disciples Peter and John are described as uneducated, common men.) "To know letters" can mean simply to be literate, but it can also refer to higher learning; and from the immediate context it is not clear which is intended, although the Jews' astonishment implies the latter and thus justifies the NRSV's preferred translation. Already Jesus' discussion of Moses (5:39-47) implies that he can read

Scripture. This is certainly the view of Luke in 4:16-20 (cf. Luke 2:41-51; also Matt 19:4; Mark 2:25). Already in John 1:38 he is called "Rabbi," which is translated immediately as "teacher." Whether Jesus was a rabbi depends a great deal on what is meant by the term. That he had formal, rabbinical training is indeed doubtful. Paul was in a better position to make such a claim (Gal 1:14; cf. Acts 22:3). The exclamation of the Jews may, however, reflect the perception that Jesus was an insightful and literate teacher grounded in Scripture.

Nevertheless, no sooner has Jesus received this acclamation than he turns it aside (v. 16). One recalls Jesus' similar statements in 5:19-20. Jesus continues to talk in terms of his teaching (Gk. *didachē*) and its origin. A true judgment about the origin of that teaching (v. 17) is not to be made on the basis of prior standards or criteria, however, but can be based only on a genuine intention to do God's will (cf. the discussion with Nicodemus in 3:1-21). Such knowledge of the truth of Jesus' teaching is knowledge about his origin with God. God speaks through Jesus, so in contrast to others Jesus seeks not his own glory but God's, and is therefore entirely true (v. 18). Underlying these statements is the distinctly Johannine notion that the revelation of God in Jesus is self-authenticating.

Quite suddenly, but in the context of the discussion of the truth of the claim to divine revelation, Jesus raises the question of Moses and the law (v. 19). Instead of attacking either, however, Jesus assumes the validity of the Mosaic law and charges his enemies with looking for an opportunity to kill him (cf. 5:18; 7:1). In John's view the law of Moses is valid, if one understands that it testifies to Jesus (5:39-47; cf. 1:45). Moreover, Jesus will argue (vv. 21-23) that he has acted in accordance with the law. The crowd, apparently feigning ignorance and innocence, protests that Jesus has a demon (v. 20; cf. 8:48). This charge is related to the accusation found in the Synoptics, that he casts out demons by the power of Beelzebul, the ruler of demons, that is, Satan himself (Mark 3:22-23). Perhaps not coincidentally, there are no demon exorcisms in the Gospel of John, for exorcisms laid Jesus open to this accusation. At this point the crowd, whose role is ambivalent (cf. vv. 12-13), seems to speak from the standpoint of the Jews. Indeed, the question of whether the crowds in John are to be equated with the Jews is a real one, and needs to be examined in each individual case. Of course, the informed reader knows that the Jews are trying to kill Jesus, and, indeed, that their goal will be realized.

The work to which Jesus refers (7:21) is, of course, the healing at the pool of Bethzatha (5:2-9). The crowd's astonishment apparently has to do with the fact that the healing occurred on a sabbath (5:9-10, 16-18) and was therefore offensive. It is worth remembering that the Jews began by accusing the healed man of working (carrying his mat) on the sabbath, but their attention quickly turned to Jesus, whom they accused of sabbath-breaking (5:16; 7:23), and then of making himself equal to God (5:18). Jesus now defends what he has done, but not on the basis of his unique, self-authenticating authority, as one might expect, but on the basis of the Jews' own practice and Mosaic law (7:22-24).

Jesus' statement that Moses gave circumcision (v. 22) is corrected—whether by Jesus himself or the evangelist is a moot question. Abraham himself was commanded to practice circumcision (Gen 17:10-14). Moreover, the Mosaic law specifically commands circumcision on the eighth day (Gen 17:12; Lev 12:3; cf. Luke 2:21). According to the Mishnah, the command to circumcise precisely on the eighth day overrides even the sabbath (*m. Shab.* 18.3; 19.2; *m. Ned.* 3.11). Although the Mishnah was committed to writing a full century after the Gospel of John, Jesus' testimony here indicates this was a practice of long standing. Jesus then argues from this practice to his own sabbath healing (v. 23). It is a good example of the argument from the lesser to the greater (*a minori ad maius* or *qal wa-ḥomer*). (For citation of relevant rabbinic material see Barrett 1978, 320.) Jesus implies that his own work is greater than circumcision, yet he does not dismiss the importance of circumcision in obedience to the law. (According to the NRSV Jesus says he has healed the man's whole body, but the Greek would be more accurately translated, "I made the whole man well.") Finally, Jesus calls upon his hearers to make a right judgment (v. 24). Will their judgment be superficial or true? Here a right judgment will take into account Jesus' claim, but it does not simply proceed from that claim. It will invoke a proper assessment of what has happened, precisely with respect to Mosaic law and Jewish tradition. Thus Jesus is portrayed as turning the Jews' basis of authority against them. What he has done is perfectly appropriate under Mosaic law.

7:25-52: The crowds, the people of Jerusalem, the temple police, and the Pharisees (among whom was Nicodemus) will all react to Jesus' claims. The reaction of all except the Pharisees, who remain unalterably opposed to Jesus, ranges from ambivalent to positive.

Thus the response of the Jerusalemites (vv. 25-27) is basically positive and open to Jesus, except they wonder whether he is the Messiah, because they know where he is from; as it turns out, Galilee (cf. vv. 41, 52). In fact, that Jesus was from Nazareth in Galilee is public knowledge from the beginning of this Gospel (1:45-46). Moreover, that the Messiah's origins would be unknown seems to conflict with the expectation that the Messiah would come from Bethlehem (7:42). There is a strand of tradition in which the identity and origin of the Messiah are a secret until he is revealed as such. In Justin Martyr's *Dialogue with Trypho* 8.4 the identity and origin of the Messiah are said to be unknown until Elijah comes and anoints him. (On the hiddenness of the Son of Man, see *1 Enoch* 48:6 and 4 Ezra 13:51-52.) The hiddenness or obscurity of the Messiah until he is revealed as such does not necessarily conflict with his birth in Bethlehem. That is, he could be born there and then emerge as Messiah from some other quarter. Of course, the people are entirely wrong if they think that Jesus' origin in Nazareth, or Galilee, accounts for him. It is a recurrent theme of this Gospel that Jesus' obvious, earthly origins do not explain him, although people are constantly deceiving themselves that they do (cf. 1:46). Exactly the Jerusalemites' claim that they know where Jesus is from sets in bold relief the fact that they do not.

At least to the crowd, Jesus' response (v. 28) is quite mysterious. The NRSV takes Jesus' initial sentence as a statement, although it could be taken as a question, in which case Jesus would be explicitly challenging their knowledge of him. In any event, Jesus fundamentally questions their knowledge of the God who has sent him (vv. 28-29). Who then tried to arrest Jesus (v. 30) is not entirely clear. Apparently not the whole crowd, for many of them believed in him (v. 31). Quite possibly this statement simply points ahead to the next attempt to arrest Jesus (vv. 32-52). That the effort failed reflects the fact that Jesus' hour has not come (cf. 2:4; 12:23). In any event, Jesus' signs are having a positive impact and effect (v. 31; cf. 2:23-25; 11:47-48). As had already been noted (above, p. 94 and Martyn 1979, 95-100), however, the performance of signs, in the sense of healings or miracles, was not expected of the Davidic Messiah. Yet the crowd's question at least has the effect of showing that Jesus has more than fulfilled messianic expectations. Thus the crowd has reason to suspect that the authorities (Gr. *archontes*) really know Jesus' identity and for whatever reason are concealing it (v. 26).

Now the chief priests and Pharisees get serious about arresting Jesus, sending the temple police (literally, servants or officers) to bring him in (v. 32). The very combination of chief priests and Pharisees is typical of John; these are not the people who characteristically conspire together against Jesus in the Synoptics. There one typically sees the chief priests and scribes (Mark 14:1) or the chief priests, elders, and scribes (Mark 14:53). It is not unthinkable that some Pharisees could have plotted with chief priests in Jesus' own day, but their absence from the synoptic accounts of Jesus' Jerusalem stay is remarkable. Even in John, where, uniquely, Pharisees are present in the party that arrests Jesus (18:3), they disappear from the account of Jesus' trials and execution. Probably the Pharisees of this account are the Pharisees known to John's community, who represent Jewish opposition to Jesus' claims, or claims about Jesus.

Jesus utters a riddlesome saying about his death and departure (v. 33), similar to one he will repeat to his disciples (13:33), who will also fail to comprehend him, as the Jews do here (vv. 35-36). Nevertheless, their speculation about Jesus' going to teach the Greeks (v. 35) is profoundly true. After his death the teaching about Jesus will be disseminated to the Greeks, that is, to the Gentile world. Hence when the Greeks at Passover seek Jesus (12:20-21), he knows that the time of his glorification, or death, has come (12:23). The Jews say more than they know, even as the high priest will when he prophesies that Jesus will die for the nation (11:50-52). There are no stereotypical Passion predictions in John comparable to those in the Synoptics (e.g., Mark 8:31; 9:31; 10:33), but Jesus throws out such hints and indications of his approaching death, which are quite clear to the knowledge-able reader (see also 3:14-16; 12:32-33).

Jesus makes a solemn, revelatory proclamation on the last great day of the festival of Tabernacles (vv. 37-39). (On whether John means the seventh day of the feast, which was technically the last day of the feast proper or the eighth day, the day of the closing of the festival, see Barrett 1978, 326.) In any event, Jesus' procla-mation (vv. 37b-38) is the main matter. Yet it presents problems, because it can be read in more than one way. The NRSV's read-ing is possible, but there are alternatives, as the notes indicate. (The RSV reads: "If any one thirst, let him come to me and drink. He who believes in me, as the scripture has said, 'Out of his heart shall flow rivers of living water.') The bodily organ named *(koilia)* is more likely the belly than the heart *(kardia)*, although *koilia* can mean the "innermost recesses of the human body" (Bauer 1979) and therefore, presumably, the heart. More impor-tant is the question of whether to take "he (the one) who believes in me" with "drink" (NRSV) or with the following sentence (RSV). If one follows the NRSV on this point, then the heart or belly could be taken to be Jesus' own. But the NRSV's "out of the believer's heart" is an interpretation, and a questionable one, for there is in the Greek text only the pronoun "his" *(autou,* modify-ing *koilias,* "heart"), but no word for "believer" at all. So given the theology of John, the most natural reading of the sentence would then be, "Out of his (Jesus') heart shall flow rivers of liv-ing water." (This translation matches neither the NRSV nor RSV.) Obviously, in any case Jesus must be the ultimate source of this living water (see 4:14; 19:34), and the water imagery fits the feast of Booths. For according to the Mishnah *(m. Sukk.* 4.9) there were daily libations at the altar of the temple, using water brought from the pool of Siloam (cf. John 9:7).

The Scripture quotation also presents problems. If one follows the rendering of the passage just suggested, it is natural to suppose that (unlike the NRSV) Jesus' statement ends with the verb "drink" and that the Scripture quotation is the narrator's, applied to Jesus. No known scriptural passage conforms exactly to the Johannine citation, but the metaphor of drinking, and the quenching of thirst, is biblical. For example, Isa 55:1 ("Ho, everyone who thirsts, come to the waters...") and the entire chapter are about God's deliverance (cf. Isa 12:3; 44:3; 49:10; Zech 13:1 and 14:8; note also the Booths setting in Zech 14:16-19). The evangelist's fondness for Isaiah makes passages from that prophet particularly relevant (Carson 1991, loc. cit., explores many possibilities). Of course, Jesus has already presented himself as the source of living water (4:14; cf. also Rev 22:1-2).

We next have a scene (vv. 40-44) in which the crowd gives its final reaction, and perhaps not surprisingly this reaction is split (v. 43). Indeed, those whose reaction is positive seem not to agree as to whether Jesus is the prophet or the Messiah (vv. 40-41). Yet, as we have observed, the Johannine Christ partakes of qualities of the Deuteronomic prophet-like-Moses while fulfilling the hope for a Davidic Messiah. The claim that he is the Messiah is, however, countered by the fact that he is from Galilee, not from Bethlehem, David's city (vv. 41-42). Of course, according to the birth narratives of both Matthew (2:5-6) and Luke (2:4, 15), Jesus was born in Bethlehem, of the lineage of David (Matt 1:1; Luke 2:4). Either John does not know this or does not embrace these facts as warranting Jesus' claim to messiahship. Interestingly, Paul knows and accepts the tradition that Jesus was of Davidic lineage (Rom 1:3), while Mark has no birth narrative but reports that blind Bartimaeus hailed Jesus as Son of David (10:47, 48). Yet also in Mark, Jesus seems to question the Messiah's Davidic sonship (12:35-37). Quite possibly John knows the tradition of Jesus' Davidic lineage, but does not correct those who seem to be ignorant of it, because it is not Jesus' geographical origin or his ancestry that warrants the claim that he is the

Messiah, even when the claim of that ancestry or origin is based on Scripture. Again, some want to arrest Jesus (cf. v. 32), to no avail (v. 44); but then the authorities, who have all along intended his arrest, reenter the story (7:45-52).

The temple police (literally, "the officers") who had been sent out by the authorities to arrest Jesus (v. 32), now return empty-handed (v. 45). Here, as previously, the authorities are described as chief priests and Pharisees. These are the parties who in John consistently array themselves against Jesus and plot to have him put out of the way (cf. 1:19, 24). Finally, it is the chief priests and "Jews" who succeed in convincing Pilate to execute Jesus (18:28–19:16). They are perplexed and presumably angry that the temple police have not fulfilled their orders, but the latter have apparently themselves fallen under Jesus' spell, and their assessment of Jesus' speech is, from the evangelist's perspective, entirely apposite. It is unique (v. 46).

The response of the Pharisees to them (vv. 47-48) is contemptuous, as we might expect. First the temple police have obviously been deluded (v. 47). Those who know and are in positions of authority have not believed (v. 48)! (Indeed, by definition they would not.) Because they are ignorant, the crowd, unlike the authorities and Pharisees, is accursed. (Obviously, the police agree with the crowd.) Commentators have long seen here the equivalent of rabbinic disparagement of the "people of the land," that is, the common people, who are not meticulous in their knowledge and observance of the law. (Barrett 1978, 332, has collected notable sayings of the sages about the people of the land.) The underlying question is Who is able or competent rightly to understand and assess Jesus? The authorities assume that they are. It is precisely that assumption that John intends to call into question.

Now Nicodemus, himself a Pharisee ("who was one of them"), reappears (v. 50; cf. 3:1) to suggest that according to the law, Jesus deserves a fair hearing (cf. Deut 1:16). On the one hand, Jesus stands above the law. Yet the law, fairly interpreted, even if it is not understood as pointing to Jesus, nevertheless approves him, and his actions (cf. 7:21-24). Nicodemus the Pharisee here represents such a balanced, fair interpretation of the law. If he does not yet understand Jesus, he is not, like his colleagues, biased against him. He will, of course, return later to bury Jesus (19:39), as he perhaps comes closer to understanding and believing in him. Having dared to speak up for Jesus, Nicodemus now feels the brunt of the authorities' contempt (v. 52). Galilee is also held in contempt, even as the common people are. Although in the Gospel of John, Jesus' ministry is centered in Jerusalem, the Fourth Gospel recognizes his Galilean origin (cf. 1:46).

That no prophet hails from Galilee is not explicitly said in Scripture, and it is not clear that the Pharisees' statement is true. The verb (NRSV: "is to arise") is actually present tense: "No prophet arises from Galilee." At least Jonah (cf. 2 Kgs 14:25) was from Galilee, and Capernaum means in Hebrew "village of Nahum," presumably the prophet of that name. Yet Scripture does not support the expectation of a messianic and prophetic figure from Galilee. The Messiah will, of course, come from Bethlehem in Judea (v. 42). Part of the crowd has hailed Jesus as "the prophet" (v. 40), presumably the Deuteronomic prophet like Moses (Deut 18:15), and at least one ancient, papyrus manuscript (P^{66}) has "the prophet" in verse 52. If the latter is the original reading, and not an assimilation to verse 40, the authorities' statement is not telling, for Scripture does not say from where the Deuteronomic prophet will arise. (Following P^{66} and the present tense of the verb "to rise," the REB has "the Prophet does not come from Galilee.") Of course, the authorities are referring to scriptural predictions and are denying that Jesus of Galilee can fulfill Scripture. They have a point, but if Jesus was born in Bethlehem their argument collapses, as we have seen.

◊ ◊ ◊ ◊

The question of messiahship, raised as Jesus gathers his disciples (1:29-51) and emphasized toward the narrative's end (20:31-30), now receives a thorough airing against the background of opposition to Jesus, which has been building. At the beginning and the end his disciples and the evangelist acclaim him. Here his opponents denigrate him. It is particularly significant that objections to Jesus' claims are advanced on the basis of traditional messianic expectation based on Scripture (vv. 41-42; 52), which he is assumed not to fulfill. Does the irony of the situation arise from the fact that Jesus was actually born in Bethlehem and does fulfill such expectation, as Matthew and Luke make clear? Or does it instead arise from the fact that although Jesus does not fulfill such expectation he is nevertheless the one sent from God as his unique and final emissary? In John's view either irony works, but in different ways.

How far traditional, national, or related expectations are from comprehending Jesus is marked by his reaction to his uncomprehending brothers (vv. 1-9), which is similar to his earlier reaction to his mother (2:4), who nevertheless is portrayed somewhat more favorably. Jesus walks to his own drumbeat, and is in no case subject to human prompting, as he eventually does what his mother and brothers suggest, but at his own initiative. His closest kin do not sway him.

Clearly this episode shows that not all Jerusalemites are dead set against Jesus. Indeed, one gains the overall impression that most people are still open to him, if not actually favorably disposed (vv. 12, 31, 40, 46, 50-51). It is not even clear that every response of "the Jews" is unfavorable. Yet there lurks in the background the mortal threat against Jesus, which while disavowed (v. 20) is nonetheless real, as the knowledgeable reader will understand. With his death in view Jesus points ahead to the time when he will become for the believer the source of living water, and of the Spirit (vv. 37-39). Water imagery abounds in this Gospel, but it may be that Booths, with its ceremonial pouring of water, provides the occasion for the invocation of water as the metaphor of the salvation that flows from Jesus.

The Jews Contest Jesus' Claims (8:12-59)

Chapter 8 is a distinct literary unit with only a loose connection with what precedes and with what follows, as the Jews attempt to stone Jesus and he eludes them, departing from the temple (v. 59), and seemingly ending the scene. In 8:20, Jesus is said to be teaching in the temple (cf. 7:14, 28; 8:59), the center of Jerusalem. The evangelist doubtless deemed this setting appropriate for the discourses of Jesus and the ensuing disputes, but otherwise it plays no explicit role in the episode. Even the succeeding episode is set in a location that is not far from the temple (see 9:7), although it is not mentioned. The shepherd discourse of chapter 10 may be presumed to take place in the temple as well (10:23). Indeed, Jesus is in the environs of the temple in chapter 5 (see v. 14). So with the exception of chapter 6, which possibly once actually preceded chapter 5, we have a series of episodes in which Jesus speaks and debates in Jerusalem and in or near the temple (chaps. 5, 7–10). Appropriately the subject of discussion is his own status and role.

The loose connection of chapter 8 with the preceding narrative is underscored by the fact that most manuscripts, but not the most ancient, insert at the beginning the story of the woman caught in an act of adultery who is brought before Jesus in the temple (8:2). There is no question that it was not a part of the original Gospel. In fact, a few manuscripts place it elsewhere, for example, at the end of the Gospel or after Luke 21:38. The woman is brought by the scribes and Pharisees, a pairing familiar from the synoptic Gospels. Although the Pharisees appear frequently in John, scribes are otherwise absent. The obviously later insertion of this pericope makes a certain sense, however, for it provides an episode, an encounter of Jesus with a sinful woman and Jewish authorities, which can be viewed as a springboard for the ensuing discussion. The temple setting is the same, and the theme of judgment takes up 7:24, 51 and is continued in 8:15-16, 26, 50. Moreover, Jesus confronts the Jewish authorities and accepts their challenges to his authority (8:5). Some such encounter often provides the background and basis for discussion in John (cf. chaps. 5, 6, 9, and 11). (Because the pericope is not Johannine, many commentators do not address it. A helpful exception is Schnackenburg 1980, 162-71).

Although there is no explicit narrative thread from chapter 7 into 8, there is, as noted, a common temple setting. In addition, the question of Jesus' role and authority, which stood at the center of discussion between the Jewish authorities, the Jerusalemites, and finally Nicodemus, is developed further, as Jesus now enters this conversation. Heretofore, people have reacted to Jesus' words. Now the Pharisees, the Jews, and the Jews who had believed in him enter directly into conversation with Jesus, rejecting his claims. Thus while the connection back to chapter 7 is loose enough, it is nevertheless intelligible (see below, pp. 180-81, 185-86).

The introduction of "the Jews who had believed in [Jesus]" (v. 31) is surprising, particularly since they almost immediately demonstrate that they are not really his disciples. Their appearance raises the question of whether there were fissures within the Johannine community, or between it and other Christian communities (as proposed by Brown 1979, *passim*), as well as the division between Johannine Christians and "the Jews." The question of the source of the polemic of this chapter is intriguing, for it does not represent the kinds of polemic or issues that exist between Jesus and his opponents in the Synoptics. That was much closer to the historical situation of Jesus himself. On the other hand, it is difficult to imagine the evangelist's creating this controversy out of thin air. The polemical situation originating within the synagogue in which Christ-confessors and their opponents confronted one another in an ever-increasing crescendo of hostility provides the setting that makes these bitter exchanges intelligible.

◊ ◊ ◊ ◊

8:12-21: This episode begins with Jesus' announcement that he is the light of the world, who offers the alternative to walking in darkness (v. 12). Thus the typical Johannine dualism is invoked. If the Booths setting is to be presumed, Jesus' statement fits that festival well, for the first day of the feast was marked by the lighting of four enormous candlesticks that were said to illumine the entire city as men with torches in their hands danced before them (*m. Sukk.* 5.2-4). That Jesus speaks "again" appears to make connection with the preceding Booths episode, although rather generally. ("Again" [Gk. *palin*] occurs rather frequently as a connective in John, e.g., 8:21; cf. 1:35; 4:46.)

The background of light symbolism is otherwise deep and extensive in Scripture and in Judaism. In the Bible light symbolizes God and divine truth: "The LORD is my light and my salvation; whom shall I fear?" (Ps 27:1); "in your light we see light" (Ps 36:9). Not surprisingly, light symbolism plays a large role in the Dead Sea Scrolls, so that the very phrase "the light of life" is found in the Community Rule (1QS3:7). Barrett, probably correctly, suggests that it there refers to the Law. (For an excellent, brief essay on the backgrounds of "light" in this passage, see Barrett 1978, 335-38.) "Light" appears as symbolic of God also in contemporary non-Jewish sources: "'That light' said he, 'am I, Mind, thy God'" (*Corpus Hermeticum* 1.6). In Plato's Allegory of the Cave (*The Republic* 7.1-11) the light is the divine reality that projects shadow images on the wall of the cave.

Elsewhere in the New Testament "light" appears as a symbol of the salvation Jesus brings, for example, in Matt 4:16 (quoting Isa 9:2). In John, after speaking of himself as light, Jesus invites his followers to become sons of light (12:36), a phrase he also uses in Luke 16:8. Such language is reminiscent of the *War Rule* of Qumran, which describes the eschatological war between the Sons of Light and the Sons of Darkness. In 2 Cor 4:4 Paul speaks of "the light of the gospel of the glory of Christ," and then plays variations on this theme (4:6). Finally, in the book of Revelation we read that the Lamb's servants will have the Lord God as their light (22:5), so that they will need neither lamp nor sun.

Not surprisingly, after Jesus claims to be the light of the world the Pharisees reject him as a false witness (v. 13). One cannot testify on one's own behalf. The biblical background of their charge is the requirement of at least two witnesses in a capital case (Num 35:30; Deut 17:6; 19:15). But the Mishnah apparently becomes more rigorous: "None may testify of himself" (*m. Ketub.* 2.9; cf. *m. Rosh HaSh.* 3.1). The Mishnaic formulation, or something like it, seems to underlie the Pharisees' rejection of Jesus. Thus the

Pharisees' response to Jesus rejects his "I am" saying on legal grounds as illegitimate testimony on his own behalf.

Jesus seems to concede they have a point (v. 14): "Even if I testify on my own behalf..." (RSV: "Even if I do bear witness to myself..."). Yet he has an overriding consideration: He knows his origin and destination, while they do not. On the face of it, this is a mysterious statement, but as such it is entirely typical of the Fourth Gospel. Characteristically, the Jews, or Pharisees, do not know where Jesus really comes from (cf. 9:29), although they may claim they do (6:42; 7:27). Even his disciples-to-be may at first dismiss him because of his place of origin (1:46). Of course, Jesus' origin is God, and he does only what the Father has given him to do (5:19-24). Moreover, he is going to God (3:13; 7:34; 14:1-4). Against this background, the meaning and implications of Jesus' statement are perfectly clear, but to the Pharisees with whom Jesus now speaks they can scarcely be. Their fundamental problem and deficiency is that they know neither Jesus' origin nor his ultimate destination. In other words, they do not know he is the one whom God has sent on a unique revelatory mission (cf. vv. 19-20).

Having stated their fundamental problem (v. 14), Jesus next turns to the specific objection of verse 13. The basis of their judgment is called into question (v. 15). They judge by human standards, knowing neither Jesus' origin nor his destination. (Presumably by "human standards" Jesus refers to their own traditions, or even interpretations of Scripture, which they regard as authoritative, but he does not.) Jesus' further statement that he judges no one is true with respect to his and God's intention (cf. 3:17), although not with respect to the effect of his coming (3:18-21). Having said that he does not judge, Jesus immediately qualifies that statement (v. 16), referring to his origin, and his solidarity with the Father who had sent him. Therefore he does not judge alone. There are then two witnesses, as the law requires, but the character of these witnesses is strange indeed: Jesus and the Father who sent him (v. 18). Jesus manifests knowledge of the law, but complies with it in a way his interlocutors could scarcely regard as satisfactory; he must know this.

Their answer perhaps betrays their ignorance (v. 19), although it is a question whether at this point in the narrative their ignorance should be construed as innocent. Conceivably, they may be understood as already knowing, and therefore rejecting, Jesus' claim. Jesus' response is true from his standpoint, naturally, but it may also be true from theirs. That is, they are now determined to know neither Jesus nor the Father of whom he speaks. Of course, from the Johannine Jesus' viewpoint that means they do not know God. Obviously, Jesus' opponents would not concede that they do not know God, but they would readily admit they do not know the one Jesus represents as God. The chasm between the parties is so broad now that it extends to the question of the nature and identity of God (cf. vv. 54-55). In fact, that question lies at the root of Johannine theology. Jesus claims that to know him is to know God and the Jews emphatically reject that claim. Although they do not here make that rejection explicit, knowledge of their rejection underlies this discussion and makes it intelligible. The extent of the gulf between them will become evident in the conversation that immediately follows (vv. 21-30).

For the moment there is a pause. The narrator tells us where Jesus was and why he was not yet arrested (v. 20), although the intent to arrest him was clearly already present earlier (7:32). Jesus has been teaching in the temple for a while (chaps. 5, 7) and will continue to do so (chaps. 9, 10). It is an appropriate place for him, the center of Judaism. Yet the questions of why he was teaching in the treasury, where that would be, and whether one might likely teach there are difficult (see Barrett 1978, 340). Possibly John wishes to portray Jesus as occupying various parts of his temple (cf. 10:23). Jesus' hour is obviously the moment of his death, which is anticipated and awaited throughout Jesus' public ministry (2:4; 12:23). That Jesus' hour had not yet come obviously could have been known only in retrospect.

8:21-30: Jesus speaks now of his destiny and imminent departure, and while the Jews' guess at his meaning is off base, it is not totally wrong (v. 22). Jesus will, indeed, die. Of course, that Jesus has said to them that they will die in their sin is indicative of the distance between him and them. The knowledgeable reader will know that while they die in their sin, by contrast Jesus dies in fulfillment of the Father's will. While he does not kill himself, he lays down his life willingly (10:17-18). By suggesting suicide "the Jews" at once manifest their ignorance and feign their innocence (cf. 7:20, 34-36).

Jesus states the distance separating him from the Jews in the most extreme, dualistic terms (v. 23). "The Jews" in John are defined by unbelief, the price they will pay for not believing is total (v. 24). The Jews ask a question that is innocent on the face of it, but can scarcely be so at this point in the narrative (v. 25). Jesus' answer is difficult because the Greek is obscure. Probably the RSV's "Even what I have told you from the beginning" fits the context and renders the Greek better than the NRSV's "Why do I speak to you at all?" (see Barrett 1978, 343). Moreover, the NRSV's rendering scarcely allows Jesus to continue as he does in verse 26. He intends to continue speaking and judging in the presence of the Jews. But they do not understand what or who he is talking about (v. 27). Because they do not receive the Son, they cannot understand what he says about the Father.

The statement of Jesus in verse 28 presents a problem. Even Jesus' disciples only understand and appreciate Jesus' revelatory claims after he has been lifted up, that is, after his crucifixion and resurrection. But will the Jews also know? (Verse 29 is a typical Johannine embellishment.) Perhaps the fact that many of the Jews now believe in him (v. 30) to some extent relieves the difficulty. Those who believe will know. Yet will those who believe remain with him? As the narrative develops, it quickly seems they will not.

8:31-59: The discussion will now center on descent from Abraham, as the tension between Jesus and his newly found Jewish believers quickly becomes apparent (vv. 31-33). Although they have believed in Jesus, they apparently do not wish to concede that their descent from Abraham now means any less to them. The freedom that Jesus brings they already had. The motifs of freedom and slavery, which now come to the fore, sound quite Pauline (cf. Rom 6:17). Since slavery is slavery to sin (v. 34), freedom is apparently freedom from sin. Obviously, Jesus' word of admonition or warning to them (v. 31) is not heeded.

The fact that these believers reject Jesus so soon presents a real and severe exegetical problem. D. A. Carson (1991, 346-49) helpfully outlines alternative interpretations, and points out that in John fickle faith is a recurring theme (cf. 2:23-26; 6:60). That apparently is what we see here. The Jews who have believed very quickly show themselves unwilling or unable to continue in Jesus' word, as their protest (v. 33) immediately demonstrates. (The Greek verb is *menō*; cf. 1:39; 15:4.) The transition from belief in Jesus to hostility is sudden.

Jesus' response to them (vv. 34-38) makes clear that they are not truly his disciples, and, indeed, never have been (as in 2:23-25 and 3:2-3). The contrast between slave and son (v. 35) again reminds one of Paul (cf. Gal 4:21-31), although there is no clear evidence of direct dependence. The Son here is Jesus himself, as the subsequent statement (v. 36) makes clear. Again Jesus refers to their effort to kill him (5:18; 7:19), so we rightly infer that these believers are no different from the other Jews. That is the only possible inference since they trace their free status not to Jesus but to Abraham. This being the case, there is no place in them for Jesus' word (v. 37). Jesus now says that he declares what he has seen in his Father's, that is, God's presence (v. 38). The preexistence of Jesus with God (1:1-2; cf. 17:5) is here assumed. The second half of this statement is difficult and there are different manuscript readings. In contrast to the NRSV, the RSV has "you do what you have heard from your father" (i.e., the devil, as in v. 44). But the most ancient witnesses (P[66] B) support something like the NRSV's rendering, which takes the verb to be a present imperative: "You should do what you have heard from the father." This is possible, although it could be an indicative, simply stating what they do. Quite possibly the construal of the verb as a present indicative led to the insertion of "your" (missing in some ancient mss.) to modify "father," for it would be inconceivable that these opponents of Jesus actually did what they had heard from God the Father. Thus "your father" anticipates the statement that the devil is their father (v. 44). This reading and construal actually fits better, since there is no explicit discussion of what they have heard from the Father.

These Jews do not, apparently, understand Jesus to mean that God is their father. At least, Jesus' statement ("You should do what you have heard from the father") leads them to reiterate that Abraham is their father (v. 39), and in doing so they perhaps inadvertently deny that God is their Father in favor of Abraham. But, of course, Jesus then asserts that their intention to kill him proves they cannot be children of Abraham (v. 40). When Jesus further says they are not doing what Abraham did, but what their father does (v. 41), he is already implying that the devil is their father (cf. v. 44). This leads them to assert that God is their father, and at the same time seemingly to call in question Jesus' paternity. That they deny that they were "born of fornication" (RSV; NRSV: "illegitimate children") may imply a belief that Jesus was. (Barrett 1978 and Hoskyns 1947 follow Origen in thinking the Jews are here casting aspersions on Jesus himself by evoking rumors that he was of illegitimate birth.) For his part, Jesus has just implied that their claim to be children of Abraham is false, and that their father is someone else. Therefore their response may be defensive and at the same time evoke rumors of Jesus' illegitimate birth. In any event, they now assert that God is their Father (v. 41), so that their claim and Jesus' clash sharply. Jesus obviously understands this and denies their claim; the correctness of his denial is proved by their conduct: rather than loving Jesus they are trying to kill him (v. 42; cf. v. 40). Only those who acknowledge Jesus truly know God as Father (cf. v. 19). Jesus then makes a play on words that is difficult to capture (v. 43): "What I say" translates *lalia* (speech, what is uttered), while "word" renders *logos* (communication and, according to 1:1-18, what Jesus is). It is not too much to say that because they do not accept Jesus they do not really know what he is talking about.

Jesus then proceeds to denounce his opponents in the strongest possible terms (v. 44). If they have questioned his legitimacy in a veiled way (v. 41), he now exposes their ancestry explicitly and mercilessly: Their father, the devil, is a murderer and a liar. Although there were serious differences and debates between them, no such hostility dominated the relationship between the historical Jesus and other Jews. We see here rather the reflection of the mortal tension between the Johannine community and the Jews who had rejected their claims. They are seen as the heirs of the temple authorities who in all probability did play a significant role in Jesus' trial and death (see below, pp. 229-31, 346). It follows from what has been said of Jesus' opponents that they would reject the truth (v. 46). This rejection is then explained in terms of origin. We have repeatedly seen that this sort of explanation is characteristic of this Gospel (v. 47). Jesus and his opponents have different origins, God and Satan. At this point in the narrative it is—or appears to be—that simple. John sometimes seems locked into a thoroughgoing, ontological dualism such as is found in later Gnosticism. Yet at the same time it is clear that John regards people's decisions as meaningful and even crucial.

The response of the Jews (v. 48) is, from their point of view, not excessive or unreasonable, for what Jesus has said is in their view outrageous and can be accounted for only on such terms. Jesus has not previously been accused of being a Samaritan, but he has shown an extraordinary openness to them (4:4-42). But his complaint that the Jews are seeking his death has once before evoked the response that Jesus has a demon (7:19). It is sometimes suggested that the accusation that Jesus himself has a demon accounts for the absence of his demon exorcisms in John. In Mark, where they are prominent, Jesus is accused of casting out demons by the power of Beelzebul, the prince of demons (3:22). Thus by implication he is demon-possessed. Of course, in John's view the pretended innocence of Jesus' opponents only masks their malice of intent. Jesus naturally denies that he has a demon and reasserts his accusations against the Jews and his claims on his own behalf (vv. 49-51). Because the Jews dishonor Jesus, by implication they also dishonor the God who seeks Jesus' glory, by revealing himself through him, and that God is the final arbiter of these matters, that is, the judge (v. 50).

Jesus' general word of promise (v. 51), now scarcely addressed to these hearers, nevertheless gives them the opportunity to underscore their lack of comprehension (vv. 52-53). It is now clear to them that Jesus is demon-possessed and his word of promise (v. 51) shatters against the fact that Abraham and the prophets all died. The question about Jesus' status vis-à-vis the fathers (v. 53) of Israel has been heard before (4:12; cf. Matt 12:42/Luke 11:31). Those who know who Jesus really is know the answer to that question, but others do not. Only God the Father is greater than Jesus (14:28). The conversation continues as if progress could be made, but of course it cannot. The fundamental tenet of the Johannine christological argument is set out first (v. 54). The crucial term is of course "glorify," which has an obvious meaning, but also a hidden and specifically Johannine one. When Jesus speaks of seeking his own glory (v. 50) or glorifying himself (v. 54) the meaning is the more obvious or commonsense one. When he says the Father seeks his glory or glorifies him, the meaning is decidedly different. It means the Father reveals himself through Jesus and specifically through his death (12:23-25). This is the distinctly Johannine (and esoteric) meaning. These two poles of the Johannine meaning of "glory" are elsewhere well represented in 5:44 and 12:43. (Note that *doxa*, "glory," can also be translated "honor," although the more common term is *timē*; cf. 5:23.)

Jesus concedes that the Jews intend the same reality when speaking of God the Father (vv. 54-55); the difference is that Jesus actually knows him, while the Jews claim to know him but in reality do not. Apparently the Johannine Jesus cannot resist calling the Jews liars one more time (v. 55). We learn repeatedly that Jesus' sonship and messiahship derive from his obedience rather than his arrogance: "But I do know him and I keep his word" (cf. 5:19, 30; as well as the view of Jesus in Phil 2:6-11). Then, Jesus goes on to claim Abraham for his cause (8:56) as he has already claimed Moses (5:39, 45-46). In doing so Jesus seems to assert his own personal knowledge of Abraham, which from the Jews' point of view is uncanny, and claims Abraham's blessing (v. 57). Understandably the Jews are perplexed, and in effect they misunderstood in a typically Johannine way, seeing Jesus only as a man less than fifty years old. Of course, while Jesus is that, he is also more than that. (On Jesus' age in John cf. 2:20-21; John possibly considers Jesus to be somewhat older than the thirty years attributed to him in Luke 3:23.) Jesus sets them straight with a typical "I am" saying (v. 58), referring, of course, to his preexistence, as the Johannine reader will well understand. The Jews can only comprehend this as arrogance in the extreme. That is, Jesus claims his own glory. Understandably then, they take up stones against him, presumably to stone him for what was, if not technically blasphemy (cf. Lev 24:16), a near equivalent (cf. 10:30-31). Quite possibly the "I am" is taken as an indication Jesus is usurping divine prerogatives (cf. Exod 3:14; Isa 43:13 for use of *egō eimi* by or of God).

The theological themes of the Gospel of John, particularly its Christology, are repeated many times and developed in different settings in the course of the narrative. The claims made by or for Jesus are at first veiled (2:13-22; 3:1-10) and evoke perplexity. Then they become overt and mortal hostility surfaces (5:18). Yet even when he refers to the threat against his life, his charge is brushed off (7:20-21); he is accused of having a demon, he is paranoid! Toward the end of chapter 7 (vv. 40-44, 51), reasons for rejecting messianic claims for Jesus are set out.

In this episode (chap. 8) Jesus enters into direct and extended discussion, and polemic, with his Jewish adversaries. Although Jesus still does most of the talking, as he does throughout the Gospel, his opponents are now allowed to speak their piece. (In some contrast with Justin Martyr's *Dialogue with Trypho* where the tone is relatively polite, particularly as Justin and Trypho say farewell, here the disagreement is sharp as gross insults are traded.) Earlier the Jews had accused Jesus not only of breaking the Sabbath but of making himself equal to God (5:16-18). Now they imply Jesus was illegitimate (8:41), accuse him of being a Samaritan, and again of having a demon (vv. 48, 52). Moreover, those Jews who had believed in him now renege (vv. 33, 39), for they can claim Abraham as their father, and that is quite enough. Specifically, they reject the salvific work of Jesus. He has not freed them, for as descendants of Abraham they have always been free (v. 33). The issue then increasingly becomes Abrahamic sonship, until Jesus shockingly announces that he has priority over Abraham (vv. 56-58), at which point his adversaries attempt to stone him. As the conversation unfolds it becomes evident that its bitterness derives from the kinship of the antagonists, but neither will grant the other a share of the legitimate lineage. It is either one or the other. If there were need of demonstration or confirmation that John's theology was hammered out in the heat of conflict, we have it here. Yet Jesus and his opponents continue to appeal to the same God (vv. 54-55), as Jesus concedes, even as he claims complete knowledge of that God while denying it to them. That the Jewish opponents of the Johannine Christians were intolerant of them is probable. That the Johannine Christians were intolerant of their opponents is virtually certain.

Apart from its polemical edges and thrusts, however, chapter 8 does not go beyond what has earlier been said of and about Jesus. It does not advance those claims but sets them over against the sharpest opposition.

Jesus and the Blind Man (9:1-41)

Chapter 9 consists of a single episode that begins with Jesus' healing a blind man (vv. 1-7) and concludes with his opponents reflecting on the significance of what has transpired (vv. 40-41). The hostility that began to emerge so sharply after Jesus' healing of the man at the pool of Bethzatha, has reached an apex in chapter 8. In this episode, however, the initial hostility toward Jesus himself is not so sharp, or the focus has changed just a bit. The object of the opponents investigation, and ultimately their wrath, is the blind man to whom Jesus has given sight. Typically in the Gospel of John a miracle story not unlike those found in the Synoptics (cf. Mark 8:22-26; 10:46-52) provides the beginning point and basis for a subsequent discussion of Jesus and his work (cf. chap. 5). (Interestingly, hostility against Jesus rises sharply again in chapter 10 but declines in chapter 11, at least through the story of the raising of Lazarus.)

As closely woven as this episode is, the narrative connections with those preceding and following are rather loose. Jesus escapes the opponents who seek to stone him at the end of chapter 8, and leaves the temple. At the beginning of our episode he is said to be walking along, a typically vague way of beginning a miracle story in the Synoptics (cf. Mark 2:13, 23). In actuality the temple area was not far from the pool of Siloam of old Jerusalem, where Jesus sent the blind man to wash (9:7, 11). (As the pool of Bethzatha was just north of the temple area, the pool of Siloam was directly to the south, at the foot of the ancient city of David.) So at least the events of chapters 8 and 9 take place in close proximity to each other. The Pharisees of 9:40-41 may be presupposed as the audience of Jesus' shepherd discourse of chapter 10, and one must recall that the present textual divisions were not introduced until many centuries later. Yet the division marked by the present chapters seems real enough.

9:1-7: The healing story begins as Jesus sees the man blind from birth. How the disciples knew his condition was congenital is not said, but this fact becomes important as the story develops. The belief that illness or misfortune is the result of sin (vv. 2-3) is an ancient one (cf. Exod 20:5; Luke 13:1-5), and dies hard: "What did I do to deserve this?" It is important to maintain the moral balance of one's personal universe. Jesus, however, rejects the notion that the man's blindness is the result of sin (v. 3; also Luke 13:1-5; but cf. 5:15; Mark 2:5, 9). But Jesus' explanation for its existence is scarcely more acceptable to modern sensibilities (cf. 11:4). Now Jesus subtly alludes to his coming death (vv. 4-5) as he will in the Lazarus story (11:9-10, 16). Both aspects of the stories, the explanation for the existence of the subject's dire condition in the first place and the unmistakable allusion to Jesus' coming death, are characteristic of the Gospel of John. Jesus' work displays God's glory (see 2:11), but that glory is finally not manifest until his death. That these reminders occur at the beginning of each of the Gospel's two final miracle stories is scarcely coincidental. The scene is set theologically, as well as otherwise, for what Jesus will do.

That Jesus now says he is the light of the world (v. 5) recalls 8:12 (cf. 1:5, 9). It is rather curious that this saying seems to put a limit on the period in which Jesus is the light of the world, as if that is something he would be only during the period of his earthly ministry. Something similar may be said of Jesus' statement in 11:9-10. Yet in the context of the Gospel as a whole, such statements can hardly mean that Jesus' function as light of the world will be terminated with his death and exaltation. Probably, the import of the time constraint really applies to Jesus' hearers, his opponents—their opportunity to believe and confess—rather than to Jesus (cf. 12:35-36). There is an urgency about recognizing who he is. Yet Jesus' own ministry is under a time constraint: he must get his work on earth done before his hour of departure arrives (v. 4). He must be about his mission with dispatch.

The healing, that is the giving of sight, is described briefly (vv. 6-7). As in Mark 8:23 Jesus uses spittle, but here he makes a paste, mud, with the spittle to apply to the man's eyes. Because Jesus sends him away to wash in the pool of Siloam, apparently nearby, the healing actually takes place when Jesus is not present, although the man returns with sight (v. 7). The meaning of the Hebrew name *Silōam* is then explained. It means "sent," being derived from the Hebrew verb *shalaḥ* ("send"), and Jesus is described in John as the one God sent (e.g., 3:17). Although the significance of the name is noted, John does not elaborate upon it. Water for the ceremonies of Booths (chap. 7) was drawn from this pool. The fact that the miracle takes place "off stage" is reminiscent of the changing of water into wine; the actual transformation is not described; suddenly, however, it has happened (2:9). Perhaps the succinctness of the narrative, even in comparison with synoptic miracle stories, bespeaks its primitive character.

9:8-34: The narrative continues with an investigation of whether the man has actually been given sight. Miracle stories often end with some proof of healing (5:9; Mark 2:12). Here the man is said to return from Siloam able to see (v. 7). While there is no immediate acclamation of the crowd, a discussion of what has transpired now occurs (vv. 8-9). Typically in John, Jesus' work results in division of opinion, and that is the case here. The neighbors cannot agree whether the man who now sees was actually the blind man they were accustomed to see begging. The man himself settles the matter by saying, literally, "I am he" *(egō eimi).* The NRSV's "I am the man" is a smooth translation and correct in its present context, but loses the obvious connection with the "I am" sayings of Jesus. The neighbors now launch an informal investigation; "kept asking him" correctly renders the Greek imperfect tense (v. 10). The man answers succinctly (v. 11), and in doing so virtually repeats the brief miracle story. What this man has experienced he knows, and he will not deny or renounce his knowledge. Yet he makes no pretense of knowing more than he has experienced (v. 12). The opening episode now simply ends, but the investigation and discussion will continue.

There are several more or less separate interrogations concerning the once blind man. After his neighbors have questioned him (vv. 8-12), he is brought before the Pharisees (vv. 13-17). Also called "the Jews," they summon his parents (vv. 18-23). Then "they" (Pharisees/Jews) summon the man himself a second time (vv. 24-34). This episode provides a good example of the way John tends to speak of Jesus' adversaries as Jews or Pharisees interchangeably. The Pharisees are the only party of the Jews John mentions. Sadducees, Zealots, and Essenes no longer existed as distinct groups after the Roman war (BCE 66–70) that resulted in the sacking of Jerusalem and the destruction of the temple as well as the Essene community of Qumran. Nor are scribes mentioned.

The Pharisees, to whom the healed man is brought, will now appear as judges to straighten out the perplexities into which the man's neighbors have fallen. Their role here corresponds to their dominant position in postwar Judaism. For the first time we hear that Jesus performed this deed on the sabbath (v. 14). In the synoptic Gospels Jesus is several times accused of violating the sabbath (cf. Mark 2:23-28; 3:1-6) and already in John the issue has been raised (5:9-10; 7:22-23). Presumably the making of mud specifically violates the sabbath (vv. 14-16), as earlier the healed man had violated the sabbath by carrying his pallet (5:10). Once again the man succinctly narrates what transpired (v. 15). Interestingly, even the Pharisees are at least initially divided in their opinion (v. 16). Some insist on sabbath observance as the criteria; others find his signs impressive, if perhaps not decisive (9:16; cf. 2:23-25 and Nicodemus's positive assessment in 3:2). Therefore, at this point they put the ball in the healed man's court (v. 17). He continues his positive testimony (cf. vv. 9, 25). Indeed, the Pharisees have momentarily conceded that he is in a position to speak authoritatively, and he does: "He is a prophet." The woman of Samaria had said the same of Jesus (4:19). Nicodemus had said that he was a teacher come from God (3:2), and both are right as far as they go, even if they do not go far enough. "Prophet" can mean someone sent by God on a mission, and Jesus is certainly that. Of course, the term "prophet" evokes the Deuteronomic prophet like Moses (Deut 18:15; see Martyn 1979, 102-28; Meeks 1967, *passim*). That this figure is already in view is suggested by the comparison, albeit hostile, between Jesus and Moses in 9:28. In the context of the narrative this is the first stage of the man's confession, which will become complete in verse 38.

The opponents of Jesus (Jews/Pharisees) wish to disprove the miracle, presumably by showing that the man who now sees is not the same as the blind man who begged (v. 18). Thus they turn to his parents in order to establish his identity. The conversation with the parents (vv. 18-23) is probably the single most important bit of evidence for the circumstances of the Gospel's origin. The parents speak very cautiously, although truthfully, because they fear the consequences (v. 22). There can be no doubt that this is their son, who was born blind, who now sees (v. 20). It is painfully clear, however, that the parents want to avoid saying anything about how he was healed or who restored his sight (v. 21), lest "the Jews" suspect them of being followers of Jesus and put them out of the synagogue (v. 22). Clearly they wish to remain Jews in good standing, that is, to remain within the synagogue. The threat to followers of Jesus of being put out of synagogues is reflected also in 12:42 and 16:2 (see Martyn 1979, especially 37-62; above, introduction, pp. 35-38).

The synoptic Gospels do not speak of such a threat. (Luke 21:12 mentions followers being delivered up to synagogues after Jesus' death, but not of expulsion even then.) For one Jew to believe another was the Messiah, or to believe his claim to be the Messiah, was no crime, even if the claim proved to be false. The famous rabbinic sage Akiba, who flourished during the time the Fourth Gospel was composed and for several decades thereafter, is said to have acclaimed the ill-fated Bar Kokhba as Messiah and even to have suffered martyrdom at the hands of the Romans when his rebellion failed in 135 CE. Yet his standing was not thereby diminished. It would certainly have been exceptional for Jesus' disciples or followers to have been expelled from the synagogue, and presumably from Judaism (or at least from good standing as Jews) because during Jesus' lifetime they believed he was the Messiah or Messiah designate. Of course, if Jesus himself had made the claims for himself that he is described as making in the Gospel of John, such expulsion might have occurred. But just such claims are characteristic of the Fourth Gospel rather than the Synoptics, suggesting they are postresurrection claims of Jesus' followers, that is, the church. It is interesting and probably significant that in the Gospel of John, Jesus is not portrayed as a Jew, except somewhat incidentally (4:9), and is himself not threatened with expulsion from the synagogue. The Johannine Jesus is already beyond the synagogue, another indication that he is the postresurrection Jesus.

If John assumes a postresurrection setting in which claims for Jesus are being sharply rejected and confessors punished by "the Jews," can the specific historic setting be identified? Martyn and others have suspected that the promulgation of the Twelfth of the Eighteen Benedictions of the synagogue service is related in an important respect to the setting of the Gospel of John. The Twelfth Benediction is in effect a condemnation of "Nazarenes" (Christians?) and "heretics" or sectarians (also Christians?). The crucial question that has occupied some Johannine and rabbinic research is when the form of the Twelfth Benediction that pronounces this condemnation was formulated. (There are other, different versions of the same benediction.) If Samuel the Small, the sage to whom it is attributed, issued this version at Jamnia (the rabbinic college) in the mid-80s of the first century (as proposed by Martyn, as well as Davies 1966, 256-315, especially 270-77), the timing fits the probable date of origin of the Gospel of John very well (as Brown 1966 has shown, lxx-lxxv, lxxxv).

There is little doubt that the research bringing together the threats of expulsion from the synagogue in John and the Twelfth Benediction have brought us close to the originative setting of the Fourth Gospel. Yet there are problems with the proposals that have been made.

For one thing, the dating of this version of the Twelfth Benediction remains a matter of some uncertainty and dispute, together with the question of whether, or how, it was used against Johannine Christian heretics. Moreover, did the Jamnian college have the authority that seems to be ascribed to it in 9:22? Nevertheless, it remains altogether probable that this thesis corresponds closely to the dynamics of church-synagogue dialogue—initially dialogue within the synagogue—assuming that 9:22 points to a real and not imaginary situation. (See now the statement of Meeks 1996, 317-28, especially 320: "The members of this Jesus sect, who liked to think of themselves as 'Galileans' rather than 'Judeans' and perhaps included some Samaritan converts as well, were expelled from the synagogues of their town." Relatively few exegetes now working on the Gospel of John would disagree. On the scholarly discussion of the evidence on the Jewish side, see D. Moody Smith 1990, especially nn. 47, 17.)

Whatever the historical circumstances behind this scene, it is important to John that one not only believe in Jesus but be willing to confess him as Messiah and bear the cost of that confession. Nevertheless, at this point in the narrative, no one has yet confessed Jesus in such a hostile setting, but we are being prepared for what is to come. The man born blind, under pressure from the Jews, will not deny his experience and is, in a real sense, driven to decide and confess who Jesus is.

The second and definitive direct interrogation of the man (vv.

24-34) now gets under way as he is summoned by the interrogators (presumably the Jews/Pharisees). Their opening statement is a bit curious, divided as it is into two parts (v. 24). The second is clear enough. They have already arrived at a decision about Jesus before their interrogation begins (cf. 7:50-52, where Nicodemus warns Jesus' opponents not to proceed hastily against Jesus). The judgment that Jesus is a sinner stands in sharp contrast to Jesus' previous statement to his opponents that they will die in their sins (8:21) if they do not believe (8:24). Perhaps their initial, peremptory order to the man is a kind of "swearing in" of a witness or one accused (cf. Josh 7:19): "Admit the truth" (Barrett 1978, 362).

Confronted with this candid condemnatory judgment, the man's classic response has become proverbial (v. 25). He cannot yet render a theological judgment about Jesus, but he knows for sure what his previous condition was and how it has decisively changed. The interrogators now alter their tune just a bit. In verse 18 they did not believe the miracle had really happened; now they ask how (v. 26). The man has indeed already described the event (v. 27), once to his neighbors (v. 11), then to the Pharisees (v. 15), who are presumably the same as this group of interrogators. But there is a sharp edge to his response. His questions, particularly his asking whether they want to become disciples is probably not entirely innocent, although it could be read as such.

The man's question is taken as sarcastic and derisive, probably correctly, so they revile him (v. 28). Their statements are weighty and telling, doubtless reflecting where things now stand between the synagogue and the Johannine Christians. The alternative of Jesus or Moses is clearly laid down by the Jews. One might assume that the Johannine community would accept it. But according to Jesus' statement of 5:45-47 they would not, for the Christ-confessors also lay claim to the testimony of Moses. In a real sense the question is whose appeal to Moses is justified. The opponents then render their judgment about Moses and Jesus (v. 29). The Johannine Christians would agree about Moses, but not about "this man" (Jesus). On the contrary, they know where he has come from, that is, from God. The opponents, in saying they do not know where Jesus comes from, express their genuine ignorance. At the same time, their statement is derogatory and dismissive. This entire scene is rich with irony.

The once blind man now makes a telling, explicit argument (vv. 30-33). The sarcasm becomes deeper and more hostile (v. 30). One thinks of Jesus' question to the puzzled Nicodemus (3:10), where relations were not nearly as strained. The tension between their ignorance and the man's knowledge of his healing becomes unbearable and reflects badly on them. The fact that Jesus was able to give sight to one born blind, something previously unheard of, proves that God authorizes him and therefore hears him (vv. 32-33). He cannot be a sinner, but rather is one who truly worships and obeys God (on true worship, cf. 4:22-24; on Jesus' obedience to the Father, cf. 5:19, 26; 17:4; 19:30). The point is that this miraculous deed vindicates the claim that he is from God. Jesus is the one who gives light and sight to human beings, even as he gives life (5:19-29). The one who receives such light and life knows that Jesus is from God. (In the broader narrative context, Jesus' deed and the healed man's confession justify Jesus' claims against Jewish opposition in chap. 8.)

The opponents fire back a withering retort (v. 34) to the man's stubborn faith and simple logic. His brazen effrontery is that he should, on the basis of his experience, presume to teach the authorized teachers. Yet the question is, "Who are the authorized teachers?" Or, "Who authorizes them?" Obviously the questioners believe that they are the teachers whom God through Moses has authorized, but that is precisely what is at issue. Their reply harks back to 9:2-3 and the question of whether the man's blindness was the result of sin, whether that be the man's or his parents. Obviously the opponents assume that it was. Particularly in this narrative context, his being cast out by them implies that he is expelled from the synagogue (v. 34; cf. v. 22).

9:35-41: In the final scene of this episode Jesus finds the man who has been expelled and asks him a decisive question (v. 35; cf. 5:14). The suspense caused by the fact that the man knows what has happened to him and who his benefactor is, but not much more about him (except that he is a prophet, v. 17) is maintained as Jesus puts his question in terms of the Son of Man rather than himself directly. "Son of Man" is the term Jesus characteristically uses of himself in the other Gospels as well. Its background and exact meaning remain somewhat mysterious, despite efforts of modern scholars to explain it. (For bibliography and a unique explanation of the term in John see Burkett 1991.)

Perhaps not surprisingly, the healed man is somewhat mystified by the title (v. 36), even as the crowd in the concluding scene of Jesus' public ministry seems puzzled by it (12:34). The man's intentions are entirely good as he asks Jesus for an explanation— or to identify himself—so that he may believe. Whether he addresses Jesus as "sir" or "Lord" is a good question, for either is a possible rendering of the Greek vocative *kyrie*. Perhaps the ambiguity is intentional, for the word is both the polite form of address and the christological title. Jesus then identifies himself (v. 37), and the man's response is immediate and unrestrained (v. 38). Clearly "Lord" is the proper translation now as Jesus is recognized for who he truly is. In effect, we suddenly shift to a postresurrection perspective, for the title "Lord" is characteristically applied not to the historic figure of Jesus, but to the exalted one. That perspective now sheds light back upon all that has happened, and readers may now wonder whether they have read about an event in the life of Jesus or in the postresurrection life of the church and its missionary activity. In fact, Martyn (1979, *passim*, but especially 30) quite aptly speaks of two levels in this chapter, and in this Gospel: that of the historical Jesus, who according to an ancient tradition performed such an amazing healing, and that of the missionary preacher, who represents Jesus as the one who opens the eyes of the blind, perhaps figuratively and spiritually. The one level is apparently superimposed on the other, but they are, in John's view, inextricably related.

Such an interpretation of Jesus' work of bestowing sight is, in fact, now suggested (v. 39). Startlingly, Jesus says that he has come not only that the blind may see, but also that those who see may become blind. That Jesus is going to blind people physically is absurd and grotesque. One may then legitimately ask whether his enabling those who do not see to see is meant only, or even primarily, in a physical sense. Almost certainly it is not. Jesus' giving sight to this one blind person symbolizes his role as the giver of light and sight to all who believe.

The Pharisees' question (v. 40) is somewhat surprising, if only for its mildness. Indeed, there is a certain pathos about it. Naturally, by their light they are not blind; they see, but their light is not the light of the world (8:12). Jesus' reply to them confirms their worst fears (v. 41). Their question about their own blindness was framed so as to anticipate a negative answer. "No, you are not blind." But had they been blind, they would have been like the blind man who received sight. Thus they would not have sin. Yet the very claim to see by someone or something other than the Light of the World means that their sin is not taken away. It remains and they remain in it.

Beneath this outwardly rather strange conversation lurks the Johannine concept of revelation, as well as sin. Jesus' coming reveals who people are. All are really in darkness and need the giver of sight and light. Those who own up to their need accept Jesus as Revealer and the giver of light and sight. Those who insist they see, already, when in fact they do not, are locked into the estrangement from God that is sin. In Johannine theology it is finally through the revelation of God in Jesus that sin is defined. This revelation is thus genuinely a *krisis,* a crisis, or point of division among human beings, for weal or for woe. This story shows how it happens. In many ways it is an archetypical Johannine narrative.

Yet the episode is distinctive in that the protagonist is the man upon whom Jesus has performed an astounding work, a sign (v. 16). He stands out, although his role is not wholly unique in the Fourth Gospel. The man healed at the pool of Bethzatha responded to hostile questioners that Jesus had healed him and commanded him to carry his mat, thus violating the sabbath (5:10-16). Whether the man testified to Jesus or fingered him for his Jewish opponents (v. 15) is, however, the question. The woman of Samaria testified to Jesus' knowledge of her, raised the messianic question and caused her fellow Samaritans to flock to Jesus (4:29-30). Lazarus, raised from the dead by Jesus (11:1-44) is not described as testifying to Jesus, but his very presence is such testimony, threatening to the authorities (11:48) and ultimately perilous to Lazarus (12:9-11), for a great crowd has seen the sign that Jesus performed (12:17-19).

The man born blind is unique in that he carries on a discussion with Jesus' opponents. In doing so he does not expound Christology. In fact, like the man healed at Bethzatha, at first he does not know the identity or name of Jesus (cf. 5:13). His ignorance on that score makes all the more impressive his testimony to having been given his sight (v. 25). He cannot and will not be dislodged from his firm knowledge of what happened to him. The story is eloquent testimony to Jesus' power to deliver a victim from whatever oppresses him or her. The man's belief is grounded in firsthand experience that speaks louder than any theological assertions based on tradition received at second hand. Jesus' origin, the recurring issue in this Gospel, can be inferred precisely from what he has shown himself able to do (vv. 32-33).

The historical, theological significance of this episode was brought to the center of attention by Martyn (1979), who suggested that the fear of expulsion from the synagogue revealed something significant and germane about the roots of the Fourth Gospel, its earliest setting in life. A determination on the part of certain Jewish authorities to exclude Christ-confessors from synagogues leads parents of the man born blind to answer the Jews cautiously, if truthfully. Their caution, if understandable, is not commended by the evangelist, who wants believers to become confessors, even at the expense of exclusion (12:42; cf. 16:2; 20:19). The son, who has been given sight, boldly confesses, not doctrine about Jesus, but what Jesus himself has done for him. Presumably the life of the Johannine community, a community of Jesus' disciples and their heirs, was based upon such a brave and incautious confession.

As we have noted, the narrative connections with the preceding episodes (chaps. 7–8 particularly) are slim. Yet there are important thematic connections. The overarching christological theme is obvious. Moreover the image or metaphor of Jesus as the Light of the World (9:5) continues the claim he has made earlier (8:12). Of course, sight and light are intimately related. In the background of chapter 7, and perhaps chapters 8 and 9 as well, since no change in time or season is indicated, is the festival of Booths (7:2). The ceremonial water drawing of that festival is clearly alluded to (7:37-39), but there was also the lighting of the four enormous candlesticks (above, p. 180), which although not mentioned hovers in the background.

Jesus the Shepherd and the Gate (10:1-42)

Chapter 10 presents the reader with a rich variety of materials and themes, all centering on the role and function of Jesus, who describes himself both as the gate or door of the sheep and their shepherd (10:1-18). In this opening section Jesus mentions opponents or false leaders, but they do not appear on the scene until he has finished speaking (v. 19). Apparently the occasion for Jesus' presence in Jerusalem is the festival of Dedication (v. 22), or Hanukkah, which occurs in December and commemorates the rededication of the temple by Judas Maccabeus in the second century before Christ. (It is thus a postbiblical festival.)

The controversy that erupts between Jesus and his enemies over his messianic claims and role becomes acute once again as Jesus claims oneness with God. Understandably, they accuse him of blasphemy and attempt to stone him (v. 31) and, failing that, to arrest him (v. 39). The accusations against Jesus are reminiscent of the trial before Jewish authorities in Mark (14:53-65) after his arrest, a scene that is missing from John at that point in the narrative.

The sequence of chapter 10 after 9 is not problematic in the sense that either might better be placed somewhere else. (Moreover, 10:21 refers back to the sign of chap. 9.) Yet even as Jesus, who is speaking at the end of chapter 9 (v. 41) continues to talk (10:1), the imagery changes abruptly, from sight and blindness to shepherds and sheep, as the subject becomes the identity of the true shepherd or representative of God. Of course, the question of Jesus' identity and role underlies chapter 9 as a whole, and, indeed, the whole Gospel. In any event, chapter 10 marks a new beginning in Jesus' discourse and a new stage in controversy with his opponents.

At the end of chapter 10 there is a transitional paragraph (vv. 40-42) that clearly marks the end of this narrative and apparently prepares the way for the account of Jesus' raising of Lazarus from the dead. Yet it would serve equally well as a transition to the Passion Narrative. Quite possibly at an earlier stage of the Gospel's development this marked the end of Jesus' public ministry and a transition to the Passion. There is a second withdrawal of Jesus in 11:54, which also seems to mark the end of a public ministry, after which he goes directly to Jerusalem. Here he withdraws across the Jordan, soon to return, if not to Jerusalem to Bethany on its eastern outskirts. If there are indeed parallel conclusions to Jesus' public ministry, this only matches the Gospel as a whole, which has parallel concluding chapters (see Gaventa 1996, 240-52; on the possibility that in an earlier recension 10:40-42 concluded the public ministry, see Lindars 1972, 375-76, 377-78, as well as Brown 1966, 413-15; on the possibility that this was a summary that originally stood at or near the end of a sign source, see D. Moody Smith 1984, 62-79, especially 75-77).

The internal unity of chapter 10 is less than clear, in contrast to 4:1-42 and chapters 5, 6, 7, 9, as well as 11:1-44. As Barrett (1978, 371) comments: "There is much variety in this discourse—for example, on no interpretation can 'I am the door' and 'I am the shepherd' be made to fit neatly together." Jesus does not directly address his disciples. His sheep are spoken of in the third person throughout, and Jesus is presumably alone with his opponents and others (vv. 19-21). Actually, although his disciples were with him at the beginning of the episode of the man born blind (9:1), at some undesignated point they disappear, so that at the end Jesus alone approaches the man who has now been cast out (v. 35) and is accosted by some of the Pharisees (v. 40). In the narrative as it stands before the reader, these Pharisees must be presumed to be the hearers of Jesus' discourse in 10:1-18, and in verses 19-21 they speak—except they are now called "Jews" (cf. v. 31). (See von Wahlde 1989 on Jews and Pharisees as criteria of source criticism, especially 31-36.) So there are elements of continuity as well as discontinuity between chapters 9 and 10. When they are read together, the relatively innocent question of 9:40-41 becomes the mortal hostility of 10:31-39. Yet this represents the direction in which the attitude to Jesus is moving as he encounters his fellow Jews.

◊ ◊ ◊ ◊

10:1-18: The shepherd discourse (which runs through v. 18) begins on a decidedly negative note (v. 1). Naturally, one asks Who is the thief and bandit? The Pharisees of 9:40-41? Possibly, although Jesus does not address them directly and they have said little to provoke such a retort. (Yet Jesus' sharp words to Nicodemus are not provoked by anything the latter actually says.)

This discourse has sometimes been referred to as the parable of the Good Shepherd (cf. the parable of the True Vine in 15:1-11). Yet neither Jesus nor the evangelist uses the term "parable" (Gk. *parabolē*) here or elsewhere. Rather, the term "figure of speech" *(paroimia)* is used (v. 6; cf. 16:25, 29). Synoptic parables are best not regarded as allegories (in which figures within the parable represent persons or realities external to it); but as a rule they make one, central point. If we seek to identify these bad shepherds (i.e., the bandits of vv. 1, 8; the hired hand of vv. 12-13), we are, of course, treating this figure of speech as an allegory, and that may be what we are invited to do. If so, who are they? Are they Pharisees of the preceding discourse, who have been poor shepherds to the blind man, or others, for example, messianic pretenders (Acts 5:33-39; cf. John 6:15) or savior figures generally? Obviously, in this discourse they serve as foils to the true shepherd, who appears in verse 2. The shepherd of the sheep, who enters by the gate (v. 2), will in due course be identified as Jesus (v. 11), although that identification is for the moment withheld. The characterization of how this shepherd calls and leads the sheep (vv. 3-5) clearly corresponds to the work of Jesus (cf. 6:37, 39; 18:9, as well as v. 14).

It has often been said that the behavior of the sheep and shepherd corresponds to actual pastoral practice (see, for example, Schnackenburg 1980, 282-83). The metaphor is biblical. Ezekiel (chap. 34) upbraids the failed shepherds of Israel, as the Lord God is presented as the True Shepherd. Clearly this text lies in the background of the Johannine Jesus' discourse. One should also note Num 27:16-17 and Moses' description to the Lord of the need for a leader of the people so that the congregation will not be "like sheep without a shepherd" (cf. 1 Kgs 22:17). (Joshua is then appointed.) That last phrase particularly is found in the Synoptics (Matt 9:36; Mark 6:34), where the sheep clearly denote the people of Israel. Interestingly, "sheep" is used of the people several times in Matthew (9:36; 10:6; 15:24) and of the community of Jesus' followers specifically in John (21:16-17, as well as this discourse). The portrayal of the people as sheep and Jesus as shepherd has a long and rich history in Scripture and elsewhere (see on v. 11 below), which will extend into the period of the church and, indeed, is still alive today.

Jesus' hearers do not understand (v. 6). We have already noted the difficulty in knowing exactly who these hearers are. One might think they are his disciples, although in the literary context they can only be "the unbelieving Jews" (Schnackenburg 1980, 283). That Jesus' opponents do not understand is altogether characteristic; and often his disciples do not either.

Although the gate (or door) has already appeared in this figure of speech (v. 2) the focus of the imagery now shifts decidedly (v. 7). With an "I am" saying (egō eimi) Jesus identifies himself as the gate for (or of) the sheep. This identification turns out to be puzzling not only because Jesus already seems to be the shepherd (vv. 3-5; cf. v. 11), but also because it leaves more or less unaccounted for the figure of the gatekeeper (v. 3). Perhaps the reader should take warning and not try to press the figure(s) of speech into an allegory.

That Jesus is the gate, or door, is not an unprecedented metaphor, but probably one much less common than shepherd. ("Door," as in the RSV is probably a more accurate translation of the Greek thyra than "gate"; Gk. pylē.) The fact that Jesus speaks of the sheepfold or the courtyard *(aulē)* of the sheep has probably affected the NRSV's choice of words. Perhaps Jesus is thought of as the gate because of the shepherd's practice of lying across the gateway to protect the sheep from intruders or to keep them from going out into the dangers of the night. In any event, Jesus as either gate or door is more difficult to imagine than Jesus as shepherd. Of course, in connection with the image of Jesus as gate one recalls such Johannine sayings as "I am the way, and the truth, and the life. No one comes to the Father except through *(dia)* me" (14:6). Obviously the concept of Jesus as the way is not unrelated to that of Jesus as the gate or door.

The ancient, mythical concept of a door to heaven is perhaps involved here (see Barrett 1978, 372). Indeed, in an ancient text obviously known to John (cf. 1:51) we read of the gate of heaven. Jacob says (Gen 28:17): "How awesome is this place! This is none other than the house of God, and this is the gate of heaven." He is speaking of the place he will call Bethel ("House of God"), where he has experienced a theophany. (The Greek term used here in the Septuagint, is *pylē,* which means "gate" rather than "door," but the essential point is the same.) Yet it is possible to read too much into this text, and especially into John's use of *thyra.* It clearly suggests, however, that Jesus provides the one true access to God. That at least is its principal meaning, as verses 8 and 9 confirm.

Who are those who came before Jesus (v. 8)? Abraham, Isaac, Jacob, Moses, and the prophets? Hardly. John has made every effort to secure their support for Jesus (5:45-47; 8:56), and he seems confident that he has it. Almost certainly the same figures are in view as in the case of the thieves and bandits of 10:1: Messianic prophets and pretenders, perhaps the present Jewish leaders who were, in a sense, before Jesus. The fact that "thieves and bandits" appears in both cases would seem to clinch the identification.

That the sheep did not listen to these leaders strongly implies that "sheep" is a designation of Jesus' followers specifically, not of all the people. Jesus reiterates that he is the gate (v. 9; doubtless to God and to the benefits of his salvation). He says, literally, "If anyone enters *through* (Gk. *dia*) me," taking the imagery of the gate or door farther than the NRSV actually indicates. The going in and going out echoes Num 27:17, where leader and people go in and out. Finding pasture obviously means to be fed, a metaphor for the salvation just spoken of. Again Jesus is contrasted with the thieves (v. 10; cf. vv. 1-2). The word translated "kill" is *thyō*, highly appropriate for the slaughter of animals. Being saved, finding pasture, and having life all amount to the same thing. The NRSV follows a long tradition of interpretation in speaking of having life "more abundantly." Brown (1966, 384) says "have it to the full." The point is that there is no limit to the gift of life that Jesus dispenses. The contrast between the good shepherd and the bad one will be drawn out in what follows.

The "I-am" saying (v. 11) that one has been led to expect now appears, as Jesus proclaims himself the Good Shepherd. This is obviously a recognition formula (Bultmann 1971, 225-26, n. 3: "Who is the Good Shepherd? I am he."). Among many—or at least more than one—shepherds Jesus is the one good, true shepherd. The figure of the shepherd as not only leader but provider is assumed in the Gospel of John (cf. 21:15-17). It is a manner of speaking well known in antiquity, and, as we have observed, in Scripture. (Schnackenburg 1980, 295, acknowledges its widespread use in antiquity, but believes John is here relying on its biblical background.)

Numbers 27:16-17 and Ezek 34 have already been noted. One should think also of David, the progenitor of the Messiah, who was by trade a shepherd before he was called to lead Israel (1 Sam 17:15, 34, 40; cf. Ps 78:70-72). Moreover, in the Bible the hoped for heir of David's rule is described as a shepherd (Ezek 34:23-24; Mic 5:4). Unfortunately, in the Old Testament, as in John, there are bad shepherds as well as good (see Zech 11:4-9, as well as Ezek 34:1-10). In fact, Ezekiel's classical description of the evil, selfish shepherds is a virtual antitype of the portrayal of the good shepherd in John 10:1-18 (see Dodd 1953, 358-61). They are the leaders of Israel who have failed to care for and feed the sheep, but rather have allowed them to be scattered and to fall prey to wild animals.

In the synoptic Gospels Jesus takes up the shepherd imagery of Scripture in contemplating his own mission. We have already noted the use of Num 27:16-17 in Mark 6:34 as Jesus sees the crowd, who are "like sheep without a shepherd." According to Matthew (15:24) Jesus says that he was sent only to the lost sheep of the house of Israel, to whom he also sends his disciples (Matt 10:6). In the prediction of Peter's denial, Jesus is clearly referring to himself as in Mark 14:27 when he cites Zech 13:7: "I will strike the shepherd, and the sheep will be scattered." This same passage seems to be in view also in John 16:32, although it is not cited explicitly. Obviously, the presumption is that Jesus himself is the shepherd, but outside the Gospel of John Jesus is explicitly called the shepherd only in the Epistle to the Hebrews (13:20: "the God of peace, who brought back from the dead our Lord Jesus, the great shepherd of the sheep ... ").

Not surprisingly the good shepherd's role in the economy of salvation corresponds to Jesus' actual fate (v. 11; cf. 15:12-13). The description of what Jesus does—from the standpoint of the Gospel what he has already done—stands in contrast to the behavior of the hired hand (vv. 12-15; cf. vv. 1, 8), which is foreshadowed already in Ezek 34:1-10 (especially vv. 5-6, 8, 10). The NRSV translation, that the hired hand "does not own the sheep" (v. 12), is less literal than the RSV, but accurate and to the point. Jesus "owns" his sheep, because they have been given him by the Father (6:37, 39; 17:6; 18:9). Unfortunately the NRSV's "does not care for the sheep" (v. 13) can be misconstrued, because the English idiom could mean simply that he does not tend them. He obviously does not tend them, but the RSV's "cares nothing for the sheep" or "the sheep are of no concern to him" would be better. In light of what is said in this Gospel about Jesus' relation to his sheep, his disciples, verse 14 comes as no surprise. The relationship of Jesus to his own is analogous to the Father's relationship to Jesus (v. 15; cf. 14:18-24). Jesus now reiterates what he, in contrast with the false shepherd, the hired hand, will do.

That Jesus then mentions "other sheep that do not belong to this fold" (v. 16) is somewhat puzzling, not because Jesus should not have such "other sheep," but because it is difficult to identify them with certainty. The note of unity struck here is again sounded in Jesus' final prayer (17:20-23), but does not help us identify the "other sheep" unless Jesus' later, postresurrection disciples (17:20) are meant. Probably most commentators think of the Gentile mission in this connection (but cf. Martyn 1996, 129). Yet these sheep already belong to Jesus, and Martyn argues (pp. 128-30) that they represent other Jewish-Christian communities. Martyn believes we are here dealing with an allegory in which the players are to be identified with figures in the Johannine community. Yet to identify the players at this distance is a daunting task. Jesus' enigmatic statement points to the openness and eventual universality of his mission (cf. 4:42; 12:20-21; 17:20; 20:29).

The essential point about the good shepherd is already made with verse 15. What remains is, in effect, commentary (vv. 16-18), which makes clear the scope of Jesus' mission (v. 16), the Father's relationship to Jesus in light of his decision for death (v. 17), and Jesus' own volition and intention in his death and resurrection, which is nevertheless his response to the command he has received from God (v. 18). A great deal of Johannine Christology comes to expression, or is reiterated, here (cf. 5:19, 30; 17:4, 7-8). Why the Father should love Jesus for laying down his life in order to take it up again (v. 17) is explained by the final statement of verse 18: Jesus has received, and accepted, the command from his Father. This command puts in an entirely different light what otherwise might seem an arrogant statement by Jesus to the effect that he causes his own death and resurrection.

10:19-21: The division that Jesus typically causes among the people now appears (vv. 19-21; cf. 7:40-42). The charge that Jesus has a demon (v. 20) has been heard before (8:48). The counter to this charge (v. 21) recalls the statements of the blind man (9:25, 31-33). Obviously, this interlude relates the whole episode to the immediately preceding account of Jesus' bestowing sight upon the blind man and confirms the reading of it in light of that event. In turn, the giving of sight dramatically portrays Jesus as the light of the world (8:12) and recalls the celebration of lights at the festival of Booths (7:2).

10:22-39: The scene shifts to the festival of Dedication (v. 22), as the discussion with opponents now centers on Jesus' claims. Since chapter 6 Jesus has been in Jerusalem and presumably in the temple area, as he was in chapter 5 (which arguably originally *followed* chapter 6). Thus Jesus has been in Jerusalem and in the vicinity of the temple for some time. Indeed, we learn that the episode of chapter 7 took place at the festival of Booths or Tabernacles (7:2, 37), which would occur in our month of October. Dedication, which is in Hebrew Hanukkah (renewal), comes in December, about a couple of months later. It celebrates the renewal or rededication of the temple area by Judas Maccabeus after the Seleucids were driven out. In another, different, but not unrelated sense, Jesus brings renewal to the temple. In fact, he is the new temple or dwelling place of God (1:14; 2:21). This would, of course, be winter, and the comment to that effect could be intended to call attention to the wintry weather. Solomon's Portico (v. 23), on the eastern side of the temple area, is also mentioned in Acts 3:11 and 5:12. Presumably a large number of people could gather there, as they do in Acts 5:12 and in this episode. (For the location of Solomon's Portico, see Josephus *J.W.*, 5.184-85; *Ant.* 15.396-401 and 20.221.) The scene is now set for the Jews to ask Jesus the crucial question (v. 24).

Their question may actually seem curious in the Gospel of John, for Jesus' messiahship has been known from the beginning (1:41), at least to his disciples and the readers of the Gospel. Yet despite Jesus' extensive discourses, which deal with his status and role, he manifests a certain reticence about the title Messiah or Christ itself. Of course this is true of the Synoptics, especially Mark, but it is surprising to find this reticence also in John. Jesus does, however, reveal himself as Messiah to the Samaritan woman (4:26), and Martha confesses him as such (11:27). (Significantly, in both cases a woman confesses Jesus' messiahship.) The NRSV here, as ordinarily in the Gospels, translates *christos* as Messiah to indicate that Jewish messianic expectations are in view. This would be historically correct, of course, and that obviously corresponds to this scene, where, as in a number of others, a Jewish (rather than a strictly Christian) context is in view.

Jesus' answer (v. 25) might have been anticipated, although it is not nearly as obvious as one might assume that Jesus has already revealed himself specifically to the Jews as Messiah. That his works, presumably his signs, prove him to be Messiah is axiomatic for John (5:36; 20:30-31), who also knows, however, that they did not have this desired effect upon his own people (1:11; 12:37). (Martyn notes that signs or miracles were not expected of the Davidic Messiah [1979, 95-100].) The explanation of their unbelief is finally God's choice (v. 26).

As we have observed, John lays alongside one another statements that affirm or imply that human decision for or against Jesus is an absolutely crucial matter and others that explain belief or unbelief as grounded ultimately in God. In this, John is not unique (cf. Mark 4:11-12; Acts 28:25-28; Rom 9–11; as well as John 12:37-41). What Jesus says here about the safety and security of his sheep in his own hand (v. 28) is the logical conclusion of what he has already said about his role as shepherd (vv. 2-5, 11-15) and agrees with other statements about his relation to his own (6:37, 39; 17:6, 12). The concluding assertion on this theme (v. 29) is unclear. The NRSV's translation follows the twenty-seventh edition of *Nestle-Aland* (1993) and some ancient manuscripts, preeminently Vaticanus. Other ancient manuscripts read "My Father... is greater than all" (so RSV), which makes a great deal more sense, particularly in view of verse 30, which stresses Jesus' equality with the Father. (One can scarcely imagine that the sheep are "greater than all"!) Yet had that been the original reading, it is difficult to see why the other readings would have arisen. Barrett (1978, 381-82) has an excellent discussion of this difficult reading and the reasons why the evangelist must have meant—if he did not clearly write—that the Father is greater than all.

Jesus' statement (v. 30) that he and the Father are one is shocking by any other standard, but particularly to Jewish sensibilities, as immediately becomes evident (vv. 31-39). Yet by Johannine standards it is exactly what he might be expected to say (cf. 1:1, 18; 5:18; 14:8-11; 20:29). John walks a very narrow path indeed. Jesus is equal to God, but precisely because he does nothing other

211

than the Father's will. He fulfills the commission that he has been given (5:19, 30). Jesus' final word on the cross (19:30), "It is finished" also means "It is accomplished." (John's position on Jesus' accomplishment of his mission and work may profitably be compared with Isa 55:10-11, and specifically what is there said about the word's accomplishment of its God-given mission.) John emphasizes the unity of Jesus with God, the Son with the Father, but at the same time honors the importance of the distinction between them (see Meyer 1996, 254-73).

The Jews' questioning of Jesus about his possible messiahship is reminiscent of the high priests' question to Jesus at the (synoptic) trial before the Sanhedrin (Mark 14:61). When in Mark, Jesus affirms that he is the Messiah, the Son of the Blessed One, the confession leads directly to his condemnation to death because of blasphemy (Mark 14:64). Similarly here, the question and ensuing discussion lead to the Jews' trying to stone Jesus to death because of his blasphemy (v. 10:33; cf. 8:59). (Not surprisingly, Anton Dauer 1992, 307-39, suspects that the synoptic account of the Jewish trial of Jesus has influenced the formation of John 10.) The Jews' determination to stone him causes Jesus to reply in wounded innocence (v. 32), at which point they accuse him directly of blasphemy (v. 33). In Mark (14:61-64) it is more difficult to see the grounds for the charge of blasphemy in Jesus' claiming to be the Messiah. In John, however, the blasphemy, if it be that, is much clearer. Jesus has claimed divine status or standing (cf. 5:18). Indeed, he has just claimed that he is one with the Father (v. 30). That this is blasphemy seems obvious, particularly in Judaism, where even to name the name of God would invoke the death penalty (see *m. Sanh.* 7.5). There seems, however, to be no scriptural prohibition against claiming to be God, but that does not mean that such a thing would be taken lightly. Rather, it was unthinkable. What Jesus claims seems just that; it is beyond the pale. (See Barrett 1978, 384-85, for a concise presentation of relevant Jewish texts.) Of course, stoning was the typical Jewish, even biblical, form of execution (see Lev 24:10-16 on stoning for blasphemy specifically).

Jesus' defense against the charge seems almost capricious (v. 34), but it is actually a piece of biblical exegesis. He invokes "your law," Ps 82:6 (cf. also Gen 3:5), a passage that in itself would cause trouble for the strict monotheist. (John often writes "law" in referring to Scripture; cf. 12:34; 15:25.) John here cites it exactly according to the Septuagint, as he proceeds to draw out its implications for his own claims (vv. 35-36). The Hebrew word is *elohim* and the Greek *theoi* (both plurals), so there is no doubt what is being said. Moreover, the same Psalm verse continues, "[you are] sons [RSV] of the Most High." Curiously, Jesus does not continue the quotation. Of course, the logic of the argument does not seem to accord with John's Christology: it should not be offensive if I make myself God, because we are all gods. Although such reasoning does not sound Johannine, Brown (1966, 410) suggests a plausible, Johannine line of argument, from the lesser to the greater: "If it is permissible to call men gods because they were vehicles of the word of God, how much more permissible is it to use 'God' of him who *is* the Word of God." As strange as Jesus' argument seems initially, both to Judaism and to the Fourth Gospel, the closer one looks the more cogent it appears. That Jesus says that "the scripture cannot be annulled" may also seem strange (and the important ms. P[45] even omits the phrase). Yet in John's view Scripture is affirmed by, and affirms, the mission and status of Jesus if only it is properly read and understood.

It is finally God who authorizes Scripture and Jesus (cf. vv. 37-38) and God does not contradict himself. While John, or Jesus in John, sometimes veers in the direction of implying that the God of the Jews is not the same as his God (cf. 8:18-20, 27, 38)—a later Marcionite and Gnostic position—Jesus' basic contention is that he represents the same one and only God the Father whom they now no longer apprehend, because they do not believe him, that is, Jesus, and hence no longer understand Scripture. Jesus here claims to his antagonists that he is doing the works of his (and their) Father, that is, of God. Jesus' works, if only they be acknowledged, authenticate him. (Of course, in chap. 9 Jesus' work of giving sight is not acknowledged.)

We again see the delicate balance of Johannine Christology that seems paradoxical. Jesus claims the highest conceivable status and role in relation to God. Yet the justification of his claim is that he does only what the Father has commanded him to do. He does all of it, but nothing other or more. In principle then he does what any human being can do.

But are not his works extraordinary, spectacularly unique? So they seem, and so he appears to be saying here. On the other hand, he promises his followers that they shall do greater works (14:12) in his name. The works he does are, after all, the Father's and not his own. Despite Jesus demurral, the Jews try to arrest him, as they have on previous occasions (e.g., 7:30, 32, 44) but, of course, to no avail. Although readers are not explicitly told that his hour had not come, they may legitimately infer that.

10:40-42: There is now an interlude ending this episode, as Jesus departs across the Jordan to the place where John had earlier baptized. This must be Bethany beyond the Jordan (1:28), a place that can no longer be located with certainty. Jesus remains there (v. 40). That many come to him presumably means he is the object of their quest (Painter 1993, especially 343-466). Their quest is successful, as many believe (v. 42).

Significantly, John the Baptist enters the picture again at this point. He is now spoken of as a figure of the past (cf. 5:33-36), although in 3:22–4:1 he was portrayed working alongside Jesus. Unlike the Synoptics (cf. Mark 6:14-29), the Gospel of John does not describe or even mention the execution of John. He has, of course, appeared at the beginning of the Gospel narrative (1:19). As he has testified about Jesus, now his testimony is mentioned again, in what seems to be a kind of inclusion. That is, John, or John's witness, brackets the public ministry of Jesus. What is said about John is, from the standpoint of this Gospel, certainly true: he did no sign, but everything he said about Jesus was true. His final testimony evokes faith (v. 42). Indeed, only John seems to have possessed full, postresurrection knowledge of Jesus, perhaps along with the Beloved Disciple, although John actually has much more to say about Jesus in the Gospel itself than does even the Beloved Disciple.

◊ ◊ ◊ ◊

This episode has established finally the hostility of the Jews, basically the Jewish authorities, to Jesus, even though there are apparently those who continue to be impressed by his works (v. 21), to which Jesus appeals again (vv. 37-38). Yet the judgment of the Jews is finally condemnatory (v. 39). We have noticed that Jesus' claims, offensive though they may be to the sensibilities of the Jews, do not entail his setting himself up over against their God. Rather, he claims that because of his fulfillment of God's command (v. 18) and his accomplishment of God's work (v. 37) he is the definitive manifestation or revelation of God. This the Jews deny. The issue could not be more sharply drawn.

The common, consistent factor in Jesus' opening discourse (vv. 1-18) is the use of the sheep metaphor to describe Jesus' disciples (see also vv. 26-29). Jesus himself is both the gate and the good shepherd, as he uses the characteristic "I am" formula to describe himself. The discourse does not advance Christology so much as ecclesiology. Like the parable or metaphor of the vine (15:1-11), it conveys something significant about Jesus' followers and their relationship to him. He is their leader (vv. 3-4) and protector (vv. 11, 15, 17), their access to God and salvation (v. 9). They are intimately known by him as individuals (v. 3). By way of contrast there are other shepherd figures whose relationship to the sheep only serves their own ends (vv. 10, 12), whose access to the sheep is illegitimate (v. 1). In crisis they flee the sheep and leave them to a dire fate (v. 12); the sheep are not secure in these shepherds' hands—quite the contrary (v. 10). Even as the shepherd knows the sheep, so the sheep know the shepherd (vv. 4-5). Their security is grounded ultimately in their having been given to Jesus, chosen, by the Father (vv. 28-29). Those who do not believe are not among those chosen sheep.

The ominous false shepherds, already described in Scripture (Ezek 34:1-10; Zech 11:4-10), are not explicitly identified. In the context, however, they must be closely related to—if not identical with—those who deny Jesus' sight-giving power (chap. 9) and accuse him of blasphemy (vv. 31-39). When Jesus says that "all who came before me are thieves and bandits" (v. 8), he obviously does not mean the fathers and prophets of Israel, but these contemporary religious authorities who have immediately preceded Jesus and who challenge and reject him. They will appear at the end of the following episode to condemn him (11:45-53), as they successfully conspire to have him put out of the way.

The Raising of Lazarus (11:1-44)

After the transitional passage, in which Jesus goes away across the Jordan (10:40-42), the reader is prepared for his entry into Jerusalem. Yet this does not happen immediately. Instead, we have the beginning of what seems to be a miracle or healing story (11:1; cf. 4:46; 5:2-5; 9:1), but first there is a fairly lengthy depiction of Lazarus and his sisters, followed by a conversation between Jesus and his disciples (vv. 7-16). At length Jesus and his disciples journey to Bethany, just outside Jerusalem, where the ill man, who has now died, had lived. Again there are conversations, now between Jesus and first Martha (vv. 17-27), then Mary (vv. 28-37), before Jesus himself acts (vv. 38-44).

There follows a reaction of the witnesses (vv. 45-46), not unlike what is found after other miracle stories (cf. 4:53; Mark 2:12). This reaction, partly positive (v. 45), but then negative (v. 46), leads over into the following episode, which is a formal meeting of the council or Sanhedrin, called in order to determine what to do about Jesus (vv. 47-53). With this hearing the wheels are set in motion that will eventually carry Jesus to his death. Jesus gives life and his enemies decide to put him to death. There are important connections between this scene and the synoptic trial of Jesus before the Sanhedrin (14:55-65), which in turn is related to the interrogation of Jesus in chapter 10, particularly verses 22-38.

The raising of Lazarus is not found in the synoptic Gospels, although there are stories of apparent resuscitations (Mark 5:35-43; Luke 7:11-17). A fragment of the recently discovered (1958) *Secret Gospel of Mark,* found in a letter attributed to Clement of Alexandria (c. 200), contains a similar, but less elaborate narrative, in which Jesus in Bethany raises a young man from the dead at the behest of his sister. The manuscript discovery has itself raised serious questions (for the original publication see Morton Smith 1973; for brief discussion and subsequent bibliography see Schneemelcher 1991, 106-9). If genuine, the fragment could present an earlier form of the Lazarus story. At least it would attest to the circulation of such a story in the early church.

That the Gospel of Luke contains a parable of Lazarus (16:19-31) would be interesting if only because of the appearance of the same name, but there are other remarkable similarities. The rich man, condemned to torment in Hades finally asks Father Abraham to send Lazarus, who reposed in Abraham's bosom, to warn his five brothers to repent and thus avoid his own fate. But Abraham refuses, saying that if the brothers do not attend to Moses and the prophets they will remain unconvinced even if someone (i.e., Lazarus) rises from the dead. In John, of course, Lazarus does rise from the dead, and the Jews manifest no change of heart toward Jesus. Did John turn Luke's parable into a resurrection story? Lukan elements are, however, missing in John, particularly any explicit reference to the Jews not attending to Scripture and repenting. Did Luke then construct a parable out of John's story? Again, the lack of specific precedent puts a question mark over this view. At most the Johannine story may have suggested, or influenced, the Lukan parable or vice versa. (A good discussion of the problems of the tradition-history of this episode is found in Schnackenburg 1980, 340-46, who does not, however, mention the similar narrative in *Secret Mark,* which when he wrote [German original 1971] had not been published.)

The Gospel of John affords interesting and important evidence of how complex the literary and tradition history of the Gospel materials may have been. The story of the woman taken in adultery (7:53–8:11) obviously circulated independently before finding a place in most manuscripts of this Gospel. Now we have a story not unprecedented in the other canonical Gospels, which has a possible parallel or forebear in an early version of Mark and significant points of contact with a Lukan parable.

◊ ◊ ◊ ◊

11:1-16: The death of Lazarus is reported by Jesus and discussed with the disciples. Lazarus of Bethany is first identified, along with his sisters (vv. 1-3). Moreover, Bethany is said to be the village of Mary and Martha, who have not yet entered the narrative; and Mary is identified with reference to an incident that has not yet occurred (cf. 12:1-8), as if the story would already be known to the reader. In Luke's narrative a similar incident occurs earlier (7:36-50), but there the woman who anoints Jesus' feet is not named. Again in Luke, Jesus enters an unnamed village, where he meets sisters named Martha and Mary (10:38-42), and we are told Mary listened at Jesus' feet while Martha worked. Strikingly, later on in John, Martha will serve (12:2) while Mary anoints Jesus' feet (12:3).

As at many other points some connection between the Gospels of Luke and John is obvious, although its exact nature is not. Here (John 11:1) John may seem to identify the village of Mary and Martha mentioned but not named in Luke (10:38). Yet it would then seem strange that he does not identify them with reference to the Lukan incident, but rather identifies Mary only, and with reference to the Johannine anointing narrative that is still outstanding (12:1-8). The sisters' sending for Jesus is explained by the close relationship of Jesus to Lazarus (v. 3), and to his sisters as well (v. 5). Jesus loved them all.

The Greek verb for love used here *(phileō)* is the one used of friendship, and, indeed, the noun *philia* commonly means "friendship." In John *agapē* and the verb *agapaō* are often used of self-giving love, but *erōs* (sexual love) does not appear. The verbs *phileō* and *agapaō* seem, however, to be used interchangeably (cf. 20:2 and 21:7 where each is used of the Beloved Disciple, with no apparent difference of meaning). Interestingly, the noun *agapē* occurs in the Gospel, but not *philia*, although *philos,* friend, appears also in 15:14-15, where it clearly refers to Jesus' followers.

Do Lazarus and his sisters belong to Jesus' own, his disciples, or are they his personal friends? The latter can easily be imagined and that fact makes Jesus' conversations and reactions intelligible. It is hard to conceive of the Johannine Jesus having personal friends. Yet it is equally hard to conceive of his tiring on a journey (4:6), much less weeping in grief (11:35). This story seems to depict the three as Jesus' friends as well as his followers, even as his true followers are his friends. Thus there is a rationale for the use of *agapaō* and *phileō* interchangeably.

Jesus now offers a theological explanation of the nature and reason for Lazarus's illness (v. 4) that reminds the reader of what was said earlier of the blind man's condition (9:3). Part of the suspense of the narrative results from Jesus' statement (v. 4) at first seeming false (cf. v. 14), but then profoundly true. God's glory is seen, of course, in the revelation of God through Jesus, which glorifies, or reveals, the Son even as the Son reveals the Father. As it turns out, Jesus does not go to his ill friend Lazarus immediately, but stays put, in effect allowing him to die. But precisely through this death life will be revealed.

Jesus in due course will lead his disciples back to Judea (v. 7), but over their protest (v. 8), which refers back to the Jews' earlier unsuccessful attempts to stone him (10:31), and anchors this event in its broader narrative context—something that happens more frequently in this Gospel than in the Synoptics. Here, as earlier (e.g., 9:2), Jesus' disciples call him "Rabbi," which as we are told, means teacher (1:38). Such usage is distinctive of the Gospel of John. In fact, John is among the earliest witnesses to the use of this title for a teacher, even in Judaism (see Brown 1966, 74).

Jesus' response to his disciples' honest question and warning sounds mysterious (vv. 9-10) and this is deliberately so. Jesus' speech, even to the disciples during his ministry, is figurative, parabolic, not open and plain (cf. 16:29). Of course, the informed reader knows that Jesus is the light of the world (8:12). Again, what he says here is reminiscent of the beginning of the story of the blind man (cf. 9:4, 5) and presents the same problem: A limitation seems to be placed on the time period of Jesus' work. This limitation can only refer to his historic ministry. There is an element of urgency that impels him and those who come in contact with him. Yet it would contradict John's theology at a fundamental level to suggest that Jesus means he will no longer be the light of the world when his earthly, historic ministry concludes.

Next Jesus reveals to his disciples Lazarus's fate, but in two stages (vv. 11, 14). Falling asleep is a euphemism for death (cf. 1 Cor 15:6), but the disciples seem not to get it (v. 12). Their response, if taken quite literally, however, is true: "If he has fallen asleep, he will be saved." (The NRSV's "will be all right" is what the disciples thought, but misses the characteristic double meaning of John.) So presumably the disciples say more than they know, as will Caiaphas in the subsequent episode (11:51). Jesus then tells the disciples what Lazarus's condition really is (v. 14), and continues, apparently letting the disciples know why he delayed going (v. 15; cf. v. 6). On any commonsense human accounting, Jesus' delay is incomprehensible, or even inhumane (v. 15). But perhaps this is just the point. Jesus does not act in accord with common sense or even by standards of what is generally regarded as humane. He and his revelation of God are unique, once for all, not subject to other standards. The delay has been for the sake of the disciples' faith. But now Jesus will go to Lazarus (v. 15, "to him," not simply to Bethany, the place of his death).

Thomas now appears for the first time in the narrative. He is named in every list of the twelve (Matt 10:2-4; Mark 3:16-19; Luke 6:13-16; Acts 1:13), but never outside John called the Twin (but see the beginning of *Gos. Thom.*). (John, of course gives no list of the twelve, although he knows of their existence.) "Thomas" represents the Hebrew for "twin," of which the Greek is *Didymus* (v. 16). Thomas's statement is actually ambiguous, although normally he would be taken to mean "Let us die with Lazarus." Because commentators know that Jesus is to die on this trip to Judea and Jerusalem, they take Thomas to express his willingness to die with Jesus. Possibly this ambiguity is deliberate, and indicates that Lazarus's destiny is an anticipation of Jesus'. Thomas proposes dying with Lazarus, whereas it is Jesus who is to die. Yet the disciples have already indicated that for Jesus to return to Jerusalem puts him in danger of his life (v. 8), so Thomas's exhortation recalls their warning if it applies to Jesus. Commentators sometimes note that Thomas is portrayed as lacking understanding (see Bultmann 1971, 400). Yet he at least manifests a loyalty to Jesus in the face of death that Peter will later espouse (13:37), but then betray (18:15-18, 25-27). As Charlesworth (1995) has maintained, the portrayal of Thomas in the Fourth Gospel is much more positive than most exegetes have allowed.

11:17-27: Jesus converses with Martha (vv. 17-27) and Mary (vv. 28-37), who come out to meet him, in rapid succession. First, Jesus arrives in Bethany to find Lazarus already dead for four days (v. 17). We know Jesus delayed starting for two days (v. 6). Indications of passage of time are otherwise lacking. Possibly it took Jesus and his disciples more than two additional days to reach Bethany from beyond the Jordan (10:40; cf. 1:28). We are simply not told. In any event, four days assures that Lazarus is really and truly dead. (According to rabbinic lore, the spirit of the dead hovered nearby for three days; see Brown 1966, 424). The location of Bethany in relation to Jerusalem (v. 18) is accurately given; it is on top of the ridge of the Mount of Olives east of the city. A tomb of Lazarus is still shown to visitors there. It may seem strange that "the Jews" now come to console Martha and Mary (v. 19), since in this Gospel they are otherwise hostile to Jesus and presumably to his friends. Yet *Ioudaioi* may be translated "Judeans" as well as "Jews." Elsewhere that translation is sometimes clearly inadequate (cf. chap. 6, where the *Ioudaioi* are in Galilee), but here it works, for Bethany is, of course, in Judea. Martha's meeting Jesus (v. 20) prepares the way for their conversation. Practically speaking, it is understandable that only one of the sisters goes out to meet Jesus; the other must stay at home with the mourners. But John characteristically portrays Jesus as meeting individuals one-on-one.

Martha's statement (v. 21) is only natural and underscores the fact that Jesus, far from rushing to the side of his sick friend, has delayed until Lazarus was certainly dead. Yet Martha in her knowledge of, and incipient faith in, Jesus still has grounds for hope (v. 22). Jesus, in response to her lament and affirmation, offers assurance (v. 23), which Martha accepts as an expression of Jewish, and early Christian, eschatological expectation (v. 24; cf.

Dan 12:2; Mark 12:18-27; 1 Thess 4:13-18). Such a view is apparently also found already in John (5:28-29). Yet from her lament, statement, and the tenor of his rejoinder it is apparent that she had hoped for more. Jesus delivers a promise of more (vv. 25-26), although on the basis of what he actually says at this point in the narrative it is not yet apparent how he will deliver on that promise. But one recalls such sayings of Jesus as 5:24-26, where the gift of life is clearly a present, as well as a future, reality (cf. 3:16-21). In the farewell discourses it will become plain that Jesus' promise of life (14:6) will become accessible to believers when he is glorified.

At the moment the crucial point is that Jesus is the resurrection and the life. One might infer that he does not fit into an apocalyptic, eschatological scheme already established, but breaks it open or radically revises it. The choice between life and death is the same as the choice about Jesus. This is quite plain. Yet Jesus even now continues to speak in a mysterious way (vv. 25b-26a). The person who believes will live even if he dies, but the person who lives and believes will never die. Barrett (1978, 425) is probably correct that verse 25b refers to physical death and spiritual life, while verse 26a refers to both spiritual death and spiritual life (cf. 6:49-50). (On this passage see also Carson 1991, 412-14.) The NRSV translation "will never die" (v. 26) is good idiomatic English and is found in similar form in the RSV. Yet the Greek preserves a Hebrew idiom that is not reflected in the English. One would translate literally: "Everyone who lives and believes in me will by no means die into the age." "Into the age" means "into the age to come," given traditional Jewish and early Christian eschatology. Schnackenburg (1980, 331) translates verse 25b "He who believes in me, though he die, yet shall he live"; and verse 26a "and whoever lives and believes in me shall not die to eternity." His translation removes the seeming perplexity and does not invoke the dichotomy between spiritual and physical, which is not expressly a part of this text. John seems to be saying something like this: Whoever believes in Jesus, although he will die, will nevertheless live; that is, whoever while living in this world believes, will not die with respect to the next.

When Jesus asks Martha whether she believes this, he is presumably not asking whether she shares this eschatological scheme, or any eschatological scheme per se, but whether she believes in his crucial status and role. Martha does believe (v. 27), and says what she believes about Jesus. All that she affirms about Jesus is certainly true and necessary to affirm, but whether she even yet responds in a fully adequate way may be an open question. Jesus is the Messiah or Christ (Gk: *christos*), the Son of God (cf. 20:31). "The one coming into the world" is a curious phrase, but this is not the first time we have seen it used of Jesus in this Gospel (cf. 1:9; 6:14; and cf. 3:19; 12:46; 16:28; 18:37; also Matt 11:3 and Mark 11:9). It may be a primitive expression, perhaps relating to the expectation of the prophet like Moses (6:14; cf. Deut 18:15), perhaps to the (synoptic) expectation of the Messiah. The woman of Samaria has spoken of a Messiah (Greek here actually *messias*) who is coming and Jesus has revealed himself to her as that one (4:25-26). Probably Martha's answer is correct as far as it goes, but does not quite touch Jesus' own fundamental eschatological role, a role that shapes and refocuses eschatology per se. Like other friends and followers of Jesus, Martha is on the right track, but cannot be said to have yet arrived. Yet until Jesus' hour has come and he has been glorified, he cannot be fully comprehended, although those who are willing can acknowledge him as the one sent by God. Martha has gone about as far as anyone can go.

Yet Martha's conversation with Jesus has been of crucial significance, for it has allowed Jesus to offer a new, altered eschatology that is christologically centered. Christology determines eschatology rather than the other way around. (Käsemann 1968, 19-21, but especially 16: "Christology determines eschatology and eschatology becomes an aspect of christology.") This is an important point in the Gospel, although as we saw, the revised eschatology was suggested earlier in the narrative. It will again become the subject of discussion in the farewell discourses (chaps. 14–16).

11:28-37: Mary's conversation does not carry quite the same theological weight as Martha's, but moves the action forward toward its culmination. Martha goes back to the house, where the Jews are still offering consolation (vv. 19, 31) and the sisters in effect exchange roles (v. 28). That Martha's understanding is still incomplete may be reflected in the fact that she calls Jesus "the Teacher." (The NRSV's caps are a modern editorial device.) Yet this is not a title that Jesus, or the evangelist, would reject (see 13:13-14).

Not surprisingly, Mary responds quickly to Jesus' call (v. 29). Jesus himself typically moves at his own pace (v. 30), so that he is still at the place where he had conversed with Martha. Mary is now accompanied by the Jews, or Judeans, who have been visiting the sisters to offer consolation (v. 31). Their action and their thoughts about what Mary was about to do add an intriguing bit of color and concreteness to the story. That Mary on meeting Jesus kneels at his feet (v. 32) is an act of veneration, if not worship, and is perhaps typical of her (12:3; cf. Luke 10:39). Her statement, lamenting Jesus' absence before Lazarus's death (v. 32b), echoes exactly what Martha has said (v. 21). Jesus sees Mary weeping (v. 33); we are to understand that she has been weeping all along (cf. v. 31). That the Jews are portrayed as also weeping is, in all probability, a means of portraying them sympathetically. Obviously they are not people who are unremittingly hostile to Jesus, and to understand them as "Judeans," residents of the area, is certainly appropriate. One should not too quickly assume that John always and everywhere portrays "the Jews" negatively. Moreover, at the end of this episode there will be the same kind of division among the Jews that we have seen more than once in this Gospel (vv. 45-46).

Jesus himself is now said to be disturbed, and a strange Greek verb *(embrimaomai)* that can mean literally "to snort," and usually conveys anger and emotional display is now used of Jesus (cf. Matt 9:30; Mark 1:43, although the verb's use is not clearly reflected in the NRSV). Jesus evidently participates in the mourning and sadness over Lazarus's death. The flat statement that Jesus wept (v. 35) would confirm this. Nothing is said about Jesus' irritation because of the Jews' unbelief, or about their forcing his hand by putting him into the position of having to perform a miracle that as a self-revelation would lead immediately to his death. The best explanation would seem to be the obvious one: Jesus shares the sadness of his friends and their neighbors. Thus the Jews' interpretation of Jesus' weeping (v. 35) is not a misunderstanding, but is rather true. Jesus loved (and loves) Lazarus. (The verb is again *phileō*.) The final statement of some (v. 37) reflects misunderstanding, but not more than the statements of Martha (v. 21) and Mary (v. 32). All assume the time has passed when Jesus could have been of help to Lazarus, but that, of course, is not the case. The time has not passed, but has only just arrived.

Although Mary's conversation does not, like Martha's, lead to a major theological point, it does bring closer the moment when Jesus himself will act, even though he so far has not moved. One could imagine that Jesus himself had arrived near Bethany not far from the tomb (cf. vv. 17, 31, 38); he never goes to his friend's house at this point, only later (12:1-2). Jesus understands the grief of Mary and the mourners, and is himself deeply touched, having loved Lazarus. When the Jews say about Jesus' weeping, "See how he loved *(phileō)* him," they utter a profound truth. Quite possibly their statement is true at two levels. They may be imagined to perceive this manifestation of love by one man for another, a love they to some extent share with his sisters. At the same time they are witnessing—perhaps they do not know it—the love of Jesus the Son of God for his disciples. Having loved his own who are in the world, he loved them to the end (13:2). What Jesus is about to do is not only a manifestation of his God-given and godlike authority and power (5:19), but also is a manifestation of his love, which is the love of God (3:16; 14:21). Love *(agapē)* is an action as well as a state of mind.

11:38-44: Jesus will now raise Lazarus to life. Each party to the discussion, Martha, Mary, and the Jews, has so far suggested that, if Jesus had arrived on the scene earlier, the death of Lazarus would have been averted. At the same time, the reader is aware why he did not: Jesus deliberately delayed his arrival, seeming to allow time for Lazarus to die. Yet Jesus had also declared, "This illness does not lead to death..." (v. 4). The tensions of the story and within the story have stretched to the breaking point.

Obviously, the disappointed expectations about what Jesus could have done are based on his reputation as a healer, a miracle worker. Readers of the synoptic Gospels will take this reputation for granted, but it is reflected also in John, whether or not the others are presupposed (John 2:23; 6:2; 11:47; 12:37; 20:30). Doubtless whatever else Jesus did or claimed to be he was a *thaumaturge,* a miracle worker, who healed the sick and cast out demons. In the synoptic Gospels his opponents do not question his extraordinary power, only its source (Matt 12:24; Mark 3:22; Luke 11:15).

As Jesus comes to the tomb (v. 38), the informed reader will scarcely doubt what he will do. The tomb is perhaps very much like the one in which Jesus himself would be buried, with a stone blocking the vertical entrance. When Jesus commands the stone to be taken away (v. 39), this is done by human beings (v. 41), not by angels or supernatural powers (Mark 15:46; 16:3-4; cf. Matt 28:2). So at this point the Lazarus story differs from the empty tomb narrative. Martha's famous protest (v. 39), "He stinketh" (KJV), simply underscores the fact that Lazarus, having been in the tomb for four days (v. 17) is really dead. Jesus' response (v. 40) refers to his previous statement to Martha, although he has not said exactly this. Yet at the beginning, Jesus has declared that the illness was for God's glory and the glorification of the Son (v. 4), and in their conversation Jesus has certainly promised Martha that belief in him will lead to life (vv. 25-26).

When the stone is rolled away, Jesus addresses God (v. 41), as his prayer actually anticipates what will happen. Then Jesus seems to reassure God—and the reader!—of his confidence in their relationship (v. 42). Actually, this statement is one of several in the Fourth Gospel that clarifies to the reader Jesus' confident knowledge (6:6) or his firm relationship to the Father (12:30). With the reader now confident of what Jesus will accomplish through the power of God, he commands Lazarus as if he were alive. Lazarus emerges still bound with grave clothes, which match those Jesus would leave in the tomb (20:6-7). It is pointless to ask how Lazarus could have walked out so bound. That Jesus commands that he be unbound and let go is strongly symbolic. By Jesus' word Lazarus is released from the bondage of death.

◊   ◊   ◊   ◊

The raising of Lazarus is an appropriate conclusion of the public ministry of Jesus. It is his culminating sign (cf. 12:18). Moreover, it symbolizes, or better, gives concrete manifestation to, the life-giving work of Jesus, who does what God has given him authority and power to do (cf. 5:19, 30). Jesus' words about the dead, or those who are in the tombs, hearing the voice of the Son of God (5:25, 28) now seem to foreshadow this spectacular event. Even some of the Jews have implied a comparison between Jesus' gift of sight to the blind man and the possibility that he might have prevented Lazarus's death (v. 37). Then, of course, Jesus overcomes Lazarus's death by raising him from the dead, an even mightier sign.

Probably the question of the historicity of the account is for most readers decided on the basis of considerations of what could or could not happen: Obviously, no one can bring the dead back; or, obviously Jesus could do precisely that. If, however, one brackets out that question, it is worth observing (with Schnackenburg) that the story's absence from the Synoptics does not necessarily militate against it in the sense of showing that it is a later composition. Aside from *Secret Mark*, there is Luke's story of the son of the widow of Nain (Luke 7:11-17), also restored to life by Jesus, which is not found in any other Gospel. Apparently such stories about Jesus circulated in early Christian circles. Whatever their specific historical basis, their credibility rested upon Jesus' broader reputation.

Even in John there is an incongruity of the story with the evangelist's theological point about Jesus as the giver of eternal life. The Johannine Jesus speaks of believers' passing from death to life, that is, even now entering into eschatological life. The raising of Lazarus symbolizes this eschatological gift, but only imperfectly. Lazarus seems to resume ordinary day-to-day life. He eats (12:2), as the risen Jesus does in Luke (24:42-43), but apparently not in John (cf. 21:9-14). He is subject to death, or at least the opponents of Jesus assume so as they plot to kill him (12:10), "since it was on account of him that many of the Jews were deserting and were believing in Jesus" (v. 11). Lazarus is a type of Christian preacher who leads other Jews to believe in Jesus. The NRSV's "desert" (cf. the RSV's more literal "going away") implies leaving the Jewish community, that is, the synagogue (see Martyn 1979, 66, 94, who relates this statement to the world's going after Jesus in 12:19). As such a witness to Jesus, Lazarus is a person who has received life from him. John has taken a tradition of Jesus' raising a dead man and used it symbolically to dramatize Jesus' work, and its results. There are people given life by Jesus who are instrumental in bringing others to him. According to John's tradition this man, perhaps somewhat inconveniently for his symbolic value, hangs around, eating and drinking at his sisters' house, and is perhaps finally done to death by "the Jews" (cf. 12:10-11). Yet his story gives the most concrete and memorable expression to Jesus' life-giving work.

Judgment Against Jesus (11:45-54)

The story now takes a decidedly ominous turn. Jesus gives life to Lazarus, but the reaction to him is mixed (vv. 45-46), as it so often is (cf. 7:40-44). The authorities, the chief priests and Pharisees, will now call a council and plot to put him out of the way. John's account of the plotting of the priests corresponds to the brief notice in the synoptic Gospels (Mark 14:1-2 par.), but it is much longer and more detailed. (Its position, immediately prior to Jesus' anointing in Bethany, is in that respect the same as in Mark.) In John, Caiaphas takes the leading role in the proceedings. In Matthew and Mark the high priest Caiaphas (named only in Matthew) plays such a role when Jesus himself is arrested and brought before the council (Matt 26:57-68; Mark 14:53-65). No such formal trial, with a culminating death sentence, is found at the same point in John. Yet John will here depict the council pronouncing such a sentence on Jesus in absentia, before he is arrested.

◊ ◊ ◊ ◊

The positive reaction of the Jews (or Judeans) who have seen Jesus' deed is matched by others who report Jesus to the Pharisees (vv. 45-46; cf. 5:15). Immediately the chief priests also appear (v. 47) and the council (Gk. *synedrion* = Sanhedrin) is called together. Quite possibly the chief priests represent the Jerusalem opponents of the historical Jesus, who played a role in doing him in, while the Pharisees are principally the opponents of Jesus' followers in the Johannine community, although their opposition to Jesus himself cannot be excluded. (Bammel 1970, 21, observes that as scribes Pharisees would have been present in such a council.) Thus we see here a hint of John's two levels (Martyn 1979): Jesus and the Johannine community.

The problem before the council is stated in a quite Johannine form: Jesus does so many signs (v. 47). That the Messiah would do signs in the sense of miracles was not a part of traditional (Davidic) messianic expectation; thus the statement looks distinctly Johannine but scarcely historical. Yet as Moses had performed signs before Pharaoh, so the Mosaic Prophet-Messiah might be expected to perform signs (Martyn 1979, 111; cf. Gray 1993, 112-44). Thus the complaint about Jesus' many signs relates not to the uniquely Johannine portrait of Jesus but also to the Jewish expectation to which that portrait answers.

The latter expectation affords basis for the fear of Roman intervention, which would scarcely be aroused by a charismatic healer of no political significance (v. 48). The fear of the intervention of the Romans to destroy the temple and the nation raises important questions about the time and circumstances in which the Gospel was written, as well as that of Jesus. ("holy place" aptly translates the Greek "the place," which in Jewish usage referred to the temple, as in 4:20; Acts 6:14; 21:28; 2 Macc 5:19.) Does this fear reflect knowledge, after the fact, of what the Romans were to do in the war that culminated in the destruction of the city and its temple? That the highest Jewish authorities are represented as fearing this outcome suggests that the statement was written in the knowledge of what transpired a generation or so after Jesus' death. Of course, Jesus was put out of the way, and the Romans intervened anyhow. Ironically, the dreaded outcome came upon them despite the drastic measures taken against Jesus.

The high priest Caiaphas now appears for the first time in this Gospel (v. 49). Caiaphas is specifically named as the high priest at the time of Jesus' execution only in John and Matthew (26:3, 57). He is called "high priest that year" (as he is again in 18:13), although the high priesthood was not an annual office. (Appointment was for life, but under foreign domination there were sometimes frequent changes.) "That year" probably means the year of Jesus' death. Caiaphas, who held the office for nineteen years (c. 18–36) was, in fact, the high priest at the time of Jesus (see Josephus *Ant.* 18.35, 95). (See the helpful table of high priests in the NT period in O'Day 1995, 807.) Caiaphas's advice (vv. 49-51), beginning with a none too positive assessment of his colleagues, speaks to the fear of Roman intervention. (O'Day 1995, 697, cites Josephus *J.W.* 2.166, to the effect that such rudeness was not uncharacteristic of discussion in the council.) His statement, in which he advocates the expedient course for the sake of the survival of the people and nation, is politically understandable and certainly, from his perspective, correct.

Whether this scene conveys something about the political situation and dynamics of the time of Jesus himself is a good question (see Bammel 1970, 11-40). Obviously, the evangelist has composed it, and he scarcely had recourse to a protocol of what happened on this occasion, assuming such a hearing actually took place. But whether such a meeting actually occurred does not decide the more basic historical question about the forces at work in the execution of Jesus. Yet an actual meeting of the Sanhedrin at this juncture, before the feast has begun, is actually more plausible historically than the Sanhedrin meeting on Passover eve depicted in Mark (14:55-65) but omitted by Luke.

Although John's portrayal of the scene can scarcely be taken as a verbatim account of the proceedings, it obviously sets some store on the high priest's actually having made this prophecy (v. 51) and on its being true, albeit in a sense far different than he intended. (On Caiaphas's prophecy and the whole scene, see Dodd 1963, 24.) At the least John supplies a plausible motivation for the chief priests' having decided that Jesus should be put out of the way. He represented a danger to the status quo, to whatever unofficial concordat existed between them and Roman authority. Thus to the Jewish authorities John ascribes a motive that is not dishonorable or malicious; at worst it may be prudential and self-serving. It is noteworthy that the decisive word is given by Caiaphas, as representative of the chief priests (and therefore of the Sadducees) and not by the Pharisees, who are mentioned at the beginning of the scene. Here again, if John does not intend to write history, what he presents accords with the likely historical situation at the time of Jesus. It was the chief priests, not the Pharisees, who played a leading role in doing Jesus in (Sanders 1993, 265-73).

Obviously "the nation" (v. 50) means the Jewish nation. The NRSV's "dispersed children of God" (v. 52) represents the more literal "children of God who are scattered abroad" (RSV). If John alludes to converts from among Jews of the Diaspora or Dispersion, as contrasted with the nation in Palestine, the NRSV's translation conveys this meaning best, although it is not limited to it. Two themes or emphases of Johannine thought are here suggested. First, John holds that all who believe, of whatever origin, become children of God by faith; they are born of God (1:12-13). In the prologue and here, virtually the same phrase for children of God *(tekna theou)* is found. Second, John emphasizes the importance of the gathering and unity of and among believers, that is, the community or church of Jesus' followers (10:16; 17:20, 22). The idea of gathering the scattered people of God is a biblical one, and is picked up from Scripture by the New Testament and early Christian writers. (On the gathering of Israel: Isa 43:5-7; Jer 23:1-4; Ezek 37:21-22; on the gathering of the Gentiles: Isa 56:6; Zech 14:16-17; in the New Testament aside from John: Jas 1:1; 1 Pet 1:1; cf. also Eph 2:11-18.) Both themes are found here. In conclusion, the authorities decide to have Jesus put to death (v. 53; cf. Mark 14:1). One reads the remainder of the narrative with this knowledge firmly in mind. Of course, the decision only confirms a disposition on the part of the authorities that has been evident and building through the narrative of Jesus' public ministry (5:18; 7:32, 45; 8:59; 10:31, 39).

Jesus' withdrawal (v. 54) is again noted (cf. 10:40-42). In some contrast to 10:40-42, the city and region to which Jesus here withdraws can be located. Ephraim was only a dozen or so miles north of Jerusalem. That this is "near the wilderness" corresponds somewhat with the earlier retreat across the Jordan to where John had been baptizing (10:40). Jesus is there with his disciples, presumably preparing to return to Jerusalem for Passover. But they do not go just yet. The scene shifts to Jerusalem as we read about the people's purification (cf. Num 9:1-14) for Passover (11:55), the question about Jesus' attendance (v. 56), and the order given by the authorities (v. 57). This is now the third Passover mentioned in John (cf. 2:13; 6:4), whose festival calendar and itinerary of Jesus differ from the synoptic Gospels, where only the final Passover is mentioned (except for Luke 2:41-42, where the family of Jesus takes him with them to Passover when he is twelve).

The Passover pilgrims both look for Jesus and doubt that under the circumstances (cf. v. 57) he will show up, as their anticipation heightens the tension of the narrative (v. 56). Again it is the chief priests and Pharisees who are in league against Jesus (v. 57; cf. v. 47; 7:32). The narrative preparation for Jesus' entry into Jerusalem seems complete, but there will be yet another interlude before the entry into the city actually takes place (12:1-11).

The Conclusion of Jesus' Public Ministry (12:1-50)

Chapter 12 marks the end of Jesus' public ministry. At the outset he is anointed in anticipation of his death, and then enters Jerusalem triumphantly. At the end he issues a proclamation that summarizes his message. There then follows the distinctly separate scene of the Last Supper in chapter 13. The beginning of this chapter also signals a separate scene; there is an indication of time and a change of place as Jesus comes to Bethany six days before Passover. The anointing and Jesus' entry into Jerusalem have clear parallels in the synoptic Gospels. Otherwise, although one is reminded occasionally of an incident or motif that appears elsewhere, there are no entire narratives parallel to the Synoptics.

There is, however, quite clearly a progression in the narrative as a conversation develops in which the theme of Jesus' approaching death becomes prominent (vv. 20-36a). Then, as the public ministry concludes, it is pronounced an apparent failure, but this "failure" is then explained as in actuality the fulfillment of Scripture (the prophet Isaiah) as well as the revelation of human faithlessness (12:36-43). Finally, Jesus ends his public ministry with a declaration about himself and his mission that in effect brings it to an end. The conclusion of chapter 12 thus becomes the major watershed of this Gospel.

Mary Anoints Jesus (12:1-8)

Jesus now comes again to Bethany six days before Passover (12:1). John does not enumerate the days before Passover, but given the Johannine placing of Passover on Friday evening/Saturday (see below on 13:1), this supper would presumably fall on Saturday evening, at the end of the sabbath (the next day being reckoned as beginning on Saturday evening). The meal would not itself occur on a sabbath (see Barrett 1978, 411). "The next day" (12:12) would then be Palm Sunday, although no day of the week is given either in John or in the other Gospels, and despite the fact that by Jewish reckoning it would still be the same day. (O'Day 1995, 704-5, has an excellent chart of the Passion and Resurrection Narratives in the canonical Gospels.)

Lazarus is now identified by what Jesus has done for him. Lazarus and his sisters are the hosts of the dinner (v. 2). (Martha's serving corresponds with her role in Luke 10:40.) Obviously, Lazarus has once again taken up the normal functions of life. Mary now performs the central, pivotal act (v. 3).

Mary's deed (v. 4) bears similarities to the other narratives in which Jesus is anointed, but has its own distinctive character. In Matthew (26:6-13) and Mark (14:3-9) an unnamed woman anoints Jesus' head rather than his feet as he sits at table; this happened also in Bethany but in the house of Simon the leper. In Luke (7:36-50), while Jesus is still in Galilee, an unnamed woman anoints his feet, presumably with ointment or perfume (10:37), which is mixed with her tears as she wipes Jesus' feet with her own hair. This takes place in the house of a Pharisee, whose name turns out to be Simon (7:40).

Except for the fact that Jesus' head rather than his feet is anointed, the Markan and Matthean accounts are much closer in content and wording to John's than is Luke's. Although also set in Bethany during the period of Jesus' Passion, the Markan and Matthean accounts differ from John's in that they follow rather than precede the triumphant entry into Jerusalem. In all three cases there is a protest at the expenditure of costly perfume, which could have been sold, with the proceeds given to the poor (12:5; Mark 14:4-5; Matt 26:8-9). (If one denarius was a day's wages for a laborer, three hundred would have approximated his yearly income.) In the Synoptics the protesters are, however, unnamed, while in John the unfaithful Judas assumes that role. In all accounts the Bethany anointing somehow prefigures Jesus' own death, as he himself says in defending the woman's action (12:7-8; Mark 14:5-8; Matt 26:10-12). Only Matthew and Mark, however, conclude the episode with Jesus' saying the woman's deed will be told wherever the gospel is preached in memory of her (Mark 14:9; Matt 26:13). Curiously, she remains anonymous in the Synoptics while John, who lacks this nice rounding of the story, identifies her so she could be remembered (v. 3). But the description of the perfume used to anoint Jesus—stranger in the original Greek than in the NRSV translation—is quite close to what is found in Mark (14:3), suggesting that John took it from Mark or from a similar source.

Yet if John had Mark before him as he wrote, the reasons for his changes are not obvious. On the one hand, Jesus' statement about the poor (v. 8) is similar to Mark's, although without Mark's implied exhortation to do good to them (14:7). On the other, John's statement about Mary's keeping it (presumably the perfume) for the day of his burial is much less clear than the NRSV's rendering, where a note indicates that the phrase "she bought it" is actually an interpretative addition to the text, apparently to soften the harsh contradiction of the original, which reads, "Let her alone, let her keep it for the day of my burial"

(RSV). How could she keep it when she has just poured it out? Mark says simply that she has anointed Jesus beforehand for burial, which makes perfectly good sense. It is not evident why John should have made such a change in Mark. Such differing details of the narrative are not improvements on Mark, but if anything the opposite (see Coakley 1988).

The Plot to Kill Lazarus (12:9-11)

Lazarus, as well as Jesus, attracts the attention of large numbers of Jewish people (v. 9). Thus the chief priests plan to put Lazarus to death as well as Jesus (v. 10; cf. 11:53). Lazarus has become, in effect, a witness to Jesus (see above, p. 228). This apparently means that as one to whom Jesus gives life Lazarus then leads fellow Jews to belief in Jesus. "Deserting" (literally, "going away") implies they are leaving the synagogue and going over to the now separate communities of Jesus' disciples (see Martyn 1979, 66, 94). The plot against Lazarus is then a concrete example of what Jesus will say to his followers about their misguided opponents who will try to kill them, thinking that thereby they are performing service to God (16:2).

Jesus' Triumphant Entry into Jerusalem (12:12-19)

The account of Jesus' entry into Jerusalem is found in all canonical Gospels (Matt 21:1-9; Mark 11:1-10; Luke 19:28-38). In John, of course, this is the third time Jesus has gone to Jerusalem (cf. 2:13; 7:10), although previously there has been no fanfare. John's narrative of this final entry is quite similar to the synoptic accounts, in which it is Jesus' single climactic entry into Jerusalem at the conclusion of his ministry. In each of the Synoptics there is a story of Jesus' dispatching disciples into a nearby village to procure his mount for the entry. How Jesus knows the animal will be there is never explained. This is the kind of supernatural, or at least mysterious, knowledge that one would expect Jesus to display in John, but surprisingly the story is not found here.

John's account squares with his portrayal of the Jerusalem

crowd's expecting Jesus (11:56-57). Thus a "great crowd," the festival crowd, goes out to meet Jesus, whereas in the Synoptics, the crowd seems to be approaching the city with Jesus. The account of the entry itself (vv. 13-15) is quite similar to what is found in the Synoptics (Matt 21:1-10; Mark 11:7-10; Luke 19:28-40) except that in John the crowd's acclamation (John 12:13) precedes rather than follows the description of Jesus sitting upon the animal. In John too the crowd's shout takes up Ps 118:25-26. "Hosanna" simply transliterates the Hebrew word meaning "to save." Like Matthew (21:4-5), John explicitly cites the apposite Zechariah text (v. 15; Zech 9:9) to which the whole episode seems to be related. Whether the prophetic text inspired the narrative or the event was later seen to match the text is a good question, which John actually seems to have thought of (v. 16), as he states that only after Jesus was glorified (i.e., crucified and risen) did the disciples "remember" the event and the prophetic text. Although Zech 9:9 is the dominant text, "Do not be afraid" seems to be influenced by Isa 35:4 and 40:9, where a similar phrase appears (also Zeph 3:14-20, especially vv. 14, 16). (Interestingly, the influence of the latter texts is missing from Matthew's version, where Isa 62:11 comes into play.)

Again, as in the case of the anointing of Jesus, there are problems in understanding the Johannine version simply as a redaction of the synoptic, or even the Matthean. But certainly John at least draws upon a parallel and similar tradition (see D. Moody Smith 1984, 97-105; originally *JBL* 82 (1965): 58-64). What may be seen as a characteristic Johannine redaction, however, is the disciples' later recollection and understanding of the event (v. 16). Something very similar is said about the temple cleansing (2:17, 22). This postresurrection knowledge involves more than the advantage of retrospection; it is made possible by the gift of the Spirit (14:26; cf. 7:39). John more than any other Gospel makes clear the fact that the disciples' full and true knowledge of Jesus only became possible after his physical departure from them. The messianic secret (cf. Mark) was until then a necessity, which the disciples *could not* overcome. As is often the case, what is implicit in Mark, and the Synoptics generally, is made explicit in John.

We have observed that in John there is a crowd in Jerusalem already (11:55-57) that goes out to meet Jesus (12:12-13). Now, not surprisingly, we learn that they went out to meet him because of the sign he performed on Lazarus (v. 18). Yet there is also a crowd from Bethany that had witnessed the raising (cf. v. 9). (The RSV's "bore witness" is preferable to the NRSV's "testify"; the latter does not quite do justice to the crowd's having both seen and spoken, which is implicit in the concept of witnessing.) On John's terms there would then be two crowds rather than one as in the Synoptics. If one presupposes John's knowledge of the Synoptics or their tradition, basis for the accompanying crowd from Bethany might be found there. It is the Jerusalem crowd that is distinctive of John.

It is interesting that the Pharisees now appear to utter an evaluation of the situation that is typically cynical, but nevertheless entirely true (v. 19). The element of cynicism among Jesus' adversaries is noteworthy and typical of John (cf. 11:50; 18:38). Their comment here recalls Luke 19:39-40, where the Pharisees admonish Jesus to rebuke his demonstrative disciples and he replies that if they were silent, the stones would cry out. John's account, in which we find not one crowd but two—they are coming out of Jerusalem to meet Jesus as well as going in with him—affords an appropriate backdrop and motivation for the Pharisees' commentary. The Pharisees were last heard from when they (with the chief priests) gave the order that anyone who knew Jesus' whereabouts should report the same in order that they might arrest him (11:57). As it now turns out, everyone knows Jesus' whereabouts and for the moment the Pharisees can do nothing about it, but their opportunity will come (18:3).

The Coming of the Greeks and of Jesus' Hour (12:20-36a)

Although it remains a matter of uncertainty among interpreters, "Greeks" attending Passover would presumably be Greek-speaking Jews. Yet the word used, *Hēllenes*, simply means "Greeks." (It is the same word used of Greeks in 7:35.) Possibly John has used this word here and in 7:35 because he wants to suggest the coming worldwide mission (cf. 10:16; 12:32; 17:20). If John meant Greek-speaking Jews, something similar may be seen in the Pentecost scene of Acts 2:5-13, where people of different origins and languages are nevertheless called "Jews" (2:5). Certainly they prefigure the worldwide mission, although they are not called Greeks. That these Greeks approach Jesus through Philip, from Bethsaida (cf. 1:44), who then approaches Andrew, is not surprising, since the two bear Greek names. (Only in John, 1:40-45 and 6:7-9, do Andrew and Philip appear together.)

When these disciples speak to Jesus, presumably telling him of the approach of the Greeks, Jesus immediately says that the hour of his glorification has come (v. 23), something that has not been said to this point. From the beginning of the narrative of Jesus' public ministry the reader has learned of the approach of this hour (2:4; 4:23), of Jesus' coming glorification (7:39). Now it is here. Yet it is as if time will now be put on hold as the final events of Jesus' ministry are played out (cf. 12:27-28; 17:4-5). Jesus' disciples have beheld his glory (1:14), but do not fully appreciate what they have seen until he has been glorified, lifted up (3:14-15). As for the Greeks, what becomes of them or whether they ever see Jesus, we do not learn. They have introduced a crucial turn of events and now simply disappear from the scene.

The sayings of Jesus immediately following obviously draw on early Christian tradition. The commonsense, natural analogy of the grain of wheat (v. 24) was used by Paul, also of the Resurrection (1 Cor 15:36). The saying about loving one's life and losing it (v. 25) has more than one synoptic counterpart. Mark has it in 8:35 (followed by Matt 16:25; Luke 9:24), but it occurs again in Matt 10:39 and Luke 17:33, presumably a Q-source parallel. The subsequent saying (12:26) about serving and following Jesus is perhaps a subtle Johannine parallel to the saying about taking up one's cross and following Jesus (Matt 16:24; Mark 8:34; Luke 9:23). The cross-bearing saying in turn also has a Q parallel (Matt 10:38; Luke 14:27; in Matthew it is paired with the other saying, as in Mark; in Luke it is not). We are here dealing with a saying of Jesus that has multiple attestations; that is, it appears in three streams of tradition: Mark, John, and Q. This is in itself some indication of how important it was deemed to be as a key to Jesus' teaching. The saying about cross bearing is clearly found with it in Mark and Matthean Q, although not in Lukan Q and not in such explicit form in John. When we see the parallels in the Synoptics, the Johannine form of the same saying is easily recognizable as such. It could have been derived from the Synoptics. Yet, like every other Johannine saying with a synoptic parallel that is not demanded by its immediate context (e.g., "One of you will betray me" can only occur in the prediction of Jesus' betrayal), it is differently situated in the Gospel narrative. On the whole we seem to be dealing with common tradition, also found in Q, rather than with John's use of other canonical Gospels.

We next come upon a saying that is paralleled in other Gospel narratives rather than sayings (v. 27), namely, the Gethsemane story, which portrays Jesus in anguish (Matt 26:36-46; Mark 14:34-42; Luke 22:39-46; cf. Heb 5:7-10, which like this Johannine saying, seems to have the Gethsemane experience of Jesus in view). Possibly John and Hebrews knew a tradition about Jesus' agony without knowing the story as we find it in the Synoptics. As quickly as Jesus is troubled and asks how he should pray (cf. Mark 14:36), he answers himself in Johannine terms, praying the Father to glorify his name (v. 28a), and perceives an immediate response (v. 28b). The past and future glorifications probably refer, respectively, to the earthly ministry and to his coming death and resurrection respectively.

The crowd's estimate of what has happened, or what they have heard, typifies their obtuseness or their inability to comprehend. It also nicely illustrates John's appreciation of the ambiguity of historical revelation. It is not just a matter of seeing signs (or hearing sounds) but of being able to apprehend what is really going on. God may thunder from heaven (1 Sam 2:10; 7:10), but there is little indication the crowd has understood this. That an angel has spoken to Jesus is not, so to speak, right on target, but neither is it altogether wrong. Somewhat curiously, Jesus' initial response could be taken to mean God's effort to communicate with the crowd has failed, inasmuch as God spoke for their benefit and not for Jesus' (v. 30). But what Jesus says accords with what we have heard all along, namely, that Jesus is in such close union with the Father at all times that he needs no special communication from God (cf. 11:41-42).

Jesus' pronouncement (vv. 31-32) marks the conclusion of his public ministry and is a kind of Passion prediction (cf. 3:14-15). In his death the judgment of this world occurs already. (Cf. Luke 10:18: "I watched Satan fall from heaven like a flash of lightning.") Jesus has already spoken of the condemnation (literally "judgment") of those who do not believe (3:18-19). The culmination of Jesus' coming is his death, which is the judgment of this world. Yet that culmination is already prefigured in the public ministry so that John can say that judgment comes with Jesus throughout his ministry. As Jesus' coming is judgment for the world, for unbelief, so it is salvation to all who believe (v. 32). Jesus speaks of his death by crucifixion as being lifted up (as the aside of v. 33 makes clear). Already he has used this word (Gk. *hyposoō*) of his crucifixion, but in an esoteric or enigmatic way (3:14; 8:28). Now the narrator explains, at least to the reader, that Jesus is alluding to his crucifixion.

The crowd's response (v. 34) would seem to indicate that they now actually understand what is meant by being lifted up, for they contrast that with remaining forever. Where the law says the Messiah will abide forever is a good question. One thinks of Pss 89:29-37; 110:4; or Isa 9:6, all of which refer more to the Davidic line than to the Messiah per se. Later sources may, however, imply the Messiah will endure forever, for example, *1 Enoch* 49:1; 62:14; *Pss. Sol.* 17:4 (see Barrett 1978, 427). In any event, that theme is less prominent in Judaism than their statement would suggest. The contrast between the Messiah's abiding forever and the Son of Man's being lifted up is very sharp indeed. In fact, what the crowd may be noting is the sharp contrast between traditional messianic expectation and the fate of Jesus the crucified, whom his followers claim to be the Messiah. According to the logic of the narrative, the crowd understands that Jesus is speaking of himself (cf. v. 32), as he clearly is, so that when they then refer to the lifting up of the Son of Man they equate Jesus with that figure (v. 34). Their question about the Son of Man cannot therefore be a question about his identity—they know he is Jesus—but about the meaning of the mysterious title and Jesus' own role. How can Jesus, who claims to be Messiah, speak of himself as being lifted up, that is, taken away by death? Significantly, in the synoptic Passion predictions, it is always the Son of Man who will suffer (Mark 8:31; 9:31; 10:33 par.). Perhaps John's presentation here reflects knowledge of that tradition of Passion prediction, if not of Mark itself.

Jesus now makes a concluding exhortation (vv. 35-36), which should not surprise the reader in view of what he has said earlier (cf. 9:4-5; 11:9-10). Again, in light of John's understanding of the total scope or extent of the life and work of Jesus Christ, it is inconceivable that this should mean that after Jesus' death the light and life that he brings will vanish. Rather, this statement to the crowd is Jesus' final exhortation to the Jewish, or Jerusalem, public. Thus it corresponds with 1:11: "He came to . . . his own, and his own . . . did not accept him." Although their final questions mirror their puzzlement and perplexity, Jesus knows that the decisive word will be rejection. The phrase "children of light" (literally, "sons of light") occurs in Luke 16:8 and 1 Thess 5:5 (cf. Eph 5:8) and is also a title for the faithful members of the community in the Dead Sea Scrolls (e.g., 1QS1:10), where in the War Rule it has particular prominence (e.g., 1QM1:1).

Jesus' Ministry Ends with Apparent Unbelief (12:36b-43)

Again Jesus withdraws (cf. 10:40; 11:54). This time it is final, as Jesus hides himself "from them" (cf. 8:59). The antecedent would have to be the crowd, with which Jesus has just been speaking. The statement about Jesus' withdrawal (v. 36b) could be taken as the conclusion of the preceding paragraph, as it is in the Aland critical text (1993). Yet the NRSV (following the RSV) makes the statement the beginning of this paragraph; it then appropriately introduces the largely negative result of Jesus' ministry (v. 37). Although Jesus' enemies in John are called "the Jews" characteristically, here one is left to assume that not just the Jewish authorities, who are usually denoted by the term, are meant, but the Jewish people generally (cf. Rom 9:1-5, where Paul seems to assume that most Jews have not believed the message that Jesus is the Messiah).

The characterization of Jesus' ministry as "signs," when much of it has been his own discourse, has suggested to some interpreters that this statement once concluded a collection of miracle stories that have been incorporated into the Gospel (Bultmann 1971, 113, 452; cf. Fortna 1988, 137-39). Possibly 20:31, which can be read as summarizing Jesus' ministry in terms of signs, once belonged to this source as well. If the Gospel of John as we possess it developed on the basis of an early collection of Jesus' miracles and a primitive narration of his trial and death, we may also see in this paragraph the nexus between them (D. Moody Smith 1984, 80-93, particularly 90-93; originally *JBL* (1976): 231-41).

The Scripture testimonies (vv. 38, 40) from Isaiah are interesting in this connection. For one thing, the second citation (v. 40; Isa 6:10) omits Isaiah's reference to ears and hearing, which would have been quite appropriate to this point in the Gospel, in which Jesus has said a great deal. On the other hand, the omission, and reference to eyes and seeing (as well as the heart) makes sense as the conclusion of a collection of signs, particularly if seeing the signs was intended to lead to faith. (Admittedly, readers would hear, or read about, the signs as well; nevertheless seeing is appropriate to Jesus' signs as hearing is to his words.)

These Isaiah quotations are pivotal in the structure of the Gospel. As Jesus has just announced the impending end of his ministry (vv. 35, 36), now with the help of Isaiah, he interprets its seeming failure. Both Isaiah quotations appear elsewhere in the New Testament, and are used for a similar purpose, to explain unbelief or the rejection of Jesus' messianic claims, particularly by his own people. Isaiah 53:1 (cited in v. 38) is used by Paul in Romans (10:16), where it is applied to those who have not believed the preaching of the Gospel. Isaiah 6:10 (or 6:9-10) is used in Mark 4:11-12 of the hearers' inability to comprehend Jesus' parables (cf. Mark 8:17). In Acts 28:26-27 it is used of unbelief among Jews, and it is alluded to in Rom 11:8 for somewhat the same purpose. These citations of Isaiah at this turning point of the Gospel do not stand alone. In John 6:45 Jesus clearly cites Isa 54:13. John 12:15 probably combines Isa 35:4 (cf. 40:9) with Zech 9:9. John 16:22 reflects the Septuagint of Isa 66:14. Other statements in John may echo Isaiah (e.g., John 8:12 and Isa 60:1, 3).

Arguably the theological conception that Jesus is the revelation of God's glory, which we have seen throughout this Gospel, is based upon the book of Isaiah. As John here says, "Isaiah said this because he saw his glory and spoke of him" (v. 41 RSV). The theme of God's glory is one that holds together the three major parts of the book of Isaiah (chaps. 1–39, 40–59, 60–66). Perhaps most characteristic of the book are the opening statements of Second and Third Isaiah. In 40:5 we read, "And the glory of the LORD shall be revealed, and all flesh shall see it together, for the mouth of the LORD has spoken" (RSV). Or in 60:1: "Arise, shine; for your light has come, and the glory of the LORD has risen upon you" (RSV). Twice in Second Isaiah the Lord declares that he will not give his glory to another (42:8; 48:11). Although this might seem to conflict with the Johannine revelation of the glory of God in Jesus, actually it does not. Precisely *God's* glory is revealed through Jesus as his oneness with God is made manifest. (On John's use of Isaiah, see Young 1955.)

The exact, textual source of John's use of Isaiah is a difficult, technical matter. His second, longer quotation of 6:10 replicates neither the Hebrew nor the Septuagint, although it is perhaps closer to the Hebrew. The quotation of Isa 53:1 is word for word like the Septuagint, which, however, seems to be a pretty literal rendering of the Hebrew. The fact that John has "Lord" at the beginning, which is found in the Septuagint and not in the Hebrew, is an indication that it is John's source. (Of course, the Septuagint could represent a different, underlying Hebrew textual tradition.)

That Isaiah actually saw the glory *(doxa)* of Jesus (v. 41) is an astounding assertion, but perhaps no more so than that Abraham would rejoice to see Jesus' day (8:56). This seems clearly a reference not to the text explicitly cited, but to its larger context, that is, the vision of Isa 6:1-10 in which Isaiah sees the Lord (6:1, 5) and hears that the whole earth is full of his glory (v. 3). Isaiah, in fact, forms a kind of exception to the Johannine, and general Jewish, maxim that no one has seen God (1:18; 1 John 4:20). John apparently interprets this theophany to be a vision or revelation of the preexistent Christ, rather than of the Father per se. This statement of the evangelist is all the more interesting and significant because it would seem to indicate that John not only cites Scripture as prooftext, but understands and appreciates its context.

"Nevertheless" (v. 42) refers not to the immediately preceding statement, but to the whole situation just described, namely, that his people did not believe in him. Yet many of the authorities did believe. The word used here, *archōn,* is exactly the one used of Nicodemus (3:1; translated there "leader"). As the parents of the man born blind fear the Jews and their threat to cast people out of the synagogue who confess Jesus, so the authorities here fear the Pharisees. Obviously for John, "the Jews" and Pharisees are closely allied, if not the same. This text, with 9:22 (q.v.) and 16:2, strongly suggests that the threat of being expelled from the synagogue functioned as a deterrent to confessing Jesus. Such a threat, directed against those who might confess Jesus as Messiah or Christ, fits a postwar setting of Judaism and early Christianity better than the time of Jesus himself (see above, pp. 194-96). It is tempting to see Nicodemus himself as one of these leaders who believes but does not confess. Although it is never explicitly said that he believed, he defends Jesus against his detractors (7:50-51), and his participation in Jesus' burial (19:39) might be construed as a confession. Nicodemus does not quite fit in either respect. Yet his presence or role has already suggested that there were synagogue leaders who were sympathetic to Jesus. Because of their sympathies their own good standing might be jeopardized.

John has accounted for unbelief as the fulfillment of Scripture, and therefore in a sense foreordained. But those who do not believe are not guiltless (cf. 3:18-21). By the same token those who believe but do not confess show that they are still under the power of sin, loving "human glory more than the glory that comes from God" (v. 43). The RSV translated this verse "the praise of men more than the praise of God." Another possible rendering would be "human opinion more than the glory (praise or opinion) of God." Obviously John here plays to advantage upon the several meanings of *doxa*. In 8:31-38 Jesus has argued with "Jews who had believed in him" about whether they were free apart from his work, and they have taken the position that they were (v. 33). The issue here is different, but one wonders whether these two groups are related, if not the same.

Summary of Jesus' Message (12:44-50)

Although the issue of Jesus' public ministry has now been decided, he makes one final public proclamation or appeal (v. 44). That he "cried aloud" indicates the public nature of Jesus' discourse. (The same Greek verb, *krazō*, is used in the Baptist's proclamation in 1:15 and of Jesus in 7:28 and 37.) What Jesus now says aptly summarizes his message all along. Perhaps it is only a question of whom Jesus is now addressing. It is conceivable that his contemporaries, either those who have rejected him or those who have believed but not confessed, are given one more chance. More likely, however, this summary statement looks more to the future (17:20) than to the past. We have then a standard form of the Johannine proclamation of Jesus as the Christ and what his advent may mean to those who confront him.

The opening assertion about Jesus' relationship to the Father (vv. 44-45) is typical of what Jesus has said all along (cf. 5:19, 30; 10:30; 14:8-11; 17:4, 7-8). Jesus says or does nothing other than what the Father has given him to say or do. His speaking or acting is his obedient response to what the Father has commanded. Thus his oneness with God, his perfectly manifesting God, follows from his obedient response to what God has commanded him (vv. 49-50). Commentators are understandably hesitant to use obedience as the fundamental quality of the Johannine Jesus' relationship to God because of John's exalted Christology. Yet this tension between Jesus' unique status and his unique obedience is fundamental to John's Christology, particularly to its paradoxical character. It is true that John does not speak of Jesus' obeying the Father, but at a crucial point of the Gospel narrative he says Jesus does as the Father has commanded him (14:31). That would seem to be a definition of obedience.

That Jesus is the light of the world (v. 46) takes up a fundamental theme and metaphor of the Gospel (cf. 1:5; 3:19-21; 8:12; 9:5; 11:9-10). Whether one remains in darkness seems to be up to the individual's decision. Echoing the concluding words of the Nicodemus discourse, Jesus once again affirms that the purpose of his coming is not to judge the world but to save it (v. 47; cf. 3:17). Of course, Jesus can also say that he has come for judgment (9:39; cf. 5:27), but such statements should be viewed more as expressing result than purpose. When the Son comes to save, or give life, and is rejected, the judgment or condemnation of those who reject him is inevitable. Such paradoxical statements are similar to statements of Jesus that affirm the possibility of a meaningful decision of faith, which in turn stand alongside statements that express a predestinarian view. There is a seeming contradiction, and one has to decide what is more fundamental in the evangelist's purpose (see Keck 1996, 274-88).

Rejection brings judgment (v. 48) and by virtue of the very word that was intended to save. The initial clause of verse 47 prepares the way for this statement about judgment by the word. The reference to the last day may seem discordant in view of John's earlier assertions that both life and judgment are already present with Jesus' coming (3:18-21; 5:24; see Bultmann 1971, 219, 345, n. 6; cf. Schnackenburg 1980, 423-24, who tends to agree with Bultmann as to the redactional character of the phrase, but does not think it contradicts the evangelist's thinking). Judgment takes place now, but it will also find eschatological confirmation ("on the last day").

Jesus then concludes his final public oration by once again asserting his absolute obedience to God (vv. 49-50). If Jesus brings the commandment of God, which is eternal life, and in obedience delivers that commandment, he in effect becomes God for us. That is his claim, and its paradoxical nature makes it all the more offensive to those disposed to reject him. One might call his Christology *subordinationist*. Exegetes shy away from the term, perhaps because it evokes an ancient Christian heresy. Yet it is quite appropriate to the Gospel of John, or at least to one pole of its Christology. The other pole is, of course, the preexistent, exalted nature of Jesus Christ. Both poles are neatly captured in John's talk about the lifting up of the Son of Man (3:14-15; 12:32, 34). Precisely the lifting up of Jesus is both his crucifixion and his exaltation; there is a nice but real polarity. It is easy to overlook this polarity because of John's seemingly extravagant and even excessive statements about the role and dignity of Jesus, but it is necessary always to bear in mind that this is but one aspect of John's Christology. The exaltation aspect ("Christology from above") can scarcely be missed, particularly when John is read alongside the Synoptics. Therefore it is easy to give the other pole ("Christology from below") short shrift. Yet it is equally important, and John's Christology cannot be adequately understood without it. So, quite appropriately, Jesus' concluding statement emphasizes both.

The conclusion of Jesus' public ministry is thus clearly marked. The Johannine account of Jesus' ministry is shot through with this bipolar Christology, which becomes the theme of Jesus' works and words. There is a sense in which the end, as it is now described, is known from the beginning. What happens is a playing out of the inevitable: "He came to his own home, and his own people did not accept him" (1:11). Yet the ministry of Jesus did happen, and its having happened is of fundamental significance: "And the Word became flesh and lived (or dwelt) among us . . . " (1:14). From the retrospective position of the narrator of the Gospel the outcome is known, and knowledge of the outcome has become an aspect of the narrative itself. One might expect the Gospel to project a closed system of predestination or inevitability, for individuals as well as for historical events, but it does not (Keck 1996). The ministry of Jesus presented real possibilities for another outcome, had people made different, true, and proper decisions about Jesus, but with the end of his ministry such possibilities have been closed off.

In retrospect, however, it can be seen that God was at work in the seemingly dismal outcome. Yet such happier possibilities have not disappeared, but have been removed to an expanding future, in which people will still have the opportunity to believe in and follow Jesus (20:30-31; cf. 1:13; 17:20-23).

THE REVELATION OF THE GLORY BEFORE THE COMMUNITY (13:1–20:31)

In the second major part of the Gospel Jesus turns away from the world as he gathers his disciples about him to bid them farewell and to instruct them in what they will need to know as they face the world without his physical presence among them (13:1–17:26). Then he turns outward, to face the world once more as he goes to his arrest and ultimately to his death (chaps. 18–19). Jesus is again in full public view, and his glory will be revealed in his death, but only his disciples will see it as his glorification, and then only in light of his resurrection (chap. 20). Only disciples, or those who will truly become his disciples, see him risen from the dead and believe in him.

Jesus' Farewell to His Disciples (13:1–17:26)

As Jesus withdraws from his confrontation with the world and with those who turn out to be his enemies—called "the Jews"—he meets one last time with his disciples. This meeting falls into two major parts, defined by parallels with the synoptic Gospels, or lack thereof. The Last Supper (chap. 13) is clearly recognizable from the other Gospels, while the farewell discourses (chaps. 14–16) and final prayer (chap. 17) are not, although they may represent related interests or motifs. Nevertheless, the setting of 13:1–17:26 is the same, the Supper (cf. 14:31), although this fact is not emphasized explicitly in the discourses or prayer.

The Last Supper (13:1-38)

John's account of the Last Supper parallels the synoptic Gospels (Matt 26:17-29; Mark 14:19-25; Luke 22:7-38), but is longer and differs in important respects. Of course, John does not narrate the preparation for Passover; in John the meal is not a Passover meal (13:1). Yet it is nevertheless an occasion of great importance for Jesus and his disciples, and it is hard to understand why John does not mention Jesus' seemingly uncanny advance knowledge of the arrangements if he knew of it. (Similarly, John has omitted Jesus' advance knowledge of arrangements for the entry into Jerusalem; cf. Mark 11:1-6 par.) Otherwise Jesus' foreknowledge is underscored (13:1).

In Matthew (26:30) and Mark (14:26) the Supper clearly ends with the singing of a hymn, after which the party goes to the Mount of Olives. At this point there is a curious agreement between John and Luke, neither of which mentions the singing of a hymn; but both portray continuing table conversation between Jesus and his disciples. Only at John 18:1 do Jesus and his disciples go out across the Kidron Valley into a garden. (Although one commonly speaks of the Garden of Gethsemane, the place is called a garden only in John, where it is not named Gethsemane!) John envisions the discourses of Jesus (chaps. 14–16), as well as the final prayer (chap. 17), as having occurred at the Supper. In fact, Jesus' command, "Rise, let us be on our way" (14:31), presumes they are still at table. Yet there is a break at the end of chapter 13, where clear parallels to the Synoptics end with the prediction of Peter's denial, and a fresh beginning with chapter 14. (Thus chapters 14–16 are known as Jesus' farewell discourses.)

The contents of the Johannine account of the Last Supper are as recognizably similar to the other Gospels as they are also distinctly different. The most obvious differences are that only John describes Jesus' washing his disciples' feet while omitting any account of his instituting the Lord's Supper. Not only do the other canonical Gospels know such an account, but Paul as well (1 Cor 11:23-26). In the Synoptics the prediction of the denial of Peter comes just after they have gone out (Matt 26:30-35; Mark 14:26-31), while in John (13:36-38), as in Luke (22:31-34), it happens at the Supper itself. Then, Luke, like John, also has Jesus continue at table with his disciples after the prediction of Judas's betrayal. Of course, it is only in John that Jesus, toward the end of the Supper, gives the disciples the new commandment that they should love one another (13:34-35). Yet in Luke, likewise immediately after the prediction of Judas's betrayal, Jesus exhorts his disciples to be servants of one another (22:26-27).

Inasmuch as the Supper is the narrative setting for Jesus' farewell discourses and prayer, it becomes clear that in the Johannine version Jesus begins and ends with an exposition of his ministry and mission. At the beginning there is the footwashing (13:1-20), in which Jesus interprets his death in relation to his own mission and the disciples'. At the end, in the prayer (chap. 17), Jesus announces what he has done and prays for the success of his ministry among his disciples.

13:1-20: Jesus washes the disciples' feet and gives two related interpretations of the deed. In the opening statement we are given three important facts: what time it is by the Jewish calendar; what time it is in Jesus' ministry; and Jesus' own disposition and intention. It is an extremely important statement, in which emphasis falls on Jesus' love for his disciples.

That the Last Supper occurs before Passover and is not a Passover meal is consistent with the chronology of this Gospel in the Passion Narrative (cf. 18:28; 19:14, 31, 42). Possibly John alters the date so that Jesus will be crucified when the Passover lambs are slain, but he does not otherwise make a great deal of this coincidence. Initially, Jesus is called "the Lamb of God who takes away the sin of the world" (1:29; cf. 1:36), a title that does not exactly fit the Passover lamb, which is not a sin offering (see commentary on 1:29), although it obviously is drawn from the same cultic realm and the imagery of the lamb is significant. Paul speaks of Christ as the paschal lamb who has been sacrificed (1 Cor 8:7), and for him it is quite clear that his death is conceived in terms of the temple sacrifice for sin (Rom 3:25). That Jesus dies for the people or his disciples is frequently stated in John (e.g., 10:11, 15; 11:50; 15:12-13), but usually not in terms of the sacrificial altar.

Jesus' ministry has reached its climactic hour, as is now clear.

His death is his departure to God (13:1), as will become more evident in the course of the narrative.

His love for his disciples is nothing other or less than the expression of God's love (3:16; 2 John 3:16; cf. Rom 5:8). Jesus' loving of his disciples is more than a human emotion, if it is that at all. One must remember that the *logos*, who is incarnate as Jesus Christ (1:14), is said to be *theos* (God) (1:1) as is Jesus himself (1:18; 20:29). With respect to his revelatory function, he is no different from the Father (10:30; 14:9). The Father makes himself known through Jesus, and, as far as John is concerned, only through Jesus. (On the identity and differences of Father and Son in John, see Meyer 1996, 255-73). Jesus' love for his disciples has been expressed all through his ministry, but particularly and most important in his death (cf. 15:12-13). It is only from the standpoint of Jesus' death that the true nature and extent of his love can be seen: that it is God's love and that it is universal. That Jesus loved his disciples "to the end" is a literal translation of a Greek phrase that could, however, be rendered "completely." The NRSV, however, rightly preserves the temporal sense, since Jesus' death is in view.

Jesus now prepares to wash the disciples' feet (vv. 2-4). One recalls that just a few days before Mary had anointed Jesus' feet (12:1-8). The stories, while obviously differing in function, are not unrelated. During supper (v. 2) he arose, stripped for work (the RSV's "laid aside his garments" is more literal than the NRSV; cf. 21:7), girding himself with a towel (v. 4). The devil is now said to have inspired Judas to betray Jesus (v. 2). Judas's action can only be explained as the work of the most powerful and sinister force (cf. Luke 22:3; where the devil is said to enter Judas for the same purpose). Three times in John, and only here, Judas is called the son of Simon (see also 6:71; and 13:26), a man about whom there is no other information. "During supper" can mean that the supper was already underway when Jesus started the footwashing; thus one could imagine this happened after Jesus had given the words of institution found in the Synoptics— although this is a harmonization not suggested by the text.

Before Jesus' actions are described, we are told what he knew

(v. 3), which is what he has known all along. At no moment in his ministry has Jesus lacked knowledge about himself, his relation to God, or his mission. About these things Jesus is omniscient; he never needs to be told anything (cf. 6:6; 12:30; cf. 21:17). One might infer some such knowledge, or foreknowledge, from some synoptic accounts (cf., for example, Mark 2:8; 11:2-6; 14:12-16), but there Jesus can even ask about his own identity in Peter's confession (Mark 8:27). John is consistently different.

Jesus' action is briefly described (v. 5). The washing of feet was a custom in Judaism as in other cultures (see O'Day 1995, 722). But *Midrash Mekhilta* on Exod 21:2 says that even a Jewish slave could not be required to wash his master's feet (see Barrett 1978, 440). *Joseph and Aseneth* (a pseudepigraphical Jewish book) tells the story of the Egyptian maiden Aseneth, who is betrothed to the Hebrew (biblical) Joseph, washing Joseph's feet over his protest (20:1-5). The story is not exactly analogous to Peter's reaction in John, but close enough to merit our attention. Thomas (1991, 26-60) shows that in antiquity, whether Jewish or Greco-Roman, the washing of another's feet is an act of servitude, ordinarily performed by a person of inferior rank or status. Exceptions are rare and in the nature of the case significant. This finding explains Peter's reaction (vv. 6, 8), which in all probability most readers would take as natural and normal—that is, needing little explanation.

Jesus' words (vv. 7, 8), however, require explanation. When Jesus tells Peter he does not know now but will understand later, a familiar Johannine motif is evoked (cf. 2:17, 22; 7:39; 12:16; 14:29). Who Jesus is and what he has done can be fully understood only after his crucifixion and resurrection. What does it mean that unless Peter allows Jesus to wash his feet then he has no share with him? Does footwashing become a kind of saving, sacramental action? Or, does it symbolize the saving work that Jesus accomplishes through his death? Jesus' statement obviously implies the latter. Peter's reaction (v. 9) is then normal, as well as typical of Peter, although he does not yet understand. If an allusion to baptism is to be found here, as it may be, it is understood as in Rom 6:3: a baptism into Jesus' death.

Jesus' response (v. 10) presents a difficulty for interpreters, because Jesus has apparently declared to Peter that unless he allows him to wash his feet he cannot be saved. Therefore, as most commentators agree, footwashing must symbolize the salvation Jesus effects, preeminently through his death (see C. Koester 1995, 116-17). How can Jesus then say that he who has bathed *(ho leloumenos)* does not need to wash *(nipsasthai,* the word heretofore used for the washing of the feet) except for his feet? In that case the footwashing, which must symbolize Jesus' saving work in its totality, culminating in his death, would be reduced to a subsidiary action. Some manuscripts (notably Sinaiticus) lack the phrase "except for the feet." If that shorter reading is original, the bathing of which Jesus now speaks is the same as the washing of the feet, and would symbolize Jesus' saving work. Thus we should read: "One who has bathed does not need to wash, but is entirely clean." It is then apparent that Peter has misunderstood Jesus, failing to understand that Jesus is speaking all along of his saving work under the metaphor of footwashing. His death, like the washing of another's feet, is an act of humiliation and servitude (cf. Phil 2:6-11). Peter, however, can only see the violation of social propriety.

The phrase "except for the feet" would have been added by a scribe, or scribes (there are actually several slightly different readings), who was thrown off by the use of a Greek verb for "bathe" *(louō)* other than the one *(niptō)* used of footwashing up to this point. The washing *(niptō)* of the feet, is of course, necessary, as Jesus has said to Peter. Yet, given the longer reading, he who has bathed must wash his feet. But what then is the meaning of bathing, or having bathed, and how is it effected or enacted? That becomes hard to say. The argument for the omission of "except for the feet" is, on substantive grounds, strong (see the arguments of Bultmann 1971, 469-70, n. 2; Barrett 1978, 441-42; O'Day 1995, 723-24).

A case for the retention of the phrase "except his feet" becomes more plausible if footwashing was actually practiced in the Johannine community or churches liturgically as a kind of recapitulation of the love and saving work of Jesus and of his command that his disciples should love one another as he has loved them (vv. 14-15). It would then be an essential symbolic act. Evidence of the footwashing as a liturgical act in the early church is, apart from this text, disputed (Bultmann 1971, 469-70, n. 2, asserts that "there is no evidence for such a sacrament before Augustine"). Yet Thomas (1991, 129-30), who accepts the longer reading, thinks that the liturgical practice of footwashing is actually first attested by Tertullian, only a century or so after the Fourth Gospel (see his valuable collection of patristic texts, 158-172). On balance, the shorter reading still seems preferable. Yet this is a good example of how text-critical and exegetical problems intertwine.

Jesus, of course, knows that not all his disciples are clean, but that Judas will betray him (cf. 6:64, 70-71). An omniscient Jesus cannot have been deceived by Judas. With verse 11 the salvific interpretation of Jesus' washing the disciples' feet concludes. Its implications for the obedience and behavior of the disciples will now be drawn, as Jesus puts his clothes back on, takes his place at the table, and asks his disciples if they understand the meaning of what he has done (v. 12). Clearly the disciples are to emulate Jesus' humble act (vv. 13-15). Does this mean they should wash one another's feet literally or liturgically? If it does mean that in the context of the Gospel's interpretation the act would still be symbolic of the service that disciples render to each other in emulation of Jesus. That service is graphically described in 15:12-14 (v. 14, "What I command you" refers, of course, to 13:34, the new commandment).

Probably we are at a point where we can suggest why John does not have Jesus institute the Lord's Supper. Clearly John 6 presupposes this sacrament, as in all probability do allusions to Jesus' blood (19:34), to the vine (15:1-8), or to wine (2:1-11). Of course, the feeding of five thousand (John 6:1-15) has eucharistic overtones, as do the parallel narratives of the other Gospels. There is in the *Didache* an entire early eucharistic service (chap. 11) with no reference to the night on which Jesus was betrayed or to the Last Supper. Yet it is difficult to believe John would have had no knowledge of the Last Supper setting, even if he did not know the synoptic Gospels, or was not using them as his source(s). Perhaps a generation earlier Paul obviously knows the tradition that the Lord's Supper was established on the night Jesus was betrayed (1 Cor 11:23). Assuming that this tradition was widespread and known to John, we must ask why he did not repeat it.

Clearly John underscores as central the love of God for the world, not only exhibited but effectuated in Jesus' death, and insists that the true disciples recapitulate that love in their own life through concrete deeds. They lay down their lives for one another (15:13) as Jesus has laid down his life for them (cf. 1 John 3:16). That this may have actually happened in a Johannine community under duress and persecution is not hard to imagine (cf. 16:2). In fact, 1 John takes up this emphasis and makes plain that the true disciples express their love in concrete acts; otherwise it is not love at all (3:17). In other words, 1 John draws out the practical, day-to-day implications of Jesus' "extreme" command to lay down your lives for your friends. In a different way this is also done in the footwashing scene. In the washing of the feet, the most humble of services, one can find symbolized Jesus' humble service in death (cf. Phil 2:7, 8) as well as the loving service that the disciples must perform for one another.

One can scarcely overstress the centrality of love, divine and human, in the Fourth Gospel. If Jesus' followers do not in their daily lives recapitulate Jesus' love for them, their allegiance to him is specious. John underscores both points, and they are integrally related, in the footwashing scene. It is apparently deliberately allowed to displace the words of institution of the Lord's Supper, but not because John denies or disparages that rite. Rather, because at this crucial moment he does not wish to portray Jesus' giving himself for his disciples in a way that does not implicate them in an analogous self-giving. Thus John here presupposes the synoptic and Pauline traditions, if not the synoptic Gospels. Jesus then sets for the disciples, all disciples, an example (v. 15), which he underscores by defining their place and role (v. 16). (It is noteworthy that here the term *apostolos*, "apostle" is translated in the NRSV as "messengers.") It is important, indeed necessary, to know, but equally crucial to act (v. 17). Thus Jesus' action at table in John, in some contrast to the Synoptics, is one that the disciples may not only receive but must replicate.

The reference to Judas (v. 18) is something we have come to expect (cf. vv. 2, 11), as Ps 41:9 is quoted to show that his deed is comprehended in God's purpose. The fact that the disciples will only come to a realization of who Jesus really is after his death (v. 19), a recurring and central motif of this Gospel, is now reiterated (cf. v. 7). The relation of the disciple/apostle (cf. v. 16) to Jesus is analogous to the relation of Jesus to the Father (v. 20; cf. Matt 10:40; Mark 9:37; Luke 10:16). The high Christology of the Gospel is accompanied by an equally high view of the apostolate, and the church.

13:21-30: In a long and dramatic scene, Jesus identifies his betrayer (note Brown 1994, 1399-1401, on Judas's betrayal). In Matthew and Mark the prediction of Judas's betrayal (Matt 26:20-25; Mark 14:17-21) precedes the institution of the Lord's Supper (Matt 26:26-29; Mark 14:22-25), whereas in Luke it follows (22:15-20, 21-23). In John there is, of course, no institution of the Lord's Supper per se, but the prediction of betrayal follows the footwashing. If one were to suppose that the footwashing has replaced the words of institution, this would constitute an agreement of John with Luke against Mark and Matthew but one should not rush to this conclusion, so different is the Johannine account.

That Jesus is "troubled in spirit" (v. 21) is reminiscent of John 12:27, where Jesus, obviously facing the onset of the events leading to his death, says, "Now my soul is troubled." (The Greek verb, *tarassō*, is in both cases the same.) Jesus' opening statement, "Very truly, I tell you, one of you will betray me," is virtually identical with his opening word in Matthew (26:21) and Mark (14:18). Yet the scene as John portrays it is much more detailed and elaborate. Understandably the disciples look at one another (cf. Luke 22:23), wondering whom Jesus meant. In Matthew (26:22) and Mark (14:19) they begin to say to Jesus individually, "It is not I, is it?" (Their question expects a negative answer: "No, it is not you.") The effect in John is similar.

We then have a typically and uniquely Johannine stage within the episode, as the Beloved Disciple acts as an intermediary between Peter and Jesus (vv. 23-26). The Beloved Disciple (literally, "The disciple whom Jesus loved") makes his appearance for the first time in this Gospel. He is unique to the Gospel of John and obviously an important figure (see Introduction, pp. 24-27). The fact that he here mediates between Peter, as well as the other disciples, and Jesus indicates the importance of his overall role. He reclines next to Jesus. Literally, he is in the bosom (Gk. *kolpos*) of Jesus, as Jesus is in the bosom *(kolpos)* of the Father (1:18). (By not translating literally in either case, the NRSV conceals this connection; the KJV preserves the connection by translating "bosom" in both places.) The clear implication of the use of the same term in both places is that the Beloved Disciple is to Jesus as Jesus is to the Father. As Jesus makes the Father known, so this disciple makes Jesus known. Thus the Gospel is ascribed to him (21:24; cf. 19:35). He is somehow the one through whom the community gains, and maintains, access to Jesus. At the end of the Gospel, when the Beloved Disciple appears for the last time, again alongside Peter, he is identified by reference to this scene (21:20).

John gives a play-by-play account of the interchange between the Beloved Disciple and Peter (vv. 24-26), which is unique to this Gospel. Jesus identifies the betrayer in somewhat the same fashion as in the other Gospels (v. 26), but in John alone is he at this point in the narrative said to be Judas (cf. Mark 14:20; but also Matt 26:25, where at the end Judas is explicitly fingered). Readers of the Synoptics would, however, know that the betrayer was Judas, because there Judas's act of going to the chief priests in order to hand Jesus over has already been narrated (Matt 26:14-16; Mark 14:10-11; Luke 22:3-6). Nevertheless, it is significant that in this account the Johannine Jesus explicitly identifies Judas, manifesting his typical omniscience. The disciples, apart from the Beloved Disciple (v. 26), seem to get no answer to their, or Peter's, question (v. 24). Tellingly, they do not understand Jesus' instruction to Judas (vv. 27-29), although the Beloved Disciple has been told by Jesus how he will identify the betrayer

(v. 26). Presumably he knows, but we are never told that he tells Peter or the others. John's account clearly goes beyond what we are told in the Synoptics. Yet it also presupposes that Judas has still not committed the dreadful deed, so that Jesus himself commands him to do it (v. 27), a typically Johannine motif. Again we are told that Judas was, in effect, the treasurer of the group (v. 29; cf. 12:6)—very likely a historical fact, since John otherwise seizes every opportunity to denigrate him.

What motivated Judas to betray Jesus has been a subject of never-ending fascination to readers of the Gospels. According to the synoptic Gospels it was apparently greed; he was to be paid off by the chief priests (Matt 26:15; Mark 14:11; Luke 22:5; cf. Acts 1:18; Matt 27:3-10). Strangely, despite John's denigration of Judas, he does not report this base motivation. Perhaps John does not want to portray Jesus as having been betrayed for such trivial, as well as base, reasons. Satan, after all, is the root cause of Judas's deed (vv. 2, 27).

That some disciples imagine that Jesus has told Judas to buy supplies necessary for the festival of Passover (v. 29) of course fits the Johannine chronology, according to which this is not the Passover meal, as in the Synoptics, but the evening meal on the day immediately preceding it (18:28; 19:14, 31). The fact that Jesus might have instructed Judas to give to the poor (cf. 12:5-6) is perhaps a mark of the traditional basis of this narrative. The departure of Judas into the night (i.e., darkness) at Jesus' command (v. 30) has obvious symbolic, dualistic overtones, which, however, John does not elaborate. (Cf. 3:2 where Nicodemus's approach to Jesus by night has symbolic overtones that are not developed; similarly, the meaning of the name of the pool of Siloam, "sent," in 9:7 is mentioned but not exploited.)

13:31-35: Jesus now gives his disciples the love commandment, which characterizes his teaching, but there is no immediate preparation or build-up to it. Indeed, Jesus has been discussing his glorification and departure from his disciples (vv. 31-33), and after the command (vv. 34-35) that subject is resumed (vv. 36-38). At first glance, the love command may seem to be an interjection or interpolation. Yet, coming as it does at the conclusion of the narration of Jesus' actions at the meal, particularly the footwashing, and before the longer discourses with the disciples (chaps. 14–16), it is appropriately placed. What Jesus has demonstrated he now commands.

Jesus' statement about his glorification (vv. 31-32) resumes an important and now familiar theme (cf. 12:23), which will be repeated (17:4-5). That the Son of Man "has been glorified" (NRSV) translates the Greek aorist tense in the obvious way, as referring to past time.

Glory in the biblical sense belongs to God; it is his distinctive quality as God (see above, p. 243). Jesus is glorified precisely in his abdication of worldly glory as he freely chooses death on the cross in obedience to God (10:17-18). Thus he glorifies God and reveals God. The switch from past to future tense in verse 32 may indicate that Jesus' revelatory work in his earthly ministry was in view in verse 31, while his imminent crucifixion and exaltation are now envisioned. That the latter event is anticipated in the very near future is clear from Jesus' next statement (v. 33; his similar statement to the Jews is found in 7:33-34). Jesus' disciples are imperceptive until he has been glorified, although their lack of comprehension is, of course, not marked by hostility and rejection.

Simon Peter will return to the question of Jesus' going away (v. 36), but now Jesus interjects his new commandment (vv. 34-35). That Jesus' disciples should love one another as Jesus has loved them is, of course, fundamental to Johannine theology and ethics (cf. 15:12-13; 1 John 4:7-11). This love has been exemplified in the footwashing scene, as Jesus tells his disciples he has given them an example (13:15). The Jesus of John teaches love, but, in some contrast to the other Gospels, avoids specific concrete injunctions (but cf. 1 John 3:17; 4:20). Many interpreters have seen in the Johannine version of Jesus' love command an apt summation of his teaching. In fact, the command to love the neighbor (Mark 12:28-34) or even the enemy (Matt 5:43-45) is attributed to Jesus in the synoptic Gospels; and Paul prominently displays the command to love the neighbor (from Lev 19:18), as if it were axiomatic for believers (Rom 13:8-10; Gal 5:14) in their relation to one another, although he does not attribute it to Jesus. Significantly, both John and Paul understand the love commandment as applying primarily, if not exclusively, to relations among believers (D. Moody Smith 1996b).

Mutual love is to become the hallmark of Christian community (v. 35), and presumably the key to Christian mission—a role attributed to unity, a closely related theme, in 17:21, 23. The multiple attestation of the love command means at the very least that it was assumed to go back to Jesus.

13:36-38: Peter then returns to the question of where Jesus is going (v. 36), as the Last Supper concludes with an episode parallel to the Synoptics. Jesus' response to Peter is typically enigmatic. "Afterward" points ahead to the time after Jesus' death and resurrection (cf. 13:19). What specifically Jesus has in mind by "afterward" becomes apparent in his postresurrection conversation with Peter where he foretells his destiny (21:18-19; cf. 2 Pet 1:14). Now Peter's response reflects perplexity (v. 37), and there is a touch of irony in the fact that while Peter will not lay down his life for Jesus at this crisis point in Jesus' ministry, but will rather deny him, later on, "afterward," he will die a martyr's death. The scene concludes with Jesus' announcing that Peter will deny him three times. This, of course, parallels the synoptic episode (Matt 26:30-35; Mark 14:26-31; Luke 22:31-34). In every case it occurs after the meal proper, although in John and Luke the party is still at table, while in Matthew and Mark the announcement is made as they depart to the Mount of Olives. In each Gospel Jesus predicts Peter will deny him three times before the cock crows, but only in Mark does he say "before the cock crows *twice*" (14:30). In Matthew (26:31) and Mark (14:27) Zech 13:7 is quoted in somewhat altered form: "I will strike the shepherd, and the sheep will be scattered." John (with Luke) does not cite the passage here, but Jesus alludes to it at the end of the farewell discourses (16:32). Although there is no citation, John knows a tradition that associates Peter's denial with this prophetic saying. In any case the Zechariah text is taken to refer to the flight of all the disciples, and not just Peter. Peter's denial is a specific and extreme instance of the disciples' defection. John, of course, will later narrate the denial (18:13-24), as do the other Gospels (Matt 26:57-68; Mark 14:53-65; Luke 22:54-71). But only John will depict a scene in which Peter is apparently restored to Jesus' good graces (21:15-23). Also only John identifies Jesus' defender at the arrest, the man who strikes with the sword (18:10), as Peter. Perhaps this is another touch of Johannine irony, for at that point Peter does seem willing to lay down his own life. Yet within a few short hours he will deny Jesus (18:17).

◊ ◊ ◊ ◊

The Last Supper scene does not so much advance the theology and ethics of the Gospel as express it in dramatic, narrative form. Jesus' washing of the disciples' feet takes the place of the words of institution of the synoptic Gospels. There is ample reason to suppose that John was written in a community that shared the flesh and blood of Jesus in a sacramental rite (cf. 6:52-58). Moreover, Jesus' washing of the disciples' feet symbolizes the cleansing from sin that the Eucharist effects. In fact, refusing this service seems to be tantamount to refusing the benefits of Jesus' death (13:6-8). Like the Eucharist, the footwashing embodies Jesus' self-giving service to the disciples (or believers) in his death, "he loved them to the end" (13:1).

More graphically than this sacramental act, however, Jesus' washing of the disciples' feet has clear ethical implications for the disciples, which are drawn out in Jesus' second interpretation of the footwashing (13:12-20). What Jesus has done for them they must do for one another. Not only does Jesus then give the love commandment (v. 34), but later on, in instructing his disciples he tells them that their willingness to lay down their lives for one another must match his own (15:12-13). In John, as in Paul's writings, the ethical imperative is grounded in the theological, or christological, indicative. What Jesus' disciples are required to do for one another is no more than Jesus has already done for them. Because of its ethical, as well as theological implications, the washing of the disciples' feet is the narrative centerpiece of the Last Supper, and its message is underscored once more toward the end of the scene as Jesus issues his commandment that his disciples should love one another.

Jesus' prediction of his betrayal by Judas (vv. 21-30) and denial by Peter (vv. 36-38) are known to us from the synoptic tradition, although both have been subjected to a distinctly Johannine shaping. In the former episode Judas's perfidy is underscored even more strongly than in the other Gospels, even as Jesus' foreknowledge and his initiative are emphasized. Similarly, Jesus proclaims to Peter not only his denial, but his subsequent return. Even Jesus' telling question to Peter (v. 38) could in Greek also be read as a statement: "You will lay down your life for me." The knowledgeable Johannine reader would understand (cf. 21:18-19) that despite Peter's denial, apparently to save his life, he would finally lay down his life as a martyr for Jesus.

Jesus' Farewell Discourses (14:1–16:33)

The farewell discourses of Jesus take place at the Last Supper (chap. 13). No change of venue is indicated at the beginning of chapter 14. Chapter 13 closes with Jesus' prediction of Peter's denial, and although Jesus apparently begins a new discourse at 14:1, he also makes connection with what he has said toward the end of the preceding scene (cf. 13:36; 14:2-3). Although the Last Supper in John contains several episodes with synoptic parallels, so that as a whole it is clearly the counterpart of the synoptic scene, the same cannot quite be said of the farewell discourses. In a very general sense, however, their content corresponds to the synoptic apocalypse (Matt 24:1-44; Mark 13:1-37; Luke 21:5-33) in that Jesus reveals future events to his disciples. (On thematic and other parallels with the Synoptics, see Brown 1970, 595.) What is revealed, and the conversational, dialogical manner are, however, quite different. As far as we can tell, the supper setting continues through chapter 17, the final prayer of Jesus. Yet the discourses are obviously coming to a conclusion in 16:29-33, and there is a clearly transitional statement in 17:1.

The fact that in 14:31 Jesus tells his disciples to get up and depart, but they do not, has suggested to many commentators that there has been some disarrangement of the text (Bultmann 1971, 459, 595) or that chapters 15–16 (17) have been added later (Brown 1970, 586-88; Barrett 1978, 454-55). The latter view is the simpler and more feasible alternative, and the one followed in this commentary. Yet we shall read these discourses as a whole, on the working hypothesis that in their present form they manifest a certain coherence, whether or not they were composed in stages. (See Segovia's important work *The Farewell of the Word* [1991, vii-ix, 20-58, 283-313]; yet Segovia [319-28] also believes that the discourses arose in stages.) We have frequently noted the retrospective character of the Johannine narrative, which is nowhere more evident than in these discourses. Indeed, in the farewell discourses Jesus explains how, through the Spirit-Paraclete, illumination will take place (14:26). Another characteristic of John's Gospel is repetition. Already, fundamental theological themes have been reiterated. Arguably, the farewell discourses offer a culminating example of John's repetitiveness. As far as the composition of the discourses is concerned, their repetitiveness does not necessarily bespeak later, redactional additions. And even if it does, the virtue of repetition may be seen as brought into play by a later editor, for good reason.

While John 14–16 is the Johannine counterpart of the synoptic apocalypses (see Barrett 1978, 455), on many crucial points it differs. To begin with, the synoptic apocalypses occur before the Last Supper, while the Johannine discourses are set at, or after, the Supper. So their positions in the narrative are different, although similar in that they both occur as the end of Jesus' ministry comes into view. The basic general theme of the future the disciples will face after Jesus' departure may be said to be the same, but it differs in two important respects. First, the vivid apocalyptic language and conceptuality of the Synoptics is missing in John, except that the basic idea of Jesus' coming again, his future presence, is very much at the center of attention, as it is in the culmination of the synoptic apocalypse. In the Synoptics, of course, we read of the coming of the Son of Man (Mark 13:24-27 par.) rather than Jesus, but it is the assumption of the evangelists and of the narrative, here and throughout the Gospels, that the Son of Man is Jesus. Second, the Johannine narrative is concerned with the manifestation and continuing presence of Jesus among his disciples specifically, and not to the world (14:22). That Jesus should be manifest in glory to the world, including the disciples, is very much the essence of Christian apocalyptic (cf. 1 Thess 4:13-18; Rev 1:7; as well as the synoptic apocalypses).

In this connection, it is also worth observing that the farewell discourses occur in the presence of all the disciples. (The fact that the twelve are not specifically mentioned may imply that more, rather than fewer, disciples are presumed to be present.) In Mark (13:3), by contrast, Jesus takes with him the inner circle of four (Peter, James, John, and Andrew) and goes up on the Mount of Olives across from the temple (only Mark mentions both places). Interestingly, Matthew and Luke omit these names, implying that Jesus addresses all his disciples. This change, which brings them closer to John, is a natural one. That in the Synoptics the disciples are on the Mount of Olives across from the temple is quite appropriate. National and apocalyptic hopes centered about the temple (Isa 44:28; 66:6; Ezek 40–48; Mal 3:1). John, on the other hand, has the disciples gathered with their teacher and Lord (13:13) at, or after, the meal. What Jesus will reveal concerns them only, or at least primarily, and not the world. Yet while the synoptic apocalypse describes public cataclysms and events, it too is given for the benefit of the disciples. It is a revelation to them only.

Ancient Jewish and other literature provides close parallels to John's farewell discourses in the testament of farewell of a dying hero. Segovia provides a helpful summary of analyses of farewell scenes that fall into a recognizable pattern (1991, 2-19). In Greco-Roman literature the archetypal farewell scene is Socrates' farewell to his disciples as recounted by Plato in the dialogue entitled *Phaedo*. As Segovia points out (6, n. 6), this scene contains elements that become common to most such scenes:

> First, there is a conversation between the dying man and his confidants in his last hours. Second, within such a conversation are a

number of fixed and recurring elements: forebodings or prophecies of death, final instructions regarding the care of those left behind, the appointment of a successor, a prayer of thanksgiving to the gods, words of farewell and consolation for the intimate circle, an account of past activities, teachings and exhortations for the wider gathering, and political and philosophical testaments.

Particularly if one includes John 13 and 17, which belong to the total farewell scene, virtually every item mentioned by Segovia is included.

Within the Old Testament the most significant parallel to John's discourses is Moses' address to the people in Deuteronomy. With its emphasis on obeying God's commandments Deuteronomy itself prefigures a similar emphasis in the farewell discourses of John. It is a kind of testament of Moses, as he prepares Israel for his death and departure. After their forty years of wilderness wandering they are about to go over the Jordan and possess the promised land. Moreover, in Deut 18:15-22 there is the promise of the prophet like Moses, which Jesus fulfills in the Gospel of John. Probably the earliest biblical exemplar of this genre is Jacob's blessing of his sons, the fathers of the twelve tribes of Israel, just before his death (Gen 49). Such biblical testaments gave rise to a flourishing genre of testaments in the period of Christian origins (see Charlesworth 1983, 773-995). Of these the most notable are the *Testaments of the Twelve Patriarchs* (the sons of Jacob), which were in the process of composition about the time when the Gospel of John was being written (Charlesworth 1983, 775-828).

Within the New Testament, Luke comes closest to constructing such a farewell of Jesus (22:14-38), even as he depicts Paul delivering a farewell address to the Ephesian elders on the island of Miletus (Acts 20:17-38). Interestingly, Luke knows, and lets the reader know, that the hearers will never again see Paul alive (20:25, 38). Such scenes, like John's, are in some respects closer to the typical farewell type-scene than to the synoptic apocalyptic discourses.

How many such scenes the evangelist himself knew we can only guess, but he doubtless knew at least the biblical (Old

Testament) precedents. Probably he knew also traditions concerning the Last Supper, at which the discourses are set (as in Luke 22:14-38). The question of whether he knew the synoptic apocalypses is a part of the larger issue of John and the Synoptics, which continues to be much debated. Two points may, however, be made with a high degree of certainty. First, if John had known the Markan apocalypse he would scarcely have taken it up in the way Matthew and Luke did. On eschatology more than anything else John is writing revisionist history. But second, even if John did not know Mark, he surely knew the apocalyptic temper of much early Christianity, which is what he seeks to revise (11:24-25; 14:22; 21:22-23). In all probability the apocalypse of Mark 13 developed over time, and it has parallels and perhaps even some basis in other apocalyptic utterances, particularly 1 Thess 4:15-17 (which Paul ascribes to a word of the Lord) and 1 Cor 15:20-28; then there is the Revelation to John and whatever traditions may lie behind it.

As original as they may seem, the Johannine discourses emerge from, and presume, rich eschatological and testamentary traditions.

Jesus' First Farewell Discourse (14:1-31)

As we have observed, chapter 14 comprises a complete unit of discourse, after which one could easily move to the emergence of Jesus and the disciples into the garden (cf. 14:31; 18:1). In this discourse Jesus assures the disciples that they will not be separated from him, despite his departure to the Father, with whom he lives in closest unity. Their unity with Jesus and the Father will be assured on two sides, the divine and the human. On the one side, God will send the Advocate or Paraclete, the Spirit, who will effect the continuing presence and guidance of Jesus. On the other the disciples must respond by continuing obedience to Jesus' word. Given these conditions, one grounded in God's initiative, the other contingent on the disciples' response, the disciples may be confident that Jesus' peace, which is the peace of God, will abide with them.

◊ ◊ ◊ ◊

14:1-7: In these opening words Jesus promises his disciples they will always be with him (cf. 17:24). Again in 14:27 he will tell the disciples that their hearts should not be troubled, and when the risen Jesus first greets his disciples he offers them first a word of reassurance (20:19: "Peace be with you").

Right at the outset (v. 1) there is a translation problem, reflected in the NRSV note. The Greek can be translated in either of two ways. The reason for choosing the translation of the text over that found in the note is theological; either is possible since the present indicative and imperative are the same in Greek. In John's view belief in God entails belief in Jesus: access to God is now only through Jesus (cf. 14:6). Belief in Jesus is not an add-on to belief in God.

Jesus next assures the disciples that there is room for them in his Father's house (v. 2). "House" reflects the Greek *oikia* (rather than *oikos*, the building), and can mean "household" or "family." Probably the choice of the term is significant. The dwelling places *(monai)* are denoted by the nominal form of the verb frequently used by John of abiding in or with Jesus (*menō;* cf. 6:56; 15:4-10; also 14:23, where the noun is used again: "make our *home* with them"). One comes to dwell in God's house, his dwelling place.

The closing sentence of verse 2 presents the more serious translation problem. Again, the translation given in the NRSV note (cf. KJV) is possible and perhaps preferable. The difficulty with the translation adopted in the text is that Jesus has not yet told the disciples in the narrative that he is going to prepare a place for them (so also O'Day 1995, 741). (The Greek conjunction *hoti* can either be translated "for," with the note, or "that," with the text.) In any case John's purpose is to stress the certainty of what is said (Bultmann 1971, 601). Jesus then elaborates his word of reassurance (v. 3), and in doing so alludes to what he has just said to Peter (13:36). Peter, of course, was speaking of the immediate future; Jesus now speaks of the eschatological future, beyond death (as Bultmann 1971, 602, also clearly recognized; cf. 17:24).

Jesus then attributes to the disciples knowledge of the way home, to the Father's house (v. 4). The alternative reading in the note, attested in at least one very early manuscript (P[66]), makes little substantive difference. Thomas, who has spoken earlier (11:16), admits ignorance and asks the key question (v. 5). The motif of the disciples' misunderstanding or, closely related, ignorance, is something we have seen earlier (13:9, 36-37) and will see again shortly (14:8, 22). Whether Thomas's question reflects some irritation or is simply a straightforward and necessary inquiry is impossible to decide on the basis of the framing of the question itself, but must be determined in the interpretation of the context. (As Segovia 1991, 86, points out, Jesus seems to respect Thomas's question.) It can reasonably be taken as a necessary and important question that allows Jesus to say what he must (see Charlesworth 1995, 262, 316, 319, 335, 429, who emphasizes this way of reading Thomas's question). Indeed, Thomas's question allows Jesus to respond with a definitive revelatory proclamation (v. 6).

Jesus' statement affirms not only the validity, but the exclusivity of his claim. One thinks immediately of Jesus' statement to Martha that he is the resurrection and the life (11:25), but there he does not deny any other valid access to God, as he seems to do here. The terms Jesus uses are typical and important in John, especially truth *(alētheia)* and life *(zōē)*. We see them already prominently displayed and emphasized in the prologue (life in 1:4; truth in 1:14, 17). It is no surprise that Jesus says that he is truth and life.

"Way" *(hodos)* is less prominent in John, in fact it is used only here of Jesus, quite clearly because the subject is access to the Father. How does one gain it? Jesus is the way. Interestingly, the same term is used of the Christian movement in Acts (9:2; 19:9, 23; 22:4; 24:14, 22). There it is not a christological title, yet it is not hard to imagine a connection. While the term in Greek, as in English, basically denotes a road or path, it was widely used symbolically to refer to a way of life, a practice. The latter usage has biblical precedent (Prov 4:11; Jer 5:4). In the Qumran literature "way" (Heb. *derek*) is often used similarly (1QS9:16-21), as the members of the community apparently referred to their discipline as the Way. Also in early Christian literature there appears the concept of "two ways" (i.e., of life and death), particularly in the

Didache (especially chaps. 1 and 5). Perhaps closest to John 14:6 in New Testament usage is Heb 10:20, where Jesus is said to open a new and living way through the curtain (i.e., his flesh) into the sanctuary of the tabernacle, which is God's presence. (On the background of "way" here, see Brown 1970, 628-31, as well as Bultmann 1971, 603-7.) Although this background and the Christian and Jewish parallels are relevant to understanding what John means, his use of the term for Jesus, and as a virtual title for him, would seem to be unprecedented, although it is not surprising in John.

The identification of Jesus himself as the way squares with the radical claim of Johannine Christology, which is made quite explicitly here: "No one comes to the Father except through me" (v. 6; cf. Heb 10:20). This statement reflects a severe exclusivity, even intolerance. It should, however, be seen in light of John's presupposing a bitter polemic between Christ-confessing and Christ-denying Jews, in which confessors are being expelled from synagogues for their belief (9:22). Moreover, such polemic and mutual rejection were not unprecedented within ancient Judaism. (On such polemical tensions against and within Judaism see Luke Johnson 1989). One can, minimally, appreciate this statement of Jesus as assurance that he provides access to the Father. That no one else does is, of course, the obverse, but not a necessary obverse. The assumption that there is no way to the Father, and that Jesus has opened one (Heb 10:20) and has become himself that way is probably a more accurate reading of this statement than the assumption that there are many ways to the Father and that the Johannine Jesus is closing off all save one, himself. Jesus, in fact, gives his disciples the assurance that he has done just that (v. 7).

14:8-14: Philip's question again raises the issue of Jesus' relation to the Father. Following Jesus' assurance (v. 7), his request seems to manifest a kind of obtuseness, because Jesus has just said he has shown the disciples the Father (cf. Philip's perplexity in 6:7). All this conversation harks back to 1:18, where the classical Jewish belief that man does not see God is reflected. (See Exod 33:20: "no one shall see me and live," meaning no human being shall see the face, or presence, of God and live.) In this regard, Exod 24:10 is extremely interesting, for the Hebrew simply says that Moses and those with him "saw the God of Israel," while the Septuagint reads, "They saw the place where the God of Israel stood." The Old Testament does, if rarely, speak of men seeing God—as in Isa 6:1, 5—but as we come down to the period of Christian origins this becomes an intolerable idea in Judaism.

Philip's demand therefore seems impertinent against this background, as well as obtuse after what Jesus has just said. But, as is so often the case in the Fourth Gospel, the conversation partner's dullness opens the door for Jesus' clarifying, revelatory statement (v. 9; cf. 14:5 and 6 above). The ignorance of the twelve is a major motif of Mark's Gospel. Yet in a somewhat different form it also appears in John. Philip has been with Jesus all along, since the day Jesus called him (1:43; cf. 6:7; 12:21), yet he can still ask this question. Is Jesus' counterquestion to be read as a reflection of his actual astonishment and irritation with Philip? Possibly, but all along, and even in these final discourses, the disciples, although they have believed and followed Jesus, still do not understand him. Jesus uses the occasion to ask a probing question (v. 10a) and reiterate the Johannine Christology (vv. 10-11).

The Christology Jesus reiterates has been stated and restated, most recently in 12:44-45, 49-50. Heretofore Jesus has said it publicly, now he says it to his disciples, who seem to need to hear it as much as anyone. Yet there is now a change, for here Jesus expresses an even closer unity with the Father. Not only does he say what the Father gives him to speak, but the indwelling Father thereby does his works, and Jesus goes on to assert his unity with the Father, their mutual indwelling (Countryman 1987). He asks the disciples to believe him as he asserts that unity. Here (v. 11) the verb becomes plural, as Jesus addresses all his disciples; in verse 10 it is singular, as there Jesus is portrayed as still in conversation with Philip only. Then there is a curious turn as Jesus seems to contemplate the possibility that the disciples will not believe him, and says in effect, "All right, then believe me because of God's works." He has said something quite similar to his opponents already (10:37-38).

This statement puts at center stage the question of God's works. Earlier on Jesus has said that he must complete the work of God (4:34). In his concluding prayer he says he has completed the work God has given him to do. His final word on the cross, as he expires, is "It is finished," doubtless a double meaning in which John delights. Jesus' life is finished; he dies. But at a deeper level his work, God's work, is finished. Jesus' work is so closely aligned with God that he can say that the Father who dwells in him does his work. In Acts, Jesus' miracles are the work of God (10:32; cf. 10:38). Not only does Jesus do the work of God, his works, that is, his ministry, are the works of the God who speaks through him. Bultmann (1971, 609) equates Jesus' or God's works with words, but in the context of the whole Gospel it is more natural to think the works God does through Jesus include deeds, signs. Carson (1991, 495) thinks the reference is primarily to signs. Von Wahlde (1989) believes that the use of "signs," rather than works, and "Pharisees," rather than "Jews," for the religious authorities is characteristic of an earlier form of the Gospel. As the Gospel now stands, "works" often seems a broader category that includes signs, but is not exhausted by signs.

Jesus then turns from his own works, which are the works of God, to the works of his followers (v. 12). The first hint of disciples doing the works of God comes when Jesus is asked how to do the works of God after the feeding of five thousand (see 6:28): the answer is to believe in the one God has sent (v. 29). His disciples do believe in him and thus already do the works of God. Thus Jesus' promise that they will do the works he does comes as no surprise. He does the works of God: God works in him, and as believers they will do the works that he does (v. 12a). And they will do greater works because Jesus goes to the Father (v. 12b).

Probably a great many readers have been perplexed by Jesus' concluding statements in answer to Philip (vv. 12-14), because he promises his disciples first that they will do greater works than he does and then that anything they ask in his name he will do. The problem is, of course, that these promises exceed and defy any reasonable expectation, not that the promises themselves are hard to understand. In fact, there are similar assurances and promises of Jesus about answered prayer elsewhere (e.g., Matt 7:7-8; Mark 11:24; Luke 11:9-10; cf. Jas 4:2-3; 1 John 3:22). The interpreter should leave aside the question of whether or not these promises are realistic and ask what they mean in this Gospel.

The problem raised already by Jesus when he tells the disciples, "Where I am going, you cannot come" (14:33), leads into the theme of the discourses. Seemingly, the disciples are told exactly what Jesus has told the Jews (7:34). So the discourses address the fundamental question raised by the separation of Jesus from his disciples by death. From their standpoint this problem may seem insurmountable; from Jesus' standpoint, to which the reader is introduced also, it is no problem at all. Only Jesus' departure presents the possibility of his abiding with them eternally, a possibility that otherwise, or heretofore, did not exist. Eschatologically speaking, the disciples still live in the present age, which is passing away (cf. 1 Cor 7:31), while Jesus speaks from the standpoint of the coming age, into which he has already passed. He invites disciples to join him there, but they have not as yet.

Jesus is now about to promise them the Spirit-Advocate, really the means of his continuing presence with them (vv. 15-17). In light of this promise, with all that it entails, what Jesus says about the works they will accomplish and the fulfillment of their petitions is not surprising. Key phrases in this connection are "because I am going to the Father" and "whatever you ask in my name." It is Jesus' unity with the Father that will enable his disciples to do "greater works," which are really the continuing works of Jesus. Not anything they ask will be granted, but only what they ask in Jesus' name. The name in biblical and Johannine thought is the empowering reality and presence of the divine.

Jesus' promise raises the issue of what should be asked in his name. Seemingly Paul struggles with such a question in Rom 8:26; almost certainly 1 John 5:14-15 deals with this issue in light of Jesus' promise in the Gospel. Two thousand years of praying more or less perfunctorily "in Jesus' name" may be based upon this text, but it scarcely does justice to its profundity. Jesus is addressing disciples whom he has invited to live in, and out of, the resources of another age. There, in unity with him and the Father, they will do "greater works" and receive "whatever they ask." This reality sets aside all other, worldly conceptions of what believers will pray for and what may be realistic.

14:15-26: Now for the first time Jesus promises the disciples the Spirit or Advocate (see also 14:25-26; 15:26-27; 16:7-15). The future tense (v. 16) means this promise will be fulfilled after Jesus' departure. Indeed, in the Gospel narrative the risen Jesus, meeting with his disciples, will bestow on them the Holy Spirit (20:22). Of course, at the very beginning the Spirit has descended (and will remain) upon Jesus, who, it is said, will baptize with the Holy Spirit (1:33). The promise of the Spirit now fulfills the word of God to John the Baptist, as the disciples will be baptized with the Holy Spirit. One need not suppose that John believed, or intended to say, that otherwise God's Spirit had never been present in Israel or among human beings. Now, however, Jesus speaks of a new and distinctive manifestation of the Spirit. (See Burge 1987, especially 3-45, 205-15. More briefly, D. Moody Smith 1995, 78-80, 139-44, on Spirit and *paraklētos* in John.)

Jesus first states the condition of the Spirit's coming: the disciples must love Jesus by keeping his commandments (v. 15). Loving Jesus has been mentioned, if only fleetingly (8:42), but now becomes the central theme (as Bultmann 1971 notes, 612): To love Jesus is to keep his commandments. (Bultmann's insight has been taken up and developed by Miranda 1977, who gives full credit to him and emphasizes the importance of his insight.)

Jesus will return to the theme of love, but now he gives the promise of the Spirit-Advocate. Jesus' confidence that the Father will give him what he asks should not surprise us at this point. That he speaks of "another Advocate" may. Who was the first? The answer seems to be Jesus himself, who in 1 John (2:1) is called "an advocate with the Father." So already there is the suggestion that the Advocate will continue Jesus' work. (Note that in 1 John 2:1 "advocate" is not capitalized in the NRSV because it denotes a function; it is capitalized in John 14:15 because it is a title or proper name.)

There is, however, a problem of translation. As we noted, the

Greek word is the same here and in 1 John 2:1, where "advocate" is obviously the proper translation. Indeed, *paraklētos* means literally one called to the side of, an advocate or attorney. This meaning fits 1 John's use of the term quite well, but whether it fits the Gospel's (as in the NRSV) is a good question. This *paraklētos* does not function so much to advocate the disciples' cause before God as to mediate the presence of Jesus to the disciples. Unlike the earthly Jesus, the *paraklētos* abides forever. "As Jesus' successor among the disciples ... the Spirit-Paraclete is portrayed as having the same provenance and role as Jesus, except that its stay among the disciples will not be temporary but permanent" (Segovia 1991, 96). Here Segovia resorts to a transliteration of the Greek (Paraclete) so as to allow the term to be defined from the Gospel's context and avoid the danger of importing a foreign meaning through the choice of one word to translate it (so also O'Day 1995, 747). This is a reasonable procedure in view of the difficulty. (The KJV translates the term "Comforter," the RSV "Counselor," which implies an advocate, but has broader connotations. The NRSV's alternative translation, "Helper," which is a well-attested meaning, might actually serve better than "Advocate.") In any event, this particular case demonstrates well the problem of translation. One cannot ignore the etymology of a word, what it is derived from and what its components mean. At the same time, usage and function in context should be decisive. In this case etymology and usage stand in some tension with each other. Earlier use of the term or its putative equivalent in other sources is not particularly helpful in shedding light on its meaning in John, although commentators have ransacked the possibilities (see Bultmann 1971, 566-72 on possible Mandaean precedents; Barrett 1978, 462, on its use, in transliterated Hebrew, in rabbinic texts, where it means "advocate").

That the Spirit is called the Spirit of truth (v. 17) is quite appropriate. Jesus is himself the truth (14:6), and the Paraclete is in effect the Spirit of Jesus in the Johannine community, given only to those who know and have believed in Jesus. This Spirit will be in the community of believers ("in you"); probably "in" has a range of meaning from "within" to "among" (the NRSV alternative translation). "You" here is plural, so the statement does not necessarily mean within a person. This Spirit, as the presence of Jesus, will be pervasive among his followers after his departure.

Jesus now speaks directly of his continuing presence. "I will not leave you orphans," would be a literal translation of the Greek (v. 18), as Jesus repeats his promise to come to the disciples (cf. v. 3). He will take them into his Father's house (v. 2). His word and promise (v. 19) are reassuring but nevertheless enigmatic. The ending clause (v. 19*b*) is actually clearer than the opening statement. Obviously the disciples' living is dependent on Jesus' living. But what exactly is meant, or what exactly does Jesus refer to, when he says, "because I live"? Obviously Jesus does live; that is the conviction that makes possible the writing of this Gospel, as well as the early Christian faith and mission. But does John refer here to Jesus' resurrection, his future coming, or the coming of the Spirit? Fundamental is the reality of Easter (Bultmann 1971, 619): it is the risen Jesus who is coming to the disciples now (v. 18), meaning already in the time in which the Gospel is composed. Only his disciples will see the risen Christ, not the world (v. 19) for which he is dead and gone. (Contrast *Gos. Pet.* 9:34–11:49, in which Jesus' enemies see him rise from the dead and decide to suppress the information!) "That day" (v. 20) must then be Easter, which will confirm all that Jesus has said about his relation to the Father, as well as his own coming relationship to his disciples. (See Countryman 1987 on mutual indwelling and mysticism in John.)

Again, love for Jesus is said to consist of keeping his commandments (v. 21; cf. vv. 15, 24), as, indeed, Jesus has followed the commandment of God (12:49-50; 15:10). Any thought of love for Jesus as an emotion or attitude that is not strictly and closely tied to keeping Jesus' commandments is excluded. Love then is not so much a way of feeling as of doing. "Commandments" (plural) leads the reader to expect more than one. Yet the only commandment that has been singled out as such is the commandment to love one another (13:34; cf. 15:12). Love is reciprocal; and Father and Son are equivalent. Those who love the Son by keeping his commandments will be loved by the Father, as well as the Son. (On Jesus' commandments in 1 John, see von Wahlde 1990.) The promise of continuing revelation will really be fulfilled by the Spirit-Paraclete.

The Judas who now asks a question (v. 22), a Judas other than Iscariot, is otherwise mentioned only by Luke (6:16; Acts 1:13), who calls him the "son of James." (There is no list of the twelve in John, but we may perhaps assume that he takes this Judas to be among them. A caveat, however: John never explicitly states that only the twelve were present at the Last Supper.) Judas rightly understands that Jesus is speaking of a revelation or manifestation to disciples only, and is thus excluding the kind of public revelation that Christian apocalyptic texts speak. Easter or the Paraclete could be in view. We should think of the kind of revision of eschatology we saw in Jesus' conversation with Martha (11:23-26).

Jesus' response (vv. 23-24) is, in effect, to repeat what he has already said and make clear that love for him is expressed in keeping his commandments or words and, as we have seen, in no other way (cf. 1 John 1:3, where the term *fellowship* [Gk. *koinōnia*] is used of the relationship of Father, Son, and believers that is being described here). Now Jesus promises that he and the Father will come and make their home *(monē)* with the true disciples. In 14:3 Jesus has spoken of coming and taking them to himself. There also Jesus has spoken of a dwelling place or home *(monē)*. There is really no difference, except that in 14:1-3 Jesus may have the disciples' future in view as well, whereas here he is speaking principally of their present existence in the world. Where Jesus will be, there the disciples also will go. Where the true disciples are, there Jesus and the Father will come. Again, Jesus declares (v. 24) that the word he speaks is not his, but originates with the Father who sent him. (On God's sending Jesus, or the Father's sending the Son, see Meyer 1996, 255-73, especially 261-64.) Jesus' equality to God becomes manifest in his obedience to God.

That Jesus' and the Father's presence to the disciples will take the form of the coming of the Spirit-Paraclete is now made clearer (vv. 25-26). Jesus has said things to the disciples during his earthly ministry that they do not, even yet, understand. Although their present lack of understanding is not mentioned explicitly here, it is suggested elsewhere (see 13:37; 14:5, 8; 16:12, 29-33). The function of the Spirit-Paraclete, who is sent in Jesus' name, will be to teach and remind the disciples of Jesus (v. 26). The Spirit's reminding the disciples immediately recalls such statements in the narrative of Jesus' ministry as 2:22 and 12:16, where the disciples remember (and presumably understand) after Jesus has been raised from the dead or glorified. Presumably this recollection was to be inspired by the Spirit (cf. also 7:39). It is not just a retrospective view, although it is also that. The Spirit-Paraclete, one might say, inspires a theologically informed recollection of the true meaning of Jesus' ministry.

14:27-31: Jesus now apparently takes his leave. This brief section seems to conclude the discourses and, as matters now stand, brings the first stage to an end. Jesus will now say (v. 31), "Rise, let us be on our way," as if they will go out immediately. Yet the discourses continue (chaps. 15–16) and Jesus offers a long prayer (chap. 17).

The formal bestowal of peace (v. 27) signifies Jesus' farewell and approaching departure, as Jesus differentiates his peace from the world's. Again in 16:33, as the discourses actually close, Jesus speaks of peace, and when in resurrection scenes he encounters his disciples his greeting is "Peace be with you" (20:19, 21, 26). "Peace" was a greeting quite common among the first Christians, as Paul's letters show (Rom 1:7; 1 Cor 1:3; 2 Cor 1:2; Gal 1:3; 2 John 3; 3 John 15). Actually, "Peace be to you" seems to have been a form of greeting in biblical times (1 Sam 25:6), or one says, "Go in peace" (1 Sam 20:42; cf. Jas 2:16). That Jesus distinguishes his peace from the world's is reminiscent of Jeremiah's "peace, peace, when there is no peace" (6:14; 8:11), although John does not refer to the prophet directly. Jesus' leaving his peace with the disciples implies they will be secure in him (cf. 16:33), even though the world may be at war with them (15:18–16:4). Peace (Gk. *eirēnē*; cf. the proper name Irene) is in Hebrew *shalom,* a word that encompasses a large range of meaning, from health or well-being through prosperity. It alludes to and encompasses the benefits of God's care and deliverance (Luke 2:14; cf. 1:79; 2:29). When Jesus leaves his peace upon his disciples he is assuring them of the benefits of his saving work, which protects them from the world. Therefore, their hearts need not be troubled or afraid. With this reassurance, he here returns to the theme of the beginning of this chapter (14:1), so that an inclusion is formed, marking the integrity of this section or discourse.

Jesus then summarizes for his disciples what he has just been telling them in the discourse (v. 28a). His commentary on what he has said (vv. 28b-29) again reveals the retrospective character of the narrative. Jesus has told the disciples what will happen before it occurs, before they can know and, in the full sense, believe (v. 29). Thus he tells them what they can only later understand. The if-clause of verse 28b is actually a contrary-to-fact condition, which does not imply that the disciples will not love Jesus, but rather that they cannot love him fully or properly until his departure, his death, and glorification. He goes to the Father, who is greater than he is (v. 28). He does what the Father commands (v. 31) and thus demonstrates his love for the Father, even as disciples love Jesus in doing what he commands (vv. 15, 23-24). Jesus' ministry, his obeying the Father's command in arising and going on his way to his death, will show the world his love for God. Then perhaps even the world may know God's love for it (3:16). Jesus will return to the subject of the world, and what the world may know, in his final prayer, where he prays for the unity of his disciples "so that the world may believe that you have sent me" (17:21, 23). Although the world is arrayed against Jesus and his disciples, they do not reciprocate the world's hostility.

Jesus draws his discourse to a close with an announcement that the ruler of this world is coming (v. 30) and his exhortation to his followers to set out with him. The ruler of this world is Satan (cf. 12:31), who plays an active role in the death of Jesus, motivating Judas to hand him over to the authorities (13:2, 27). Judas's action can only be explained as the work of the most powerful force of evil. Although Satan seems to cause Jesus' death, through Judas' betrayal (cf. 19:11), he really does not, for Jesus determines his own destiny (10:17-18; cf. 13:27).

The Allegory of the Vine (15:1-17)

Jesus seems to begin afresh with the figure of the vine, as if the preceding chapter were not there. (Segovia 1991, 123-67, treats 15:1-17 as the Second Discourse.) Yet there is a connection. In chapter 14 Jesus has assured the disciples that they will be with him, and indeed that they may and must have union with him and the Father (vv. 20, 23). Now he will dwell on the nature and purpose of that union (15:1-17), which stands in contrast to the hostility of the world (15:18–16:4). Jesus speaks without interruption throughout this discourse, indeed, through 16:16, although the subject changes (15:18; 16:5). In fact, from this point on the disciples say very little (but see 16:17-18, 29-30).

The *figure* of the shepherd is explicitly called that (10:6: *paroimia*), although the vine is not. Yet at the end of the discourses Jesus says that he has spoken to the disciples in "figures of speech" (16:25). But after his statement that immediately follows (16:26-28) the disciples say that he is now speaking "plainly" (Gk. *parrēsia*) and not in any "figure of speech" (16:29). The figures of the good shepherd and the vine are sometimes considered the two parables of the Gospel of John, with the proviso that they are unlike the synoptic parables, which are, on the whole, not allegories. We have already observed that 10:1-18 both invites and resists treatment as an allegory. Although Jesus is clearly the good shepherd, as well as the door, it is not so clear who the other characters are. Here, by way of metaphor, it is made quite clear who the vine, the branches, and the vine grower are: Jesus, his disciples, and the Father. Again, the metaphor of pruning is understandable and quite appropriate, although one may ask what is meant by burning or, indeed, by the disciples' bearing much fruit. In sum, it is understandable why the figures of the shepherd and the vine are considered to be of the same genre, while also different from the synoptic parables. (On their character, see Brown 1966, 390-91; 1970, 668-72, who notes that the broader Hebrew concept of *mashal* covers both the synoptic parables and John's use of figures of speech. The Hebrew noun is derived from the cognate verb meaning to liken or compare. Note also Schweizer 1996, 208-19, on Johannine "parables.")

It is worth observing, however, that scriptural (Old Testament) parables could have an allegorical dimension, as Nathan's famous parable of the ewe lamb shows (2 Sam 12:1-6). While there are good reasons for seeing in both the vine and the shepherd vehicles of John's theology, it is not correct to decide on the basis of genre, particularly their allegorical aspects, that they are hellenistic and late and therefore could have no basis in the Jesus tradition. They have clearly allegorical aspects but the difference from the Synoptics (and from the Old Testament) may lie more in the explicit Christology that finds expression in them.

Jesus declares himself to be the true vine, using for the last time the "I am" formula that is characteristic of John (15:1; cf. 10:11 and the other instances cited there). Here again we seem to have what Bultmann calls the recognition formula (1971, 225-26, n. 3; cf. Schweizer 1996, 208-19, especially 214-15), meaning that Jesus is to be recognized as the *true* vine in contrast to false ones, like he is the good shepherd in contrast to bad ones. Just as shepherd and sheep symbolize Israel and her leaders in Scripture (e.g., Ezek 34), so the vine or vineyard can be a symbol for Israel (Ps 80:8-16; Isa 5:1-7; Jer 2:21; Ezek 17:6-8; 19:10-14). In Hos 10:1 Israel is a "luxuriant vine that yields its fruit." There are other appearances of the vine as a symbol in ancient religion (Bultmann 1971, 530, n. 5), but the many points of contact between John and Scripture make it the obvious first place to look. By presenting Jesus and his followers through the use of such biblical metaphors for Israel as flock and vine the Gospel implies that they are the new people of God. This is certainly what John intends to say, and, that being the case, the biblical background and basis of the language and conceptuality constitute a natural fit.

In the synoptic Gospels Jesus speaks of drinking of the fruit of the vine at the Last Supper (Matt 26:29; Mark 14:25; Luke 22:18) and Jesus tells the parable of the vineyard at the end of his ministry (Matt 21:33-43; Mark 12:1-12; Luke 20:9-18). His saying about the fruit of the vine concludes the words of institution of the Lord's Supper in Matthew and Mark and is associated with them in Luke, as well. The parable of the vineyard is the one christological parable of the Synoptics, for there Jesus expresses in parabolic form what becomes a major theological motif of the Gospel of John, namely, the Father's sending of the Son. (In Greek the word for vine is *ampelos* and vineyard *ampelōn*, so the terms resemble each other even more in the original than in translation.) Indeed, in the parable the vineyard seems to be Israel, as in the prophets, although this is not explicitly said. (This parable, incidentally, invites allegorical interpretation.) It is tempting to interpret John against this biblical and synoptic background. Moreover, John's use of the term vine evokes the words of institution of the Eucharist (cf. Mark 14:25: "I will never again drink of the fruit of the vine…"), in which wine plays a prominent role, and it seems all the more reasonable to ask about the eucharistic implications of Jesus' being called the true vine, presumably while he and the disciples are still at the scene of the Supper.

Yet the closest synoptic parallel to the vine discourse, and particularly the fruit imagery appears toward the end of the Sermon on the Mount/Plain (Matt 7:15-20; Luke 6:43-44). Although "vine" does not occur here, but rather "tree," the emphasis on the importance of fruit is quite similar. Moreover, in the Matthean version Jesus speaks of cutting down and burning the tree that does not bear good fruit (cf. John 15:2, 6). In the synoptic (probably Q) context "fruit" stands for good deeds accomplished through obedience to God, or more specifically, to the words of Jesus. If one reads John against this background, a similar meaning of "fruit" is suggested, and this would appear to be appropriate, with a distinctly Johannine twist. In John, obedience to Jesus' words or commands is love. Moreover, in the Synoptics Jesus tells his disciples that by their fruit people will know them (Matt 7:16, 20; Luke 6:45), while in John he says that by their love for one another (= obedience to his command = fruit) people will know that they are his disciples (John 13:35). While it is a stretch to suggest that John is playing off the words of Jesus in Matthew (or Luke), this discourse suggests familiarity with that tradition.

Although these connections are not irrelevant, the reader should first appreciate what John has actually written, for the text is a consistent metaphor, or arrangement of related metaphors.

After the opening statement John gives a good description of what the vine grower, who is the Father (Gk. *geōrgos*, which can simply mean "farmer"), actually does (Brown 1970, 675). Commentators have noted that John here seems to reflect knowledge of actual viticultural practice, even as in 10:1-18 he knows how shepherds relate to their sheep. The synoptic parables generally reflect the rural, small-town life of first-century Palestine. Although, John's parables or figures of speech are quite distinctive (Schweizer 1996, 208-19, especially 209-13), they too seem accurately to reflect this culture of ancient non-urban Palestine. Perhaps this is all the more surprising since John is the most urban of the Gospels, much of the action taking place in Jerusalem (2:13–3:21; 5:1-47; 7:14–10:39; 12:12–20:31; and in chap. 11 Jesus is in Bethany, just outside Jerusalem). The story of the Samaritan woman (4:1-42) takes place just outside Sychar, a Samaritan city; the bread discourse of 6:25-59 is set in the synagogue of the major town of Capernaum (6:59), which also figures prominently in the Synoptics.

Although the vine grower does what any farmer would (v. 2), his actions have patent symbolic significance as John makes clear. Unproductive branches are cut out; productive ones are pruned (or cleansed) so that they may bear more fruit. The meaning of individual figures, the vine grower, should not be pressed, but the idea that the branches are judged in terms of their productivity by the vine grower is certainly stressed. The true import of the pruning is now brought out. Jesus' disciples have been cleansed by his word (v. 3). Crucial to the analogy between branches and disciples is the key word *kathairō,* "to prune," which can also mean "to cleanse." The branches will be pruned/cleansed. The disciples are already cleansed (pruned) by the word Jesus has spoken. Actually, in verse 3 the term used of the disciples is the related adjective *katharos,* which would not typically mean pruned, but rather cleansed. But the play on the word stem is clear enough, and obviously intentional. The true disciples are those branches who have been cleansed/pruned by Jesus' word, not those that have been taken away, that is, cut out or removed completely. The disciples have heard, believed, and obeyed Jesus' word, although they may not even yet have comprehended it fully.

The analogy between the branches and the disciples becomes quite explicit (vv. 4-5), but now the point shifts from the pruning, cleansing, disciplinary work of the vine grower to the fundamental importance of the organic relationship of the branch to the vine, and of the disciple to Jesus. Obviously, the purpose of the branch is to bear fruit, and the disciples must bear fruit. Of what does their fruit bearing consist? It is an obvious question that does not receive a direct answer in this text. As Jesus' discourse develops, however, emphasis falls increasingly on the indispensability of love, which should find expression at the level of everyday life in their love for one another (v. 12). It is therefore a reasonable inference that these fruit are works of love. Yet it may be a mistake to ask about the fruit specifically, as if, in allegorical fashion, it represents one specific thing or even theme. Bultmann (1971, 532-33) stresses the general nature, as well as the more specific focus, of the expectation of fruit: "The nature of the fruit-bearing is not expressly stated; it is every demonstration of vitality of faith, to which, according to vv. 9-17, reciprocal love above all belongs."

The statements "I am the vine you are the branches" and "Apart from me you can do nothing" are complementary, the obverse of each other. Thus those who abide bear much fruit. Throughout the entire discourse, from the very beginning on (v. 2), the strong element of warning or admonition is, however, evident. Now it is emphasized by the description (v. 6) of the dire fate of branches (disciples) who do not abide in the vine (Jesus). At this point the death of the branch seems to precede its withering and being thrown away. Here the viticultural image may break down, unless we have in view branches that die naturally. But in the case of disciples it is a matter of their willingly, or knowingly, not abiding, even while they are nominally a part of the vine. The key to abiding in the vine is the fulfillment of Jesus' commandments (v. 10; cf. 14:15-16, 23), and that commandment (really singular) is mutual love. To those who abide, Jesus reiterates the astonishing promise we have already heard (v. 7; cf. 14:13-14). Such is the importance of the disciples' abiding in Jesus, and their mutual indwelling with one another and with the Father (14:20, 23), that it is an essential aspect of the glorification of the Father, even as Jesus' death is (v. 8). Obviously, Jesus' death is the key moment of glorification, which takes place on Jesus' initiative at God's command, but apart from the disciples' fruitful obedience and their union with Jesus, it remains incomplete. As Carson puts it (1991, 518), "the fruitfulness of believers is part and parcel of the way the Son glorifies his Father."

The chain of love, which begins and has its source in the Father's love for the Son, extends through the Son to his disciples (v. 9) and is the living form and substance of their unity over against the world. That love is not simply a disposition, much less a mere feeling, is then made entirely clear (v. 10). To love means to obey, and apart from such tangible obedience there is no love. Probably the primary exposition of what Jesus means here by love is found in 1 John 4:7-21, in which the priority of God's love is stressed. Indeed, God is love (4:8, 16), but also this implies the necessity of human love as the proper response to God's love (4:11). Moreover, the necessity of love's finding concrete expression is stressed (3:17), as well as the vacuousness of any talk of loving God apart from showing love to one's sister or brother (4:20).

The intensity of Jesus' speech is suddenly relieved by his sudden reference to joy (15:11). "Joy" is a significant Johannine theme. John the Baptist's joy is fulfilled with the presence of Jesus (3:29). The author of 1 John writes to complete the joy of his readers (1:4). Jesus in his final prayer speaks of the completion of the disciples' joy (17:13). Evidently, joy is an essential aspect of the eschatological life that Jesus has brought. Not coincidentally, Paul wishes his readers joy (Rom 14:17; 15:13, 32), as though it were an essential aspect of their existence as Christians. It is as if the stern warnings and solemn commandment need to be put into their proper context. Jesus has said these things for the sake of joy, that his joy may fill the disciples. It is worth noting that in his relation to the Father Jesus himself has joy. He will emphasize the theme of the disciples' joy toward the end of this discourse (16:16-24).

But now Jesus returns to the basic theme of love (15:12), reiterating the commandment already given earlier (13:34), and adding again the key phrase "as I have loved you." This time, however, he alludes to his own demonstration of his love for the disciples (v. 13). As the knowledgeable reader will recognize, Jesus here brings into view his own death. (See 13:34 and the references to Jesus' love commandment in the Johannine letters, e.g., 1 John 2:7-11; 3:11, as well as the Gospel.) In doing so, Jesus obviously points to the extreme, self-sacrificial character of the love he commands. One thinks of the word of Jesus about losing one's life and keeping it (12:25; cf. Mark 8:34-35 par.), which although it does not mention love specifically stresses that following Jesus entails self-sacrifice. It should come as no surprise that being Jesus' friend means keeping his commandment(s). The word used here is the standard Greek word for friend, *philos* (verb, *phileō*, to love; noun, *philia*, friendship or love), not a term used lightly, as Jesus will immediately spell out (v. 16) as he draws the distinction between servants and friends. Here the term for servants *(douloi)* can also mean slaves, and probably does. So if one asks when or where Jesus has previously called his disciples servants or slaves, the answer is in 13:16, where he also calls them apostles *(apostoloi;* NRSV: "messengers"). It is quite remarkable that Jesus defines friendship as being in the know, knowing what Jesus himself is doing; this sets them apart from slaves, who do not know. The disciples, like Jesus, the evangelist, and, indeed, the knowledgeable reader, will know what Jesus is doing. Jesus has revealed fully what the Father has revealed to him. Yet although Jesus has already made this known, they will not actually understand until after he has been glorified.

Jesus again makes an abrupt turn as he asserts his own initiative and freedom in choosing and appointing his disciples (v. 16). Interestingly, this statement works on two levels. First, Jesus obviously makes a theological point that is important to John (cf. 1 John 4:10); actually, it is ultimately the Father who has given these disciples to Jesus (see 6:37, 39; 17:6; cf. 18:9). The freedom and priority of Jesus' decision and act underlie all that takes place at the historical level, and, of course, Jesus acts only on behalf of God, following his command, rather than on his own behalf. But, second, Jesus has chosen and appointed his disciples, particularly the twelve, as the synoptic Gospels also make clear (Mark 3:13-19 par.; Mark actually says that Jesus called and appointed the twelve). This is something that in all probability happened during his public ministry, as the other Gospels report.

What Jesus is saying is now tied back into his discourse on the vine by the reference to bearing fruit (v. 16). Coming as it does on the heels of the command to love, it reinforces the interpretation of fruit as love, as does the idea of the fruit's abiding.

After Jesus once again promises to answer all petitions made in his name (cf. 14:13-14), he reiterates the love commandment (13:34; 15:12). The return to the theme of bearing fruit, along with the love command, forms a kind of inclusion with the opening parable or figure, after which bearing fruit is gradually interpreted as love. Love is obedience to Jesus' commands—the disciple obeys Jesus as Jesus obeys the Father—and not simply an attitude or feeling. At the same time, love cannot be adequately described in terms of ethics or as existing only on the horizontal, human level. God is love (1 John 4:8, 16), and to abide in love is to abide in union with God the Father and with Jesus his Son (14:21-24). There is no other way.

Although John does not here use the word "church" (Gk. *ekklēsia,* which appears in no Gospel except Matthew) there is an obvious sense in which the vine and its branches are a metaphor for Christ and the church, the Christian community. It is sometimes likened to Paul's use of the term "body of Christ" when he is obviously speaking of the church (1 Cor 12; cf. Rom 12:3-8). Paul's body imagery evokes the fundamental idea of interdependence among members, and one can easily imagine that Paul chose "body" for that very reason. The Johannine imagery lacks precisely this essential connotation of "body." A branch can be lopped off without materially affecting the whole, something that could scarcely be said of the eye or the ear (cf. 1 Cor 12:16-17). In this respect, John's choice of imagery is deficient in comparison with Paul's (see Via 1961, especially 181-85). If, however, the vine's fruit, of which Jesus speaks, is really the fruit of love, the expression of love in obedience to Jesus' own command, the element of mutuality is introduced, and is indeed essential, although it is not graphically embodied in the symbol itself, as in Paul's usage.

The World's Hatred (15:18–16:4a)

The preceding section (15:1-17) is about the disciples' relation to Jesus and to one another; it is about love. This section is about hatred, the world's hatred of the disciples of Jesus. (Segovia 1991, 169-212, treats this as the Third Discourse.) The transition from love (v. 17) to hatred (v. 18) is abrupt, but entirely understandable. Hatred is of course the opposite of love. The world's hatred of Jesus has been, or will be, obvious to the disciples, and they can expect nothing different. The full expression of the world's hatred of Jesus, his death by crucifixion, has not yet been narrated. The world's hatred follows upon its hatred of Jesus and his choice of the disciples "out of the world" (v. 19). Their election is discussed at some length by Jesus in his final prayer (17:6-19), as well as the fact that "the world has hated them" (17:14). If the world loves its own, as it does, it must hate Jesus and his disciples.

Here the Johannine dualism comes into play. It is clearly and integrally related to the disciples' love for one another, which is grounded in Jesus' (and God's) love for them on the one hand as well as to the world's hostility for his community of Jesus' followers on the other. Quite likely this sharp division is the basis, rather than the product, of this dualism (Meeks 1972, 71-72). The community of Jesus' disciples exists in deep alienation from other expressions of Judaism, which reject its claims for Jesus, even as it responds with rejection of any claim to know God apart from Jesus (vv. 23-24). Thus the Jews are equated with the world (cf. 16:2; see Bultmann 1971, 86-87; Ashton 1991, 134-35, agreeing with Bultmann). The setting of the Gospel is reflected here, since during his ministry the world did not hate Jesus' followers—not even the world of Judaism. Interestingly, in the opening chapters of Acts (chaps. 1–5), Jesus' disciples, notably Peter and John, incur the wrath of the temple authorities, but not the people per se. Whether that representation is historical is a good question, but it is arguably accurate, particularly with regard to where historic Jewish opposition to Jesus and his disciples lay, if not in the suggestion of the entire people's approbation.

Jesus recalls his earlier word (v. 20; cf. 13:16; in both cases "servant" or "slave" is singular, as the NRSV has resorted to the plural so the language will be inclusive). Such backward references (analepses) are not uncommon in John (18:9; cf. 6:37, 39). Jesus anticipates the world's hostility toward his disciples and prays God's protection for them in his last great prayer (17:6-19). The persecution of Jesus' disciples is almost a foregone conclusion. Perhaps more surprising is the possibility that some in the world will hear their word and believe, but there are actually hints that this may happen (3:16; 17:20, 21, 23). The preaching of the gospel of Jesus to the world is still not purposeless or pointless. What about preaching to Jews who are representative of the world? That John advocates preaching to Pharisees, who epitomize Jewish opposition to Jesus, is unlikely, although Nicodemus, who keeps coming back to Jesus, is a Pharisee (3:1). Yet John portrays many Jewish people, aside from the twelve, as believing (7:31; 7:40, 43; 8:31; 10:21; 12:11). The Jewish believers of 8:31ff. turn on Jesus, it is true, but should they be the key to interpret all other instances of Jews' believing in Jesus, or is this an isolated instance? In any event, the fact that many Jews are said to believe in Jesus during his ministry suggests that the Johannine community's mission to Israel is not yet complete or at an end. Some may keep the disciples' word.

Jesus' next statement deals with those who persecute Jesus and his followers (v. 21). Their opposing Jesus and his followers is tantamount to opposing God, and therefore not knowing God, because it is God who has sent Jesus. This theme is emphasized, if not exhausted, in the present paragraph. It is found at least as far back as 5:37-38 in this narrative of Jesus' public ministry, and the tension and hostility are heightened in the dreadful polemic between Jesus and the Jews, even some of his Jewish followers, in chapter 8. Jesus' disciples pray in his name; his opponents persecute his followers on account of it. Whoever hates Jesus hates the God who sent him (v. 23). Of course, the Jews might well protest that they do not worship the God who sent Jesus; so this ultimately becomes a dispute about God. Who is God really? An ultimate impasse is reached.

Even as verse 23 goes with verse 21, so verses 22 and 24 express the same basic ideas. One could caricature what is actually written by saying that Jesus, or the coming of Jesus, is the cause of sin, since his coming is what led to sin (cf. Jesus' response to the Pharisees' question about blindness in 9:40-41). A kind of narrative description of the coming of the Son into this world and its effects is found in 3:17-21. There the light comes into the world and people react to it by shunning it or by coming to it, depending on whether their deeds are evil or true. As was suggested (pp. 100-101), there are different ways to understand this brief narrative. Perhaps the most obvious is that it describes the way in which the light shows people for what they are. Thus the light would have revelatory, but not salvific, significance. That is, Jesus would reveal who was doing what God approved, but would not actually effect any change. But (following Bultmann 1971, 157-60) it is preferable to understand the text as meaning "that in the decision of faith or unbelief it becomes apparent what man really is and what he always was" (159). And only then. Thus the decision of faith determines both past and future. This understanding of 3:20-21 makes sense of what is said here (15:22, 24), as well as at the conclusion of the episode of the man born blind (9:40-41).

The world does not exist in a sin-free state until the advent of Jesus, whose coming introduced sin. Jesus after all is the light that shines in darkness (1:5); he comes to take away the sin of the world (1:29). It is rather that with the coming of Jesus the history of humankind has a new start. To believe is to pass from death to life. Not to believe is to incur judgment (5:24). With the coming of Jesus God is revealed and people are confronted and challenged. It is then a question of one's response to Jesus, and rejection of him, his words (15:22) and his works (v. 24), sin and condemnation. This rejection of Jesus is hatred not only of him, but of God the Father, who at least in Jesus they have now seen (v. 24). It is important to remember, however, that these words have in view not humankind in the abstract, but the enemies of Jesus and his followers, those who hate him. And their hatred is gratuitous—without cause.

Psalm 35:19 or 69:4 is quoted, although the Johannine version is identical neither to the Hebrew nor to the Septuagint. That the psalms are counted as law probably means that it is a part of Scripture, which is considered "law." It is not called "their law," because John and his community reject it (cf. 10:35) but this way of talking is an indication of the tension between the two communities. Perhaps this is the equivalent of saying in "the law as they [the Jews] read it" (cf. 8:17). Scripture still reveals God's plan; otherwise their hatred would be without explanation. What sinners do does not contradict or fall outside of God's will.

What Jesus has been saying to his disciples about the world's hatred to this point (vv. 18-25) is basically in the present tense or mode. Now Jesus shifts into the future tense as he speaks of the Advocate or Paraclete (v. 26). Yet what he has already been telling them really applies to their future rather than the present time, that is, the time of Jesus' own ministry. (On the term *Advocate,* see the discussion of 14:16.) Again the Advocate (or Paraclete) is said to be the Spirit of truth, which is the special mode of the Holy Spirit in the aftermath of Jesus' glorification. Earlier the Paraclete is said to be sent by the Father (14:26; cf. 14:16), but now Jesus is said to send the Paraclete from the Father. There is no essential difference. Now, however, the function of the Paraclete is somewhat differently defined as testifying (NRSV) or bearing witness (RSV).

"Testify on my behalf" fits the NRSV's juridical translation of *paraklētos* as Advocate. Moreover, the disciples are here set against the background of the world's hostility. Therefore the Advocate will testify on Jesus' behalf, as will the disciples (v. 27).

John uses the term *martyreō*, "testify" or bear "witness." Perhaps in verse 27 "bear witness" (RSV) is a bit better, because it implies seeing as well as saying (cf. 21:24). The disciples have been with Jesus "from the beginning." Thus the phrase "from the beginning" is also quite important in 1 John 1:1; 2:7, 13, where it signifies the beginning of the Christian tradition, and revelation, in Jesus. They are therefore competent to bear witness, to testify. A similar interest in being present with Jesus as a requirement for bearing witness competently is found in Acts, where the use of the noun "witness" implies both seeing and testifying (1:22).

Jesus now explicitly states he is warning his disciples in advance (16:1) to keep them from stumbling, obviously when these things start happening. The same word, here translated "stumble" (passive) appears also in 6:61, where the active is rendered "offend." There Jesus is questioning disciples who are about to fall away from him (6:66). (The Greek term s*kandalizō* is the basis for the English word "scandalize," and it means literally "to stumble.") Apparently Jesus wants to head off defections among his followers by warning them in advance of what will happen (cf. v. 4), for the temptation or danger of defection will be real in light of the depredations Jesus is about to describe (v. 2).

As Martyn (1979) and others have argued, ejection from synagogues was a significant threat intended to discourage belief in Jesus as the Messiah (9:22), so some Jewish believers were careful to keep their allegiance secret (12:42). Only here in John does Jesus mention the mortal threat to his disciples, although such a threat may, as Martyn suggests (1979, 67-68, 71), lie behind the constant menacing of Jesus (e.g., 5:18; 7:1, 19; 10:31). Although the Synoptics indicate that there was opposition to Jesus during his public ministry, and doubtless there was, it is not set in the context of such explicit christological controversy as it is in John (but cf. Matt 5:11; 10:18; Mark 13:6-11; Luke 6:22; 12:11-12). As we have seen constantly, the controversies between Jesus and his opponents have to do with claims made for himself, and this is distinctive. Historically such claims became explicit not with Jesus, but with his followers in the postresurrection period.

Mortal or similar threats to Jewish believers in Jesus by other

Jews are attested occasionally, if rarely, in the New Testament, although none quite correspond to what is envisioned in the Gospel of John. Stephen's speech (Acts 7) and the accusations against him led to his death by stoning (Acts 7:54–8:1) in the presence of Paul the Pharisee, who says that he himself persecuted the church of God violently and tried to destroy it (Gal 1:13; cf. 1 Cor 15:9). According to Acts (9:1-9; 22:4-11; 26:12-18), Paul was off to persecute the church in Damascus when he himself was encountered by the risen Jesus. In the context of telling his story in Acts Paul once says that when Christians were on trial for their lives in Jewish courts he voted against them (26:10). In writing to the Thessalonians Paul compares their trials to those of the churches of God in Judea that suffered at the hands of their fellow countrymen, the Jews, or Judeans (the Greek word *Ioudaioi* is the same in either case), who opposed preaching to the Gentiles (1 Thess 2:14-16). Paul himself says that he was once stoned, presumably by his fellow Jews (2 Cor 11:25), for whom stoning was the traditional form of execution. Although we cannot be certain that this was an attempted execution that for some reason was aborted, Paul in this context is writing about punishment he had received from his fellow Jews. In cases involving Paul, the issue was often preaching to Gentiles, but as far as we can see, this was not the case in John. Here it was basically an inner-Jewish dispute over the status to be accorded Jesus. Perhaps the closest correspondence to Jesus' prophecy is found in Justin Martyr (*Dial. Trypho* 95.4; 110.5; 133.6), who explicitly links Jewish responsibility for Jesus' death to that of his followers.

While the Johannine situation is not exactly paralleled in all these texts, they do afford the background against which to view it. It should be emphasized that we do not have here, or in any of these instances, a case of Christians being put to death by Jews. In John and in all the instances just cited we are dealing with inner-Jewish controversy, albeit over the Messiah or over what the Messiah's coming means for Jews or Judaism. That those who would kill the disciples of Jesus believe they are offering worship or service to God shows that other Jews are apparently meant.

Despite their belief, their actions show they know neither the Father nor Jesus (v. 3). People who have never actually seen Jesus may be in view, but in any case such persons would not really know Jesus because they would not know his true origin with the Father. Of course, not to know Jesus in this sense is not to know God.

Again Jesus emphasizes why he is telling the disciples these things before his departure (v. 4): so that when these things happen they will remember that Jesus had told them, so that they will not stumble (v. 1). The retrospective character of this Gospel has more than one dimension. The disciples look back and remember what Jesus did in his public ministry (2:22; 12:16), and they also can remember that Jesus had predicted what is now happening to them. In the evangelist's scheme the Spirit-Paraclete illumines the period of Jesus' ministry, while Jesus illumines the period of the postresurrection church, even its suffering.

Jesus' Final Discourse: His Departure and Return (16:4b-33)

This is the fourth unit of the discourses (see Segovia 1991, especially 215-17). As Segovia observes, the second (15:1-17) and third units (15:18–16:4*a*) introduce new material and themes, whereas this unit reiterates the themes of the departure and return of Jesus. Moreover, here, as in the first unit, Jesus' disciples interact with him. Jesus alone has been speaking throughout the second and third units, but now they again question him (16:17-18; they speak a second and final time in vv. 29-30). The other Judas had been the last disciple to address him (14:22). With the interchange with his disciples (16:29-32) and Jesus' word of warning and exhortation (v. 33) the discourses come to an end.

Now Jesus will further describe the work of the Spirit. But at the beginning (16:4*b*) he is continuing his statement (v. 4*a*) about why he is saying these things to the disciples at this point. Yet verse 4*b* obviously leads into Jesus' next statement (v. 5) as well as referring back to his previous one. At the same time it sheds light on verse 4*a*. Jesus distinguishes not only between the time before the hour of his glorification and the time after, but between the period of the discourses and the time "from the beginning" when "I was with you." The discourses then represent a unique stage of Jesus' relationship to his disciples, the particular moment or time of his departure from them.

The question about where Jesus is going, which he says they have not asked, has, however, been dealt with already (13:33, 36–14:7), and Peter has, in fact, asked exactly that question (13:36; cf. 14:5). Bultmann 1971, 558, n. 2, has alleviated this difficulty in his rearrangement of the text, according to which 13:36 (and 14:5) actually follows 16:5. But if, as on other grounds seems likely, this discourse is an alternative version of 13:33–14:31 the difficulty is similarly resolved. Here the question is eventually answered by Jesus, who tells them he is going to the Father (16:10). Jesus knows their questioning, however, and their sorrow (Gk. *lupē*; grief), which is, of course, occasioned by Jesus' death. So Jesus' word of consolation stresses the *advantage* to the disciples in his departing: he will send the Advocate-Paraclete (v. 7; cf. 14:16, 26; 15:26-27). Already he has told them that they should rejoice that he goes to the Father (14:28), having just promised the Paraclete (14:26).

Jesus now in effect gives two promises of the Paraclete, one having to do with the world (vv. 8-11) and the other with the disciples, the church (vv. 12-15). The function of the Paraclete with respect to the world is more difficult to understand, for Jesus has said the world cannot receive the Spirit (14:17). In fact, it is not now a matter of the world's receiving it, but rather of the Paraclete's judging the world. The Paraclete's work must, however, be carried out through the church, where the Paraclete is received, presumably in the church's preaching. Here the term translated "prove wrong" (v. 8; Gk. *elengchō*) means also "bring to light," "expose," or "convict" (RSV). As the difference between the NRSV and RSV translation shows, the meaning is not unclear but the best translation is debatable, although recent translations such as the NRSV and REB have tended in the direction of "prove wrong." Certainly the world is wrong in each of these respects: about what sin is, about where righteousness lies, and about who is judged.

The first respect in which the world is proved wrong is the failure to believe in Jesus (v. 9). That is obvious enough. (Moreover, to do the true "works of God" is to believe in Jesus [6:29].) The world is wrong "about righteousness" (v. 10) because contrary to the world's expectation the Jesus whom the world crucified goes to God the Father, and is vindicated as righteous rather than condemned as a blasphemer. (In his exalted status he appears as the Risen One and sends the Paraclete to his disciples.) It is something of a problem that Jesus says, "*You* will no longer see me," rather than "the world will no longer see me," as we might expect. In fact, in verse 17 he promises the disciples they will see him, apparently referring to the Resurrection. Yet clearly John presumes Jesus will no longer be accessible to ordinary sight, even to those who believe in him (20:29). Thus he emphasizes the importance of the earthly Jesus' having been seen (1:14; 19:35; 21:24; 1 John 1:1, 3). At the same time the farewell discourses take as their primary datum Jesus' departure, and therefore his physical inaccessibility. Here Jesus' emphasis falls on his going to the Father, as the demonstration of righteousness over against the world. Their not seeing him then comes in as a kind of afterthought that inevitably follows from his departure and creates the need for Jesus to communicate with his disciples before he goes. He must assure them of the new mode of his continuing presence.

The judgment of the ruler of this world (v. 11) has already been announced (12:31). Here the text literally reads "about judgment, because the ruler of this world has been judged" (NIV: "stands condemned"). The Paraclete-inspired preaching of God's vindication of Jesus is the judgment, that is, condemnation, of this world, which had judged or condemned him. (One thinks of what Paul wrote in 1 Cor 2:8 about the rulers of this age crucifying the Lord of glory.) Presumably they had judged him and found him guilty, as a sinner, one who defied God's righteousness. Obviously, in John's view he was none of these things, but just the opposite, and the Spirit, which inspires the church's proclamation, effects a radical reversal of the world's judgment, showing that it was exactly wrong and in need of overturning. Indeed, it has been overturned.

The coming of the Spirit-Paraclete, which can only be received by the disciples, the church, nevertheless convicts the world in the sense that it condemns the world's rejection of Jesus. The church's proclamation about Jesus means that the world's judgment of him was radically wrong, for his righteousness has been affirmed in his going to the Father, and therefore the world's disbelief is a manifestation of its sinfulness. But the world is not simply condemned to hopelessness and destruction, for God did not send the Son to condemn the world, but finally to save it (3:16; 12:47). Therefore the Spirit-inspired proclamation of Jesus condemns not the world, but the world's condemnation of Jesus. It is still a sign of hope to the world. It is the ruler of the world, that is, Satan, who has been condemned.

Jesus then turns to the work of the Spirit in the community of Jesus' disciples (vv. 12-15), as he now will reiterate and expand upon, what has already been said (cf. 14:16, 26). Even at this late date there are some things the disciples cannot "bear." It is worth noting that Jesus tells them things now, in the discourses, that he had no need to tell them earlier (16:4). Yet there are apparently things he still cannot tell them. They cannot bear or endure them; presumably they cannot understand them (see Brown 1970, 707; also Schnackenburg 1982, 133, who writes that the later situation of the community "is still beyond the grasp of the disciples who are present with Jesus . . . "; Lindars 1972, 504, says that we have here a metaphorical use of *bastazein*—found also in Rev 2:2-3— "to carry a burden," which is certainly the case). The contrast with the future time of the Spirit (v. 13) sheds light on what must be meant. Then, as opposed to now, the disciples, the church, will be able to comprehend "all the truth" into which they will be led, as the Spirit unfolds the future to them.

The function of the Spirit of truth (another point of connection or contact with the Qumran community, 1QS3:19) is defined in a way that seems to go beyond what has already been said (14:26). Earlier the Spirit-Paraclete has been called the Holy Spirit, identifying it with a rich biblical, Jewish, and Christian tradition. Its function is to teach the disciples everything, primarily by way of *reminding* them of what Jesus has said. So no new teaching is implied. Now, however, the Spirit will go beyond what Jesus has said in his earthly ministry, and this is apparently a profound difference. It is not coincidental that the Spirit is again called "the Spirit of truth" (v. 13; cf. 15:26) just at the point where its function is to lead the disciples into all truth.

The truth is in John always the truth of Jesus, yet that does not mean it is confined to what Jesus has said during his public ministry. On the other hand, what he will speak will be said on the authority of Jesus (vv. 14-15), as is put rather elaborately and with great emphasis. Quite correctly, the NRSV refers to the Spirit here as "he," although the term in Greek *(pneuma)* is neuter, while in Hebrew *ruach* is feminine. Taken literally, verse 13 reads: "When that man [masculine demonstrative pronoun] comes, the Spirit of Truth...." The noun *parakletos* is, like *logos* (word), masculine and appropriately so, for both are surrogates for Jesus himself. Yet that the Spirit "will speak whatever he hears" apparently sets the Spirit as a separate individual over against Jesus, and in this respect differs somewhat from other references, in which the unity of Jesus and the Paraclete is emphasized. Clearly the Spirit is here envisioned as an intermediary between Jesus and the church.

Although the Gospel does not tell us how the Spirit mediates the truth of Jesus to the church, there are hints elsewhere. First John 4:1-3 speaks of false prophets and urges his readers to test the spirits as to whether they are of God. The test is a christological, doctrinal one (4:2). Obviously, there are true prophets who are possessed of the true Spirit of God. (Here we are quite close to the Qumran dualism of true and false spirits, seen in 1QS3:17-4:31.) It is important to be able to distinguish the true Spirit from false spirits, and thereby true prophets from false (cf. also 2 John 7). Perhaps similarly, in the book of Revelation the exalted Jesus speaks (see 2:1) through the Spirit to the specific churches named (2:7, etc.; in every case the formula is essentially the same). Apparently this John, who describes his work as prophecy (1:3; 22:7, 10, 18, 19), considered himself a prophet also (22:9). His message to the seven churches (chaps. 2–3) is mediated in writing through the "angel" of each church. The meaning of *angelos* (angel) is literally "messenger," and it is a good question whether a supernatural figure (angel) or a human messenger is in view. In any event, we have in both 1 John and Revelation evidence for the authoritative role of the Spirit's and/or the exalted Christ's addressing the Christian community. This is what we also find in the Gospel, except that the Gospel describes what is going to happen from the standpoint of Jesus. The epistle and Revelation describe what is presently going on in the churches with which they are concerned. First John 4:1-3 reflects the dangers inherent in claims of spirit inspiration or spiritual authority—albeit Jesus is not named as the ultimate authority there as in Revelation. Yet it is hard to imagine that such prophets claiming the inspiration of the Spirit did not believe they also had Jesus' authority and authorization, as Revelation claims. That claim could be justified on the basis of these Johannine words of Jesus about the Paraclete. (See Boring 1978/79; Ashton 1991, 181-82, 394, 420-25; Minear 1984, 3-13, on prophecy and Spirit inspiration in the Gospel.)

Although it is sometimes said that "evidence for retrojecting words of the exalted Jesus back into the mouth of Jesus as he speaks in the narrative of the ministry is lacking" (Witherington 1995, 265), in the nature of the case such evidence would be hard to come by. Of course, Paul receives words of the exalted Jesus (2 Cor 12:8-9) although he does not put them into a narrative of Jesus' life, but of his own. In the Gospel of John one would hardly expect the author to say more than he has in the Paraclete sayings. On the one hand, the Paraclete speaks for Jesus, effectually making his presence real. On the other, he both reiterates what Jesus has said (cf. 14:26) and says more (16:13). What more he says is all the truth, and all God's truth (v. 15). The statement, "All that the Father has is mine," must in Johannine terms mean that there is no valid revelation of God that Jesus has not given. The revelation of Jesus given by or through the Paraclete is believed to be entirely consistent with the historical revelation given during Jesus' ministry, but, of course, such revelation was not itself complete or comprehensible as such until Jesus' glorification. As John puts it, "He will glorify me, because he will take what is mine and declare it to you" (v. 14). To do this he must say things Jesus did not say during his ministry, not for the sake of expanding the historical revelation, but to clarify it.

Unless one wishes to argue that John gives the words of Jesus verbatim or, alternatively, that John simply composes words of Jesus *de novo* according to his judgment and assessment of the theological necessities of the moment, it is important to ascertain how and why the peculiarly Johannine conceptuality and speech patterns took shape. One can scarcely be certain, but given what John writes, as well as what we find in 1 John and Revelation, it is reasonable and likely to surmise that Spirit inspiration and prophetic speech have deeply affected his presentation of the words of Jesus. This is not to say that the Spirit, any more than the evangelist, simply makes things up. Such passages as the saying about loving one's life (12:25), or indeed the love command (13:34), show how traditional words of Jesus can assume Johannine dress, and presumably become more relevant to the Johannine community.

Here we probably encounter one of two important factors that have influenced the composition and character of the Fourth Gospel. We have earlier and all along taken note of the role played by "the Jews," that is, the Pharisaic authorities, in opposing Jesus and his followers. But in their continuing danger and struggle, his followers have not been left alone (14:18). The Spirit-Paraclete, who is their Advocate-Counselor-Helper, is with them because he has been sent by the Father (and by Jesus). He is nothing less than the continuing presence of Jesus, who brings the power and word of Jesus to bear on the changed situation of his followers after his death and departure. These two historical-theological factors, that is, Pharisaic opposition and Spirit inspiration, do not, in and of themselves, account for this Gospel. Only Jesus accounts for this Gospel as he accounts for the gospel that is preached. They do, however, largely account for its distinctive character and composition.

Jesus utters a mysterious saying (v. 16) that his disciples still will not understand (v. 17), as he begins to bring the discourses to a close. It is similar to, if not identical with, things Jesus has said earlier (cf. 14:19; 16:10), even to the Jews (7:33-34). Jesus' disciples will lose sight of him at his death and departure, but then, when he is glorified, they will see him again. Some of the disciples repeat his saying in asking the question, referring also to what he said just earlier about going to the Father (v. 17; cf. v. 10). Apparently at this point, Jesus' disciples understand no more than the Jews or the crowds. But perhaps they feel they should, inasmuch as they now ask one another rather than Jesus about the meaning of all this. The narrator has them reiterate a part of their question, focusing on the "a little while" (v. 18), as they emphasize that they do not understand. (In v. 18 the imperfect tense contrasts with the aorist in v. 17, and might better be rendered "were saying," as if this were a continuing question that Jesus then addresses.) Jesus, of course, already knows their perplexity (v. 19). Probably we see again the Johannine Jesus' omniscience, although in the Synoptics too Jesus seems to have an uncanny sense of what people are thinking (e.g., Mark 2:8). The importance of what Jesus has said is underscored by his once again repeating the saying as he asks whether they are discussing it (v. 19). Of course, he knows.

The "little while" that the disciples do not yet comprehend will now turn out to be the period between his death and resurrection, as Jesus' description of their anguish makes clear (vv. 20-22). Again John underscores the necessary ignorance even of Jesus' believing disciples until after his glorification. His own coming again, the Parousia, may also be in view. (Bultmann 1971, 581, argues that the evangelist merges Easter and Parousia as he reinterprets eschatology.) But Jesus' departure is first of all his death, and the sorrowing depicted here goes with the death of a loved one (v. 20; cf. 11:31). Correspondingly, their joy results from knowledge of his resurrection, which, interestingly enough, is described as Jesus' seeing the disciples (v. 22) rather than the other way around. It is really Jesus who comes back and sees them; it is not just a matter of their seeing him.

By way of comparison, John likens their experience to a woman's giving birth. (On John's figurative or parabolic speech see 5:17; 10:1-18; 15:1-9.) That the moment of birth is called "the hour" can scarcely be coincidental in John. As Barrett points out (1978, 493), giving birth can represent the onset of the eschatological new age (cf. also Bultmann 1971, 579, n. 4 for hellenistic as well we Jewish parallels). Significantly, in Isa 26:16-19 the agony of the people is described as the agony of a woman in travail and is juxtaposed and likened to death and resurrection. Again in Isa 66:7-11 birthing imagery is used with eschatological meaning—the rebirth of the people (cf. also Mic 4:9-10). Another related scriptural image of childbirth with eschatological significance is found in Rev 12: the woman who gives birth to the male child (12:13), who is apparently Jesus or the Messiah, and who is caught up to God or to his throne (v. 5). The more general depictions of Isaiah are easier to understand as the background of what the Johannine Jesus says than is the difficult text of Revelation. As we have seen, the language and themes of Isaiah are frequently echoed in John. The use of birth imagery of the coming of the Messiah is also found, impressively, in the Qumran Hymns (1QH3), which perhaps afford a closer background to Rev 12 than to the Gospel.

It is worth noting that John is apparently fond of the imagery of birth, and uses it at crucial points to describe the disciple's coming to faith in Jesus (see 1:13; 3:3-8). Their individual birth from above or rebirth is paralleled in the corporate birth or rebirth of faith when they realize that Jesus is not dead and gone, but still present among them.

John delights in wordplay and the use of terms that have more than one meaning. (Thus in John 3 *anōthen* means "from above" as well as "again," and *pneuma* means "spirit" as well as "wind.") Here the disciples are said to have pain, as the woman in childbirth does (so the NRSV translates in vv. 20-22). The RSV had translated the same Greek term, *lypē,* sorrow. "Grief" is another possible translation. Obviously, John has chosen a term with a range of meaning extending from the physical pain experienced in childbirth to the sorrow or grief experienced at a loved one's death. The NRSV has seized one pole of meaning, the RSV the other. Both are appropriate, but neither by itself is quite adequate.

The woman's joy after giving birth corresponds exactly to a universal human, albeit female, experience (v. 21). It is a worldly model of the disciples' experience at Jesus' resurrection (v. 22). Here again Jesus speaks of the disciples' joy, clearly an eschatological motif, which no one will take away. The contrast with the natural human joy, even at a birth, which fades in time, is implicit, but perhaps intended. In any event, John underscores the unfading joy of disciples of the risen Jesus.

Jesus proceeds to describe briefly their new relationship to him "on that day" (vv. 23-24). First, he says the disciples will ask him nothing or ask him no question *(erōtaō)*. They will then understand, as they now do not. Although in late Greek usage the distinction between *(erōtaō)*, to ask a question, and *aiteō*, to ask for, had broken down, here it seems to be maintained, for in the very next statement Jesus is clearly speaking of their asking the Father for something (cf. v. 26, where asking—*aiteō*—clearly means petitioning). The translation in the NRSV note (v. 23) therefore seems preferable. Then once again, Jesus gives the incredibly generous offer and encouragement to his disciples (cf. 14:13-14). Only the new relationship makes this possible.

Is Jesus here describing a possibility of asking and receiving in this age or in the age to come? The suggestion that Easter and Parousia motifs here merge is attractive (Bultmann 1971, 581), because Jesus might then be talking about a possibility available to disciples in the age to come. But such a merging means for John that the age to come, that is, the possibility of eternal life, is already present for believers. That Jesus already brings to fruition the promises of God for the future helps explain such language, even if subsequent generations of readers find their minds boggled. The possibility of now asking in Jesus' name, which had not previously been done, is quite crucial (v. 24). The turning of the ages that already takes place with, and in, Jesus, creates the conditions under which it is possible to pray in his name with the expectation of comprehensive fulfillment. The disciples' joy is complete in the access to God that is described as asking and receiving (Barrett 1978, 495). In a real sense this is eschatological joy, available now.

Jesus begins to conclude these discourses by telling his disciples he has been speaking to them in figures of speech (v. 25, *paroimia;*

cf. 10:6). Earlier, they have been perplexed (v. 17) and Jesus' subsequent statement (vv. 19-22) took the form of a figure of speech, namely, the imagery of a woman's giving birth. All that Jesus has been saying is, moreover, still beyond the disciples' comprehension at this stage, as we shall again see (vv. 31-32). But Jesus now speaks of a time in which he will tell them plainly *(parrēsia)* of the Father. The contrast between *paroimia* and *(parrēsia)* is obviously deliberate. The *paroimia* (figure of speech) is basically a proverb (Heb. *mashal*), but its meaning is not now clear to the disciples (cf. 10:6). In the time after the glorification Jesus will speak plainly, but this does not necessarily mean he will say something different. The Jews have already asked Jesus to tell them plainly *(parrēsia)* whether he is the Christ (10:24) and he said he has already told them and they did not believe. Paroimia refers to the riddlesome character of Jesus' speech for those who do not, or as yet cannot, believe or believe with understanding. To Jesus, the evangelist, and the knowledgeable reader, Jesus' meaning is already plain. But at this stage his meaning is veiled even to his disciples. Their comprehension still depends on the glorification of Jesus and the coming of the Spirit. The plain speaking to which Jesus refers must be his speaking through the Spirit, telling them what he has told them, but now with their understanding. As now read in John's church, this Gospel represents such plain speaking.

"On that day" (v. 26) the disciples will have direct access to God so that they apparently will not even need Jesus' intercession. Jesus now points ahead to the time when the Paraclete will have come, the One who creates that new access to the Father so that further petitioning is not necessary. From the standpoint of the Gospel that time has already arrived, as the fulfillment of faith and love indicates (v. 27). (Of course, their love and faith finds expression in obedience to Jesus; cf. 14:21-24.) Jesus concludes with a very brief statement of (Johannine) Christology (v. 28).

The disciples respond (vv. 29-30) as if what Jesus has just said is finally plain and understandable to them. (Note the rather curious form of the statement of the disciples in v. 30 that *Jesus* has no need for anyone to ask him a question, which probably underscores his omniscience. See Brown 1970, 726.) Yet Jesus has been saying such things all along, particularly to the disciples in these discourses. How is it that the disciples only now say that he is speaking plainly *(parrēsia)* and not in any figure of speech *(paroimia)*? In fact, what he has just said about coming into the world and leaving it (v. 28) is purely mythological unless interpreted against the background of the whole Gospel narrative, including the Passion and Resurrection, which have not yet occurred. The disciples' statement is almost a bit of bravado that sets Jesus up to put them in their place! The disciples know that Jesus knows all things and that he has come from God (v. 30). But can it be significant that they say nothing about his going to God (see O'Day 1995, 783)? Quite possibly, because only through death on the cross will he go to God, and they will prove themselves unprepared for his encountering that dire fate (v. 32).

Throughout the discourses Jesus says things that are plain enough to knowledgeable readers, because the narrator has given us the proper cues. We share his retrospective view of the ministry of Jesus, which the disciples do not, and cannot, yet share. Thus Jesus tells them essential things that they will only understand with the unfolding of the story. John is not simply recounting history, much less the *ipsissima verba* of Jesus. Yet the portrait of the disciples as coming to faith in Christ only after his death, and in light of his resurrection, is grounded in history and in their experience. (On the narrator's perspective in relation to the disciples and the reader, see Culpepper's important observations [1983, 36-43].) The discourses would seem to move toward a happy ending, but now Jesus throws his disciples' facile affirmations into question (v. 31). His words are in themselves construable as a statement, "You now believe." But given what Jesus says about their subsequent scattering (v. 32), it probably should be read as a question (as in the NRSV and RSV). "In effect, the disciples' claims have been completely deflated, and the irony of the situation has been sharply underscored" (Segovia 1991, 273).

Here John betrays knowledge of Jesus' prediction of the scattering of the disciples, based on Zech 13:17 and found in the Synoptics in connection with the prediction of Peter's denial (Matt 26:31; Mark 14:27, but curiously missing in Luke in this episode, as it is in John 13:36-38). The most one can say is that John clearly presupposes knowledge of the event of the disciples' desertion recounted briefly in Mark (14:50; Matt 26:56, but again not in Luke). Yet he does not narrate it at the point of Jesus' arrest. Perhaps this is because he wants to have Jesus himself dismiss the disciples (18:8), so that his earlier word may be fulfilled (18:9). The phrase "to his own home" is exactly the same as in 1:11 (see the NRSV note). In fact, that is where the disciples seem to have gone after the crucifixion (21:3). Jesus will have been left alone. Yet the Father is always with him (v. 32), regardless of what the world may think or the human eye see (contrast Mark 15:34, which John seems to contradict).

Jesus quite briefly takes leave of the disciples (v. 33), saying that the purpose of his words are that they may have peace in him. Once before as he appeared to be about to leave his disciples he gave them his peace (14:27), and the two statements are worth comparing. There Jesus gives his peace, but not as the world gives peace. Here peace in Jesus contrasts with persecution (which is probably what is meant, although the RSV's "tribulation" is the more literal rendering) in the world. "Persecution" certainly fits after the extensive description of the manifestation of the world's hatred in 15:18–16:4. The little conjunction "but" is emphatic (Gk. *alla*). Despite persecution in the world, Jesus has overcome the world, so there is a basis for encouraging the disciples to take courage. Jesus conquers the world, proleptically, in his death. It is tempting to see here an inclusion with 1:5. "The light shines in the darkness, and the darkness did not overcome it." The RSV therefore translates (in 16:33): "I have overcome the world." This is in all likelihood a basically correct insight, but the Greek verbs are actually not the same, and the NRSV's "conquer" in 16:33 is more accurate. Moreover it squares with the frequent use of the verb *nikaō*, "conquer," in other Johannine writings, particularly 1 John (2:13-14; 4:4; 5:4-5) and Revelation, where the believer is described as the one who conquers (e.g., 2:7, 11, 17, 26). There are hints that the one who conquers is the Christian martyr, who conquers and sits on the throne of Christ as Jesus conquered and sat down with the

Father on his throne (Rev 3:21). Jesus' death by crucifixion is the conquest of the world. Jesus is not encouraging his followers to think they shall escape suffering and death in this world. If they must suffer and die, they will conquer the world with Jesus. (That the disciples share Jesus' destiny is a basic thesis of Minear's *John: The Martyr's Gospel,* 1984.)

Jesus' farewell discourses now end. He has told the disciples what they need to know, although they cannot understand what he is telling them at the moment they hear it. They will understand only that Jesus is glorified, and the first moment of that glorification will be his death by crucifixion. Only when they have experienced that, or at least know that it has happened, will they hear with understanding what Jesus has said. Previously they could not understand, as Jesus himself tells them, yet he tells them nevertheless. Quite likely what is recounted as Jesus' farewell discourses in the narrative of the Gospel itself reflects the disciples' later apprehension and understanding, under the guidance of the Spirit-Paraclete. Yet, even as the mortal opposition of their opponents is perceived as rooted in the original opposition to Jesus, so this understanding of the meaning of his death and departure is understood as rooted in his historic ministry. Gnostic revelation discourses of Jesus are commonly discourses of the risen Jesus (e.g., *Dialogue of the Savior, Apocryphon of James, Pistis Sophia;* see H. Koester 1990, 173-200). The Johannine discourses, while obviously similar to such Gnostic discourses, are set forth as discourses of the earthly, historical Jesus, and this is telling. If they are Spirit-inspired, so is what Jesus says of the function and role of the Spirit-Paraclete (14:26; 16:14). That is, they all are words of Jesus to his disciples calculated to explain why what has happened to him is finally for their benefit. Thus they express a distinctive early Christian conviction that was as unthinkable before it happened as it was unthinkable apart from the historic figure and mission of Jesus.

◊ ◊ ◊ ◊

In the farewell discourses Jesus both reassures and instructs his disciples, preparing them to live in the hostile environment of the world for an indefinite period after his own departure. In some respects these discourses are like the apocalyptic discourses of the Synoptics (Matt 24–25; Mark 13; Luke 21:5-36), which are compilations of sayings attributed to Jesus but assembled later for the purpose of instructing, warning, and reassuring the postresurrection church.

Yet the synoptic discourses obviously espouse an apocalyptic eschatology not unlike that reflected in many of Jesus' sayings about the coming kingdom of God (e.g., Mark 1:15; 9:1). In John, however, such eschatology is being reinterpreted (cf. 11:24-26). The synoptic apocalypses look toward the return of Jesus, that is, the coming of the Son of Man in glory, as a public, revolutionary event of world history (cf. Mark 13:24-27). But in John, Jesus is asked how he will reveal himself to the disciples and not to the world (14:22). The Johannine community obviously knows that Jesus' return was expected by his disciples (cf. 21:22-23), and that he had not returned in a manner that answers to that expectation.

It is often suggested that John reformulated Christian eschatology in light of the passage of time and the failure of Jesus to return (the "non-occurrence of the Parousia"), and from a modern perspective this may seem to have been the case. Yet the Gospel of John, and particularly the farewell discourses, are permeated with the promise and assurance of the continuing presence of Jesus. He has indeed departed physically in death; he will at some point return (John 6:39, 40, 54; cf. 1 John 2:18, 28; 3:2-3); yet in the meantime he continues to be present as the Spirit, the Paraclete (NRSV: "Advocate"; RSV: "Counselor"). This presence is scarcely comprehensible as the product of sheer theological imagination. Rather it is the assertion of a perceived reality, likely articulated through the work of Christian prophets (see above, pp. 297-98; especially also Boring 1978/79; and Ashton 1991). Typical of John's reinterpretation of eschatology is his tendency to merge, or interchange, Jesus' resurrection, his coming again, and the coming of the Spirit-Paraclete.

The Johannine community of Jesus' followers has much at stake in the continued presence of Jesus, inasmuch as it lives in a hostile environment, in which certain religious authorities, described as "the Jews" or "Pharisees," threaten their welfare and even their existence (16:2; cf. 20:19). Jesus' prediction of the hostility they face (15:18–16:4) prepares them for it and is in itself a source of reassurance. It is a fundamental premise of the Fourth Gospel that the deadly opposition to Jesus himself continues in the opposition his followers face.

There are new situations, problems, and issues to be dealt with by Jesus' followers, to which his presence through the Spirit-Paraclete speaks. Yet there is a central, constant factor in the representation of Jesus, his commandment of love (13:34; 15:12, 17; cf. 1 John 2:7-11). Often regarded as a succinct summation of Jesus' teaching, obedience to the love commandment is not negotiable. The continuing presence of Jesus is unthinkable apart from obedience to his word (14:21-23). It is entirely contingent upon it. To love Jesus is to obey him, and to obey him is to love one another. Jesus' command to love is obviously directed to his disciples, with their relation to one another primarily in view. Love of enemies (e.g., Matt 5:44) or love of neighbor (e.g., Mark 12:31, 33) is not explicitly mentioned, although of course not excluded. The Johannine Jesus does not advocate or tolerate hatred toward those who hate his followers.

The Great High-Priestly Prayer of Jesus (17:1-26)

The discourses clearly end with Jesus' exhortation to the disciples to be courageous. We have been told nothing further about the whereabouts of Jesus and the disciples since the Last Supper (chap. 13). Although Jesus once ordered the disciples to get up and leave (14:31), no departure is recounted as Jesus talks on. Only after the prayer is there any indication of their movement (18:1), and the presumption must be that Jesus remains at table with his disciples.

Jesus prays for and about his disciples, and they are a party to the prayer: their presence is presumed because of its narrative setting and at a couple of points is actually suggested (vv. 13, 25). Yet Jesus now prays for his disciples as if they had reached a state of believing comprehension that they have not attained during his ministry or even the farewell discourses. In other words, he presumes that they have passed beyond the obscurity of vision that impeded them during his public ministry into the understanding made possible by his glorification.

In all canonical Gospels Jesus prays frequently (e.g., Mark 1:35; 6:46), and particularly just before his arrest. In the Synoptics, however, he prays in anguish before his arrest in the Garden of Gethsemane (Mark 14:32-42 par.). That anguish has been suggested in John (12:27), but Jesus quickly passes beyond it, and his final prayer in this Gospel gives no hint of any anguish or deviation in purpose. Here Jesus is entirely in control, in contrast to the Synoptics, where the events leading to his own death are clearly outside his control.

The concluding prayer fits the genre of the farewell discourse (as Carson points out [1991, 550-51]), although in biblical exemplars one often finds a blessing rather than a prayer (cf. Gen 49:1-27; Deut 31:30–32:47; 33). (On the literary genre of the prayer, see Schnackenburg 1982, 198-200; for Hermetic parallels, Dodd 1953, 420-23; Käsemann 1968, 4, cites on the Jewish side *Testaments of the Twelve Patriarchs*.) In any case, there is concern for the welfare of the people or congregation. Jacob and Moses bless the tribes of Israel upon departing. Now, Jesus prays for those who have believed in him, and only for them (v. 9)—not for the world, with which the disbelieving Jews, or Jewish authorities, are now lumped. One might infer that for Jesus the church replaces Israel, or becomes Israel, but John does not here speak in those terms. The way in which the disciples are treated in the prayer, as now having entered a more complete state of faith than was manifest in the discourses, fits the present position of the prayer, after the discourses.

Although the NRSV does not divide the prayer into sections with subtitles, the prayer falls into three or four parts: Jesus' summation of his ministry (vv. 1-5); his prayer for his disciples (vv. 6-19); his prayer for the church that is to come (vv. 20-24). Finally, Jesus concludes by stating again quite briefly what he has accomplished (vv. 25-26).

◊ ◊ ◊ ◊

17:1-5: Jesus now recalls his revelatory work. The transition to prayer (17:1) is quite brief, but distinct, indicating, first of all, that Jesus has finished speaking to the disciples. He will now address God. He lifts up his eyes to heaven, as he had done when praying before the raising of Lazarus (11:41; see Mark 6:41; Luke 18:13; see Pss 121:1; 123:1 for the Jewish practice of looking heavenward in prayer). The address to God as simply "Father" is typical of Jesus' prayers (11:41; Luke 11:2; also Mark 14:36 where the Aramaic *abba* is given; cf. Rom 8:15). Jesus has been announcing the arrival of the hour since 12:23, as time seems to stand still awaiting the consummation of his glorification in his death and resurrection. God glorifies the Son in revealing himself through him, while the Son glorifies the Father in word, deed, and preeminently in his death by becoming transparent to his will. The informed reader now knows quite well that this mutual glorification represents two sides of the same coin, and Jesus will here elaborate this theme, as he does in the very next clause (v. 2). Jesus becomes God's regent, as authority over "all flesh" (Greek) is given him. "Flesh," of course, is used in the Bible for "humanity." In Isa 40:5, according to the RSV, we read: "And the glory of the LORD shall be revealed, and all flesh shall see it together, for the mouth of the LORD has spoken." Probably such an Isaiah text lies in the background of John's thought. The statement of verse 2 affords a nice example of a tension that runs throughout John between the assertions that God sends Jesus for the sake of the world, all people, but that only those given to him by God will actually find life (1:9-13; 3:16-21; 6:35-40; 12:47).

This definition of eternal life (v. 3) is often, and aptly, cited as typical of the Gospel of John. The only true God is the God who has sent Jesus Christ, and true life is knowledge of that God through Jesus. The background of this statement is the recurring polemic between Jesus and the Jewish authorities about who truly speaks for God, which begins mildly enough in the Nicodemus discourse (3:1-15) and reaches cacophonous hostility in chapter 8. The question is not just Who is Jesus? Upon that question hinges the even more fundamental question: Who is God? Only here does Jesus refer to himself as Jesus Christ (cf. 1:17). Thus the sentence takes on a creedlike aspect.

To God's sending of Jesus there corresponds his accomplishment of the work God sent him to do (v. 4), which he will allude to again in the subsequent section (vv. 6-19). That God's glory was manifest in what Jesus said and did already is suggested in the prologue (1:14) and is asserted again during and at the conclusion of his ministry (2:11; 12:37-43), so his statement to that effect comes as no surprise. Presumably the glorification of God that Jesus accomplished in his death is already suggested here, for when Jesus petitions the father to glorify him (v. 5), he clearly has final eschatological glory in view (17:24; cf. Matt 25:31; Mark 8:38; 13:26). Yet as he will affirm at the end of the prayer, such eschatological glory is nothing other or more than his primordial glory. (Käsemann 1968, 21, aptly speaks of protology being put alongside eschatology.) The preexistence of Jesus Christ with God, the fundamental and beginning point of the Gospel (1:1-2), is now strongly reasserted as Jesus prays to God at the very end of his public ministry, just before his arrest.

17:6-19: In what may be regarded as the heart of the prayer, Jesus prays for his disciples. Once more Jesus speaks of his work as the revealer of God's name (v. 6). The Greek verb found here *(phaneroō)* often appears in connection with a divine manifestation or revelation. It is telling that Jesus describes his work as revealing, manifesting, or making known the name of God. As in no other Gospel he is the revealer. That Jesus' own were given him by the Father is a characteristic Johannine theme (6:37, 39; 18:9), as John uses what later theology would understand as the language of predestination (cf. Rom 8:28-30). It has not previously been said that the disciples have kept God's word, although they have been charged to keep Jesus' word. Indeed, the promise implied in the farewell discourses (14:23-24) is here fulfilled, as the disciples are portrayed as having entered a new stage of their relationship to Jesus. They are now ascribed postresurrection knowledge, which is, in typical Johannine fashion, knowledge of origins. They know that what Jesus has said to them really is from

God (vv. 7-8), and that God has sent Jesus (v. 8). Of course, it is not to be denied that God has sent others, such as John the Baptist (1:6), but John's authority is derived precisely from the fact that he bears true witness to Jesus (1:19-34; 5:33; 10:41).

Not unexpectedly, Jesus prays specifically for his own, his disciples, and explicitly not for the world (v. 9). They are God's. If by implication the world were not God's, that would be a thoroughly Gnostic point of view. Yet at the very beginning of the Gospel it is said that the world came into being through the Word, who comes from God (1:10; cf. 1:3). The world and its people as creation are not inherently evil, but good, as John knows from the Genesis account. The unity of Jesus with God is now expressed in terms of the people they possess. Jesus' people are God's, and vice versa (v. 10). This is clear enough, but how is Jesus glorified in his disciples? (Actually both "mine" and "yours" are of neuter gender in Greek, as is the case in 6:37, 39, but in both cases are intelligible only if applied to the disciples.)

The reader has seen repeatedly that the glorification of Jesus is the death and resurrection through which he reveals God (cf. 17:1-2), because what Jesus does in death, as well as life, is the fulfillment of God's will in his mission to and for the world. Jesus is glorified in the disciples precisely as they participate in this mission of revealing God to the world (cf. 15:8). Their common mission will be explicitly stated (v. 18; cf. 20:21). In order to glorify God they do not have to die, as Jesus did, yet that may well be their fate (15:12-13; cf. 16:2). Thus Jesus prays that the disciples be protected by God in the world (v. 11) and for the first time also prays for the unity of believers, which will be essential for their mission (cf. vv. 21, 23; also 13:34-35).

That Jesus addresses God as "Holy Father" must be significant; he will later in the prayer address him as "Righteous Father" (v. 25). Nothing is more characteristic of the biblical concept of God than holiness and righteousness (Isa 5:16; on "righteousness" see below on v. 25). Moreover, the holiness of God means that his people too must be holy (Lev 11:44; cf. 1 Pet 1:16). All this is axiomatic, as Paul addresses his letters "to the saints..." that is, those who are sanctified, the holy ones. It is important to note that the adjective "holy" translates the Greek *hagios,* of which the verbal form is *hagiazō,* which we ordinarily translate "sanctify," since there is no verbal form of the word "holy." (Thus "saints" translates the Greek *hagioi.*) Later in this series of petitions Jesus will pray to God to sanctify, make holy, his disciples. Although God is not called "Holy Father" elsewhere in John, Jesus is called by Peter "the Holy One of God" (6:69), and, of course, the Paraclete-Advocate is the Holy Spirit (14:26). Holiness, as much as any other quality or aspect, sets God apart as God. He is the Holy One of Israel (Isa 1:4; God's holiness and glory are proclaimed by the seraphim in Isa 6:3). The unity of Father, Son, and disciples (church) is a unity of holiness, which sets them apart from the world, though it is still the object of their mission.

After his more general statement about the disciples he is leaving behind (vv. 6-10), Jesus prays for their well-being, first for their protection (vv. 11-12), then for the completion (NRSV) or fulfillment (RSV; REB) of their joy (v. 13). Both are themes that recur. Probably the NRSV text (rather than the note) gives the correct reading in verse 12: God has given Jesus a name, which can hardly be other than God's own. In biblical and Jewish thought the name of God became unspeakable because of its holiness, but the name of Jesus can be uttered, and Jesus is the definitive and complete representation and revelation of God. That Jesus protected the disciples while he was with them is reflected in the historical fact that although Jesus himself was arrested, they went free, and by Jesus' own instruction (cf. 18:8-9, where this point is made with explicit reference to the fact that no one was lost; also 6:37, 39). The one exception is, of course, Judas, who is not named but called "the son of perdition" (RSV; NRSV translates "the one destined to be lost," apparently to avoid sexist language; but the term is not meant to be inclusive, and, moreover, Judas was a male). That Judas was lost fits the synoptic tradition of his demise, enshrined in the entirely different narratives of his end in Matthew (27:3-10) and Acts (1:16-20), but it is not clear that his being lost refers to his death specifically rather than to his falling out of light into darkness, so to speak. The scripture that is fulfilled in Judas's betrayal, or perhaps in the

death of Jesus himself, is not cited, but perhaps Ps 41:9, cited in
13:18 of Judas's betrayal, is intended.

That Jesus is going to the Father (v. 13) has been said repeatedly in the farewell discourses (e.g., 14:12), and Jesus has already
told the disciples why he is speaking openly to them on the eve of
his departure (16:1, 4). Of course, even at that point they failed
to understand (16:31), but now it is presumed that they hear and
understand. (Apparently, Jesus prays aloud, as he does in 11:41-
42.) In the following statement (v. 14) Jesus makes clear he has
given God's word to the disciples (past tense). Earlier, they have
not been able to understand it fully. His present statement (vv. 13-
14), however, presumes that they do understand. This confirms
the postresurrection or postglorification perspective on the disciples throughout this prayer.

The completion or fulfillment of the disciples' joy (v. 13) at
Jesus' word is the fulfillment of eschatological joy, and it signifies
their having now passed into that state of blessedness (see above
on 15:11; 16:24; 1 John 1:4; 2 John 12). As the NRSV's translation note points out, "in themselves" may mean "among themselves," and the latter rendering would underscore the importance
of the community, apart from which such joy would be inconceivable. That Jesus' disciples do not belong to the world, as Jesus
does not (v. 14) is to be taken for granted, particularly after what
Jesus has told them in 15:18–16:4. Certainly neither the disciples
nor Jesus "belong to the world" (NRSV), but perhaps the RSV's
"not of the world" better reflects the Johannine theme of origin,
which recurs throughout this Gospel.

Jesus' next petition (v. 15) is telling, because it makes clear that
he is not calling them out of the world in any ascetic, much less
self-destructive sense, but rather is praying for their protection as
they live in the world (cf. v. 11). They are now, in fact, the only
instruments of God's mission to the world (v. 18; cf. 20:21). The
evil one is, of course, Satan, unless the term (*ponērou*, genitive) is
to be translated simply "evil," which is also possible (see NRSV
note). But in all probability the NRSV is correct in taking this as
a reference to Satan as the personification of evil rather than evil
in the abstract (see Barrett 1978, 510-11). In 1 John (2:13-14;

3:12; 5:18-19) the term seems to refer to Satan, and in the Gospel the ruler of this world, obviously Satan, will be driven out or condemned (12:31; 14:30; 16:11). God the Father's protection is invoked for the disciples, because Jesus, who had protected them, is departing (cf. v. 12, which follows upon the initial petition of God to protect the disciples in the world).

The prayer tends to be repetitious, as indeed the Gospel sometimes is, and Jesus' subsequent statement simply reiterates what he has just said (v. 16; cf. v. 14). But the next petition (v. 17), for the Father to make the disciples holy (the Greek verb is *hagiazō* = "sanctify") in the truth (cf. v. 19), is climactic. The Father himself is holy by virtue of his being God (v. 11; cf. Lev 11:44). To sanctify or be made holy means to be set apart for God. Thus Jesus himself is said to be sanctified (RSV: "consecrated") and sent into the world (10:36).

As one sees in reading the Gospel, truth (Gk. *alētheia*) is a concept of central importance, usually connoting the real or authentic as opposed to the lie, the unreal, or fake (Bultmann 1971, 434-36). Jesus brings grace and truth (1:17); he is the truth (14:6); the true light (1:9); the true vine (15:1). Jesus then prays for the disciples to be made holy in the truth, to be set apart for and in the truth. Then, quite suddenly the Father's word *(logos)* is spoken of as truth, but, according to the prologue (1:1-18), that word is Jesus Christ himself (1:14). We do not err in seeing here a subtle allusion to the prologue, although, as every commentator notes, after Jesus is named (1:17) he is never again called the Word in the Gospel. Of course, the statement that God's word is truth would have been agreed to by virtually every biblical writer, Old Testament or New (e.g., Isa 45:19; cf. 2:3; 40:8; 55:10-11; Ps 119:160; Jas 1:18). But it is John who identifies that Word fully with Jesus Christ in the prologue, and that identification here stands in the background.

The sending of the disciples into the world (v. 18) recapitulates the sending of the Son (cf. 20:21), and they may expect a similar hostile reception (15:20). Yet although they are not of the world (v. 14: "do not belong to the world"), their being sent into the world is an expression of God's love for the world (3:16), not his hatred of the world (cf. 12:47). Thus Jesus' sanctifying of himself and their sanctification in truth (v. 19; cf. v. 17), that is, in Jesus, are integrally related. As we noted, to be sanctified, that is, to be made or pronounced holy, implies being set apart to or for God. This is what Jesus has done in carrying out the commission and mission God has given him, making possible their being set apart in and for this truth, which implies an analogous mission. As Bultmann says of Jesus (1971, 511): "his holiness is nothing other than the fulfillment of this his being for the world, his being for his own." Their holiness, Jesus' and the disciples', is their being set apart from the world for the sake of the world. Probably Bultmann is correct in seeing also in Jesus' sanctifying himself an allusion to his death, a fate his disciples may yet share.

17:20-24: Jesus then prays explicitly for the postresurrection church. John is aware of the distinction between the disciples of Jesus' public ministry and the later church ("those who will believe in me through their word"), even as he is aware of the altered consciousness of the disciples that only follows upon his resurrection. The preaching of the gospel about Jesus is called "their word" (cf. Acts 4:4, 29, 31 and *passim;* 1 Thess 2:13; 1 Pet 1:25) in accordance with early Christian usage. Initially, Jesus prays for the unity of all his followers (v. 21; cf. v. 12), taking up the theme as a kind of summation of what he has said in the prayer and in the farewell discourses about their mutual, mystical union with himself and with the Father (17:6-10; cf. e.g., 14:20, 23). Indeed, he now reiterates the theme of what is rightly called mutual indwelling, an indwelling that will exist not only for its own sake, but as a witness to the world (cf. v. 23). In this connection two closely related themes of the Gospel are observed and emphasized: mutual love and mission.

The unity of the church is first of all a unity in love. When Jesus gives the "new commandment" of love he says, in effect, that it will be a witness to the fact that those who practice this love are his disciples (13:35). Such love is not merely a feeling or a disposition, but a willingness to give up one's self for one's fellow believer (15:12-13; cf. 12:25). In the closely related 1 John the nature of this willingness is spelled out: it finds expression in concrete acts other than martyrdom. Thus in 1 John 3:16-17 there is first a reiteration of the necessity of the willingness to give one's life, but then a spelling out of what this may mean when a brother or sister appears who is in need of the necessities of life: Help her! The unity here besought is a unity of love (14:21, 23). The substance of the mutual indwelling of which Jesus now speaks is love among Father, Son, and believers (cf. Bultmann 1971, 512-14).

This unity in love is then a witness to the world (cf. 13:35), which, despite its rejection of the revelation of God's word in Jesus, God still loves (3:16; 12:47; cf. 4:42; 1 John 4:14). Mission to the world remains a major theme of this Gospel, as Jesus concludes his prayer with the world's believing in view as the final goal (v. 21; cf. v. 23). (On mission in John see also the monograph of Okure, *The Johannine Approach to Mission: A Contextual Study of John 4:1-42, 1988.*)

Believing that God, the Father has sent Jesus is in John's understanding of origin tantamount to believing in Jesus (cf. 15:21, where Jesus tells his disciples that their enemies do not know the God who has sent him). The community's witness to the world may seem futile, in that the world rejects Jesus, kills him, and persecutes his followers. This severe hostility and alienation may even give rise to the Gospel's sharp dualism (Meeks 1972). Yet the dualism does not override the purpose of God for the world in Jesus' mission.

The unity of Father, Son, and church is also a unity of glory, descending from the Father (v. 22). But, as our reading of the Gospel to this point amply confirms, the idea of the church's basking in its glory is the farthest thing from John's mind. It is rather the glory found, and consisting in, the accomplishment of God's revelatory work on earth (vv. 1, 4; cf. Barrett 1978, 513). Oneness in glory is also oneness in love and in mission, the fundamental themes that have just found expression here. That unity in glory is unity in, and for the purpose of, mission is then quite clearly said (v. 23). The unity of the church, as John never tires of emphasizing, is a theological unity that extends through Jesus to the Father. Such unity is inconceivable as a strictly human phenomenon. This unity may come to be reflected in the world's knowledge: not only that Jesus is the one sent by God, but that God has loved the followers of Jesus, the church, even as he has loved Jesus. To know who Jesus is means to know both his origin with God the Father and his destination in the world, namely the community of believers. But really to know these things is also to know God's love for the world and, by implication, to know God himself.

Finally, an eschatological note is struck (v. 24), as John brings together eschatology and protology (cf. v. 5; see Käsemann 1968, 21). As we have seen (cf. v. 5 above), in early Christian and biblical tradition glory is also an eschatological concept. Clearly what has traditionally been called the end time is in view here. Moreover, it is obvious that Jesus contemplates for his disciples, as for himself, life beyond death. In reinterpreting apocalyptic futuristic eschatology John by no means eliminates a lively hope for the eschatological future. Bultmann (1971, 519) puts this well: "Thus the petition can only be a request that the separation from him be a temporary one, that they should be united with him again after their worldly existence." Further (520): "Death has become insignificant for them (11:25); but not in the sense that they can ignore it because their earthly life is complete and meaningful in itself; but because their life is not enclosed within the limits of temporal-historical existence." Here a traditional notion of glory as a quality that belongs to God as God clearly finds expression, although it is affected, but not eliminated, by the distinctly Johannine connotations of the term. That God loved Jesus from the foundation of the world agrees with—although it is not expressly said in—the prologue. Historically speaking, the Father's love for the Son is an inference from the entire revelatory event of the appearance of Jesus as the Messiah and the founding of the church. Theologically speaking, it is a major premise upon which all else rests: God's love for the world; Jesus' love for his own.

17:25-26: Finally, Jesus again looks back on his accomplished work, but also indicates it will continue into the future. God is now called "righteous" (v. 25). Certainly the righteousness of God is also a crucial characteristic that defines his being God (cf.

Isa 5:16; 9:7; Rom 1:17). We recall that one function of the Paraclete is to prove the world wrong about righteousness (16:8, 10) because Jesus goes to the Father (at his death). In contrast to the righteous God, Jesus' enemies do not know where he has come from or where he is going, but his disciples now do (cf. 14:4; 16:28). To know that the one true and righteous God has sent Jesus is, in fact, to know where he has come from and who he is. Of course, what the disciples know about Jesus they know only because he has made himself known (v. 26). (Here the verb, *gnōrizō*, is different from the one in v. 6, and literally means "made known," although the NRSV translation is the same in both cases.) The name of God, which is ineffable, carries with it the divine reality (cf. Gen 4:26; Exod 20:7; 1 Kgs 3:2), as does the name of Jesus his Son (John 1:12; 2:23, etc.). In making himself known as the one whom God has sent, Jesus makes known the name of God.

It is significant that Jesus says that he both has made, and will make, the name known, and this implies John's view of the revelation of God in Jesus: It occurs during his historic ministry (2:11), but again, and definitively, in his glorification, which comes "afterward" or "later" (cf. 13:7, 36). Only at this later stage, of course, do the disciples really understand (cf. 16:28-30). Moreover, the future, continuing revelation of Jesus himself to his disciples is the work of the Paraclete (see especially 16:12-15). It is all for the sake of, or for the purpose of, the dissemination of the love of God. The love with which the Father has loved Jesus "before the foundation of the world" (v. 24) thereby comes into being in (or among) his followers. The parallel between this love and Jesus himself would seem to be significant: Where this love goes, Jesus goes (cf. the figure of the vine in 15:1-17). Moreover, one could construct the following simple equation: Jesus = God = Love (1 John 4:8, 16). Of course, if that were taken to mean that "God" is a mythological code word for "love," John would not agree. But to say that love is the manifestation on the human, historical level of the reality of God is certainly what John means.

◊ ◊ ◊ ◊

The concluding prayer summarizes the revelatory work of Jesus before God and gives voice to Jesus' continuing care for his disciples, a theme already prominent in the farewell discourses as well as elsewhere in the Gospel (6:37, 39; 18:9). There is no new theological content in the prayer, although we find a new, fresh perspective on the disciples, as Jesus now speaks of them as having believed, and by implication having understood, what Jesus has made known to them. They are, in other words, the postresurrection church, in which the promise of the Paraclete has been fulfilled.

As he departs he prays for the Father's care in his physical absence from them. He will not leave them orphans (14:18). Of course, the Paraclete, as the continuing spiritual reality of Jesus in the absence of his physical presence, is to fill this void and provide for the disciples' needs. Yet it is a significant aspect of the portrayal of Jesus in John that at this point he himself expresses concern for the welfare of his own in his absence and prays the Father to watch over them. This is more than common human concern for loved ones. But such concern makes it intelligible.

The prayer also provides the opportunity for Jesus to once again state for the church and the reader for what purpose and to what end he has carried out his ministry. This is not the first time this has been done in the Gospel (vv. 4, 6; cf. 12:44-50), but it is the very last opportunity for Jesus to do so in the presence of his disciples. And so we are given this definitive statement by Jesus of his accomplishment of his mission as he turns to the cross. While Jesus speaks as if he had already accomplished his work, not until he is dying on the cross will he pronounce it finished (19:30; the Greek verbs used in 17:4 and 19:30, *teleō* and *teleioō* are closely related in form and meaning). As we observed already, the hour of Jesus' glorification stretches out through the latter half of the Gospel. The Jesus who prays here occupies the role or status of the one who has already accomplished his mediatorial work on earth. At the same time he speaks from the temporal perspective of one still living in the period immediately before his death. As Barrett says (1978, 500), the prayer "is a setting forth of the eternal unity of the Father and the Son in its relation to the incarnation and the temporary (and apparent) separation which the incarnation involved." The separation is inherent in the Incarnation, but the Incarnation was not really conceivable, or graspable, until after the historic ministry, death, and resurrection of Jesus. That is, only after Jesus' glorification was the incarnation of the Word clearly understood.

The prayer has long been called the High-Priestly Prayer of Jesus. (Barrett 1978, 500, says this title was "already hinted at by Cyril of Alexandria.") There is a sense in which the title is quite appropriate, as Jesus appears as intermediary between God and his own disciples and followers. Moreover, he sanctifies himself, so they may be sanctified. (At 17:19 both the RSV and REB translate *hagiazō* ["sanctify" or "make holy"] as "consecrate," to devote to God.) One could say that he devotes them, as he has devoted himself, to God. Yet it is finally God who is the initiator and actor both for Jesus (10:36) and the disciples (17:17). Nevertheless, the sanctification of either requires their obedient consent. As Jesus accomplishes what God wills for himself, so the disciples follow Jesus' commandment, and thus God's will for them. In all this Jesus is the intermediary between God and humanity, particularly his self-chosen disciples, and his work is brought to clearest expression in this prayer. (Jesus is actually called a mediator, *mesitēs*, in 1 Tim 2:5 and Heb 9:15; 12:24; and in 1 John 2:1, as we have seen, an advocate, *paraklētos*.) So although Jesus is not explicitly called a high priest, the title is not a misnomer.

The title is, of course, reminiscent of the characterization of Jesus in Hebrews, where the major and distinctive role and title of the exalted Son of God is high priest (see especially Heb 4:14–5:10). Indeed, this Jesus sanctifies his followers (Heb 2:11) even as the Johannine Jesus prays for their sanctification in the prayer (17:17, 19). This is not John's only affinity with Hebrews, in which Jesus also plays the mediating role in creation (1:2). The extent, nature, and origin of this relationship remains to be explored. In all probability, however, the obvious similarity between the Jesus of the Johannine prayer and the great high priest who has passed through the heavens of Hebrews (4:14) lent the traditional title to the prayer. That the Jesus who speaks in the Fourth Gospel is the exalted, heavenly high priest is not a misperception from John's point of view even though these terms are not used in the Gospel.

THE PASSION NARRATIVE (18:1–19:42)

The Gospel accounts of the events leading up to and including Jesus' death are called Passion Narratives because they describe Jesus' Passion or suffering. (The term suits the Synoptics better than John, where Jesus scarcely suffers anguish or pain.) The Passion Narrative of John's Gospel is a discrete unit consisting of chapters 18 and 19. After John's long discourse and prayer at table (chaps. 13–17), the story begins to unfold rapidly as John's narrative becomes closely parallel to the synoptic accounts (cf. Matt 26:30–27:66; Mark 14:26–15:47; Luke 22:39–23:56). (This is by far the longest section in which John runs side-by-side with the Synoptics.) Jesus enters the garden (18:1; Matthew and Mark name it "Gethsemane" but do not call it a garden), where he is to be handed over and arrested. In all the Synoptics Jesus there endures great agony at the prospect of suffering and death that lies before him (Matt 26:36-46; Mark 14:32-42; Luke 22:39-46), so that in Christian parlance "Gethsemane" has become virtually synonymous with Jesus' agony and anguished prayer that "this cup" (his death) be removed from him (Mark 14:36). John lacks this account, but in 12:27 gives a hint that he knows of it (cf. Heb 5:7). Moreover, in John (chap. 17) Jesus also has prayed immediately before his arrest, although this typically Johannine utterance finds Jesus entirely composed and in control of the situation.

The literary break preceding the Passion Narrative is sharpest in John. (In effect, Brown recognizes this fact in his exhaustive study, *The Death of the Messiah* [1994], which begins with Jesus in the garden, where he is arrested. For a briefer, but reliable, study of John's entire account, see Senior 1991.) Given the chapter divisions of the Synoptics (Matt 26–27; Mark 14–15; Luke 22–23), one might count their Passion Narratives as beginning with the priests plotting against Jesus (Mark 14:1-2). (The chapter and verse divisions of the Bible are not original, of course, but in this case reflect the apparent narrative division after Jesus' apocalyptic discourse.) The Synoptic version would then include the account of Judas's betraying Jesus to the chief priests (Mark 14:10-11 par.) and the celebration of the Passover at the Last Supper (Mark 14:12-25 par.), as well as the anointing of Jesus by the woman in Bethany (14:3-9), all of which bear directly upon Jesus' death.

In fact, there are Johannine parallels to most of these episodes: the plotting of the priests (11:45-53); the Last Supper (chap. 13; where it is not, however, a Passover meal and there is no institution of the Lord's Supper); and the anointing of Jesus (12:1-8). John actually has these items in the same order as Mark, although he omits any explicit narrative of Judas's meeting with the chief priests and, of course, gives no account of the preparation for Passover (Mark 14:12-16), since in his account the meal occurs before the Passover is eaten. At the same time, John inserts extensive conversations, that have no close Synoptic parallels, in which Jesus meditates on, or explains, his departure in death (12:12-50; chaps. 14–16). Thus events that seem to occur in rapid succession in the Synoptics are more spread out in John. Moreover, Jesus' entry into Jerusalem (12:12-19) takes place after the plotting of the priests and Jesus' anointing, whereas in the Synoptics (Mark 11:1-11 par.) it seems to occur long before them and is soon followed by the cleansing of the temple (Mark 11:15-19 par.), which occurs at the beginning of Jesus' ministry in John (2:13-22).

Such marked similarities, as well as significant differences, both in the build-up to the Passion and the Passion Narrative proper, raise the question of how John's narrative is related to the Synoptics. Is it drawn from them or an original account? Obviously, historical questions and issues are also involved. At first glance, the similarities would appear to support the basic historicity of the story, but there are also remarkable and presumably significant differences, including the astonishing difference as to the precise dating, in relation to Passover, of the Last Supper and Jesus' crucifixion.

One might ask whether John altered history, or the synoptic accounts, so as to have Jesus crucified as the supreme Passover offering while the lambs are being slain. As we have observed, Jesus presides over a last supper with his disciples, which is not a Passover meal. Of course, one could ask whether the Synoptics have made the Last Supper a Passover meal so that Jesus could lead his disciples in the celebration of that most significant of Jewish festivals. There is in the Gospel of John a kind of undertone of Passover motifs, as we shall see (e.g., 19:29, 36; cf. 1:29). Yet Jesus does not lay out such a paschal role for himself explicitly in his discourses, and in this Gospel theological issues tend to be discussed directly. Paul says of Jesus' death, "For our paschal lamb, Christ, has been sacrificed" (1 Cor 5:7), in an equation that is as explicit as can be. On the basis of this statement one could imagine that Jesus' death was moved to the day before Passover. Conversely, the historicity of that dating could have led to a statement such as Paul's. Thus John's intentional use of paschal imagery would not necessarily mean that he had changed the date of Jesus' crucifixion, or the festival calendar, so as to have Jesus die at the same time as the lambs. Brown (1994, 1351-73) cautiously decides that the Johannine dating of the Thursday night and Friday, as Nisan 14, the day before Passover, is probably correct. This acute and prominent problem, however, illustrates the difficulty of deciding historical issues as well as of deciding between John and the Synoptics.

In our treatment, the historical question must come in at two levels: the history of tradition (Is John independent?) and the actual history of Jesus' suffering and death. Up to a point, within the three synoptic Gospels the problem of the history of tradition is relatively simple. For it is clear that both Matthew and Luke used Mark as the principal narrative source in the composition of their Gospels, and this is no less true in the Passion Narratives (Brown 1994, 40-46). Because John's Gospel is so different from the Synoptics until we approach the Passion, it is sometimes suggested that at this point reliance upon Mark, or the Synoptics generally begins (cf. Crossan 1995, 20-22). Yet even here there are still problems in understanding John's narrative as based on his use of Mark or of the Synoptics. There are episodes found in the Synoptics and not in John and vice versa. Moreover, John's verbatim agreements with Mark are much fewer than Matthew's or even Luke's. The situation is further complicated by the fact that Matthew and Luke, although obviously dependent on Mark for their basic narratives, add new material or episodes (e.g., Matt 27:3-10, 62-66; Luke 23:6-12). Did they know alternative Passion Narratives? Probably not, although they may have known older traditions associated with the telling of the story (Brown 1994, 44-46).

The *Gospel of Peter*, discovered only in the late–nineteenth century, contained yet another account of Jesus' trial and death and one that does not seem in every respect to be derivative from the Synoptics (cf. debate between Crossan 1995 and Brown 1994). Also Paul, in giving the traditional words of institution of the Lord's Supper, refers to the night when Jesus was betrayed (1 Cor 11:23) and thus apparently knows, and presumes knowledge of, a narrative of Jesus' death. If so, there must have already been a tradition of telling the story as early as the 50s, when 1 Corinthians was written, and probably earlier. This commentary will not, therefore, assume John's knowledge of other Gospels, but relationships will be examined and tested at every relevant point.

With good reason some interpreters have suggested that the present, canonical version of the Fourth Gospel is based upon an earlier narrative, no longer extant, which was in many respects like Mark (Fortna 1970, 1988; Haenchen 1984). Not surprisingly, such theories vary a great deal in their treatment of material in the public ministry of Jesus, but naturally come closer together in the Passion Narrative. Moreover, form critics, for example, Bultmann (1968, 275-79), Dibelius (1935, 179-81), Jeremias (1966, 89-96), and more recently Green (1988), have argued that since the death of Jesus was a central theological theme of earliest Christian preaching (cf. Dodd 1936, 7-35), an appropriate narrative of the Passion would likely have been formed within the first Christian generation. (Perhaps 1 Cor 11:23 would be the earliest evidence of its existence.) Thus some notable exegetes (e.g., Bultmann 1971; and Brown 1970, 1994) who differ widely in their views of the character and sources of the narratives and discourse material of Jesus' public ministry, nevertheless agree that John knew and used a Passion Narrative in many respects parallel to, but distinct from, Mark or other Synoptics.

If John's Passion Narrative is independent of the Synoptics, it constitutes a separate witness to those critical events. While the historicity of the death of Jesus by crucifixion is scarcely in doubt, the same cannot be said about the details of the Passion Narrative. As we shall observe, in some instances John and the Synoptics differ. On the face of it such differences would seem to call the historicity of each into question. On the other hand some differences would be expected in independent narratives of the same events. At some points Scripture is cited. At others it may be presumed. In either case one asks whether or to what extent Scripture actually created the narrative as the early Christians strove to put together this fundamentally important story. Moreover, it cannot be assumed that if Scripture was the source of some narrative details it was the source of all. To a considerable extent different Scripture is cited in John and in the Synoptics.

Throughout the synoptic Gospels we find episodes or sayings that are more or less self-sufficient and could have been placed in a different order. In fact, Matthew and Luke sometimes change Mark's narrative order and the order of the sayings material common to them (Q). In the Passion Narrative, however, the order of the episodes can scarcely be changed. Judas's betrayal obviously precedes the arrest, the arrest the trial(s), the trial(s) the execution, and the execution the burial. So the common order of the episodes does not necessarily imply a common source.

As in this commentary we look intensively at the individual episodes, there will be opportunity to explore questions about the tradition history, as well as the historicity, of individual items. Although interpreters tend to lean one way or the other, it is important to avoid general judgments prior to detailed analysis. The initial task of the reader and interpreter is to assimilate and appreciate the Johannine version of this imposing narrative, which has had such a significant impact, for weal or woe, upon readers for nearly two millennia.

The Arrest of Jesus (18:1-12)

The story of Jesus' arrest is, of course, found in all the Gospels. John's version finds a parallel in the Synoptics that may bespeak its traditional origin. Although John's account has its characteristic features, it does not seem to be derived from the Synoptics. Obviously, the narration requires a statement about Jesus' and his disciples' journey to the place where he was to be arrested, as well as the arrest itself.

Although in the Synoptics Jesus immediately begins to pray fervently that this cup (his imminent death) be removed from him (Mark 14:36 par.), no such prayer is found in John. Yet just prior to this scene Jesus has uttered a quite different prayer (chap. 17), and there is in John 12:27 just a hint that he knows the synoptic tradition of Jesus' praying in anguish before his arrest and death (cf. Heb 5:7-8). Needless to say, such anguish does not fit John's portrayal of a Jesus who goes to die by his own intention (10:17-18).

Since the arrest is a discrete episode, complete in itself with obvious beginning and ending, on form or tradition-critical grounds it looks like a separate unit of tradition. However that may be, it is difficult to conceive of such a unit's having been transmitted independent of the broader narrative framework of the Passion of Jesus. The existence of such a framework is already suggested by Paul's reference to the night on which Jesus was betrayed, or, literally, handed over—apparently a reference to the arrest (1 Cor 11:23).

◊　◊　◊　◊

There can scarcely be any doubt as to the basic fact at the root of this story. Jesus must have been handed over, or arrested, before he was arraigned and executed. Paul already knows a tradition to this effect (1 Cor 11:23). Whatever his intention may have been, it is almost equally obvious that Judas played a key role. John's account differs from the Synoptics in details, as we shall observe. In some cases such differences reflect no discernible Johannine theological interest and are presumably traditional, and perhaps historical.

18:1: The brief phrase, "After...these words," makes connection, however briefly, with the discourses uttered at the Last Supper (chaps. 13–17). Jesus is said to go out with his disciples across the Kidron ravine, a wadi that contains running water only during the rainy, winter season. (The Greek reads, literally, "the winter-flowing Kidron.") Matthew (26:36) and Mark (14:32) say that they go to a place called Gethsemane ("oil-press" in Hebrew or Aramaic). Luke says only "to the Mount of Olives." Only John specifies that they entered a garden, which goes unnamed, or mentions the Kidron ravine.

The withdrawal across the Kidron is reminiscent of King David's retreat from Jerusalem, similarly across the Kidron, in the face of Absalom's rebellion (2 Sam 15:23). As the death of Jesus approaches, allusions to Scripture become more frequent, as was already evident in chapter 12. In John, as in the Synoptics, Jesus and his disciples have just arrived from the Last Supper at the place of the arrest. The traditional site of the Supper is the Tomb of David, just outside the present Wall of the old city in the southwestern quarter. Presumably, they would have moved around to the slope of the Mount of Olives (to the east of the temple area) on which Gethsemane is situated. There is an old Roman stairway going down from the temple mount, on which Jesus and his disciples are said to have walked. While these locations are consistent with the Gospel narratives, there is no way to confirm that the postbiblical traditions are accurate. In fact, one cannot be certain even of the exact location of the so-called Garden of Gethsemane.

The arrest of Jesus is foreshadowed by the appearance of Judas (v. 2), here, as customarily in John, described as Jesus' betrayer (cf. 6:64, 70-71; 12:4; 13:21-30). He becomes, quite literally, the one who hands Jesus over to the authorities (see Brown 1994, 1394-1418, on Judas). Judas knows the place where Jesus and the disciples often met (cf. Luke 22:39), and that is, presumably, at least one of the things that Judas betrayed. Only John indicates that Judas had this special, and crucial, knowledge. In the other Gospels Judas is described as one of the twelve, and John certainly knows this about him (6:70). As we earlier observed, only

John tells the reader that Judas was the treasurer of the group (12:6; 13:29).

In the arrest Judas clearly plays a central role, as he seems to be leading the arresting party (v. 3). In John's account this consists of a cohort (Gk. *speira*) of Roman soldiers (mentioned only in John), as well as the officers or servants of the chief priests and Pharisees. Yet John does not narrate Judas's meeting with the authorities, but presupposes it. John is distinctive in implicating Roman soldiers and Pharisees. It is improbable that a cohort of soldiers, consisting of as many as six hundred men, would have been needed to arrest Jesus. (The NRSV translates *speira* "detachment" and the RSV "band.") As the story unfolds in all the Gospels, a Roman judge and Roman soldiers effect Jesus' execution, and this representation must have some historical basis. But beyond this point Pharisees are not involved in Jesus' death in any Gospel, and only in John are they mentioned even here. (In Matt 27:62 the Pharisees join the chief priests in asking for a guard at the tomb, but when the guards report back after the Resurrection, only the chief priests are mentioned.) It is worth noting that the Pharisees, Jesus' antagonists throughout all the Gospels, are not said to be involved in putting him to death. In fact, only John mentions the Roman authority explicitly (11:48), although readers generally would have known and assumed that the governor (Pilate) and soldiers were Roman.

In the Passion Narrative John emphasizes the responsibilities of the Jewish authorities ("the Jews") and presents them in the worst possible light; therefore, implicating the Romans in Jesus' arrest does not suit his agenda but rather detracts from it. There are other indications that John may be drawing on an independent tradition. Details about the arresting party's equipment differ (e.g., only John mentions lanterns and torches and he uses a general term "weapons" rather than specifying swords and clubs or cudgels), and the differences are not significant theologically.

Although Judas leads the arresting party, Jesus seizes the initiative in a manner that is fully, and uniquely, Johannine (v. 4). Whereas Matthew (26:48) and Mark (14:44) say that Judas had indicated that he would identify Jesus by a kiss, nothing is said of this in John. The absence of Judas's kiss fits with John's sense of the dignity and authority of Jesus: the one who is betraying Jesus does not touch—much less kiss—him. Moreover, that Jesus knows fully what is to happen agrees entirely with Johannine Christology (cf. 13:1-3). Jesus' question, "Whom do you seek?" (v. 4 RSV), hints at the theme of seeking Jesus that is prominent in this Gospel (note Painter 1993, *passim*, but here especially 378-79), both among those seeking salvation (e.g., 1:38; 4:40; 6:24) and those seeking to kill him (e.g., 5:18).

The response of the arresting party allows Jesus to identify himself with the characteristic formula *egō eimi,* usually translated "I am," often with a predicate such as "true vine" or "good shepherd." But the little Greek phrase is also a customary recognition formula (Bultmann 1971, 225, n. 3; 639, n. 7). The evangelist uses the customary phrase, but the knowledgeable reader will see its further, deeper connotation. The notation of Judas's "standing with them" indicates again whose side he is on, but also denies his proximity to Jesus, in contrast to the Synoptics!

The reaction of the arresting party to Jesus' word underscores its profundity and power (v. 6) and clearly indicates it is more than a mere recognition formula. Precisely the *egō eimi* (cf. e.g., LXX Exod 3:14: Isa 45:5-7; 48:12; where God uses the phrase in identifying himself) sends the arresting party reeling backward. Of course, nothing like this is found in the synoptic accounts. It is a typically Johannine emphasis, and probably an embellishment of the traditional story. That such a thing actually happened and the synoptic accounts ignored it is scarcely conceivable historically. It is John's way of conveying theological points through narrative: the power of God incarnate in Jesus and the fact that the fate of Jesus was not determined by human hostility, but by the will of God, who intends human salvation through it (John 3:16). (Similarly, Acts 2:23 speaks of "the definite plan and foreknowledge of God.")

Jesus repeats the question and gets the same answer (v. 7; cf. vv. 4-5). The narrative has not progressed past the point where the question and answer were first uttered. (Fortna notes that this kind of repetition is a characteristic literary technique to accommodate the insertion of material into a source; 1970, 21). But now Jesus elaborates (v. 8). His request, or command, to let the disciples go corresponds on the one hand with the fact, reflected also in the Synoptics and Acts, that Jesus' disciples were not arrested with him (but cf. Mark 14:51-52), and on the other to Jesus' earlier statements about not losing those (disciples) God has given him (v. 9; cf. 6:39; 10:28; 17:12). Jesus' words, like the words of Scripture, do not go unfulfilled (also 18:32; cf. 3:14; 12:32-33). The fulfillment of Jesus' words, like that of Scripture, betokens the realization of God's will.

Then comes the moment of violence recounted by all the Gospels: with a sword someone cuts off an ear of a slave of the high priest. John's account is most specific: Simon Peter cuts off the right ear of the slave, whose name is Malchus (v. 10). Later Peter will encounter his kinsman in the high priest's courtyard (18:26). Luke also specifies the right ear. In both Matthew (26:51) and Luke the swordsman is clearly one of Jesus' disciples, and in Luke they even ask Jesus' permission to strike with the sword (22:49). He does not respond until one of them does, but Jesus then heals the severed ear (Luke 22:51). In Mark, however, the swordsman is not said to be Jesus' disciple; he is only a bystander (14:47). In neither Matthew nor John does Jesus heal the ear, but in both he admonishes the swordsman (Matt 26:52-54; John 18:11), but with different, apparently unrelated, words. Jesus' word about the cup, meaning his death, reflects the language of Mark and the Synoptics, where Jesus also uses "cup" to refer to his death (Mark 14:36; cf. 10:38-39).

Up to this point in the narrative, Jesus has not yet been taken into custody, whereas in Matthew (26:50) and Mark (14:46) he is seized immediately after Judas's kiss. Only at the end of John's narrative (18:12) is Jesus seized and bound. Similarly, Luke, who mentions Judas's kiss, without saying he actually performed it (22:47-48), has Jesus taken into custody only at the end of the episode (22:54).

Obviously, the Johannine version emphasizes the initiative and authoritative power of Jesus. Even at his own arrest he remains in control. This portrayal agrees fully with what the Johannine Jesus says about his own death. Jesus lays down his life of his own accord; no one takes it from him (10:18). Jesus' will in the matter, as throughout the Gospel, is not to be distinguished from God's. At the conclusion of the Johannine scene, Jesus says nothing about his teaching daily in the temple (Mark 14:49 par.), although he later alludes to this practice in his interrogation by the high priest (18:20).

Peter's Denial of Jesus and the Arraignment Before the High Priest (18:13-27)

The arrest of Jesus is followed immediately by his arraignment before the high priest. John continues to run parallel with Mark and the Synoptics, but with remarkable differences. All report Peter's threefold denial of Jesus centering around a hearing or trial before the high priest. In Matthew and Mark the stage is set for Peter's denial as he enters the courtyard of the high priest (Matt 26:57-58; Mark 14:53-54), but the denials occur only after the judicial proceedings. In Luke there are no judicial proceedings at this point in the narrative. John is similar to the Markan pattern, except that one of the denials occurs before and the other two after the arraignment before the high priest. Surprisingly, in Luke the authorities do not act against Jesus until the morning of the following day has broken (22:66-71).

While both Matthew and Mark on the one hand and John on the other describe an appearance of Jesus before a Jewish high priest, the similarity ends there. In Mark, with Matthew apparently following him, there is what appears to be a full-scale trial of Jesus before the Council (Sanhedrin). Charges are brought, witnesses testify, Jesus is questioned, and a verdict is rendered with appropriate punishment. In John, on the other hand, Jesus is questioned by the high priest (Annas rather than Caiaphas) concerning his disciples and his teaching, and he responds, but no council is said to be present, no formal charges are recounted, and apparently no verdict is rendered. Jesus is then sent off bound to Caiaphas, also described as the high priest. The second and third denials of Peter follow (18:25-27) and Jesus is then said to have been transferred from the house of Caiaphas to the praetorium, where he will face the Roman governor, Pilate. Nothing is said, however, about what may have transpired before Caiaphas.

Moreover, there is apparent confusion in John's narrative, for Caiaphas is clearly said to be high priest at the beginning of this episode (18:13), as he is identified by reference back to the advice he gave the Council (11:49), as well as at the end. Yet in the course of the narrative of the hearing Annas is called high priest (vv. 19, 22). True, the same Greek word *(archiereus)* can be translated either "high priest" (of which there was one) or "chief priest" (of which there were a number). Yet in context the term is used so as to imply that Annas was high priest as well as, or instead of, Caiaphas.

The relationship of John's account to the Synoptics' is puzzling. The Markan (and Matthean) trial scene, over which the high priest (in Matthew, Caiaphas) presides, and particularly its conclusion, in which Jesus is condemned to death for his allegedly blasphemous claim that he is the Messiah, fits very well with the character and cause of the mortal opposition of the Jews to Jesus as presented in the Gospel of John (cf. particularly 10:22-39, especially vv. 24, 33-36). Had John known Mark, or been using Mark, at this point, would he have passed over the opportunity to take up his narrative? The explanation that John expected the reader to supply it imputes a rather strange, and eccentric, editorial policy to John, since there are in fact, parallels to most Synoptic episodes in the Passion Narrative of the Fourth Gospel.

Our procedure will be to read John's narrative alongside the Synoptics, particularly Mark, but without assuming John's dependence upon any one of them. In this way the significant similarities and differences will be noted.

◊   ◊   ◊   ◊

Only John (18:13) reports the delivery of Jesus to Annas, Caiaphas's father-in-law, at the same time correctly stating that Caiaphas was high priest in that year (cf. 11:49). ("That year" must refer to the year of Jesus' death, for the high priesthood was not an annual office.) Annas had earlier been high priest (6–15 CE), and had been succeeded in that office by several of his sons, as well as by Caiaphas, successively (see Josephus, *Ant.* 20.198; also 18.35, 95). Caiaphas held the high priesthood for nearly two decades, beginning in 18 CE, an exceptionally long tenure. In one of many scattered points of agreement with John, however, Luke places the ministry of Jesus in the high priesthood of Annas and Caiaphas (3:2), and in Acts actually names Annas as high priest (4:6). This is incorrect, of course, although Annas was still alive and active in Jesus' day.

As he does more than once (cf. 7:19-20; 18:9, 32), John refers back to an earlier saying or episode of the narrative (v. 14; cf. 11:49-53). It is noteworthy that Caiaphas is recalled as having counseled "the Jews," inasmuch as Caiaphas, as well as Jesus, was a Jew. Once again it is apparent that "the Jews" are a special category in John.

The scene now shifts to outside the hearing room, where Peter and an unnamed "other disciple" are following Jesus (v. 15). The other disciple is not named, just as the Beloved Disciple remains anonymous. This disciple now accompanies Peter, even as the Beloved Disciple usually appears in the company of Peter (13:23-25; 20:2-10; 21:20-23; except not at the foot of the cross, 19:25-27, for by then Peter, along with the rest of the disciples, has fled). No other Gospel mentions this figure, just as no other Gospel mentions the Beloved Disciple. Since he is someone in whom the evangelist has a theological interest, it is surprising, if this episode is his composition, that John does not simply call him the Beloved Disciple. His further anonymity suggests that he belongs to tradition, if not to history. The question of his identity with the Beloved Disciple is related to the problem of the historicity of the latter, who is said to be responsible for the Gospel itself (21:24). If the disciple whom Jesus loved was a historical figure, as many exegetes now conclude (see Charlesworth 1995, 12-14, and *passim*), and was designated as such only by the evangelist, it would not be surprising that he should appear without the evangelist's sobriquet in a narrative received from tradition.

The possibility that this disciple was known to the high priest seems to militate against his identification with John the son of Zebedee, the Galilean fisherman. Yet fishermen were entrepreneurs, not common laborers at the bottom of the social spectrum (Wuellner 1967, especially 45-61). Thus the conjecture that John knew the high priest because he sold him fish is not as preposterous as it has appeared to many modern exegetes. On the other hand, the natural inference from the bare statement that the disciple was known to the high priest is that he was a Jerusalemite. So also the Beloved Disciple appears only in Jerusalem during Jesus' ministry. This coincidence encourages their identification, although it does not support the identification with John the son of Zebedee. (See Brown 1970, 822-23, for a good, succinct discussion.) The latter is not impossible, although less likely.

Obviously, this disciple has connections that Peter lacks, and thus is able to help him (v. 16). In John it is the door maid who grants Peter entrance at the behest of the other disciple who asks him about his relation to Jesus. In the Synoptics (Matt 26:69; Mark 14:66; Luke 22:56) it is also a maid who accuses Peter of being with Jesus. In John, Jesus brusquely denies the maid's question. (The question, probably for politeness' sake, expects a negative answer, which the NRSV's translation accurately reflects: "You are not also one of this man's disciples, are you?") This denial scene concludes with Peter standing by the fire, warming himself, with members of the arresting party (cf. Mark 14:54).

The scene now apparently shifts to inside the high priest's house, where he questions Jesus, not about any threat to the temple or claim to messiahship, as in Mark (14:55-65 par.), but about his disciples and his teaching (v. 19). Jesus' response (v. 20) is remarkably similar to what he says at the point of his arrest in the Synoptics (Mark 14:49 par.). Jesus then says in effect, "Why ask me? Ask those who heard me" (v. 21). The answer is not friendly or respectful, and not surprisingly elicits a blow to Jesus and an angry question (v. 22). Jesus responds as if what he has taught is by now well-known. The question seems tiresome to him. Moreover, after the end of his public ministry (12:50), Jesus no longer discusses his mission and message with representatives of the world, but limits himself to laconic answers, as he does even in his more extended responses to Pilate (18:28–19:16). (Jesus' response to the chief priest and to the police is strangely parallel to Acts 23:1-5, where Paul is struck by those standing by in response to the high priest Ananias's order.) When struck, Jesus utters a measured and reasonable request, which receives no answer at all (v. 23). Instead, he is sent by Annas to Caiaphas (v. 24), said to be high priest as in verse 13; but of course Annas has been acting in that capacity in this narrative.

To relieve the confusion, the Sinaitic Syriac version has the verses in the following order 13, 24, 14-15, 19-23, 16-18. This rearrangement makes Caiaphas the high priest referred to in the narrative, and puts all the denials after the hearing, as in Mark. Given this order of verses, however, the one that stands in almost every other manuscript witness would scarcely have emerged. Obviously, this is an attempt to make sense of the text in light of the other Gospels. Indeed, it removes the confusion from John, where both Annas and Caiaphas are said to be high priests, an impossible state of affairs.

The transfer of Jesus to Caiaphas (18:24) evokes the synoptic scene in which Jesus is tried by the Sanhedrin, presided over by Caiaphas (Matt 26:59-68; Mark 14:55-65). As we noted above, the evangelist perhaps intends the reader to supply the scene from Mark (or Matthew), but such an expectation and assumption would be rather strange in John. Yet there are similar statements elsewhere in John that have the effect of bringing this Gospel into line with the Synoptics, while breaking the flow of the narrative (cf. 2:12; 3:24; 4:2; 6:59). Of course, the Jewish authorities in John have long since condemned Jesus because of his view of his own dignity and role in relation to God and sought to put him to death (cf. 5:18; 7:19; 8:40; 10:31-39). Yet the Markan account of the trial before the Sanhedrin, culminating in Jesus' blasphemous claim to be "the Messiah, the Son of the Blessed One," fits so well the Johannine Jews' case against Jesus, its absence is remarkable. John does not in other instances shrink from repetition.

The focus of John's narrative now shifts to the courtyard where, we are reminded, Simon Peter remains (v. 25, which picks up the thread of v. 18). A second time he is questioned about his relationship to Jesus and denies it. The third and final challenge comes from a man identified very precisely (v. 26); he is a slave of the high priest and a kinsman of the injured Malchus (cf. 18:10). Of course, in no other Gospel is the man whose ear was cut off or Jesus' last challenger so identified. The latter's question is also unique in that it locates Peter at the arrest scene ("in the garden"). Peter again denies and the cock crows, fulfilling Jesus' prediction (13:38; cf. 16:32), as in the Synoptics. Remarkably, it is only in Mark that the cock crows twice (14:72; cf. 14:30). Like Matthew and Luke, John reports only one cock-crowing.

◊ ◊ ◊ ◊

John's placement of a hearing before Jewish authorities in the midst of the account of Peter's denial of Jesus (found also in Mark, and Matthew) is either given him by tradition or by the Synoptics, probably Mark. As we have seen, there are problems to be explained if John is regarded as dependent on Mark (or Matthew). (See above, pp. 322-26, 332-33.) Rather, John seems to have relied on, or been heavily influenced by, an alternative account (see Fortna 1977/78). It seems to have left a deep impression on the Gospel tradition that Peter actually denied Jesus, particularly if John is here independent of Mark (as Brown 1994, 412, argues). Like Judas's betrayal, Peter's denial creates a potential embarrassment for the early church. Is it more readily explained as a literary invention for the sake of theology or as an unfortunate event that the tradition has not suppressed? The latter is more likely, as Brown persuasively argues (1994, 614-21).

As we have noted, John's account lacks at this point a strong, formal, condemnation of Jesus in a trial before the Sanhedrin (cf. Mark 14:55-65). Officially, condemnation of Jesus by "the Jews" has already occurred more than once (beginning in 5:18) and will continue into the trial before Pilate (18:28–19:16). Indeed, it is a major theme of the Fourth Gospel. Nevertheless, at this point John's account is remarkably spare, as the Gospel omits the kind of trial and condemnation one might have anticipated.

Therefore, distinctly Johannine theological themes do not come to strong expression in this pericope. This state of affairs stands in some contrast to the Gospel of Mark, where the trial before the Sanhedrin serves as a climax of the narrative. Jesus, under questioning, admits that he believes himself to be the Messiah, the Son of God, and is therefore condemned to death by the authorities. In John, of course, the reader has known Jesus was the Messiah from the beginning (1:41), in Mark since Peter's confession (8:29). Perhaps not surprisingly, Mark's narratives of the confession of Peter (8:27-30) and the Sanhedrin trial (14:55-65) both have counterparts of diminished significance in John (6:66-69; 18:19-24), which do not have the same pivotal function in the narrative. At the same time the Johannine versions of these episodes cannot easily be explained as derivative from Mark.

Although such episodes as the denial and trial may be given by tradition and history, the typical Johannine irony shines through them. While Jesus is being arraigned before the representative of Jewish authority, his chief disciple is outside busily denying him. Jesus was handed over by one of his disciples, denied by another, and abandoned by all. Yet precisely through these events and their dismal culmination in a horrific death Jesus saves his disciples; indeed, he protects them from such a fate (17:12; 18:9).

The Trial Before Pilate (18:28–19:16a)

Even more than in the Synoptics, the trial before Pilate is the centerpiece of the Johannine Passion narrative. (John's account consists of thirty-nine verses, Mark's of only fifteen.) It is the one climactic event that decides Jesus' fate. If John knew an account of Jesus' appearance before the Sanhedrin, he has suppressed it in order to focus entirely upon the one trial before Pilate, in which the Jews, in condemning Jesus, also condemn themselves. While there are points of similarity between the Johannine account and the synoptic, as in other cases it is difficult to understand John's narrative as simply based upon, or derivative from the Synoptics.

Brown divides the narrative into seven scenes marked by the movement of Pilate inside and outside the praetorium (1994, 757-59): 18:28-32, 33-38a, 38b-40; 19:1-3, 4-8, 9-11, 12-16a. There may also be a chiastic construction centering on 19:1-3, since the first and last scenes deal with the Jews' intent to see Jesus executed (18:28-32; 19:12-16a), the second and sixth with the issue of kingship or power (18:33-38a; 19:9-11), and the third and fifth with Pilate's declaration of Jesus' innocence (18:38b-40; 19:4-8). However that may be, the Johannine account is obviously highly articulated or structured in a way the Markan is not. Pilate shuttles back and forth between Jesus inside the praetorium and the Jews outside. In this way John portrays Pilate as caught between the truth of Jesus and the relentless pressure of his Jewish adversaries.

18:28-32: In the opening scene, Pilate goes outside the praetorium, which these adversaries have just refused to enter, and begins a conversation with "the Jews." By thus identifying Jesus' accusers, the Gospel aids and abets the impression, which was to grow through the centuries, that the Jewish people generally opposed Jesus to the death. This is not historically true, and at a couple of points in the trial before Pilate Jesus' opponents are identified also as chief priests (19:15) or chief priests and police (19:6), possibly affording a valuable clue as to who really were at the root of the opposition to Jesus.

Only John speaks of a transferral from Caiaphas to the headquarters of Pilate, the praetorium (v. 28). The presumption of the narrative seems to be that there was a meeting of Jesus with Annas and Caiaphas at their houses. The location of the praetorium is a matter of dispute, whether the fortress Antonia on the northwestern corner of the temple area or the Herodian palace on the western side of the city. More probably the latter in the view of Brown (1994, 708). John may not be particularly interested in geographical loci, but here as elsewhere he projects an intelligible Jerusalem scenario.

In John, as in no other canonical Gospel, these events occur before the Passover, whereas in the Synoptics Jesus and his disciples have already eaten the Passover the evening before. Was the Jews' fear of contamination before Passover well founded (cf. Ezra 6:19-22)? John may mention this fear by way of irony, because "the Jews" do not appreciate how much greater defilement they are risking as they hound the Son of God to death. In any event, although in the view of the narrative the danger of defilement that would prevent keeping the Passover was real, it is not clear what the anticipated source of such defilement would be (cf. Brown 1994, 744-45; Barrett 1978, 532-33). Perhaps just being present in a Gentile's domicile would risk defilement.

The question of Pilate to those bringing Jesus before him (18:29) is a direct and obvious one. Their response (v. 30), on the other hand, is not direct, and it furthermore presupposes Jesus' guilt, which in their eyes has been established throughout the Gospel. It accords also with the verdict issued in the Markan account of Jesus' trial before the Sanhedrin (14:64), which is not recounted in John (but cf. 11:53). Interestingly, only in Luke's account (23:1-2) do the authorities begin by issuing before Pilate an indictment of charges against Jesus. Yet at this point in John's narrative (v. 30) the nature of Jesus' evil deed (RSV: "evildoer," translating literally) or crime (NRSV) is not given. The reader will know, but Pilate will not. In John, Jesus is repeatedly "handed over": here to Pilate (cf. v. 35); later by Pilate to the Jews (18:36; 19:16); also by Judas, who betrays, that is, hands over, Jesus (e.g., 18:5). In each case the same Greek word, *paradidōmi,* is used, as also by Paul (1 Cor 11:23). Behind all this handing over of Jesus there lies, in early Christian conviction, the will and purpose of God.

Pilate's response (v. 31) reflects a disinterest in the whole matter (cf. 19:6), similar to that expressed by the Roman proconsul Gallio, when asked by Jews to punish Paul (Acts 18:12-17). Pilate seems to assume what Gallio actually says, namely, that this is an inner-Jewish, religious matter, indeed, one concerning Jewish law, with which he does not wish to deal. (There may be a subtle irony here, for John would agree that Jesus is to be judged according to Jewish law, which, rightly interpreted, is fulfilled in him; cf. the thesis of Harvey, *Jesus on Trial,* 1976.) When the Jews respond as they do (v. 31), they once again presume Jesus' guilt and, moreover, that the crime of which Jesus is guilty deserves nothing less than the death penalty (5:18 and *passim;* cf. Mark 14:64). The reader of this Gospel will not now be at all surprised.

The Jews' statement that they are not allowed to execute anyone highlights the historical fact (v. 31) and its historical and theological significance (v. 32). The Jews would have executed Jesus by stoning (e.g., Lev 20:2, 27; 24:14, 16, 23; cf. Acts 7:58-60). They did not. Rather, he was executed by the typical Roman method of crucifixion. Thus, as Jesus himself had predicted, albeit in a veiled way, he was to be "lifted up" (12:32; cf. 3:14-15), that is, crucified. Pilate must fulfill Jesus' prophecy by having him crucified, and the Jews should not put him to death by stoning.

The Jews' statement also implies that under Roman rule they did not have the authority to put Jesus to death. True, a Jewish crowd stoned Stephen, whose preaching for good reason they found offensive (Acts 7:54–8:1), but this seems more a lynching than a legal procedure. Did the Jewish authorities in Jerusalem, that is the chief priests, have the power, which necessarily would have been granted by the Romans, to execute criminals deemed worthy of death? The Gospels create the impression, here explicitly stated, that the Jewish authorities did not have the right to carry out a death sentence, and thus needed to persuade Pilate to do it. (Brown 1994, 363-72, 747-49, discusses this much-debated matter fully with reference to the ancient sources and concludes that with few exceptions Jews in Judea were not permitted to carry out executions.) Probably the picture John paints in this conversation is historically accurate. Jesus was, finally, executed by the Romans. Yet there remains the historical question about the role of Jewish authorities, especially the chief priests, whom John portrays as instigating the execution. Jesus was not a credible threat to Roman authority per se, unless he could be portrayed as disrupting the status quo and thus threatening an unspoken concordat between the chief priests and the Romans. In fact, what is suggested in John 11:47-53 is that the chief priests saw him as such a threat (Sanders 1993, 272).

18:33-38a: The next episode centers around Pilate's interrogation of Jesus. In the Synoptics (Matt 27:11-14; Mark 15:2-5; Luke 23:2-5) Pilate simply asks Jesus whether he is the King of the Jews, and Jesus responds enigmatically, "You say so." In

Matthew (27:13-14) and Mark (15:4-5) Jesus makes no response in the face of many accusations by the chief priests, much to Pilate's amazement. By contrast, in John alone Jesus responds at some length to Pilate's question about his kingship, and his response contains distinctively Johannine features or themes (vv. 34-37). Although there are strong indications that Jesus' speech was composed by the evangelist for the occasion, it and the whole episode nevertheless have a kind of verisimilitude that is typical of the Fourth Gospel. Given the Johannine terms of discussion, people would react in some such fashion.

Thus in response to Pilate's question (v. 33), found in all the Gospels, Jesus poses a counterquestion that already suggests his knowledge of a conspiracy against him, which there is in John (v. 34). Pilate's response (v. 35) indicates that Jesus' knowledge is well-founded. Even Pilate's counterquestion to Jesus suggests that the chief priests are the source of his initial question about kingship, as he then spells out what the reader (with Jesus) will know has happened, concluding with the matter-of-fact "What have you done?"

Jesus now speaks of his kingdom (or "kingship," as the RSV translates) in terms that seem quite Johannine (v. 36). The Greek term *(basileia)* is the same one Jesus uses earlier (3:3) in speaking of the kingdom of God. Moreover, it is the same term that is translated throughout the synoptic Gospels as "kingdom" (of God). ("Rule of God" is also a possible translation.) Here the subject of this rule, the one who carries it out, is, of course, Jesus, but his rule, or kingdom, is God's. This is what Jesus, in effect, says when he declares his kingdom is not "from this world." It is surely a matter of source or origin. Repeatedly in this Gospel the question of Jesus' source or origin appears in relation to his role and authority (1:46; 9:29-30). In saying that his kingdom is not from or of this world Jesus implies that it is from God, although he does not say this directly to Pilate, who would scarcely understand if he did. In any event, the source of his kingdom—his authority or rule—outside this world explains why his followers do not offer physical resistance. Thus, in a typically Johannine way, the pacifism of Jesus' followers is explained (cf. Matt 5:38-

42; Luke 6:29-31). Ultimately, Jesus, who has been turned over to Pilate (18:35), will be turned back over to the Jews (19:16), seemingly for execution. Of course, John knows the Roman authorities actually carried out the deed, as they do in all the Gospels. That the Jews play such a role here probably reflects the continuing hostility of Jewish authorities to the Johannine Christians in the generations following Jesus' death (an essential aspect of the thesis of Martyn, *History and Theology in the Fourth Gospel*, 1979). In John's view, Jesus' disciples do not escape the hostility that was originally directed at him (15:20-21; 16:2).

With Pilate's legitimate inference from Jesus' response (v. 37) John's narrative returns to the point of his original question to Jesus (v. 33), paralleled in the Synoptics. The repetition may signal that the preceding material has been interpolated into an earlier source, whether Mark or a parallel narrative (cf. John 18:4, 7, where Jesus repeats his previous question). Now Jesus answers as he does in the Synoptics (Mark 15:2 par.): "You say...." And again Jesus expands upon the theme of his kingship in a thoroughly Johannine way. Jesus first states his purpose and mission, using characteristic Johannine terms, with which the reader is by now familiar: his own coming; world; witness; truth. Significantly, Jesus refers here to his own birth, never explicitly mentioned elsewhere in this Gospel (cf. Gal 4:4). His coming into the world is, theologically speaking, a descent from heaven (3:13; 6:33, 51), but this does not mean that Jesus was not born of a woman (cf. 2:1; 19:25-27; also Gal 4:4). John's apparently mythological language is intended to interpret, not cancel out, human, historical realities. The second part of Jesus' response brings his followers into the picture. Those who hear, really hear, and thus understand the import of Jesus' voice (cf. 10:4-5, 16) are his disciples. They belong to the truth (NRSV); they are, with respect to origin, literally "of the truth" (cf. the motif of birth from above or from God: 1:13, 3:3-7), as is Jesus. Pilate reveals his own distance from Jesus, the truth, by his question (v. 38*a*), which reveals who he is and where he stands. Ultimately, he will be unable, or unwilling, to resist the forces bent on doing Jesus in.

18:38b-40: Again the scene changes, with Pilate now going outside once again to confront the Jews. Although his seemingly naive question shows that he scarcely begins to comprehend Jesus, Pilate declares in effect that he finds Jesus innocent (18:38b) as he will twice more (19:4, 6; cf. Luke 23:4, 14, 22). Historically, a Roman procurator would have been able to sustain his verdict, and there is ample evidence that Pilate would use force in order to do so (Brown 1994, 698-705; cf. Luke 13:1-5). Yet in John he does not. Indeed, in all the Gospels Pilate expresses his misgivings, but does not prevail.

Pilate then refers to a custom by which he, as governor, released one prisoner to the Jews at Passover, and in effect suggests that he might now release Jesus ("the King of the Jews," v. 39), whereupon they call instead for the release of Barabbas, a bandit, who has not until now been mentioned. Of course, the reader of Mark (15:6-14) or Matthew (27:15-23) will have been told in advance by the narrator of the custom of releasing a prisoner at Passover, as well as who Barabbas was, and why he was in prison. The crowd then asks Pilate to release a prisoner, but when Pilate proposes Jesus, the crowd, stirred up by the chief priests, asks for Barabbas instead and ultimately calls for Jesus' crucifixion. The incident is much reduced in John (as also in Luke), with Pilate taking the initiative. John's account puts the spotlight on Pilate in order to highlight the role of the Jews in rejecting Pilate's offer and demanding instead the release of Barabbas. In John, unlike the Synoptics, the Barabbas episode is not the climax and conclusion of the trial.

19:1-3: Jesus is next flogged and mocked, as also happens immediately after the Barabbas incident in the synoptic Gospels (Matt 27:26-31; Mark 15:15-20), although not yet as preparation for crucifixion. Each of the Synoptics mentions the release of Barabbas, but John assumes or ignores it, and Barabbas, in whom John seems no longer interested, simply disappears from the scene. The Barabbas scene has taken place outside the praetorium or headquarters, but Jesus has all the while remained within, where the flogging and mocking now occur (cf. 19:4, where Pilate moves outside again).

The mocking of Jesus (19:2-3) is closely paralleled in Matthew and Mark. (In Luke this mocking occurs only when Jesus is arraigned before Herod Antipas in 23:6-12.) Jesus is now arrayed in royal garments. In John, however, the crown of thorns is mentioned first, then the purple robe. In John, as in Matthew (27:29) and Mark (15:18), Jesus is hailed as King of the Jews by Roman soldiers (19:3), even as Caesar would have been similarly greeted (Brown 1994, 868). Elsewhere, John calls Jesus the Savior of the world (4:42), a title applied also to the Roman Emperor (Barrett 1978, 244).

It is worth noting that the NRSV reads Pilate "had [Jesus] flogged" (19:1), whereas the RSV simply says that Pilate scourged (or flogged) Jesus. The latter is a translation of what the Greek quite literally says, but the NRSV is surely right to indicate that Pilate himself did not do the flogging (cf. a similar construction in 21:24).

19:4-8: Pilate comes out of the building again, this time bringing Jesus with him, apparently to declare him innocent as he now says not once but twice (vv. 4, 6). Pilate's shuttling back and forth, whether by himself or as here and in 19:13-16 with Jesus in tow, seems out of character for a Roman governor, particularly one of Pilate's proven toughness. However that may be, Pilate's behavior is an extremely effective literary device for portraying him as caught between opposing forces, as in some sense he was. Mark also reflects Pilate's doubt about Jesus' guilt (15:14), although it is not portrayed so dramatically. It may be that John deliberately emphasizes Pilate's plight and exaggerates a sense of his entrapment for theological reasons. Pilate's failure to make a decision for Jesus finally becomes a decision against Jesus. Trying to find a basis to defend Jesus other than the truth of Jesus himself is ultimately futile.

Pilate repeatedly states that he finds no cause (Gk. *aitia*), meaning cause for complaint or cause of condemnation, in Jesus (vv. 4, 6; cf. 18:38). This apparently technical, legal terminology, and the NRSV's translation is entirely apt: "I find no case against him." The innocence of Jesus before Roman law was important for early Christians to be able to affirm (cf. Luke 23:47, where the centurion's confession that Jesus was a son of God is changed to a Roman declaration of his innocence).

Significantly, in John's account Jesus has not yet been divested of his royal regalia (v. 5): he may now stand before the Jewish authorities as their king (cf. 19:15). In the synoptic account of the mocking they are immediately thereafter replaced with his own garments (Matt 27:31; Mark 15:20). John's intended effect is clear. Pilate's presentation of Jesus (the KJV translates literally: "Behold the man!") is laconic but admits of distinctly Christian and Johannine interpretation. Is this a succinct statement of the doctrine of the Incarnation? Probably. If so, in typical Johannine fashion, and with a touch of irony, Pilate is saying more than he could possibly know theologically (cf. Caiaphas's statement in 11:50).

Pilate's presentation of Jesus affords the chief priests and police opportunity to call for his crucifixion (v. 6). It is interesting that in the Synoptics it is the crowd, or the people, who call for Jesus' death (Mark 15:11-13), but in John it is a more limited group. In light of John's apparent tendency to shift the blame for Jesus' death to the Jews generally, this difference is surprising since if anything we would have expected the opposite in Mark and John. Probably the chief priests and police or officers *(hyperetai)* are actually the same group that John elsewhere calls, "the Jews," just as in other parts of the Gospel "the Jews" and "Pharisees" seem virtually synonymous. Subtly, John reflects a consciousness that "the Jews," as he calls them, are essentially those Jewish authorities who oppose not only Jesus but his disciples who formed the postresurrection church. Through his public ministry "the Jews" are the Pharisees, as indeed Jesus himself debated with Pharisees. In the Passion Narrative the Pharisees fade into the background and "the Jews" are the chief priests and the officers, as indeed Jesus himself was opposed in Jerusalem by the temple authorities.

Pilate's response to the Jews (v. 6) contains a touch of Johannine irony in that he seems to grant them permission— indeed, orders them—to crucify Jesus, that is, to carry out capital punishment, which they have expressly said they may not do (18:31)! Of course, Pilate does not really intend to give Jews the authority to do this. On the other hand, his charge to the Jews prepares the way for John's statement that Pilate turned Jesus over to them, that is, the Jews, for crucifixion (v. 16; cf. 18:36). Pilate then makes his third affirmation of Jesus' innocence, as also in Luke, Pilate three times declares Jesus innocent (Luke 23:4, 14, 22), using similar language.

The response of "the Jews" (clearly now the chief priests and police) sums up their entire case against Jesus (v. 7). The NRSV's "has claimed to be the Son of God" is an interpretation of the statement that Jesus *made* himself Son of God (cf. RSV). They have then already decided that Jesus must die and for what reason (see 5:18; 11:45-53).

That the law decrees death for anyone who claims to be Son of God in the Johannine sense of equality with God may be inferred from Lev 24:16 (cf. *m. Sanh.* 7.5; *m. Ker.* 1.1-2). The biblical and Mishnaic texts concern blasphemy and its punishment, of which claiming special sonship to God, not to mention equality with God (10:30, 33), would be an extreme manifestation, and it is precisely this of which Jesus is deemed guilty.

Enormous issues are at stake here. Pilate, who had not understood Jesus' relation to the truth (18:38) is now said to be more afraid than ever (v. 8), presumably in light of Jesus' alleged claim. How would Pilate have understood it? Probably as the claim that Jesus was some sort of god appearing in human form. As Schnackenburg puts it, "numinous terror before the divine," falls upon this representative of earthly power (1982, 260). Thus Pilate is literally awestruck. Brown, on the other hand, prefers the explanation that Pilate is being pushed into a corner, where he will be forced to make a decision about Jesus (1994, 830). As the narrative develops, the latter is surely the case. Yet the statement about Pilate's fear also appropriately underscores the awesomeness of Jesus before this wielder of the powers of this world.

19:9-11: Pilate once again shuttles into his headquarters in the praetorium (v. 9), obviously taking Jesus with him, as he again questions him. This exchange is distinctively Johannine. Yet the motif of Jesus' silence and Pilate's astonishment is found also in the Synoptics (Matt 27:12-14; Mark 15:3-5), although there in the face of the accusations of the chief priests while here vis-à-vis Pilate's questioning.

Pilate asks Jesus about his origin, a familiar Johannine motif (v. 9; cf. 1:46). The question makes sense at two levels. It is a question quite naturally put to a prisoner by a magistrate or judge. Pilate may not hear the theological overtones of his question. Yet at the same time the question connects with the statement about Pilate's fear in view of the accusation that Jesus claims to be Son of God. In this connection it is worth remembering that the text of verse 7 read, literally, *"made himself* son of God." This is what Pilate has heard, is perhaps what caused him to fear, and leads to this question, which may mean "Are you of divine or human origin?" Jesus' silence in response to Pilate's question matches his similar silence when Pilate asked him, "What is truth?" (18:38). Doubtless Jesus' silence itself speaks volumes: Pilate would scarcely be able to comprehend the theologically adequate answer. When in the face of Jesus' silence Pilate affirms his power over him (v. 10), he is saying in effect that he has power to determine Jesus' fate, but at the same time he is, implicitly, raising the question of the origin and source of his own power. Obviously, Pilate states that his power is, as far as Jesus is concerned, absolute. Jesus in effect acknowledges the correctness of Pilate's statement (v. 11). Pilate can dispose of Jesus, but in having him crucified he will only fulfill God's will.

Who is the one who handed Jesus over to Pilate and therefore is guilty of the greater sin? Of course, Judas is repeatedly described as the one who has handed Jesus over (e.g., most recently at 18:2). Caiaphas (18:28) is also a candidate. Yet the Jews have also acknowledged that they have handed Jesus over to Pilate (18:30). Even though "the one who handed me over to you" is singular, at this point in the narrative the Jewish authorities are probably meant (cf. Brown 1994, 842). Pilate evidently takes no offense at Jesus' declaration that his own power comes from God. (After all, Jesus has otherwise laid the greater part of the blame elsewhere.) Thus he once again will seek to release Jesus.

19:12-16a: To Pilate's desire to release Jesus (v. 12), the Jews respond with a scarcely veiled threat. This interchange apparently presupposes that Pilate has gone back outside, although we are not informed of that explicitly until he must fetch Jesus from within (v. 13). If the scenes are to be marked by Pilate's movements, then the final one consists of 19:12-16.

As we have noted, Pilate's doubt about Jesus' guilt plays a role in every Gospel (e.g., Mark 15:10, 14), but only in Luke (23:4, 14, 22) and John (18:38; 19:4, 6) does Pilate declare Jesus innocent. This is actually the second time in John (cf. 18:39) that Pilate has proposed releasing Jesus (cf. Luke 23:22). Also in Mark (15:9-10; cf. Matt 27:17-18) Pilate asks the crowd whether they will have Jesus released as the Barabbas episode unfolds. (The extant fragment of the *Gospel of Peter* only begins after the Barabbas scene, if there was such a scene in that Gospel.)

Here Pilate's final attempt meets what can only be construed as potentially a stinging rebuke, for the Jews call Pilate's loyalty to the emperor into question (v. 12). The thrust of the Jews' outcry is clear enough; they are in effect threatening Pilate. The only question is whether "friend of the emperor" ("friend of Caesar") was at this specific period an honorific title or category (Brown 1994, 843). If it was, then they are accusing Pilate of not living up to his status. In any case, the Jews are portrayed as bringing acute pressure upon Pilate in the one way they could.

In fixing the blame for Jesus' condemnation and death firmly on the Jews (the Jewish authorities) John brings to expression his own strong interest and belief. On the other hand, his portrayal of Pilate's behavior is anything but flattering. Pilate accedes to their wishes, although he knows better and is in a different way also quite guilty. Pilate could have stopped the execution and released Jesus, but he didn't. Indeed, his soldiers carried it out. Dodd (1963, 98-120; cf. also Rensberger 1988, 87) argues eloquently that John's account of the trial and execution of Jesus, written up though it is in John's characteristic style and with his apologetic interests in view, nevertheless possesses a superior plausibility and verisimilitude that bespeaks its claim to a higher degree of historicity than the Synoptics'. The Jews, that is, the chief priests and those aligned with them, see in Jesus a fundamental threat to the well-being of the temple and to their own authoritative status (2:19; 11:47-50). That this perception is rooted in Jesus' own time and ministry is suggested by the pervasiveness of the words of Jesus against the temple in the Gospel tradition (2:19; cf. Mark 13:2; 14:57-58; 15:29 par.; Acts 6:14), a state of affairs, which, with the so-called temple cleansing, implies that Jesus' attitude toward the temple played an important role in his demise (cf. E. P. Sanders 1985, especially 61-76). Jesus' quotation of Ps 69:9 (John 2:17) already suggests this. The fact that the picture John paints in some ways coincides with his interests does not necessarily mean that it lacks any historical basis.

Pilate responds to the Jews' challenge by mockingly presenting Jesus to them as their king (vv. 13-14), but, in accord with their wishes, he does not release him. There is a real sense in which the Jews have won the day and Pilate has lost. Ironically, as Pilate brings Jesus out again he himself sits on the judgment seat, as if he were finally judge (see Brown 1994, 1388-93, for the correctness of this translation). The name of the place, given in Greek and Aramaic, no longer identifies its location with certainty. Extant stone pavement slabs buried under the site of the ancient Antonia fortress on the northern side of the temple mount have suggested that place as the locus of the scene, although this identification is uncertain (Brown 1994, 845). More likely the site would have been the Herodian palace on the western side of the ancient city, near the still extant tower of Phasael.

John carefully notes the time: noon ("the sixth hour," reckoning from dawn) on the day of Preparation. In Mark (15:25) Jesus already hangs on the cross at the third hour and at the sixth hour, presumably noon (Mark 15:33; cf. Amos 8:9), darkness comes over the land. Once again John makes clear that Jesus is crucified before the Passover is eaten, while the lambs are being slaughtered, rather than after as in the Synoptics (cf. John 13:1, 29; 19:31). As Pilate places Jesus before the Jews as their king, his pronouncement (v. 14; literally, "Behold your King") parallels that in verse 5; both are unique to John. Significantly, Jesus has still not been stripped of his kingly array (v. 5), as he was immediately in Mark (15:20).

The Jews now cry out again for his crucifixion (v. 15) as the chief priests and police had already (v. 6). This is actually the outcry of the crowd in the Synoptics (cf. Mark 15:13-14 par.). Pilate's telling question (only in John) presumes that Jesus is king of the Jews. Mockingly, Pilate accepts Jesus' claim in the face of those who have challenged him. Their answer is the clincher: they will be loyal to the emperor if Pilate will not (cf. v. 12). This amounts to an amazing reversal of roles as John, ironically, contradicts normal expectations. Behind this statement lies an ancient history of debate about kingship (see especially 1 Sam 8). Who should be king of Israel? In desiring an earthly king the people reject the kingship of the Lord (2 Sam 8:7). Now they repeat that earlier choice by choosing Caesar, the Roman emperor, rather than Jesus. All along "Israel" and "Israelite" have been good words in John's book, but not "Jews." Now, in effect, the chief priests (perhaps significantly they are quite specifically identified and are not simply called "the Jews") deny their role as Israel, which they presumably leave to Jesus and his followers, in swearing allegiance to Caesar. It is a strange turn of events, but one that fits John's supersessionist theology. When Pilate turns Jesus over "to them" (v. 16), the antecedent can only be the chief priests or the Jews (cf. 18:36; also Luke 23:25). Yet the subsequent narrative reveals that soldiers, presumably Romans, carry out the execution.

◊ ◊ ◊ ◊

The trial of Jesus before Pilate is as clearly parallel to the synoptic versions as it is distinctively different from them. The literary structure of the Johannine episode, perhaps shaped chiastically around the central event of the mocking of Jesus as king of the Jews (above, pp. 344-45), far surpasses the synoptic accounts in both literary and theological development.

Nevertheless, the theme of kingship dominates the other

accounts as much as it does John's. In all probability, Pilate's question to Jesus, "Are you the king of the Jews?" constituted the fundamental theme as well as the historical issue in the very beginning. The claim to be the king of the Jews, or the attribution of that claim to Jesus, led ultimately to his crucifixion by the Romans. As much as Pilate may have doubted whether Jesus constituted a political threat—Barabbas was plainly a more dangerous figure—he was evidently convinced he could not take a chance on him.

Moreover, the question of kingship is also the messianic question. Did Jesus claim to be Messiah? At the very least he was executed as the king of the Jews, as the placard on his cross showed. The question of whether Jesus himself claimed messiahship is real enough. That Jesus was executed as a messianic pretender is nevertheless significant confirmation of the fact that others at least entertained the question, whatever Jesus may have thought of himself.

At the beginning of John's Gospel Jesus is hailed as Son of God and King of Israel. "Son of God" is a common title for Jesus, whether in the Fourth Gospel or elsewhere (cf. Mark 1:1; Rom 1:4). King of Israel is not so common except that it is the equivalent of Messiah or Christ, the generic title of Jesus in the New Testament, which gives the whole movement, Christianity, its name.

In John the increased prominence of the theme of Jesus' kingship is balanced by the recession of the kingdom of God in Jesus' teaching. Although the kingdom of God is mentioned in John (3:3, 5) it quickly fades into the background, whereas it is the center of Jesus' preaching and teaching in the Synoptics (Mark 1:14-15). The kingdom, kingship, or rule of God was a central element in the historical Jesus' own preaching. The same Greek word, *basileia*, would lie behind any of these three English terms. Its recession in John has to do with the prominence of Christology and the reinterpretation of eschatology in that Gospel. Insofar as Jesus in John no longer speaks about the manifestation, particularly the near advent, of the kingdom, he is by that much removed from the historical, as well as the synoptic, Jesus. One might say that kingdom eschatology, often described in modern scholarship as apocalyptic, is replaced by christological eschatology. That is, the manifestation of God in Jesus' earthly ministry, and finally in his crucifixion and resurrection (understood as glorification) is the ultimate revelatory event. Eschatological hope has, in principle, already been fulfilled. If one will believe, eternal life as a present and continuing possibility replaces kingdom expectation. Thus Christ is already king, from the standpoint of the evangelist, and therefore heavy emphasis falls upon his kingship or rule in the passion narrative. Obviously, Pilate means earthly kingship when he asks Jesus whether he is a king, but he is incapable of understanding the meaning of Jesus' kingship, which is not of this world. To penetrate to the level of Jesus' kingship, as John presents it, one must be born from above. That is, one must be given a new perspective and starting point. In human terms this is inexplicable (3:8); yet one may begin by believing (3:16).

The kingship of Christ in John replaces the kingdom of God in the teaching of Jesus, because in John, Christ is in his historic revelation, his ministry, death and resurrection, the manifestation of God (1:18). No one comes to the Father except through him (14:6). Thus "the Jews," who by definition reject Jesus, in a certain sense understand the meaning of the claims they do not accept. Pilate, on the other hand, remains uncomprehending. Whether the evangelist has thought through the theme of kingship with Christology and eschatology explicitly in view may remain a moot question. Yet the inner logic of their relationship and its relation to the theme of kingship is clear.

As we have observed, John's account of the trial before Pilate differs from the parallel synoptic accounts in its complexity, literary structure, and theological explicitness. These factors are, of course, related. In this complex and highly structured narrative the theological themes emerge largely in conversations among Jesus, Pilate, and the Jews. The Jews express their unremitting hostility and its grounds. Jesus makes guarded, but suggestive statements about himself and his ministry that accurately reflect Johannine Christology. He is a king whose power comes from on high, but he is not a king in the sense Pilate thinks, for he has come to testify to the truth. His opponents are deeply offended that he claims to be (or, literally, "makes himself") Son of God, but they know that the accusation about kingship will be most effective before Pilate. Pilate's chief role is to ask the crucial questions, whether to the Jews or to Jesus: "What accusation do you bring against this man?" (to Jews, 18:29); "Are you the King of the Jews?" (to Jesus, 18:33); "I am not a Jew, am I?" (to Jesus, 18:35); "So you are a king?" (to Jesus, 18:37); "What is truth?" (to Jesus, 18:38); "Do you want me to release for you the King of the Jews?" (to the Jews, 18:39); "Where are you from?" (to Jesus 19:9); "Do you refuse to speak to me? Do you not know that I have power to release you, and power to crucify you?" (to Jesus, 19:10); "Shall I crucify your King?" (to the Jews, 19:15). Pilate's questions serve to highlight the issues and to move the conversation and action forward.

While the Jews' motivations are patent, as they speak openly before Pilate, the words of Jesus are more mysterious and difficult, particularly from Pilate's point of view. Jesus seems to acknowledge his kingly role while distinguishing his kingship or kingdom from all others (18:36-37). That Pilate should be perplexed by his claim to testify to the truth is scarcely surprising. The same goes for Jesus' statement that Pilate's power over him comes from above, from God (19:11). The knowledgeable reader will know better than Pilate the meaning of such statements, for that reader will know the gospel message as well as this Gospel and the nature of the claims made for Jesus.

The Death of Jesus (19:16b-42)

John's narrative continues to run parallel with the Synoptics, and there are obvious similarities. In all accounts the crucified Jesus is identified by a sign on the cross naming him the King of the Jews, presumably the charge against him. Also Jesus is crucified between two criminals, but only in John does neither revile him. As in the Synoptics, Golgotha, the place of a skull, is the site of the crucifixion. In all the Gospels the dying Jesus is offered a drink. In all a group of women is within sight of the cross. Finally, in all the Gospels Joseph of Arimathea requests the body of Jesus from Pilate in order to bury him.

Yet John differs in many details. Only in John is Jesus said to bear his own cross. Only in John do we read that the sign on the cross was written in three languages and that the chief priests protested it. Only John says that the place of crucifixion was near the city. Although all the Gospels relate the dividing of Jesus' garments, only John describes Jesus' seamless robe and quotes the scripture that is fulfilled. No other Gospel reports that the mother of Jesus, as well as the Beloved Disciple, stood at the foot of the cross, where Jesus addressed them. While John alone does not report the mocking of the crucified Jesus, only John describes the incident in which the body of Jesus is pierced by the soldier's spear. Remarkably, only John does not describe the manifestations that accompany Jesus' dying in the other Gospels: the rending of the temple veil and darkness at noon. Nor does John mention the centurion's confession. Only in John are soldiers sent out to see whether Jesus is yet dead.

Those to whom Jesus is handed over, apparently the Jews (19:16), turn out to be the Roman soldiers after all (cf. vv. 16*b* and 23). That Jesus carries his own cross seems at first glance an alteration of the synoptic narratives (Mark 15:21 par.), according to which Simon of Cyrene is impressed for that task. John's Jesus should not need help! Yet it was customary for the condemned man to bear the cross, at least the crossbar, on his back (see Carson 1991, 608; and Brown 1994, 914). John's wording emphasizes that Jesus bears the cross "by himself" and perhaps implicitly reflects his knowledge of the tradition about Simon, which may well be historical. (His sons, Alexander and Rufus, were evidently known to the readership of Mark.)

The place of crucifixion is the same in all Gospels, but only John says specifically that Golgotha in Hebrew (actually the closely related Aramaic) means skull (v. 17). The site is commemorated in the Church of the Holy Sepulchre in Jerusalem, alongside the traditional tomb of Jesus. In fact, their proximity in this ancient church agrees with what is said only in John, namely, that the tomb was nearby (19:41-42).

The crucifixion of Jesus between the two criminals is narrated as concisely as possible (v. 18), and there is no mention here of their mocking or reviling Jesus (cf. Mark 15:27-32 par.). Again, the omission is typical of John, who nevertheless reported the soldiers' mocking and beating Jesus in the trial before Pilate (19:2-3). Conceivably John knows an independent tradition that is less elaborate and omits this second mocking. Remarkably, the Markan version of the mocking (Mark 15:29-32a) is replete with just the kind of irony found in John, concluding with a reference to seeing and believing that is actually quite typical of John (1:14; 4:48; 6:30, 40; 19:35; 20:8, 29). How Jesus was actually affixed to the cross is not said here, although the Johannine resurrection appearance accounts make clear that nails were driven through his hands (20:20, 25, 27). Luke's comparable appearance account mentions his feet as well (24:38, 50). The *Gospel of Peter* reports the nails' being removed from Jesus' hands as he is taken down from the cross (6:21), the only instance in which the nails are mentioned in a Passion Narrative. Psalm 22, which has extensive parallels with the Passion, mentions the piercing of hands and feet (v. 16 RSV). If the psalm were the source of elements in the Passion Narrative, the nailing of Jesus to the cross might reasonably have been mentioned there, as well as in the appearance stories. However that may be, John assumes that Jesus was nailed to the cross through his hands or forearms.

Brown (1994, 949-52) treats the matter thoroughly, documenting from other ancient sources and a modern archaeological discovery that victims were often nailed to the crossbar and concluding that it "can be deemed historically plausible" that Jesus was nailed to the cross. Probably the initial offer of myrrhed wine to Jesus (Mark 15:24) anticipates such trauma. Obviously, nails driven through the palms of the hand would not support the weight of a body, so nails must have been driven through the wrists or forearms. (On the practice of crucifixion generally, see Hengel 1977, especially 22-38.)

The inscription on the cross (v. 19), indicating the charge on which the accused was suffering, is similar to that described in all the other Gospels, although each of the four differs in wording from the others. The common element in all is "King of the Jews." Only John elaborates on the nature of the inscription, which he alone calls a title, or indicates any reaction to it. That it was given in three languages—Hebrew, Latin, and Greek (v. 20)—is John's way of pointing to its universal significance: Jesus is the savior of the world (4:42). Yet it is scarcely likely historically that the soldiers would have gone to the trouble of writing it in three languages (Brown 1994, 965). Only John mentions the place of crucifixion—near the city where many Jews could read the inscription—and in doing so seems to agree with the similar siting in Heb 13:12 ("outside the city gate"). Such a siting also fits the location of the Church of the Holy Sepulchre, which although within the present city walls would have been outside the walls in Roman times.

The protest of "the chief priests of the Jews" (vv. 21-22) is entirely understandable, and ironic, recalling as it does their statement that they have no king but the emperor (v. 15). Moreover, they are presumably troubled that many of the Jews were reading the title (v. 20). The trial of Jesus before Pilate may be read as a vigorous dispute, which the Jews appear to win, in that they persuade and even threaten Pilate, who thinks Jesus innocent, until he accedes to their wishes and turns Jesus over to them for crucifixion. (Incidentally, it now becomes obvious that Pilate is actually supervising the execution.) Yet in the end Pilate prevails in that he crucifies Jesus as their king, not merely as the one who made that claim. Thus Pilate's final retort (v. 22) has become a kind of byword, an expression of utter and complete finality. Where this episode occurred is not said, but it is presumably near the cross itself.

Now the scene shifts to the foot of the cross, where the soldiers who have just crucified Jesus gamble for his garments (19:23-25a). Again we have an episode found also in the Synoptics (Mark 15:24 par.), although what is only mentioned briefly there is here told in more elaborate detail, with Scripture (Ps 22:18) explicitly cited. Clearly Ps 22:18 is related to this episode, whether as its inspiration or confirmation. Details of the Johannine account are unique: because Jesus' tunic *(chitōn)* is seamless and cannot be divided, the soldiers cast lots for it. The scripture citation is in two lines (NRSV), the first apparently fulfilled in the dividing of the clothes (plural), the second in the casting lots for the tunic. The Greek words are similar in both lines of the Psalm quotation *(himatia, himatismon)*. (John's quotation follows the LXX.) Whether the seamless tunic represents the garment of the high priest (cf. Exod 39:27; 36:35 LXX) is debated among commentators. Josephus uses the same word, *chitōn,* to describe the high priest's robe and says that it was woven from a single thread *(Ant.* 3.161). Does John suggest, however subtly, that Jesus, who has been done in by the chief priests, is himself the true high priest? (Carson 1991, 613-14, thinks this a bit too subtle to be real.) The prayer of John 17 is often called "The Great High-Priestly Prayer," and although that term is not used of it in the Gospel itself, Jesus is depicted as performing a priestly, mediatory function. This would not be the first instance in which an undeveloped narrative detail suggests a theological point (cf. 9:7; 13:30). The final assertion (v. 25a) rounds off the episode and prepares for the next.

19:25-27: Jesus' mother and his Beloved Disciple stand together at the foot of the cross. Only in John do they appear here. John, with all the other Gospels, has women observe the crucifixion. The lists are different in each of the three Gospels (and only Luke does not name them). In the Synoptics the women are mentioned only after the death of Jesus has been described. In John they are obviously mentioned before it, because in his scenario Jesus speaks to one of them, his mother. (Brown 1994, 1016, has a useful chart showing the women who observe the crucifixion as well as the burial according to each Gospel.) The only woman mentioned in all accounts is Mary Magdalene, who later will come to the tomb of Jesus and find it empty (20:1; Matt 28:1; Mark 16:1; Luke 24:10). One may only wonder whether Clopas, mentioned in John as the husband of one of the women named Mary, is the same as the Cleopas named in Luke 24:18 as one of the two disciples who encountered Jesus on the Emmaus Road. It is actually unclear how many women John envisions as standing there; probably four. (The NRSV punctuation indicates four as does the RSV, and Brown 1994, 1016, also accepts each name or appellation as representing a different individual.)

Jesus' mother now appears for the second time during his ministry (cf. 2:2-5), and like the Beloved Disciple remains anonymous in this Gospel (see Beck 1997). His mother's appearances thus bracket Jesus' ministry, coming as they do at his first public appearance and at the end. This can scarcely be coincidental. Yet the meaning of her appearances is not immediately obvious. There is, of course, no birth narrative in the Fourth Gospel. At her first appearance Jesus seems to rebuff his mother (2:4), but she nevertheless possesses uncanny knowledge of what he can and will do. Her appearance now strangely matches her presence in the upper room, with Jesus' brothers, after the Ascension (Acts 1:14). Apparently James, Jesus' brother, became a disciple because the risen Jesus appeared to him (1 Cor 15:7), and other brothers became missionaries (1 Cor 9:5). What about Jesus' mother? The veneration of her suggested by the infancy narratives of Matthew and Luke implies that she became a disciple, as does Acts (1:14). That she would appear at the foot of the cross, presumably to comfort her son is only natural and has historical precedent at ancient crucifixions (see Brown 1994, 1029). The fact that Jesus, her oldest son, would want to provide for her, befits his character and role. (See the innovative treatment of the mother and family of Jesus in John by Van Tilborg, *Imaginative Love in John*, 1993.)

There is a certain plausibility about this whole scene as a historical event, although the fact that it is not reported in the Synoptics has caused most modern, critical exegetes to regard it as at best a symbolic narrative created by the Fourth Evangelist. (Bultmann 1971, 673: "Doubtless this scene, which in face of the synoptic tradition can make no claim to historicity, has a symbolic meaning." Barrett 1978, 551, doubts that Roman executioners would have allowed friends and loved ones so close to the cross of a rebel king.) Yet to what purpose; or what intended meaning is conveyed? Such symbolic interpretations have varied widely and are, according to C. H. Dodd "singularly unconvincing" (1953, 423). The Beloved Disciple obviously is, or represents, the witness undergirding this Gospel (21:24). Mary is frequently taken somehow to represent the People of God, Israel, and the church.

Brown, who struggles with the difficulty of this text and most interpretations of it, sees the key issue for John in the problem of the relationship between those who came to Jesus through faith, his disciples, and the natural family of Jesus (1994, 1019-26). He concludes: "it brings the natural family (Jesus' mother) into the relationship of discipleship by making her the mother of the Beloved Disciple who takes her into his own realm of discipleship" (1025). Obviously, the relationship of Jesus' family to him is a question raised by this Gospel (2:4; 7:5; cf. 20:17) as well as by the others (cf. Mark 3:31-35). That Jesus' mother should bracket his ministry, appearing at its beginning and end, says something about his earthly, human origins and dimension. He was born of a woman (cf. Gal 4:4) and has a human father (1:45; 6:42), and the existence of his family underscores this fact. It is worth observing that Jesus' earthly father is absent throughout his ministry, but of course his heavenly Father plays an important role. In John alone his earthly, human mother also plays a significant role (cf. van Tilborg 1993).

Quite possibly John knew a tradition that placed the mother of Jesus at the foot of the cross, and this fact occasioned his construction of this narrative in which she is linked most closely to the Beloved Disciple, the model disciple and witness who takes her to his home. The presence of the Beloved Disciple at the cross is not surprising, despite the fact that Jesus has predicted to his disciples that they will scatter and leave him alone (16:33; cf. Mark 14:27). This prediction may imply that the Beloved Disciple is not one of the twelve. Indeed, he only appears when Jesus enters Jerusalem for the last time. That he should appear at the cross as the final witness, who endures to the end, is altogether appropriate.

19:28-30: The death of Jesus is narrated quite briefly, again differently than in the Synoptics, and with a couple of startling omissions. Typically, Jesus is all-knowing and in control (v. 28; cf. 13:1). There will be no cry of dereliction (Matt 27:46; Mark 15:34; cf. Ps 22:1), nor will Jesus utter a loud cry as he expires (Mark 15:37 par.). He says that he thirsts only to fulfill Scripture, probably Ps 22:15 or Ps 69:21. The latter is probably the stronger candidate, in that the psalmist speaks of being given vinegar for thirst, which is exactly what happens in John's narrative. Thus it is not Jesus' statement per se but the whole event that fulfills Scripture. (The NRSV says "sour wine"; the RSV, "vinegar"; the Greek *oxos* would be the same in either case as in the LXX of Ps 69:21.)

That the sponge is placed on a branch of hyssop (v. 29) is a perennial problem, since the hyssop branch would scarcely support a wet sponge. But branches of hyssop were used to apply blood to the doorposts and lintel of the Israelites at the original Passover (Exod 12:22). A subtle reference to Passover may be intended. Mark has the same incident (15:36), but says "a stick" instead of hyssop. Quite possibly John knows a different version that contained an allusion to Passover through the hyssop. (Of course, for John the death of Jesus occurs as the Passover lambs are slain.) In Mark the soldier, or bystander, responds to Jesus' cry of dereliction by offering the drink. In both John and Mark, Jesus accepts it (19:30; Mark 15:36). As soon as he has drunk the sour wine he utters his last words and dies.

Jesus' last words reiterate what he has said already about finishing, or completing, the work the Father has given him to do (4:34; 5:36; 17:4). (Here Jesus uses a related but somewhat different verb, *teleō* rather than *teleioō*.) The statement is quite Johannine and unprecedented in the other Gospels. As in Luke (23:46) the last word of Jesus is appropriate to his character and purpose in the Gospel. Here Jesus dies with dignity and seemingly at the moment he intends. The Johannine Jesus is in control to the end (cf. 10:18). Thus Jesus bows his head and gives up his Spirit. Actually, he gives over *(paredōken)* the Spirit, as a literal translation of the Greek would say. There is almost surely a typically Johannine double meaning here. Jesus expires, gives up his breath, but at the same time gives over the promised Spirit (7:39; 14:16-17), at least proleptically. The risen Jesus will finally bestow it upon his disciples (20:22). Perhaps Jesus does not here give over the Spirit finally or definitively, but certainly John's unique wording points to the gift that is coming. (Mark and Luke use the verbal form *ekpneuō,* which the NRSV translates "breathed his last.")

John narrates the death of Jesus succinctly and impressively, but, as we noted above (pp. 355-56, 361), omits certain features found in Mark. The omission of Jesus' pained outcries is understandable, as we noted. Yet John also omits mention of the darkness at noon (Mark 15:33 par.), the rending of the temple veil (Mark 15:38 par.), and the centurion's confession that Jesus was Son of God (Mark 15:39) or innocent (Luke 23:47).

The darkness that pervades the land during Jesus' crucifixion could have been seen as an aspect of John's light/darkness dualism, in which light represents the forces of God, Jesus, and believers; and the darkness forces opposed to them (1:1-5). At the cross the darkness seems to triumph. The rending of the veil of the temple could have been seen as the end of its status as the dwelling place of the presence of God. God now dwells definitively in Jesus, whether present physically or in the Spirit (cf. 1:14; 4:21-24). The centurion's confession could have been seen as the correct assessment of who Jesus is—Son of God—by a Gentile, Roman officer, while the Jewish authorities want to put Jesus to death precisely for making such a claim (20:7). Such omissions make it difficult to understand John as having worked from a Markan or synoptic source. Rather, it seems more likely that he employed a source or traditions that did not contain these features. (On John's independence, see Brown 1994, 75-93.)

19:31-37: In John's unique chronology Jesus is crucified on Nisan 14, before the beginning of the Passover (Nisan 15) that evening. It is now the day before Passover, and this Passover evening also began the sabbath, thus a sabbath "of great solemnity" (v. 31). Leaving the bodies exposed after sundown would in any event violate the law (Deut 21:23), all the more so because this was a special occasion. Not surprisingly, "the Jews" (who here are likely equivalent to the chief priests) want them taken down to prevent such offense. The request to have the legs broken seems on the face of it to heap cruelty upon cruelty, when in fact such a procedure, horrifying as it was, mercifully hastened death, as their request anticipates. Because the crucified could no longer support his body, the weight would collapse the thorax and the victim would die of asphyxia. Thus in the *Gospel of Peter* (4:14) the legs of the criminal who defends Jesus are not broken precisely in order to worsen his torment. (On the breaking of the legs [Lat. *crurifragium*], see Brown 1994, 1175. On the *Gospel of Peter,* an early apocryphal gospel, of which a portion of the Passion narrative only is extant, see Schneemelcher 1991, 216-27; Brown 1994, 1317-49; for a view sharply different from Brown's, see Crossan 1995, 22-25, 30-31, and *passim.*)

The soldiers (presumably Roman, as Pilate is in charge of proceedings) break the legs of the two criminals crucified with Jesus (v. 33), but not those of Jesus, who has already died (v. 32). That Jesus died quickly is also suggested by Pilate's statement in Mark when Joseph of Arimathea requests the body (15:44), and is likely a historical fact. (On the physiological cause of Jesus' death see Brown 1994, 1088-92; the evangelists of course did not know the cause and it was of little concern to them.) One of the soldiers pierces Jesus' side with his spear, and blood and water come out. Exegetes have dwelt upon the significance of this effusion. Two main lines of symbolism, which are not mutually exclusive, the eucharistic and the antidocetic, have been proposed. Both are reasonable and within the bounds of Johannine theological interests. The blood, of course, is symbolized by the wine of the Eucharist, which, in Mark, Jesus calls his blood shed for many (14:24). The water would then be the water of Baptism. On the other hand, the effusion of water and blood indicates that Jesus is really dead, and, not only that, but that he was really human. He emits real bodily fluids, water as well as blood—this against any Gnostic or docetic playing down of Jesus' humanity. It is entirely possible that the scene was placed here to convey either or both of these important theological ideas. Yet the climax of the episode has not been reached.

A truthful witness now testifies to this event. Although not so identified here, such a truthful witness in 21:24 is clearly the Beloved Disciple. Moreover, that same disciple has, of course, just been addressed by Jesus in the scene immediately preceding his death, as he stood at the foot of the cross (19:25-27). This witness is obviously the Beloved Disciple. The truth of his testimony will be of crucial importance for those—the readers—who may believe because of it. Not incidentally, the clear sense of this statement is that the event just narrated really happened. It was seen and witnessed, in the sense of being testified to. In 21:24 the validity and authority of the Beloved Disciple's testimony is extended to the entire Gospel: he wrote it or caused it to be written.

Finally, the pericope closes with two quotations from Scripture (vv. 36-37). The first is similar to several Old Testament texts: Exod 12:46; Num 9:12; Ps 34:20. Yet it reproduces none of them exactly. The Pentateuchal passages refer to the Passover lamb, which in all probability is in view here. The Zechariah (12:10) quotation is alluded to also in Rev 1:7 (cf. *Barn.* 7:9). John follows the Hebrew more closely than the Septuagint (Barrett 1978, 558). The first quotation refers to verses 32-33 and the second to verses 33-34. They are apparently unrelated except as they are each fulfilled in this episode. The first, if it is based on the Pentateuchal texts, portrays Jesus as the Passover victim, a motif that we have seen with the hyssop (19:29), as well as the condemnation of Jesus at noon (19:14) when the slaughtering of the Passover lambs would have occurred, and the Johannine chronology that makes this coincidence possible. (On Christ as Passover offering, see also 1 Cor 5:7.) Moreover, Jesus is identified by John as the Lamb of God (1:29, 36), possibly the Passover lamb. Passover imagery hovers in the background, but does not become the object of theological discussion.

The second quotation seems less pregnant theologically, as it confirms the significance of this aspect of the total Passion Narrative. Jesus' death takes place according to God's will; thus the fulfillment of Scripture motif. (Not coincidentally, Jesus was first announced as the fulfillment of Scripture in 1:23, as John quoted Isa 40:3.) It is not difficult to see why these two passages were claimed as fulfilled in this last episode of the saga of Jesus' death. It is more difficult to imagine the episode being framed on the basis of these texts. Moreover, as we already observed, what happens in this episode would not have been unprecedented, and may well be historical, as the emphasis on the truthful witness certainly is intended to make plain.

19:38-42: As in all the Gospels, Joseph of Arimathea takes charge of the burial of Jesus. There are, however, several notable differences in this account, and a couple are typically Johannine. Joseph is described as a secret disciple because of "his fear of the Jews" recalling John 12:42. In each Gospel Joseph is portrayed as having had a positive relation to Jesus and his message, as he is here. The Johannine Passover context, however, gives him a good reason as a pious Jew to get Jesus quickly buried. Only in John does Nicodemus appear at all (v. 39; cf. 3:1-16; 7:50-52), so his role in assisting Joseph is unique. The day of Preparation (v. 42), if it refers to preparation for Passover rather than the Sabbath, reflects the unique Johannine chronology, which motivates the hurried burial. The proximity of the tomb to the site of the cruci- fixion (v. 41) is unique to John and, as we have seen, agrees with their proximity in the ancient Church of the Holy Sepulchre. That Jesus is buried according to the custom of the Jews (v. 40) is prob- ably assumed, but not stated in the other Gospels, all of which speak of a single linen shroud (*sindōn;* the "Shroud of Turin" is based on the Synoptics). John mentions linen cloths and spices. That the tomb is new (v. 41) is attested also by Matthew (27:60), who says it belonged to Joseph himself, and implied by Luke (23:53), who with John says that no one had ever been laid there. Since usually more than one body would be placed in a single tomb, this is a significant fact.

Exegesis has naturally paused over the role of Nicodemus, with most commentators suggesting he is continuing to move toward discipleship (cf. 7:50-51). Quite possibly he, like Joseph, belongs to the secret disciples who believe in Jesus but fear to confess him. Of course, John wants such disciples to make an open confession and leave the synagogue (cf. 12:42). The three appearances of Nicodemus in John seem to mark advances in his understanding, even if he has not yet arrived at adequate and open confession.

Brown's excellent treatment of the burial accounts (1994, 1205-41) concludes by affirming the nuclear historicity of Joseph of Arimathea and his role. Obviously his relation to Jesus has been stated in different ways according to the interests of the different evangelists. Brown notes the development in the Gospels toward the highly laudatory portrayal of Joseph as a disciple of Jesus in the *Gospel of Peter* (2:3; 6:23). For obvious reasons Nicodemus's presence at the tomb is much more problematic historically.

Typically, the Passion Narrative ends with an episode in which three kinds of elements or narrative details are mixed. First there are elements, like the role of Joseph of Arimathea, that are directly parallel to the Synoptics. Second, there are elements like the secrecy of his discipleship for fear of the Jews and the presence of Nicodemus that are characteristically and uniquely Johannine. Third, there are elements like the proximity of the tomb, which although unique to John do not embody recognizable Johannine theological interests. We have seen combinations of these elements throughout the Johannine Passion, indeed throughout this Gospel.

◊ ◊ ◊ ◊

The account of Jesus' death is, not surprisingly, replete with Johannine motifs from the point at which he set out for Golgotha, needing no help and carrying his own cross (v. 17). The sign on the cross, which as in all the Gospels identifies Jesus as the King of the Jews, is according to John written in the three relevant languages—Hebrew, Latin, and Greek—to make clear the universal relevance of what is transpiring (v. 20). Yet at the same time it becomes a bone of contention between Pilate and the chief priests (vv. 21-22), as this time Pilate holds his ground against them.

Once more, however, Jewish rejection of Jesus as Messiah is underscored. The dividing of Jesus' garments (vv. 23-25*a*) is recounted in all the Gospels, but John alone cites the relevant scripture (Ps 22:18) to indicate God's purpose is being fulfilled and characterizes Jesus' distinctive, seamless tunic, which is reminiscent of the high priest's.

Only John describes any conversation of Jesus with his mother or, of course, the Beloved Disciple (who appears only in John). The appearances of Jesus' mother at the beginning of his ministry (2:1-11) and at the end are also unique to John and remind the reader of Jesus' humanity: He is the son of Mary as well as the Son of God.

Jesus dies in complete control of the situation. No one takes his life from him (10:17-18). He gives it up as he gives over the Spirit, and his final words indicate the completion of his work (v. 31; cf. 17:4). What he says to the end fulfills God's will and, of course, Scripture (v. 28).

Missing from John's account is any reference to the mocking of Jesus, whether by the pair crucified with him or by his opponents. This is understandable, given the Johannine presentation of Jesus, as is the omission of the cry of dereliction from the cross. On the other hand, the absence of the darkness at noon, the rending of the temple veil, and the confession of the centurion are harder to understand, particularly if John knew or was following Mark.

As we have noted, the piercing of Jesus' side (vv. 31-37) has manifold theological significance. First, the issue of water and blood underscores Jesus' humanity. At the same time it perhaps symbolizes Baptism (water) and the Eucharist (blood). The appearance of the witness, presumably the Beloved Disciple, emphasizes the historical truth of the narrative while the citation of Scripture places it within God's will.

Unlike the piercing of Jesus' side, found only in John, the burial occurs in all four Gospels. Yet the theological interests of John become clear. Joseph of Arimathea and probably Nicodemus appear as would-be disciples of Jesus, apparently believing but not yet confessing, for fear of the Jews. Perhaps significantly, they appear on this side of his resurrection, putting the lifeless body in the tomb. Whether they will emerge on the other, as disciples of the risen Jesus, is at this point left to the imagination of the reader.

◊ ◊ ◊ ◊

The death of Jesus is obviously of central theological importance in this Gospel, although its importance is expressed in some ways different from the rest of the New Testament. Even in the Johannine letters (cf. 1 John 1:7; 2:2), the typical early Christian language of cultic, vicarious sacrifice is more prominent than in the Gospel. Jesus' death in John is nevertheless a vicarious sacrifice, as the Good Shepherd lays down his life for his sheep (chap. 10; 11:50-52).

The Johannine Jesus, omniscient and omnipotent though he may seem, suffers betrayal, denial, and trial. His betrayal by Judas seems to be a particularly sore point, for John repeatedly goes out of his way to show that it did not take Jesus by surprise (6:64, 70-71; 13:11, 27). As in the Synoptics, Jesus is denied by Peter (18:15-18, 25-27), and that denial is set in the context of his abandonment by the other disciples (16:32). Again, this does not take place without Jesus' foreknowledge (13:36-38). Although Jesus also predicts Peter's denial in the Synoptics (Mark 14:26-31), where the other disciples are even more directly implicated with Peter, John carries the motif of Jesus' foreknowledge even beyond what one already finds there in the denial and betrayal predictions.

Surprisingly, there is not in John an elaborate account of Jesus' trial before Jewish authorities, the Sanhedrin (cf. Mark 14:55-65), although this council does condemn him in advance, as Caiaphas the high priest directs their decision (11:45-53). Jesus then appears in a relatively brief scene before Annas (18:19-24), while an appearance before Caiaphas is noted, but not narrated. Nevertheless, the Jews pursue Jesus relentlessly by seeking his death as they argue with Pilate (18:28–19:16), for their mortal hostility had long since reached this level (5:18). They act as prosecuting attorneys, so to speak, before Pilate. With the exception of the absence of the formal trial scene, their role corresponds almost exactly to what one would have expected from the rest of the Gospel.

Through the trial before Pilate the theme of Jesus' kingship ("rule" or "kingdom") becomes the center of discussion, and Jesus has the opportunity to explain himself on this point, as he does not in the other Gospels. Jesus' rule, while ultimately the last word, does not immediately bring all human rule to an end. The statement that Jesus' kingdom is not from or of this world means that the rule of Pilate continues and the power of the Jewish authorities over Jesus seemingly prevails. The fact that this is the case, or seems to be the case, is an inevitable implication of the Incarnation. God really dwells in Jesus, who is nevertheless a human being, in ways that do not contradict his humanity or the seriousness of actual historical circumstances. Jesus' unity with God is portrayed in such elements of the narrative as the power of Jesus' word at his arrest or his consciousness and control of all that is taking place. Yet at the level of human causality events move forward to Jesus' death, which is not prevented by divine intervention or the revelation that Jesus was never human after all. In fact, the piercing of his side as well as his burial attest his true humanity.

Theologically viewed, Jesus' death in John is his exaltation, his being lifted up. John has played heavily on the "lifting up," of Jesus all along (e.g., 12:32). The Greek term *(hypsoō)*, which means just that, points both to the physical manner of Jesus' execution (cf. 18:32) and to its theological depth. His death is his exaltation from which he effects the salvation of humanity (12:32). In a similarly paradoxical way, Jesus speaks of his death as his glorification. Both usages stretch human language to the limit, but are at the same time profoundly meaningful. Jesus' death reveals God, and therefore reveals God's glory. (Here John draws on Isaiah's understanding of God's glory, as we have already observed.) But this is not the manifestation of God's glory that one might have anticipated, even on the basis of Scripture, apart from Jesus. In revealing God's glory in his death Jesus transforms not only the idea of God's glory, but in a very real and important sense, of God. The God who reveals himself in this Jesus is a God of the depths, as well as the heights, of human existence. Precisely at the depths of human experience Jesus is lifted up; he glorifies God; God glorifies him (17:4-5). The profound and radical theological idea that Paul expresses in the great meditation on the cross of Christ in 1 Cor 1:18-31 finds a Johannine counterpart. (On Jesus' death as glorification see Smith 1995, 119-22.)

Paul differs from John in that he views the cross of Christ, indeed, Christ's earthly ministry, as a movement of self-emptying or humbling (Phil 2:6-11; 2 Cor 8:9), although he can refer to the crucifixion of the Lord of glory (1 Cor 2:8). Still, that glory is in Paul basically eschatological, not yet. In John that glory is manifest, however, from the beginning in Jesus' earthly ministry (2:11), and it is the occasion of disciples' belief in him. Yet it does not override or obliterate real humanity and actual history. Nowhere is this clearer than in the Johannine Passion Narrative, where such manifestations of Jesus' glory stand beside and interpret, but do not cancel out, the reality of his humanity or the integrity of a history that runs its course on the basis of a different system of cause and effect. Only with the discovery of the tomb empty and the mysterious appearances of Jesus to his disciples is that history stood on its head or reversed. From that latter perspective, attained only through Jesus' death, his whole ministry is set in a new light, and only then understood as the revelation of glory. That is, only from this side of Jesus' resurrection can the reality of this peculiar history be properly grasped. In the conviction of the evangelist this was a really unique and pivotal historical life, but it was only revealed as such through his death and resurrection.

THE FIRST RESURRECTION NARRATIVES (20:1-31)

John's account of the resurrection appearances of Jesus is the longest in the New Testament. There are two sets of narratives, indicated by the division of chapters 20 and 21. Remarkably, each Johannine episode has a counterpart in the Synoptics. In this respect the Johannine narratives are similar to the later longer ending of Mark (16:9-20, which is not found in the oldest mss.), which pretty clearly presupposes appearance narratives of the canonical Gospels. Chapter 21 is commonly regarded as an appendix or epilogue, whether added to the Gospel by the original author or (as many exegetes think) by a later hand, and that is how we treat it here.

The colophon (ending) of 20:30-31 has every appearance of ending the Gospel (cf. 21:25, which seems to be modeled on 20:30-31). Yet there are no surviving manuscripts of the Gospel of John that do not also contain chapter 21. This chapter was always a part of the published Gospel. Moreover, it addresses questions, such as the final status of Peter, his relation to the Beloved Disciple, and the fate of both (they have apparently died), not previously entertained. It also contains the only Gospel appearance scene in which Peter figures prominently (cf. 1 Cor 15:5, where Paul reports the first resurrection appearance was to Peter, and Luke 24:34, where a resurrection appearance to Peter is reported by the disciples in Jerusalem).

Some commentators see chapter 21 as a later addition embodying interests foreign to the basic document (Bultmann 1971, 700-706). Yet the case for its integrity and authenticity has also been strenuously argued (e.g., by Minear 1983). Thyen (beginning with 1971) agrees that chapter 21 belongs to the final stratum of the Gospel, but insists that its author should be called "evangelist" rather than "redactor" and the whole book read in light of his work. In our treatment we take the position that the major seam between chapters 20 and 21 likely indicates a stage in the literary development of the Gospel, and that chapter 21 was added later. On the other hand, we shall view chapter 21 in light of what precedes, and vice versa.

There are then at least two major questions raised by the juxtaposition of these two resurrection chapters. The first we have just mentioned, namely, their relationship and role in the literary development of the Gospel narrative. The other is the source of the individual episodes. Because John's narratives parallel the Synoptics', it can reasonably be argued that they are derivative from them in the fashion that Mark 16:9-20 is apparently derivative from the other Gospels. Yet as in the case of other Johannine parallels with the Synoptics, there are remarkable differences not immediately recognizable as expressing Johannine theological interests. Remarkably, John's relationship to the synoptic resurrection narratives is quite different from the relationship to their Passion Narratives. There John generally parallels the synoptic narrative, principally the Markan, although with significant deviations. Here John follows no other Gospel(s), but can be viewed as drawing together or collating the narratives of the others. The exact relation of John's narratives to them will be considered in the exegesis of individual passages.

Moreover, the relationship of chapter 21 to the Synoptics may be different from that of chapter 20. While 20:30-31 indicates awareness of individual stories not incorporated into the Gospel, the mention of other books in 21:25 rather clearly suggests that other Gospels are known to exist. Arguably, knowledge of one or more of the Synoptics is reflected in the latest editorial layer of the Gospel, whatever its origin. Thus certain statements can be viewed as editorial notations intended to reconcile the accounts (e.g., 3:24; 4:2; 6:59; 18:24, 28).

While chapter 21 is generally taken to be later than chapter 20, a good case has recently been made for regarding them as alternative endings of the Gospel (Gaventa 1996, 242, 245-47). A precedent for that suggestion may be found in the relationship of chapters 15–16 (17) to chapter 14 in the farewell discourses, for with Jesus' statement of 14:31 the discourses seem to be at an end. Yet they continue, and the obvious, literary solution is that two versions have been juxtaposed. Something similar may have happened here. (If the Gospel for whatever reason—perhaps the evangelist's death—had been left unfinished, it is understandable that an editor would have preserved the author's literary remains as fully as possible.) Although chapter 21 contains no empty tomb story, it may be presupposed, whether from chapter 20 or some other source.

The Tomb Discovered Empty (20:1-10)

Every canonical Gospel contains the story of the discovery of the empty tomb by women or a woman; in every case Mary

Magdalene is named. In John, only Mary; also in the *Gospel of Peter* Mary clearly plays the leading role; in the other Gospels Mary is at least named first. Despite the testimony of the Gospels, however, there is no statement about the discovery of Jesus' empty tomb elsewhere in the New Testament. Paul seems to miss an excellent opportunity when he adduces witnesses and otherwise argues for the reality of the Resurrection in 1 Cor 15 (especially vv. 3-8). But Paul does not know our Gospels. The question can only be whether he knew, but did not invoke, a related tradition.

◊ ◊ ◊ ◊

All the Gospels offer differences of detail, and John is no exception. Notably, the synoptic Gospels make clear that the women saw the tomb in which Jesus was laid (Mark 15:47 par.). John lacks this detail, but in his case it would not be so important in that the tomb was hard by the place of crucifixion (19:41-42). In the Synoptics (Mark 16:1; Luke 24:1) the women go to the tomb to anoint the body of Jesus, but in John this has already been done (19:39-40). Of course, in John, Mary goes to the tomb alone (but cf. v. 2 where she says "we," perhaps an indication of knowledge of Mark's or a related account). While John clearly states it was still dark (v. 1), according to Mark (16:2) the sun had come up (Matt 28:1 follows Mark; Luke 24:1 is somewhat ambiguous). In every case the stone is seen to be already rolled away (only Matt 28:2 describes how that happened).

Mary immediately seeks out Simon Peter and the Beloved Disciple (v. 2) and says to them what she will later say to the pair of angels (v. 13). Only in John does Mary make this poignant, touching statement whose ironic dimension is obvious to the knowledgeable reader. Apparently she assumes that grave robbers or vandals have been at work. Also, only in John is the discovery of the tomb immediately reported to two disciples (but see 20:18, where she presumably reports to all the disciples as she does in Matt 28:8 and Luke 24:9). In the synoptic Gospels the women are encountered by a mysterious figure (or figures; in Matthew said to be an angel) who tells them that Jesus has risen and instructs them to inform the disciples (Mark 16:5-7 par.). In Matthew (28:8) and Luke (4:9) they do this, but in Mark they depart in fear and say nothing to anyone (16:8).

In John there is later (vv. 11-13) an encounter with two angels, but it is inconclusive, as Mary will then see the risen Jesus (20:14-18). But first there is a full report of a visit to the empty tomb by Peter and the Beloved Disciple. There is no comparable narrative in any other Gospel or elsewhere, although Luke briefly reports a visit by Peter (Luke 24:12) in a statement not attested in all manuscripts and one of the disciples on the Emmaus Road mentions a visit by "some of those who were with us" to the tomb (Luke 24:24). This is only one of the many similarities unique to Luke and John (see Matson 1998).

Typically, Peter is placed in a kind of rivalry with the Beloved Disciple, in which he fares none too well, coming in a clear second (20:3-4). The parallel statement in Luke 24:12 has Peter alone, as we might expect, for the Beloved Disciple appears only in John. The Beloved Disciple and Peter both see the linen burial cloths (cf. Luke 24:12) and enter the tomb; but the Beloved Disciple in effect waits for Peter to enter before he does (vv. 5-8). John evidently envisions a type tomb, common in Jewish burial practice, large enough for a number of bodies and therefore large enough to allow people to enter. The description of their entry may imply a cavelike tomb in the side of a small hill or rock face with a circular stone that could be rolled back, perhaps on a ramp. (For details see Brown 1994, 1247-49; also see the article "Tomb" by Meyers 1976, which has excellent illustrations.) John obviously emphasizes the details of what was seen, as we should expect, given his emphasis on the eyewitness of the Beloved Disciple. Such details are not found in the Synoptics or in the *Gospel of Peter.*

In the interplay between the Beloved Disciple and Peter, it is probably significant that the former is said to believe first (v. 8), after seeing. While Peter is said to have seen, he does not believe. That the Beloved Disciple believes on the basis of what he has seen fits John's portrayal of him as the truthful witness (19:35; 21:24).

Neither he nor Peter knows (RSV) or understands (NRSV) the scriptural prophecies of Jesus' resurrection (v. 9). That Jesus rose from the dead was early on said to be the fulfillment of Scripture (Acts 2:24-27; 1 Cor 15:4). John's statement is sometimes regarded as problematic in view of the Beloved Disciple's believing. Yet the simplest explanation suffices: the Beloved Disciple's belief is grounded in his seeing, even if he does not yet know the scriptural prophecy. Charlesworth (1995, 68-118), who believes that Thomas is the Beloved Disciple, limits this believing to what he has actually seen, in agreement with some earlier exegetes. He does not yet come to faith. But "to believe" here and elsewhere in John and the New Testament generally implies coming to faith in Jesus (1:7, 50; 3:12; 4:48, 53 and *passim*, as well as Acts 2:44; 4:4, 32 and Rom 3:22; 13:11; 1 Cor 1:21). In saying that they did not know the scripture, John once again reveals an awareness of a distinction between what disciples knew as Jesus' ministry transpired—even at the tomb—and what they only later knew and understood in light of his resurrection appearances and the advent of the Spirit. In particular, John has already noted this is true of scriptural prophecy (cf. 2:17, 22; 12:16). The disciples' returning to their homes seems appropriately to conclude the scene (v. 10).

Mary's Encounter with the Risen Jesus (20:11-18)

John's similarities to the synoptic accounts are so obvious that any differences stand out. John 20:2 is one ending of what might seem a very brief story of Mary alone discovering the tomb empty. (But even here she refers to "we," perhaps a vestige of an earlier account.) Yet again in 20:18 (cf. v. 2) Mary goes and reports to the disciples. Not surprisingly, some exegetes have suggested that in this episode at least two narratives, once independent, have been combined. Also, characteristic of John is the dramatic encounter of Jesus and Mary alone (vv. 14-18), yet even this has a synoptic parallel. In Matthew, Mary Magdalene and the other Mary encounter Jesus as they leave the tomb (28:9-10), and Jesus repeats the instruction they have just received from the angel (v. 9).

Mary now stands outside the tomb weeping (v. 11) as if the disciples, at least one of whom has seen and believed, had no further communication with her! In fact, we were not told that she had returned to the tomb with the disciples, although we naturally assume that she did. How strange that they now seem to depart without so much as a word to her. This is, however, probably an indication that the episode of the disciples' visit has been inserted into the earlier narrative of Mary's discovery of the tomb empty.

The story now returns to where we might have been at the end of 20:1 or 2, at which point Mary has already recognized that the body of Jesus is not in the tomb. At this juncture, however, Mary, stooping (cf. v. 5 and Luke 24:12), looks into the tomb. None of the Gospels agree exactly on who was there in the tomb. Mark (16:5) has a young man (*neaniskos;* cf. Mark 14:51, where the same word is used to designate the youth who flees naked after the arrest) in a white robe. Matthew has an angel, who has already descended and rolled the stone away (28:2-6). Luke has two men in dazzling clothes (24:4). John has two angels in white (v. 12) appropriately situated at Jesus' head and feet, except, of course, Jesus is no longer there. On this matter John seems to add up and combine the figures of the other accounts. There are two, and they are angels. Actually, the Greek *angelos,* like its Hebrew counterpart *malach* means messenger, without a necessarily supernatural connotation. In any case, the figures in the tomb are mysterious messengers sent from God, who are never heard from again after they perform their mission. When the angels question Mary about her weeping (v. 13), Mary responds as she had earlier reported to Peter and the Beloved Disciple (v. 2). In none of the Synoptics are the women said to weep, although they do in the *Gospel of Peter* (12:52, 54). Likewise, in *Peter* and in John, as well as Luke, the figure(s) in the tomb questions the visitor(s). As Mary turns and sees Jesus (v. 14), the narrative itself reaches a turning point. This brief episode is moving, poignant, and typically Johannine. Mary's momentary failure to recognize Jesus (v. 14) is comparable to the misunderstanding motif found elsewhere in this Gospel. Jesus repeats the question of the angel and then asks her whom she is seeking (v. 15). (On seeking, and seeking Jesus, cf. 1:38; 6:24, 26; 7:34, 36; 12:21; 18:4 and see Painter 1993.) Indeed, Mary's misperception is underscored as now, mistaking Jesus for the gardener, for the third time she indicates her belief that the body of Jesus has been removed (v. 15)—a not unnatural conclusion.

Mary's assumption has its odd counterpart in Matthew, where the opponents of Jesus guard against the possibility that the disciples will steal the body and proclaim his resurrection (Matt 27:62-66). John makes the point, more emphatically than the other Gospels, that Jesus' resurrection was totally unanticipated by his disciples and intimate followers. Thus, unlike the Synoptics (Mark 8:31; 9:31; 10:33) John does not have Jesus foretell his own resurrection unambiguously, although it is mentioned in the narrative (2:22). (In 10:18 Jesus clearly alludes to his resurrection, but in a veiled way.) Mary's natural assumption about the fate of Jesus' body effectively sets the stage for Jesus to take the initiative in manifesting himself to her (v. 16).

Mary and Jesus address each other (v. 16) in what is surely one of the most memorable encounters in the history of literature. Mary responds to Jesus by calling him teacher (or literally in Hebrew or Aramaic, "My teacher"). Immediately Jesus forbids her to touch or hold onto him (v. 17). The negative of the present imperative, found here, typically means, "Desist from what you are doing." Thus the NRSV and RSV translations imply this. Arguably, the narrative of Matthew 28:9-10, where the women take hold of the feet of Jesus, is assumed, for John has not said that Mary attempted to hold him. Most modern translations of Jesus' word are similar to the NRSV and RSV, but the old KJV has "Touch me not," and this meaning is not impossible for John. (Bultmann 1971, 687, n. 1: "The present imperative does not necessarily imply that she has already touched him, but it need only presuppose that she is trying to do it, and is in the process of doing it . . . "). If this interpretation is followed, there is an even neater contrast between Jesus' prohibition here and his invitation to Thomas (20:27). (In that case also the relationship to the Matthean version is less compelling, although still possible.)

Jesus' reason for forbidding Mary to hold onto or touch him is again unique to John, who brings resurrection and ascension together in this appearance story. Luke has Jesus ascend to heaven to conclude the resurrection appearances (24:50-53; Acts 1:1-11). References to Jesus' resurrection outside the Gospels, however, clearly conceive of it as the appearances of Jesus from heaven (1 Cor 15:3-8; Phil 2:9; 1 Pet 3:18-20). John probably represents a stage before Luke. The risen Jesus is not continually with his disciples (contrast Acts 1:4; but cf. v. 3), but appears to them unexpectedly. Jesus' admonition to Mary ties resurrection and ascension together. Mary is not to regard this appearance of Jesus as a restoration of earlier relationships between Jesus and his followers (unlike Lazarus, who according to 12:10 was apparently still subject to death). Jesus' permanent postresurrection state will not obtain until he has ascended to the Father, which he will now do. In fact, he is in the process of doing so. The ascended Jesus will then offer his hands and his side to Thomas (20:27).

By "brothers" (v. 17) Jesus clearly means his disciples (cf. v. 18), but the use of the term is not fortuitous, for in what Mary is to tell them Jesus links himself most closely to them: "my Father...your Father...my God...your God." The promise of the unity of the disciples with Jesus and God, found in the farewell discourses (14:18-24; 16:16-24; 17:6-19) is now being fulfilled. Mary then goes to the disciples, announces that she has seen the risen Jesus, and delivers his message to them (v. 18). The first resurrection appearance has been to Mary Magdalene, a woman, clearly a follower of Jesus in the literal sense of the word (cf. Mark 15:40-41). Yet she is distinguished here from the disciples, as she is again in 21:14, although probably in both those instances John has the twelve primarily in view. That women—the mother of Jesus, the woman of Samaria, Mary and Martha, and Mary Magdalene—play a large role in this Gospel is, however, obvious and significant. It doubtless reflects the fact that women played an important role in the ministry of Jesus, as well as in the earliest churches (see Brown 1979, 183-98).

Jesus' First Appearance to the Gathered Disciples (20:19-23)

This scene has two significant counterparts. One is the subsequent episode, a week later, in which Thomas, absent here, is present and demands proof that his fellow disciples have seen the crucified Jesus (20:24-29). The other is a quite similar episode in Luke (24:36-43), in which the risen Jesus shows the disciples his hands and feet as proof of his identity as their crucified leader. (So again the Johannine narrative finds a synoptic parallel.)

The opening sentence (v. 19), which sets the scene, is translated rather freely in the NRSV, for "the house where the disciples had met" represents the simple Greek "where the disciples were" (RSV). The NRSV thus implies a traditional place of meeting, perhaps the upper room where the Last Supper was held and where Jesus' followers met after the Ascension (Acts 1:13). This is actually a good historical guess, but goes beyond what is stated in the text. Moreover, it is the same day as the discovery of the tomb, Easter Sunday. The doors being locked "for fear of the Jews" is by now a familiar Johannine motif (cf. 7:13; 9:22; 19:38). Probably this reflects a later time and setting of the Johannine community. Otherwise, there is no evidence of Jewish persecution of the disciples at this early stage. Suddenly Jesus appears. In view of the locked doors his very appearance is miraculous. His greeting of "Peace be with you" has become traditional among Christians. Yet it was a conventional greeting, or benediction, in biblical antiquity (Exod 4:18; Judg 6:23; 19:20; 1 Sam 25:6; 1 Chr 12:18), and it remains so among Hebrew and Arabic-speaking people today. In this context, however, it has particular significance, taking up as it does Jesus' bestowal of peace upon his disciples as he takes leave of them in the farewell discourses (14:27; 16:33). This is, of course, God's peace, the final, eschatological peace in which the disciples will now live, as his repetition of this blessing (v. 21) shows.

Jesus' demonstration of his hands and side (v. 20) is obviously intended as proof of his identity as the Crucified One (cf. Luke 24:39, where Jesus' showing of his hands and feet means that his presence is bodily, even physical, not purely spiritual). Although the nailing of Jesus to the cross was not mentioned in any Passion narrative, it is assumed here (see above, p. 356). The disciples' rejoicing is a clear indication that they get the point. That they are said to see the Lord (Gk. *kyrios*) is significant. *Kyrios* is seldom used of the earthly Jesus, but now it can be bestowed upon him freely (cf. 20:29; 21:7).

As Jesus repeats the blessing of peace (v. 21) and sends the disciples as the Father sent him (also 17:18; cf. 15:18–16:4), the unity of Jesus with his Father and his followers finds expression in mission to the world (3:16), for which they will now receive empowerment and illumination. (Similarly, in Acts 1–2 the gift of the Spirit is linked to the mission charge.) In an important sense Jesus' bestowal of the Spirit upon his disciples (v. 22) is the culmination of the resurrection narratives. Certainly it is the climax of this particular episode. Jesus' promise of the Paraclete, the Spirit of truth, given repeatedly in the farewell discourses (14:16-17, 26; 15:26; 16:7-15) is now fulfilled. The Spirit as Advocate (NRSV) will arm the disciples against the world as they go forward. But perhaps more important, the Spirit will from now on shed light backward on Jesus' entire earthly ministry, illuminating it as the revelation of God (cf. 7:39). It is the genius of John to understand that Jesus' ministry is understandable only retrospectively, in light of his crucifixion and resurrection, and that his witness and interpreter is the Spirit—ultimately God, for God through Jesus is the source of the Spirit.

Perhaps curiously, the power of forgiving or retaining sins is bestowed upon the disciples (v. 23). Yet this is not the only point in the Gospel narratives where this bestowal occurs, for immediately after Peter's confession in Matthew, Jesus grants him the so-called power of the keys (16:19, repeated in Matt 18:18, whereas in John, it is given to the disciples as a group). In light of what is said elsewhere in John, a moment's reflection will confirm that this power is primarily for inner-community discipline, a problem and need that appears acute in 1 John. The same is true in Matthew, particularly Matt 18:18. Although the function of the Spirit as Advocate (and judge) extends also into the world (16:8-11), the sphere in which the Spirit's activity is immediately perceived and acknowledged is the community of Jesus' disciples, that is, the church. With the gift of the Spirit the church is literally inspired: Jesus breathes upon them the Spirit (literally "infused them"). The imagery of breath or wind recalls the Nicodemus discourse (3:8 particularly), as well as the death of Jesus himself (19:30), who at that point is said to give over the Spirit, obviously in anticipation of this climactic moment of his resurrection. The commissioning of the disciples for mission is, of course, an important element of the resurrection narratives of Matthew and Luke–Acts as well (Matt 28:16-20; Luke 24:49; cf. Acts 2).

Jesus and Thomas (20:24-29)

Thomas is identified as one of the twelve, called the Twin (v. 24). His name is found in every list of the twelve (Matt 10:1-4; Mark 3:13-19; Luke 6:12-16; Acts 1:12-14), and when he first appears in John, he urges his fellow disciples also to die with Jesus (11:16). Thomas plays no role in the other canonical Gospels, but is an important figure in John, where in addition to these scenes he raises a significant question for Jesus (14:5). He is also present for the final resurrection appearance (21:2). The recently discovered *Gospel of Thomas,* consisting only of a collection of Jesus' sayings, at its beginning names him as author, calling him Didymus Judas Thomas. (Actually *Didymus* represents the Greek word for "twin" and "Thomas" the Hebrew.) Few scholars would accept this attribution at face value, but it at least indicates the importance of Thomas in some early Christian circles (see H. Koester 1990, 78-80). The early Thomas traditions are likely rooted in Syria (see also H. Koester 1982, 150-54, 208). Yet in traditions incorporated in the third-century *Acts of Thomas* (39) India is said to have been his special mission field, and many contemporary Indian Christians look to Thomas as the founder of their church. Again, in *Acts of Thomas* 39 Thomas is said to have been Jesus' twin brother! The unique prominence of Thomas in John, among the canonical Gospels, suggests that John emanates from a Christian environment that overlaps the circles in which Thomas was venerated.

Thomas's absence from the scene a week earlier is left unexplained, but it allows for the following episode, pregnant with theological meaning. The disciples' report (v. 25) takes up the evangelist's statement of verse 20 (cf. Paul's claim to have seen the Lord, i.e., the risen Lord, in 1 Cor 9:1; cf. also 1 Cor 15:8). Thomas's response, specific and to the point, has earned him the title "Doubting Thomas." Whether this episode puts Thomas in a simply negative light is doubtful, although there is a long tradition of interpreting Thomas in that way. Yet his determination (cf. 11:16) could be construed as laudable, his question (14:5) as crucial, and his need for proof of the resurrection at least as understandable. Jesus does not call him Doubting Thomas, but adjures him to believe rather than doubt (v. 27), whereupon Thomas believes (vv. 28-29), uttering the fullest and most adequate christological confession in this Gospel. Charlesworth (1995) knowingly goes beyond the explicit testimony of the texts in arguing that Thomas is the Beloved Disciple, but rightly maintains that the Thomas texts have been routinely read in such a way as to reflect no credit upon him, when a quite different reading is equally possible.

For Thomas to want to see what his colleagues have reported to him is reasonable enough, but seemingly he wants further proof. Actually, when the opportunity presents itself (v. 27), Thomas will appear overwhelmed. He sees, but the text does not report that he actually touched Jesus (although 1 John 1:1, "and touched with our hands," might be read as an allusion to this episode, particularly if as tradition holds, the Beloved Disciple, who is responsible for the Gospel of John, wrote the epistles as well). Obviously, the words of Thomas go beyond the Lukan parallel (Luke 24:39-40) in mentioning the nails specifically, but, in Luke, Jesus also invites the disciples to handle him, employing almost exactly the same Greek verb used in 1 John 1:1. Thomas's request reflects awareness of Jesus' having been nailed to the cross, as well as of his side's having been pierced (19:31-37).

Not only is the piercing of the side unique to John, but according to the narrative of the Gospel only one disciple was in a position to witness it, the unnamed Beloved Disciple who was a principal in the episode just preceding (i.e., 19:25-27). Arguably, the piercing of the side was for the evangelist a known, historical fact, so that knowledge of it would not be so limited (or perhaps he would not have considered who might have known it). Yet special emphasis is placed in the truthful witness's having known it (19:35) and he is in all likelihood the Beloved Disciple. (Moreover, there is again an apparent allusion to this episode in 1 John 5:6.) The specificity of the request to examine the side as well as the hands of Jesus is actually the strongest link in Charlesworth's argument (1995) that Thomas is the Beloved Disciple, that is, if one takes the integrity of the narrative seriously.

The previous Sunday's scene is now virtually repeated (vv. 26-29). Under quite similar circumstances, with Thomas now present, the disciples are gathered; Jesus once again appears among them and utters the same word of greeting (v. 26; cf. v. 19). He then issues to Thomas the invitation to do exactly what he has said he must (v. 27; cf. v. 25). One scarcely notices that Jesus' apparent knowledge of what Thomas has demanded is uncanny, for it is no more so than the knowledge available to Jesus during his earthly ministry (cf. 1:48-49; 4:17-19, 39). Thomas's response is exactly appropriate, as he utters the confession of Jesus as Lord *(kyrios)* and God *(theos)*. This confession is typical of early Christian theology and language as far as Lord *(kyrios)* is concerned, but uniquely Johannine in its ascription of the name of God *(theos)* to Jesus as well. In 1:1 the preexistent word *(logos)* is called God *(theos)* and at the end of the prologue this most exalted title is repeated, after the incarnation of the Word in Jesus has been confessed. For the most part John withholds the designation *theos* from Jesus, but in the course of the narrative makes clear that this ascription of deity to Jesus is indeed correct and unavoidable (5:18; cf. 5:19-24; 10:30; 14:8-11). While Thomas may have once doubted, he has now made the confession that is essential and true. Jesus is Lord and God.

Jesus' response has the future church in view (v. 29; cf. 17:20). That Jesus dismisses seeing as unimportant is a possible inference from this statement, and one that is finally embraced by

Bultmann (1971, 696), who equates Thomas's position with "the common attitude of men, who cannot believe without seeing miracles." Yet is John's purpose to disparage seeing, even seeing the risen Jesus? This hardly seems credible in view of the emphasis placed on seeing elsewhere in the Gospel, and particularly with reference to Jesus' resurrection (20:18, 20, 25; cf. 1:14; 34; also 1 John 1:1-3).

Bultmann's view is, as he indicates, closely tied to his perception of John's criticism of miracle faith (which is in turn a basis of his own criticism). There is no doubt that simply seeing and believing in Jesus' signs is insufficient as faith (2:23–3:2). Yet in this Gospel sign faith may be the beginning point for adequate faith, even Nicodemus's (7:50-52; 19:39), while no one who rejects Jesus' signs is ever said to come to faith. In an important way Jesus' statement articulates this Gospel's position on the relationship between seeing and believing in Jesus. Although seeing is not believing, there is no believing without seeing, that is, without somebody's having seen. Thus, John says that "we have seen his glory" (1:14). The Baptist says, "And I myself have seen and have testified that this is the Son of God" (1:34). Jesus prays for his original disciples (17:6-19), who have certainly seen him, although this is assumed rather than said explicitly. Then he prays for subsequent generations, "who will believe in me through their word" (17:20). The blessing of "those who have not seen and yet have come to believe" (20:29) is predicated upon the fact that Jesus' own disciples, including Mary Magdalene, have seen the risen Jesus and believed in him (20:18, 20, 25, 28-29). In every case their seeing results in belief, although no one says, "I saw and therefore I believe."

No one who sees the risen Jesus does not believe, and this is as true in John as it is in the other Gospel accounts. There may, however, be a moment of wonderment as in John 21:12; Luke 24:41; perhaps Matt 28:17 is an exception, but presumably the doubters believe when Jesus speaks. In Mark 16:9-20 the risen Jesus upbraids not those who have seen him and doubt, but those who doubt the testimony of witnesses to his resurrection. Thus in a real sense there is no seeing of the risen Jesus without believing, even though the seeing is taken to be prior. So there is no believing without seeing, but in the case of the resurrection also no seeing without believing. Therefore, the seeing itself is a gift of Jesus, of course from God (cf. 9:39-41).

The Purpose of the Gospel: The First Conclusion (20:30-31)

This passage is often referred to as the first colophon, or ending, of the Gospel, the other being, of course, 21:24-25. After what is so obviously a concluding statement one does not expect more. Yet the narrative resumes in chapter 21.

The initial statement, which is perfectly clear, nevertheless does not seem quite apposite in this context, since the signs of Jesus in this Gospel have been his deeds, particularly his miracles, done during his earthly public ministry. The statement about signs in 12:37, fits much better in its context at the end of Jesus' public ministry, although it too is puzzling in that it does not mention Jesus' words despite the fact that his discourses have been quite extensive (see above, p. 242). Both statements have been construed as the ending, or part of the ending, of a sign source, a collection of miracle stories, upon which the evangelist drew (see Bultmann 1971, 452, 698). (That John drew on a source of miracle stories different from the Synoptics is an entirely plausible hypothesis, but the delineation of the source material within the Gospel has proved a daunting task.) Here the reference to signs seems out of place, although in Acts 1:3 the risen Jesus is said to have presented himself "by many convincing proofs" (not called "signs" however) to his disciples. The expression in Acts would seem to be similar, but actually more appropriate to John, where Jesus accomplishes proofs of his resurrection, but does not perform signs.

Whatever the origin of the statement of 20:30, however, it is best taken as a summation of the entire Gospel, and not of Jesus' resurrection appearances only. In that case the use of "signs" fits better, if not perfectly. Of course, if the present form of the Gospel were based on an earlier Signs Gospel (Bultmann 1971; Fortna 1970; 1988), such a summation would be quite appropriate. As it stands, it is a bit unexpected, but certainly not incomprehensible. Jesus' ministry can, in Johannine terms, be understood as a sequence of words and deeds, all signifying who he is. (So even Bultmann 1971, 698: "As with 12.37, it is at first surprising that the work of Jesus is described under the title *semeia,* but it is comprehensible in view of the unity which, in the thought of the Evangelist, 'signs' and words form.")

Interestingly, the author refers to his work as a book (Gk. *biblion;* cf. 21:25 where the same term is used of the many books that could be written about Jesus). Most commentators pass over John's use of the term, which seems unexceptional enough. What is noteworthy is that he does not use the term "Gospel," by which we know his work. In fact, that term was not applied to such documents until decades later (see H. Koester 1990, 24-31).

The final statement of the purpose of the Gospel (v. 31) would, in a general sense, be appropriate for all the Gospels. Yet, although it seems simple and straightforward, it has generated a considerable controversy that hinges on the tense of the verb "to believe." This in turn hinges on the choice of two major, alternative manuscript readings. In either case the verb is properly in the subjunctive mood (after the conjunction *hina*) and thus indicates purpose. The oldest manuscripts (P[66] B) have the present subjunctive, but most others have the aorist. In proper Greek the present implies continuous action, the aorist punctiliar. As Barrett puts it (1978, 575): "The present subjunctive (strictly interpreted) means 'that you may continue to believe, be confirmed in your faith,' the aorist 'that you may here and now believe, that is, become Christian.' " The fact that both forms of the verb are represented in many manuscripts means at least that from an early period there were differences as to how this statement should be understood. Yet even if we could determine the original reading, there would still be a question as to how the evangelist wished to be understood, or to what extent he knew and followed the rules of Greek grammar.

Most commentators are inclined to the view that John in its present form was written for Christian consumption. The farewell discourses (from the Last Supper through Jesus' prayer; i.e., chaps.13–17) would seem to have a primarily Christian readership in view. Yet aside from the question of the right reading and interpretation of the verb "to believe" in 20:31, the whole gospel presses the necessity of deciding about Jesus so urgently that the reader feels that pressure as well. Carson (1991, 661-63, citing his earlier article, 1987) argues strongly that because Jesus is anarthrous and *christos* has the article, the latter is the subject and we should read: "that you may believe that the Christ, the Son of God, is Jesus." Thus the purpose is finally to convert. Witherington (1995, 346) agrees on this point, accepting the NRSV translation ("that you may come to believe ... "), which indicates the choice of the aorist subjunctive and therefore the missionary purpose. Those who see John as a Gospel that went through stages of development (e.g., Bultmann and Fortna) believe that the missionary purpose was primary at an earlier, no longer extant, stage, but that in its present form the Gospel has Christian readers (or hearers) in view. Such a progression, although perhaps not demonstrable, is altogether plausible and also accounts for John's continuing use as both a missionary tract and the source of inspiration and edification among Christians.

It is important for the author of this Gospel that readers should believe that the Messiah is Jesus (Gk. *christos*), as 1:19-51 clearly shows. But it is equally clear, as the narrative of this Gospel unfolds, that the traditional, Jewish meaning of messiahship is being transformed and extended almost beyond recognition, as is here suggested by the title Son of God. That title, and all it entails, seriously qualifies, changes, and enriches the identification of Jesus as Messiah or Christ. It represents a development that is mainly inner-Christian and inner-Johannine, although not entirely without precedent in Judaism. As is clear from the very beginning of the Gospel (1:4), John's fundamental goal and conviction is that through the name of Jesus readers should gain life. What Jesus brings the Gospel of John now brings, the possibility of life—eternal life—for the two are the same in John. Of course, the Gospel does not bring life apart from Jesus. One might say, however, that Jesus brings life through the Gospel, that is, through this very document.

◊ ◊ ◊ ◊

The discovery of the tomb empty, the appearance of Jesus to Mary Magdalene outside the tomb, the appearance to the disciples behind closed doors, followed by a similar appearance a week later—all these narratives underscore the faith that Jesus, who was crucified, has indeed risen. What the disciples have seen is the same crucified Jesus whom they had deserted as lost and left for dead. But although truly dead, he is no longer. The tomb is empty: Jesus has been seen alive.

John believes such things happened, although a comparison of his two accounts with Luke's account of the risen Jesus' encountering his disciples (Luke 24:36-43) reveals a somewhat different perception of what has happened. In John, Jesus does not protest that he is not a disembodied spirit, eating fish to prove the point. In John, Jesus finally offers his hands and side to Thomas's touch, but one never reads that Thomas actually touched, only that he saw and believed. Clearly, John intends to establish the identity of the risen Jesus with the crucified. Paul has the same interest (1 Cor 15), even though he specifically and explicitly eschews talk of a physical resurrection. Nor does he even mention the empty tomb. John's belief and claim is, of course, that the resurrection is historical, that is, a given, in the sense that it involved Jesus as well as the perception of him. This holds true whatever modern people make of it, although consternation at this claim is not a strictly modern reaction (cf. Acts 17:32).

John 20 begins with the account of the discovery of the tomb of Jesus empty. Although the two disciples come to faith on examining it—or at least the Beloved Disciple does—Mary Magdalene remains insistent that Jesus' body has been removed, presumably stolen. Her reasonable, honest explanation is only overturned by her encounter with Jesus himself outside the tomb. Jesus appears to his disciples and shows them his hands and side in establishing his identity, before bestowing the Spirit. Thomas must, of course, be shown and persuaded separately. Thus, in this chapter, emphasis quite clearly falls on establishing the reality of Jesus' resurrection by showing the continuity between Jesus of Nazareth, who died and was scarred by crucifixion, with the Risen One. Yet after Thomas accepts the proof the risen Jesus offers him and confesses Jesus as Lord and God, Jesus pronounces his blessing upon those who have not seen and yet believe.

Fittingly, the Gospel then closes with a statement of purpose. One could scarcely hope for a more appropriate culmination and conclusion of this Gospel. John has stressed the importance of the disciples' seeing Jesus, at least for their faith, but at the same time Jesus makes clear that those who have not seen will believe because of the disciples' testimony (cf. 17:20), which is contained in this Gospel (20:31; cf. 21:24). Bultmann (1971, 701) succinctly points to the several indications in chapter 20 that the Gospel has reached its conclusion: the disciples receive what appear to be definitive and final appearances of Jesus; they are commissioned; Jesus' blessing of those who have not seen cuts off any expectation of a further appearance. The reader does not expect the narrative to continue, but it does.

EPILOGUE: RESURRECTION APPEARANCES TO DISCIPLES AND PETER BY THE SEA (21:1-25)

Because the Gospel seems already to have ended, chapter 21 must be regarded as a kind of appendix or epilogue. Actually, "epilogue" would seem the better term because this extended episode deals with the resolution of relationships involving Jesus, Peter, and the Beloved Disciple that had been left hanging (see Culpepper 1983, 96; cf. Brown 1970, 1078-79).

As matters now stand, this is the fourth appearance of Jesus, although 21:14 says that it is the third to the disciples, apparently not counting the appearance to Mary Magdalene and therefore not reckoning her a disciple. On the other hand, "the disciples" designates the group, perhaps the twelve, who are gathered in the other scenes. This appearance by the sea does not require the previous appearance narratives in order to be understood. In fact, if anything they cause a problem, for, as we shall see, this appearance seems unexpected, and, apart from the literary context, the reader would not think that the disciples had seen the risen Lord at all. (It may be relevant that our fragment of the *Gospel of Peter* breaks off as Peter and Andrew, still grieving and not yet having seen the risen Jesus, are going to the sea to fish.)

The appearance to the disciples, apparently seven in number, leads into a rather extended conversation between Jesus and Simon Peter, in which the Beloved Disciple eventually plays a role (vv. 15-23). This conversation appears to resolve the obvious alienation of Peter, who has denied Jesus three times, as Peter three times affirms his love for Jesus in response to the latter's rather insistent questioning (vv. 15-19). While this whole episode is unexpected in John's narrative, it answers to the expectation aroused in Mark (16:7; cf. 14:28) that the risen Jesus will appear to the disciples, Peter specifically included, in Galilee (see Bultmann 1971, 705, n. 5). This Markan word fits John 21 (cf. Matt 28:16), but not John 20 (or Luke 24), for it actually clashes with the tradition of initial resurrection appearances in Jerusalem, found only in John and Luke. The various accounts and reports of resurrection appearances add up to a complex and in some respects contradictory picture of what went on after Jesus' burial. Perhaps this is not really surprising in view of the extraordinary character of the disciples' experiences, claims, and belief. (On the resurrection narratives see Perkins 1984.)

John's Gospel will now end with the relationship of Jesus to Peter restored and that of Peter and the Beloved Disciple resolved. In effect, they are not to remain rivals, but each in his own way will bear testimony to the truth of the Christian message.

The resurrection scene of 21:1-14 has a recognizable parallel in Luke 5:1-11, which also centers upon a great, and surprising, catch of fish made by the disciples at the direction of Jesus, when previously they had no success. In Luke it is a call story, which stands in place of Mark 1:16-20. In John's resurrection story the disciples come to recognize the figure on shore as the risen Jesus (21:7, 12), although they seem reluctant to hail him as such. Similarly, in the Lukan Emmaus Road appearance narrative (24:13-35), disciples at first do not know the risen Jesus, but then come to recognize him (Luke 24:31-32). The relation of John's resurrection story to Luke's call story is real, but not easy to explain. They differ sufficiently that it is not necessary to assume a direct, literary relationship. (Bultmann 1971, 705, asserts that John's Easter setting is prior; Fortna 1970, 89-98, treats it as originally the third sign in his Gospel of Signs rather than a resurrection appearance. Brown 1970, 1090, neatly summarizes the points of similarity with Luke 5:1-11.) The fact that it answers to the expectation of a Galilean resurrection appearance aroused by Mark 14:28 and 16:7, and does not fit exactly the Johannine resurrection context, implies that the Johannine narrator knew it was a resurrection story and added it here, where it leads nicely over into Jesus' conversation with Peter (see Brown 1970, 1085-95).

Jesus' Appearance to Disciples by the Sea (21:1-14)

The Sea of Tiberias (v. 1) is otherwise known as the Sea of Galilee (cf. 6:1). Seven disciples are gathered there, assuming that the sons of Zebedee are James and John, as is always the case in the synoptic Gospels (cf. Mark 1:19; 3:17). Thomas is known from all lists of the disciples (in the Synoptics and Acts), but as we have seen he plays an active and important role only in John (11:16; 14:5; 20:24-29). Nathanael is mentioned only in John (1:46-49), as is the village Cana (2:1; 4:46), but we have not previously been told that Cana was his home. Nathanael appears in no list of the twelve, but since John gives us no such list we cannot be certain that he did not consider Nathanael one of the twelve. Of the two unnamed disciples one must be the Beloved Disciple, unless, of course, he is John the son of Zebedee, as tradition holds. Yet there are serious problems with that tradition, as we have seen (above, pp. 24-27). (On the development of this tradition see Culpepper 1994. Although Charlesworth [1995] argues that the Beloved Disciple is Thomas, all such proposals, whether ancient or modern, run up against John's apparently deliberate attempt to keep this disciple anonymous, for reasons that David R. Beck 1997, especially 108-36, sets forth. Beck offers an extended critique of Charlesworth's proposal; see especially 127-36.)

Why these disciples (and not others) are gathered is not said, and the reader can only conjecture. Have they assembled there to meet the risen Jesus (Mark 14:28; 16:7)? Possibly, yet nothing in John's Gospel suggests that he will appear in Galilee, and nothing in this pericope suggests he has already appeared in Jerusalem. Peter's stated intention, to fish, and the disciples' joining him (v. 3), suggests that the disciples are simply going back to work, taking up their occupations where they left off in order to follow Jesus (as is certainly the case in *Gos. Pet.* 14:58-60). To this point we have seen in John no suggestion that Jesus' disciples had been fishermen by trade, as is made clear by the Synoptics (especially Mark 1:16-20 par.). Of course, John displaces the Synoptic call story, if he knew it, by the account of John the Baptist's sending his disciples to Jesus (1:35-51). Their previous occupation may be something the author (at least the author of chap. 21) presumes as known, whether from the Synoptics or their tradition. Apparently the author of chapter 21 knows other Gospels (cf. 21:25). In any event, the disciples go out at night to fish, but are unsuccessful (cf. Luke 5:5, which indicates both that the disciples were fishing at night and that they caught nothing). That their fishing at night is Johannine symbolism is called into question by the fact that it is found also in Luke (5:5); moreover, night fishing on the Sea of Galilee may have been common (Brown 1970, 1069).

Jesus is standing on the shore at dawn (v. 4); the reader will know more than the disciples at this point. Jesus questions them; they answer that they have had no success (v. 5). Then, following Jesus' instructions, they make an overwhelming catch (v. 6). The motif of the disciples' not immediately recognizing the risen Jesus is familiar from Luke (24:13-35), where on the road to Emmaus the two disciples do not recognize Jesus until, having arrived at their destination, Jesus reveals himself to them in the breaking of bread. Now in John the Beloved Disciple recognizes Jesus and identifies him to Peter as the Lord, a typical designation of the risen Jesus (v. 7). At this point in the narrative only he and Peter apparently know who it is.

Peter then responds with typical impetuosity (cf. 13:8; Mark 8:32; 9:5-6). He is presumably stripped down for work (cf. 13:4). It seems odd that he puts on clothes to go swimming, although it is apparently a token of respect to Jesus the Lord. Brown (1970, 1072) suggests that the meaning is that Peter tucked in his outer garments. Once again, Peter has been surpassed by the Beloved Disciple, who has just recognized Jesus and has told Peter who it is standing on the beach. Now, however, Peter attempts to get to Jesus first, and apparently does, leaving the others, including the Beloved Disciple, to come along behind in the boat, which was already near the shore, dragging the net full of fish. The distance from the shore seems an irrelevant fact, except that it lets us know that the disciples in the boat were close enough to the shore to recognize Jesus.

Jesus has prepared breakfast for the disciples (v. 9). He will now feed them, as he fed the multitude of five thousand beside the sea (6:1-15). So Jesus has done two remarkable things for his disciples: he has led them to a great catch of fish; now he feeds them. The episode has eucharistic overtones. Yet while there is bread, fish seems to be the main dish, as fish were also prominent in the feeding of the five thousand (6:1-15; cf. Mark 6:30-44 par.; 8:1-10). That their number, 153, is given exactly is most perplexing and presumably has some significance. Curiously, the numbers one through seventeen add up to 153, as Augustine observed, but why this should be significant is not obvious. Through the centuries exegetes have not tired of offering explanations of the number, whose exactness is assumed to bespeak its importance (for some of these interpretations see Beasley-Murray 1987, 401-4; more succinctly, Brown 1970, 1074-5). Gematria, the symbolic interpretation of numbers, has led to no agreement or illumination, as Brown observes. His suggestion (ibid., 1076) that the exactness is intended to substantiate the accuracy of the eyewitness to the event is as plausible as any. Moreover, it supports the implication that the catch was so large it might have broken the net, but didn't. Remarkably, it is Simon Peter alone who hauls (or draws) the net ashore. The same verb, *helkō*, is used of the exalted Christ's drawing all people to himself in 12:32, and in 6:44 of God's drawing people to Jesus. Therefore, it is sometimes thought that the fish represent the "catch" of believers or churches (cf. Mark 1:17 par.: "fishers of men," as the RSV translates).

Yet this is nowhere said in John, and Jesus' command seems to consider the fish as food (v. 10).

Jesus then explicitly invites the disciples to the breakfast he has prepared (v. 12). Although he suggests they bring some of the fish they caught (v. 10), it is not clear why they were necessary, since there was already fish and bread (v. 9). There are two stages within this episode, the miraculous catch of fish and the meal. The Lukan version (5:1-11) has only the catch of fish, although later Luke also portrays the risen Jesus present with his disciples at mealtime (24:30-35, 41-42). Jesus' instruction and Simon Peter's action (vv. 10-11) bring the two stages together, but without them verse 12 follows quite well on the heels of verse 9. Not surprisingly some exegetes (e.g., Brown 1994, 1085, 1094-95) suggest that two previously independent stories have been combined in John, or perhaps in his source.

As the disciples recognize the presence of the risen Lord, their awe apparently prevents them from asking him his identity, which in any event they already know (v. 12). Of course, this recognition seems a bit superfluous after the Beloved Disciple recognizes him and tells Peter (v. 7), who leaps out of the boat into the sea. (Perhaps the incongruity results from the joining of two independent stories.) Nevertheless, the recognition of the risen Jesus at mealtime is an important resurrection motif (cf. Luke 24:35) and probably represents a historical fact: Jesus was known to have appeared to his disciples at mealtime. Moreover, the first resurrection appearances may well have taken place in Galilee, at the Sea, where Jesus conducted much of his public ministry (see Brown 1970, 1093-95). The culmination of the scene, with its clearly eucharistic overtones, is Jesus' distribution of the bread and fish to the disciples (cf. 6:11; Mark 6:41). As is often the case in the Gospels, we are here dealing with multiple layers of tradition and interpretation. The eucharistic overtones may reflect the liturgy and practice of primitive Christian communities. Yet that liturgy and practice doubtless has roots in the ministry of Jesus, who fed crowds and ate with his disciples and others. That the risen Jesus made his presence known as the disciples again ate together is highly probable, as is the location by the Sea of Galilee.

Jesus' Conversation with Peter (21:15-19)

While the previous narratives bear marks of being based on tradition, the conversation between Jesus and Peter that follows it, especially verses 15-19, is highly stylized and Johannine. Jesus repeatedly asks Peter whether he loves him and refers to his followers as sheep or lambs. Jesus' threefold question and subsequent command seem to match Peter's threefold denial of Jesus (13:38; 18:17, 25-27; cf. Mark 14:66-72 par.), and while the matchup is not explicitly made, it can hardly be coincidental.

While Peter is being sharply questioned, Jesus' commands also imply a pastoral role for him. In this connection one naturally thinks of Jesus' word to Peter in Matt 16:18-19 and the authority Jesus bestows on him there (but cf. John 20:23, where a similar authority is given to all the disciples). Clearly Peter is the leading figure among the twelve in John and in the other Gospels, as well as in Paul's epistles (where Peter is referred to as Cephas, or *Kēpha*, "Rocky," the Aramaic original of the epithet "Peter"; cf. especially Gal 1:18–2:14; 1 Cor 1:12-13; 9:5). Two letters of the New Testament are ascribed to him, and ancient tradition links the Gospel of Mark to his name. Of course, in Roman Catholic tradition he was the bishop of Rome, the first pope, buried on the site of the great basilica named for him. Some ancient, first-century bones, kept under the great altar, are venerated as his own. As questionable as it may be to read this passage in light of the position Peter later attained in the history and traditions of the church, the development of these traditions has some basis in the New Testament, and even in the career of the historical Peter, as this episode suggests.

Jesus' initial question (v. 15) is difficult, as he asks, "Do you love me more than these?" More than what or whom? (a) More than the fish, fishing equipment, and fishing business? (b) Or, more than the other disciples love Jesus? (c) Alternatively, the question could mean, "Do you love me more than you love these other disciples?" But such a question would make little sense in John, where Peter would be expected to show his love for Jesus precisely through his love for other disciples. It is easy to eliminate (c), and since (a) has no clear antecedent in the preceding context, unless it be these fish about to be eaten—which is absurd—(b) is the best alternative. The other disciples are clearly present. The question therefore seems to contemplate Peter's leadership or superior rank, whether during Jesus' ministry (cf. 13:37; Mark 14:29) or later (cf. 13:7).

Peter may justify his status by his unsurpassed love for Jesus, which has certainly been put in question by his denial. His love for Jesus will find expression in his care for Jesus' flock. Jesus is the Good Shepherd (10:1-6, 11-18) and Peter must emulate him. Love for Jesus means first of all obedience to Jesus' command to love one's fellow disciple (13:14-15, 34; 14:15, 21, 23-24; 15:12-14; cf. 1 John 4:11-12, 19-21). Jesus' threefold question of whether Peter loves him, followed by Peter's affirmation that he does, followed by Jesus' command to feed his flock is a thoroughly Johannine sequence. John scarcely anticipated that the pope would every year wash the feet of other priests on Maundy Thursday, but arguably this act is, in light of ecclesiastical developments in intervening centuries, a faithful recapitulation of what Jesus intended by his question and command. Simon Peter's office, if it may be called that, is pastoral. He shows his love for Jesus by caring for the flock, obviously out of love.

The words Jesus uses are of some interest, but the variations of vocabulary are probably not of fundamental importance. The difference between lambs (v. 15; *arnia*) and sheep (v. 16; *probata*) does not appear significant. Feeding and tending are obviously essential aspects of the shepherd's work. Jesus here also uses two different verbs for love (*agapaō* and *phileō*). The noun *agapē* and the cognate verb are sometimes thought to distinguish the peculiarly Christlike or Christian form of love. But John uses the terms for love interchangeably here (as is obvious in vv. 15-16). The play on words is a part of Jesus' playing with Peter, which finally gets to Peter, who is hurt (NRSV) or grieved (RSV) that Jesus seems not to take him at his word. Peter's response (v. 17), which attributes omniscience to Jesus, is right on target, given John's Christology and portrayal of Jesus. Why did Jesus ask in the first place? He is, of course, testing Peter's loyalty. Moreover, Peter denied Jesus three times, so he must affirm his love three times in order to strike a balance.

Then Jesus proceeds to predict Peter's earthly destiny in words that are mysterious (v. 18), and therefore must be explained (v. 19). This is probably our earliest reference to Peter's martyrdom, which is also hinted at in 2 Pet 1:14, a statement that seems to reflect knowledge of this word of Jesus to Peter. That Peter suffered martyrdom is also attested in *1 Clem.* 5:4, written at about the same time as John, although how he was executed is not said. Eusebius reports that Peter was crucified upside down (*Hist. Eccl.* 3.1.2), a legend that has become famous. Whether John's description of Peter's fate signifies crucifixion is a debated question (see Brown 1970, 1107-8). Peter's stretching out his hands could imply crucifixion, but then it is odd that the binding of Peter and his being led where he does not wish to go are mentioned after rather than before the stretching forth of the hands (as it were, on the cross). Yet an earlier interchange between Peter and Jesus (13:36) implies that Peter will follow Jesus in death, perhaps in crucifixion. Moreover, the explanatory note (v. 19) makes clear that the manner of Peter's death is in view, not merely the fact of it. It is significant that Peter's death, like Jesus', glorifies God. Jesus deals first with the question of Peter's death, but will go on to speak of the Beloved Disciple's. As for Peter, Jesus gives him the simple command that readers of Mark or the Synoptics know so well: "Follow me" (cf. Mark 1:17; 2:14).

Jesus, Peter, and the Beloved Disciple (21:20-24)

John's narratives have always impressed readers by their verisimilitude, and this extends particularly to the manner in which characters react to one another. Thus Peter has seemed irritated that Jesus kept asking him the same question (v. 17). Now Peter's response to Jesus' command is, so to speak, distracted by his noticing the other disciple, the one whom Jesus loved, who is further identified by reference to his role at the Last Supper (v. 20; cf. 13:23-25). Quite understandably, Peter asks about the fate of his rival who with one exception (19:25-27), when Peter had deserted Jesus and fled, always appears alongside him. As we have seen, he is the rival who always seems to surpass Peter. Jesus responds, in effect, by telling Peter to attend to his own discipleship ("Follow me"), and not to be concerned about his colleague (v. 22).

Jesus' reference to his own return, however, raises a theological and, as it turns out, practical question. At this point the narrator steps in to explain (v. 23), and his explanation reveals that Jesus' statement has created a problem, as we are told that it was misunderstood, perhaps understandably, "in the community" (NRSV) or "among the brethren." This whole matter needs to be viewed not only in a Johannine context, but in relation to early Christian eschatology generally. Jesus is said to have proclaimed the imminent advent of the kingdom of God (e.g., Mark 1:15; 9:1; 13:30), and Paul certainly expected Jesus' imminent return, as did his churches (e.g., 1 Thess 4:13-18). In fact, Paul is in 1 Thessalonians comforting and encouraging the church about those who have died before Jesus' return. Thus Jesus' proclamation and Paul's, as well as Paul's church's expectation, form the background of what we see here. Obviously, within the Johannine community the return of Jesus has been expected, if not within the lifetime of all, certainly before the death of the Beloved Disciple. In fact, such an expectation of Jesus' return is still alive in 1 John (2:28–3:3; cf. Rev 22:20).

As we have observed, at several points John has offered, apparently quite deliberately, a reinterpretation of early Christian, and Jewish, eschatology that moves the crucial turning point from the future to the present, or from the postresurrection church's perspective, the past (cf. 5:24-27; 11:23-25; 14:22-24). More lies behind the present text and the problem it reflects than only the puzzlement of the community about the death of their leader. That practical problem is set straight by the careful reiteration of what Jesus actually said. At the same time, we are offered an invaluable insight into Johannine circles and the development of eschatological expectation and interpretation there. In all probability the distinctively Johannine realized eschatology is the result of a development, based on experience and theological reflection, from an eschatology very much like what we find in the Synoptics, Paul's letters, and elsewhere in the New Testament. If the Johannine letters reflect such an eschatology more strongly, this is all the more true of the book of Revelation, which on grounds of its apocalypticism distances itself from the Gospel of John, while claiming to have been written by someone named John (e.g., 1:1, 4). This clarification by the narrator opens a window into the development of Johannine eschatology, as it raises the possibility that even the Revelation to John, which has interesting points of contact with the Gospel, also has some historical relationship to it (see Introduction, above, p. 34; cf. pp. 297-98).

Peter has become a martyr (Gk. *martys;* cf. Barrett 1978, 583); although the term is not used here the idea is clear. The Beloved Disciple apparently was not a martyr in the sense of dying for his faith, but he too left an indispensable testimony (NRSV) or witness (RSV), that is a *martyria* (v. 24). His witness could not be more strongly attested. The Beloved Disciple is now identified as the one responsible for this Gospel, assuming that "these things" applies to the content of the Gospel as a whole. The similarity of wording with 19:35 strongly suggests that the same witness is there in view (see Culpepper 1983, 122). In that context the witness would again be the Beloved Disciple, who with Jesus' mother stood beside his cross. His testifying, or bearing witness, was then based upon his seeing; and here also his having seen the things to which he testifies is assumed. That assumption then agrees with 1:14 ("we have seen his glory... "). How "we" know that this witness is true is actually not said here.

Moreover, it is a good question who is here speaking. Is the narrator speaking as the author of the whole Gospel, of chapter 21, or only of this statement? (On this issue see Culpepper 1983, 45-46.) Equally crucial is whether in verse 24 the Beloved Disciple is said to be the author, the one who actually wrote, or the one who authorizes and authenticates what is written.

Taking the questions in reverse order, the Beloved Disciple is said quite literally to have written these things (aorist participle of *graphō,* to write). Yet earlier on a similar construction (19:1) is translated in the NRSV "Pilate took Jesus and had him flogged."

(The RSV, translating literally, has "Pilate took Jesus and scourged him.") Moreover, the NRSV makes exactly the same translation move in 19:19, where the text says literally that Pilate wrote the title and put it on the cross. Obviously, this statement about authorship does not solve the problem as neatly as might have been hoped.

In any case, it seems on the face of it unlikely that the narrator is here referring to himself, or that he himself is the Beloved Disciple, whether or not the latter is actually thought of as the author of the Gospel. The narrator may then be the author of this chapter only and the Beloved Disciple the author, or sponsor, of the rest (Lindars 1972, 641). Bultmann, along with many other exegetes, takes chapter 21 to be the work of a later editor (1971, 700-706), a postscript added by another hand. Brown (1970, 1079-82) agrees that its addition was the work of a later editor, while nevertheless pointing out the Johannine character of the material, and arguing that because of its intrinsic relation to what precedes it should be called an epilogue.

While certainty is impossible, we adopt the view that the Beloved Disciple's witness authorized the Gospel, whether or not he himself was the author, that is, the person who finally wrote it down. With Brown we find it unlikely that he was the author in this latter sense. (There is, as we have seen from 19:1, 19, ample reason for doubting that the statement of v. 24 must mean that the Beloved Disciple himself committed the Gospel to writing.) Chapter 21 was then added by the final editor. It was not, however, composed by him *de novo,* but out of already existing Johannine tradition. Obviously the narrator of chapter 21 writes the conclusion of the whole Gospel. Therefore the real author of this epilogue intentionally forms an inclusion with 1:14. What "we" have seen the Beloved Disciple has witnessed, testified to, and caused to be written down, so "we" know that his witness is true. The "we" of 1:14 and that of 21:24 refer to a circle of disciples of Jesus of whom the Beloved Disciple is the primary and representative member, the author of the Johannine witness.

Significantly, the author emerges at the very end of this Gospel. It is often said of the Gospels that they are anonymous, and this is true particularly of Mark and Matthew. Nevertheless, an unnamed author emerges both in the Lukan prologue (1:1-4) and at the very end of the Gospel of John. Both have a similar purpose: to assure the reader of the truth, indeed, the historical truth of the narrative.

Colophon (21:25)

The final statement of the Gospel clearly echoes 20:30-31, and its author may be presumed to have known it. Yet 21:25 is significantly different. In the one case "other signs" are mentioned, here "other things," so that the referent is broader. There writing is already mentioned, not books (pl.). Here the writing of books *(biblia)* about Jesus is clearly contemplated. ("Gospels" were not called by that name for several decades; see above, p. 23. In Matt 1:1 that Gospel may be called a "book," as Senior 1998, 1-2, argues.) In all likelihood the existence of such books is known to our author, even if the statement is a conventional one with parallels in other ancient works. (See Boring, Berger, Colpe 1995, 308, who cite a number of ancient parallels including 1 Macc 9:22: "Now the rest of the acts of Judas...have not been recorded, but they were very many." Schnackenburg 1982, 374, thinks that v. 25 is the work of yet another hand; cf. Brown 1970, 1125.) At this level of composition the existence of other Gospels, presumably one or more of the synoptic Gospels, is known, as both Bultmann and Brown would agree, although they understand the purpose and perspective of the final editing quite differently. For Bultmann it is an effort to wrench the somewhat idiosyncratic Gospel of John into line with an emerging orthodoxy that has embraced the Synoptics as, in a sense, already canonical. For Brown it is the logical continuation and conclusion of the interests and theological commitments that guided the development of this Gospel from the beginning. (For Bultmann's redaction theory, see 1971, *passim,* and D. Moody Smith 1965, 213-38, where Bultmann's theory of redaction is explained and assessed. For Brown's see 1966, xxiv-xxxix, especially xxxiv-xxxix.)

◊ ◊ ◊ ◊

As we observed already (see above, pp. 370-72), the epilogue of chapter 21 addresses issues different from those central to the appearance scenes of chapter 20. There the reality of the appearances of the risen Jesus, especially his identity with the one crucified was paramount. Thus Mary's perplexity about the whereabouts of Jesus' body, which she assumes was stolen, is resolved as she finally recognizes that the figure accosting her in the garden outside the tomb is not the gardener but Jesus. Then the disciples rejoice when in seeing Jesus' hands and side they recognize that they are seeing the risen Lord. Finally, Thomas, who must have visible, even palpable, proof, is satisfied. They have all seen and believed, but Jesus pronounces a climactic and concluding benediction over those who have not seen, and yet believe (20:29).

In the epilogue, however, relationships between Peter and Jesus and then between Peter and the Beloved Disciple become matters of uppermost concern and interest. The recognition and identity of Jesus are matters already resolved at this point in the narrative. Thus the recognition and identification of Jesus, still motifs of the traditional story (21:1-14), are no longer central. Readers are left to infer that more than personal relationships between Peter and the Beloved Disciple here come into play. Obviously, the Beloved Disciple is representative of the Johannine school or community, while Peter, who appears in the Synoptics as well as John as the leader of the twelve, is probably also a representative figure (as Brown 1979, has argued, especially 25-58). Their coming to terms with each other, especially Peter's coming to terms with the Beloved Disciple, is representative of the rapprochement between Johannine Christianity and the Petrine branch of the church.

It is doubtful that the conversation between Jesus and Peter and the colophon had any existence in tradition apart from this Gospel, although the narrative of the great catch of fish and Jesus' appearance on the shore is clearly based on earlier traditions. The conversation between Jesus and Peter first of all reassures the reader, and quite likely the Johannine community, of the apostle's reinstatement to good standing. At the same time, the Johannine Beloved Disciple, who has been Peter's rival, is brought into the discussion by Peter's question (21:21). Jesus says in effect that Peter should attend to his own ministry ("what is that to you?") and discipleship ("Follow me!"). Peter obviously has a witness to bear *(martyria)*, even as he becomes a *martys* (21:18-19). So also the Beloved Disciple, who does not become a martyr, nevertheless has a witness that is incorporated into this book (21:24-25). While Peter's status is reestablished and his witness in martyrdom ratified, his followers are, by the clear implication of Jesus' words, admonished to let stand the work and witness of his colleague, who although not a martyr, has come to a good and honorable death. Thus the validity of the disciple whom Jesus loved, and his community, the community of the Beloved Disciple, is finally and emphatically endorsed. The seeming rivalry between them has come to an end.

John has more resurrection appearance narratives than any other Gospel, even Luke, whose story of the appearance of Jesus to the two disciples on the Emmaus Road is, however, the longest such account in the Gospels. Remarkably, almost every Johannine narrative, beginning of course with the discovery of the empty tomb, has a synoptic parallel. Not only does 21:1-14 find a parallel in Luke 5:1-11, but this Galilean resurrection appearance by the sea is exactly what one would expect, but does not find, in Mark (14:28; 16:7). If one counts the conversation between Peter and Jesus, which is the continuation of the appearance by the sea, as a separate account, it is the lone exception to the rule. There is nothing comparable to this in the Synoptics, although the fact that the women are instructed to tell the disciples and Peter suggests there will be some reconciliation of Jesus with the leader of the twelve who has denied Jesus under questioning. That there is such a scene in John is, on reflection, typical, particularly in chapter 21, where questions of church relations and authority come to the fore.

This scene at the end of the Gospel and, of course, the end of the appearance stories, is matched by John's empty tomb account at the beginning, where Peter and the Beloved Disciple again are found beside one another in the tomb, in an episode reported only by John. (Luke 24:12, 24 seems also to reflect knowledge of disciples at the empty tomb, although in 24:12 it is Peter alone, and in 24:24 the disciples who visit the tomb are not named. Matthew and Mark know nothing of this.) It goes without saying that the Gospel of John has a particular interest in Peter, as well as the Beloved Disciple. Although that disciple occupies a special place vis-à-vis Peter and the others, Peter's role is not unimportant. In fact, Peter plays a larger role in this Gospel than in any other, although, of course, in the book of Acts his leadership role is exceptionally important as Luke portrays it with unmistakable clarity and emphasis. It is scarcely coincidental that Peter and this other, unnamed disciple figure so importantly at the beginning of the resurrection narratives and at the end.

Moreover, without chapter 21 the Beloved Disciple would seem to exit the Gospel narrative without further, appropriate recognition or leave taking. The reader would be left unsatisfied. As things now stand a satisfying closure is attained. Beck (1997, 123, 131-33, 140-41), debating with Charlesworth (1995) argues that such a closure is obtained with 21:24; whereas Charlesworth, taking 20:30-31 to be the conclusion of the original Gospel, argues that only Thomas, who confesses Jesus in 20:29, allows the Beloved Disciple to have a proper closure and exit from the narrative. Thus Thomas should be recognized as the Beloved Disciple. Yet it is precisely the point that he is not so named in the text itself. For Beck, who regards 21:24-25 as the Gospel's conclusion, the Beloved Disciple's identification with Thomas or any named disciple is loosened, and he remains anonymous, as the evangelist intended.

◊ ◊ ◊ ◊

Despite the reservations of Rudolf Bultmann and John Ashton, two of the most prominent of interpreters, the appearance narratives are obviously of crucial significance in the Gospel of John. In Bultmann's view the appearance of the risen Jesus to the disciples is a concession to their weakness; they ought not to have needed it (1971, 696). Bultmann does not believe that the resurrection narratives can be understood as historical, that is, as representing history in any meaningful sense of the term. Yet he believes that resurrection faith as the interpretation of the history and death of Jesus is a meaningful option for modern people, including himself. There is a sense in which Bultmann, whose appreciation of the theological depth of the Gospel of John is profound, is nevertheless almost annoyed that, following tradition, John repeats stories of resurrection appearances that tend to reduce it to a historical event.

Bultmann's point of view is to a remarkable degree shared by Ashton (1991, 511-14), but not in a fashion that encourages positive theological reflection upon the Johannine texts or the question of their historicity. Ashton's sensibilities are likewise jarred by the disparity between the evangelist's theological creativity and sophistication and his apparent acceptance of the resurrection narratives as historically true and theologically important: "It is like finding Hans Christian Andersen hand in hand with Søren Kierkegaard" (511). Moreover, he finds it difficult to believe that these stories are understood by the evangelist symbolically and theologically, that he himself did not take them seriously as historical reports. In fact, there is good reason to believe he took them seriously in just that latter sense.

Unlike Plato, who used myths for their symbolic value but did not take them literally, much less historically, the fourth evangelist in all probability both used the resurrection narratives (like the sign narratives) for their symbolic value and also believed them as historical reports (Ashton 1991, 514), as hard as such belief may be for even the appreciative critic to fathom. Such belief boggles the modern mind, although Bultmann can nevertheless make positive use of John theologically by demythologizing it of its naive, first-century assumptions, so that the truth of its theology and understanding of revelation and human existence may shine through. But Ashton is unpersuaded by Bultmann's resolution of the problem, partly because of his awareness that John the narrator and evangelist would not have accepted it, but also because of his own modern, critical conviction that Jesus' resurrection itself is not historical "in any meaningful sense of the word" (1991, 511). Apparently, for Ashton the implications of this historical judgment are more negative and severe than for Bultmann, who shares it, but in effect demythologizes away the apparent historical claim in favor of the theological meaning.

It is certainly the case that the resurrection stories are something of an embarrassment to modern sensibilities, even as the Gospel of John seems actually to culminate in the death of Jesus, understood as his being lifted up (12:32) and glorified (12:16; cf. 2:22; 17:1). Thus it can be argued that the work of Jesus is actually accomplished in his incarnation and death (19:30), and the Easter events essentially add nothing, but function as signs, as the miracles did (Bultmann 1971, 632-34, especially 634). The fundamental question is raised not only by modern embarrassment but by Johannine theology itself. There is a sense in which such a sketch represents an intelligible and defensible approach to the Gospel. Yet the work of Jesus, his being lifted up and glorified, could not have been separated from his resurrection in John's comprehension, or that of early Christians generally. As a representative of the world and thought of early Christianity the Gospel narrative is in fact predicated not only on the reality of Jesus' ministry and death, but also on his resurrection. Interpreters such as Bultmann and Ashton know this, of course, but in effect see a logic in the Gospel's presentation and thought that the author himself did not see or fully draw out. For the evangelist, however, the Resurrection remains the essential and pivotal event that makes possible a Gospel narrative such as this. It is an event that happened to Jesus, not just to the disciples, although also to them.

Select Bibliography

Works Cited in the Text
(Excluding Commentaries)

Aland, Barbara, and Kurt Aland, ed. 1993. *Nestle-Aland: Novum Testamentum Graece*. 27th ed. Stuttgart: Deutsche Bibelgesellschaft.

Anderson, Paul N. 1996. *The Christology of the Fourth Gospel: Its Unity and Disunity in the Light of John 6*. Valley Forge, PA: Trinity Press International.

Apostolic Fathers. 1912, 1913. With an English translation by Kirsopp Lake. LCL. 2 vols. Cambridge, MA: Harvard University Press.

Ashton, John. 1986. *The Interpretation of John*. IRT 9. Philadelphia: Fortress.

_____. 1991. *Understanding the Fourth Gospel*. Oxford: Clarendon.

Bacon, Benjamin Wisner. 1910. *The Fourth Gospel in Research and Debate*. New York: Moffat, Yard.

Bammel, Ernst, ed. 1970. *The Trial of Jesus: Cambridge Studies in Honour of C. F. D. Moule*. SBT 13 (2nd ser.). London: SCM.

Barrett, C. K. 1975. *The Gospel of John and Judaism*. Philadelphia: Fortress.

_____. 1989. *The New Testament Background: Selected Documents*. San Francisco: Harper & Row.

Bauer, Walter. 1979. *A Greek-English Lexicon of the New Testament and Other Early Christian Literature*. Translated and adapted by William F. Arndt and F. Wilbur Gingrich. 2nd ed. Revised and augmented from Walter Bauer's 5th ed. by Gingrich and Frederick W. Danker, 1958. Chicago: University of Chicago Press.

Beck, David R. 1997. *The Discipleship Paradigm: Readers and Anonymous Characters in the Fourth Gospel*. Biblical Interpretation Series 27. Leiden: E. J. Brill.

Beutler, Johannes. 1996. "The Use of 'Scripture' in the Gospel of John." In *EGJ*, 147-62. Louisville: Westminster John Knox.

Black, C. Clifton. 1996. "The Words That You Have Given to Me I Have Given to Them: The Grandeur of Johannine Rhetoric." In *EGJ*, 220-39. Louisville: Westminster John Knox.

Borgen, Peder. 1965. *Bread from Heaven: An Exegetical Study of the Concept of Manna in the Gospel of John and the Writings of Philo.* NovTSup 10. Leiden: E. J. Brill.

_____. 1983. *Logos Was the True Light and Other Essays on the Gospel of John.* Trondheim: Tapir.

_____. 1996. "The Gospel of John and Hellenism: Some Observations." In *EGJ*, 98-123. Louisville: Westminster John Knox.

Boring, M. E. 1978/79. "The Influence of Christian Prophecy on the Johannine Portrait of the Paraclete and Jesus." *NTS* 25:113-23.

Boring, M. Eugene, Klaus Berger, and Carsten Colpe, eds. 1995. *Hellenistic Commentary to the New Testament.* Nashville: Abingdon.

Brown, Raymond E. 1961. "Incidents That Are United in the Synoptic Gospels but Dispersed in St. John." *CBQ* 23:143-60.

_____. 1979. *The Community of the Beloved Disciple.* New York: Paulist.

_____. 1982. *The Epistles of John.* AB. Garden City, NY: Doubleday.

_____. 1994. *The Death of the Messiah: From Gethsemane to the Grave.* 2 vols. New York: Doubleday.

Bultmann, Rudolf. 1955. *Theology of the New Testament.* Vol. 2. Translated by Kendrick Grobel. New York: Scribner's.

_____. 1968. *The History of the Synoptic Tradition.* Rev. ed. Translated by John Marsh. Oxford: Blackwell.

Burge, Gary M. 1987. *The Anointed Community: The Holy Spirit in the Johannine Tradition.* Grand Rapids, MI: Eerdmans.

Burkett, Delbert. 1991. *The Son of Man in the Gospel of John.* JSNTSup 56. Sheffield: Sheffield Academic Press.

Burridge, Richard H. 1992. *What Are the Gospels? A Comparison with Graeco-Roman Biography.* SNTSMS 70. Cambridge: Cambridge University Press.

Carson, D. A. 1987. "The Purpose of the Fourth Gospel: John 20:30-31 Reconsidered." *JBL* 108:639-51.

Catchpole, David R. 1971. *The Trial of Jesus: A Study in the Gospels and Jewish Historiography from 1770 to the Present Day.* Studia Post-Biblica 18. Leiden: E. J. Brill.

Charlesworth, James H. 1995. *The Beloved Disciple: Whose Witness Validates the Gospel of John?* Valley Forge, PA: Trinity Press International.

_____. 1996. "The Dead Sea Scrolls and the Gospel According to John." In *EGJ*, 65-97. Louisville: Westminster John Knox.

_____, ed. 1983, 1985. *The Old Testament Pseudepigrapha.* 2 vols. Garden City, NY: Doubleday.

_____, ed. 1990. *John and the Dead Sea Scrolls.* New York: Crossroad.

Coakley, J. F. 1988. "The Anointing at Bethany and the Priority of John." *JBL* 107:241-56.

Colwell, E. C. 1931. *The Greek of the Fourth Gospel: A Study of Its Aramaisms in the Light of Hellenistic Greek.* Chicago: University of Chicago Press.

Countryman, L. William. 1987. *The Mystical Way in the Fourth Gospel: Crossing Over into God.* Philadelphia: Fortress.

Cribbs, F. Lamar. 1970. "A Reassessment of the Date of Origin and the Destination of the Gospel of John." *JBL* 89:38-55.

Crossan, John Dominic. 1995. *Who Killed Jesus?: Exposing the Roots of Anti-Semitism in the Gospel Story of the Death of Jesus.* San Francisco: HarperSanFrancisco.

Cullmann, Oscar. 1976. *The Johannine Circle.* Translated by John Bowden. Philadelphia: Westminster.

Culpepper, R. Alan. 1980. "The Pivot of John's Prologue." *NTS* 27:1-31.

_____. 1983. *Anatomy of the Fourth Gospel: A Study in Literary Design.* Philadelphia: Fortress.

_____. 1994. *John the Son of Zebedee: The Life of a Legend.* Studies on Personalities of the New Testament. Columbia, SC: University of South Carolina Press.

_____. 1996. "Reading Johannine Irony." In *EGJ*, 193-207. Louisville: Westminster John Knox.

Dauer, Anton. 1992. "Spuren der (synoptischen) Synedrionsverhandlung im 4. Evangelium." In *John and the Synoptics,* edited by Adelbert Denaux, 307-39. BETL 101. Leuven: Leuven University Press.

Davies, W. D. 1966. *The Setting of the Sermon on the Mount.* Cambridge: Cambridge University Press.

_____. 1996. "Reflections on Aspects of the Jewish Background of the Gospel of John." In *EGJ*, 43-64. Louisville: Westminster John Knox.

Dibelius, Martin. 1935. *From Tradition to Gospel*. Translated by Bertram Lee Woolf. New York: Scribner's.

Dodd, C. H. 1936. *The Apostolic Preaching and Its Developments*. New York: Harper.

_____. 1953. *The Interpretation of the Fourth Gospel*. Cambridge: Cambridge University Press.

_____. 1963. *Historical Tradition in the Fourth Gospel*. Cambridge: Cambridge University Press.

Duke, Paul. 1985. *Irony in the Fourth Gospel*. Atlanta: Westminster.

Dunn, James D. G. 1980. *Christology in the Making: A New Testament Inquiry into the Origins of the Doctrine of the Incarnation*. Philadelphia: Westminster.

Eusebius. 1926, 1932. *The Ecclesiastical History*. With English translations by Kirsopp Lake and J. E. L. Oulton. LCL. 2 vols. Cambridge, MA: Harvard University Press.

Fortna, Robert Tomson. 1970. *The Gospel of Signs: A Reconstruction of the Narrative Source Underlying the Fourth Gospel*. SNTSMS 11. Cambridge: Cambridge University Press.

_____. 1977/78. "Jesus and Peter at the High Priest's House: A Test Case for the Relation Between Mark's and John's Gospels." *NTS* 24:371-83.

_____. 1988. *The Fourth Gospel and Its Predecessor: From Narrative Source to Present Gospel*. Philadelphia: Fortress.

Gardner-Smith, Percival. 1938. *Saint John and the Synoptic Gospels*. Cambridge: Cambridge University Press.

Gaventa, Beverly R. 1996. "The Archive of Excess: John 21 and the Problem of Narrative Closure." In *EGJ*, 240-52. Louisville: Westminster John Knox.

Goodenough, Erwin R. 1945. "John a Primitive Gospel." *JBL* 64:145-82.

Gray, Rebecca. 1993. *Prophetic Figures in Late Second Temple Jewish Palestine: The Evidence from Josephus*. Oxford: Oxford University Press.

Green, Joel. 1988. *The Death of Jesus: Tradition and Interpretation in the Passion Narratives in the Four Gospels*. WUNT 33. Tübingen: Mohr.

Harvey, A. E. 1976. *Jesus on Trial: A Study in the Fourth Gospel*. London: SPCK.

Hengel, Martin. 1977. *Crucifixion in the Ancient World and the Folly of the Message of the Cross*. Translated by John Bowden. Philadelphia: Fortress.

_____. 1989. *The Johannine Question.* Translated by John Bowden. Philadelphia: Trinity Press International.

_____. 1993. *Die johanneischen Frage: Ein Lösungsversuch* (mit einem Beitrag zur Apokalypse von Jörg Frey). WUNT 67. Tübingen: Mohr. (This is an enlarged version of *The Johannine Question.*)

Jeremias, Joachim. 1966. *The Eucharist Words of Jesus.* Translated by Norman Perrin. New York: Scribner's.

Johnson, Luke T. 1989. "The New Testament's Anti-Jewish Slander and the Conventions of Ancient Polemic." *JBL* 108:419-41.

Jonge, Marinus de. 1977. *Jesus: Stranger from Heaven and Son of God, Jesus Christ and the Christians in Johannine Perspective.* Edited and translated by John E. Steely. Missoula, MT: Scholars Press.

Josephus. 1927, 1928. *The Jewish War.* With an English translation by H. St. J. Thackery. LCL. 2 vols. Cambridge, MA: Harvard University Press.

_____. 1957–69. *Jewish Antiquities.* With an English translation by H. St. J. Thackery, Ralph Marcus and L. H. Feldman. LCL. 6 vols. Cambridge: MA: Harvard University Press.

Justin Martyr. 1930. *The Dialogue with Trypho.* Translation, introduction, and notes by A. Lukyn Williams. Translations of Christian Literature. Series 1, Greek Texts. London: SPCK.

Käsemann, Ernst. 1968. *The Testament of Jesus: A Study of the Gospel of John in Light of Chapter 17.* Translated by Gerhard Krodel. Philadelphia: Fortress.

Keck, Leander E. 1996. "Derivation As Destiny: 'Of-ness' in Johannine Christology, Anthropology, and Soteriology." In *EGJ*, 274-88. Louisville: Westminster John Knox.

Kittel, Gerhard. 1964–1976. *TDNT.* Translated by Geoffrey W. Bromiley. Grand Rapids, MI: Eerdmans.

Klassen, William. 1996. *Judas: Betrayer or Friend of Jesus?* Minneapolis: Fortress.

Koester, Craig R. 1995. *Symbolism in the Fourth Gospel: Meaning, Mystery, Community.* Minneapolis: Fortress.

Koester, Helmut. 1965. "History and Cult in the Gospel of John and in Ignatius of Antioch." In *JTC: The Bultmann School of Biblical Interpretation: New Directions?*, 111-23. New York: Harper & Row.

_____. 1982. *Introduction to the New Testament, Volume Two: History and Literature of Early Christianity.* Philadelphia: Fortress.

_____. 1990. *Ancient Christian Gospels: Their History and Development.* Philadelphia: Trinity Press International.

Krodel, Gerhard. 1983. "John 6:63." *Int* 37:283-88.

Kysar, Robert. 1975. *The Fourth Evangelist and His Gospel: An Examination of Contemporary Scholarship.*Minneapolis: Augsburg.

_____. 1985. "The Fourth Gospel: A Report on Recent Research." *ANRW* II 25:2389-2480.

_____. 1993. *John: The Maverick Gospel.* Rev. ed. Louisville: Westminster John Knox.

Loader, William. 1989. *The Christology of the Fourth Gospel: Structure and Issues.* BBET 23. Frankfurt am Main: Lang.

McNamara, Martin, trans. 1992. *Targum Neofiti 1: Genesis.* The Aramaic Bible: The Targums. Collegeville, MN: Liturgical Press.

Malatesta, Edward. 1967. *St. John's Gospel 1920–1965: A Cumulative and Classified Bibliography of Books and Periodical Literature on the Fourth Gospel.* AnBib 32. Rome: Pontifical Biblical Institute.

Martyn, J. Louis. 1979. *History and Theology in the Fourth Gospel.* Rev. ed. Nashville: Abingdon.

_____. 1996. "A Gentile Mission That Replaced an Earlier Jewish Mission?" In *EGJ.* Louisville: Westminster John Knox.

Matson, Mark Alan. 1998. "In Dialogue with Another Gospel? The Influences of the Fourth Gospel on the Passion Narrative of the Gospel of Luke." Ph.D. diss., Duke University.

Meeks, Wayne A. 1967. *The Prophet-King: Moses' Traditions and the Johannine Christology.* NovTSup 14. Leiden: E. J. Brill.

_____. 1972. "The Man from Heaven in Johannine Sectarianism." *JBL* 91:44-72.

_____. 1996. "The Ethics of the Fourth Evangelist." In *EGJ,* 317-26. Louisville: Westminster John Knox.

Metzger, Bruce M. 1992. *The Text of the New Testament: Its Transmission, Corruption, and Restoration.* 3rd ed. Oxford: Oxford University Press.

Meyer, Paul W. 1967. "John 2:10." *JBL* 86:191-97.

_____. 1996. " 'The Father': The Presentation of God in the Fourth Gospel." In *EGJ,* 256-73. Louisville: Westminster John Knox.

Meyers, Eric M. 1976. "Tomb." In *IDBSup,* 905-8, edited by Keith Crim, Lloyd Richard Bailey Sr., and Victor Paul Furnish. Nashville: Abingdon.

Miller, Ed. L. 1993. "The Johannine Origins of the Johannine Logos." *JBL* 112:445-57.

Minear, Paul S. 1983. "The Original Function of John 21." *JBL* 102:85-98.

_____. 1984. *John: The Martyr's Gospel*. New York: Pilgrim.

Miranda, José Porfirio. 1977. *Being and the Messiah: The* Message *of St. John*. Translated by John Eagleson. Maryknoll, NY: Orbis.

The Mishnah. 1933. Translated from the Hebrew with introduction and brief explanatory notes by Herbert Danby. London: Oxford University Press.

Neirynck, Frans. 1984. "John and the Synoptics: The Empty Tomb Stories." *NTS* 30:161-87.

_____. 1990. "John 21." *NTS* 36:321-36.

_____. 1992. "John and the Synoptics: 1975–1990." In *John and the Synoptics,* ed. Adelbert Denaux, 3-62. BETL 101. Leuven: Leuven University Press.

Neyrey, Jerome H. 1988. *An Ideology of Revolt: John's Christology in Social-Science Perspective*. Philadelphia: Fortress.

O'Day, Gail R. 1986. *Revelation in the Fourth Gospel: Narrative Mode and Theological Claim*. Philadelphia: Fortress.

The Odes of Solomon: The Syriac Texts. 1977. Edited with translation and notes by James Hamilton Charlesworth. SBLTT 13; Pseudepigrapha Series 7. Missoula, MT: Scholars Press.

Okure, Teresa. 1988. *The Johannine Approach to Mission: A Contextual Study of John 4:1-42*. WUNT 31 (2nd ser.) Tübingen: Mohr.

Painter, John. 1993. *The Quest for the Messiah: The History, Literature and Theology of the Johannine Community*. Rev. ed. Nashville: Abingdon.

_____. 1996. "Inclined to God: The Quest for Eternal Life— Bultmannian Hermeneutics and the Theology of the Fourth Gospel." In *EGJ*, 346-68. Louisville: Westminster John Knox.

Perkins, Pheme. 1984. *Resurrection: New Testament Witness and Contemporary Reflection*. Garden City, NY: Doubleday.

Petersen, Norman R. 1993. *The Gospel of John and the Sociology of Light: Language and Characterization in the Fourth Gospel*. Valley Forge, PA: Trinity Press International.

Philo. 1948. With an English Translation by F. H Colson. LCL. 10 vols. Cambridge, MA: Harvard University Press.

Rensberger, David. 1988. *Johannine Faith and Liberating Community*. Philadelphia: Westminster.

_____. 1997. *1 John, 2 John, 3 John*. ANTC. Nashville: Abingdon.

Sanders, E. P. 1977. *Paul and Palestinian Judaism: A Comparison of Patterns of Religion*. Philadelphia: Fortress.

_____. 1985. *Jesus and Judaism*. Philadelphia: Fortress.

_____. 1992. *Judaism, Practice and Belief: 63 BCE–66 CE*. Philadelphia: Trinity Press International.

_____. 1993. *The Historical Figure of Jesus*. London: Penguin.

Sanders, J. N. 1943. *The Fourth Gospel in the Early Church: Its Origin and Influence on Christian Theology Up to Irenaeus*. Cambridge: Cambridge University Press.

Schmidt, Karl Ludwig. 1923. Reprint 1981. "Die Stellung der Evangelien in der allgemeinen Literaturgeschichte." In *Neues Testament, Judentum, Kirche: Klein Schriften*, edited by Gerhard Sauter, 39-130. TBü 69. Munich: Kaiser.

Schneemelcher, Wilhelm, ed. 1991. *New Testament Apocrypha*. Translated and edited by R. McL. Wilson. 2 vols. Louisville: Westminster John Knox.

Schweizer, Eduard. 1996. "What About the Johannine 'Parables'?" In *EGJ*, 208-19. Louisville: Westminster John Knox.

Segovia, Fernando F. 1991. *The Farewell of the Word: The Johannine Call to Abide*. Minneapolis: Fortress.

Senior, Donald. 1991. *The Passion of Jesus in the Gospel of John*. Collegeville, MN: Liturgical Press.

_____. 1998. *Matthew*. ANTC. Nashville: Abingdon.

Smith, D. Moody. 1984. *Johannine Christianity: Essays on Its Sources, Setting, and Theology*. Columbia, SC: University of South Carolina Press.

_____. 1990. "The Contribution of J. Louis Martyn to the Understanding of the Gospel of John." In *The Conversation Continues: Studies in Paul and John in Honor of J. Louis Martyn*, edited by Robert T. Fortna and Beverly R. Gaventa, 274-94. Nashville: Abingdon.

_____. 1992. *John Among the Gospels: The Relationship in Twentieth Century Research*. Minneapolis: Fortress.

_____. 1995. *The Theology of the Gospel of John*. New Testament Theology, edited by J. D. G. Dunn. Cambridge: Cambridge University Press.

_____. 1996a. "John." In *Early Christian Thought in Its Jewish Context*, edited by John Barclay and John Sweet, 96-111. Cambridge: Cambridge University Press.

_____. 1996b. "The Love Command: John and Paul?" In *Theology and Ethics in Paul and His Interpreters: Essays in Honor of Victor Paul Furnish*, edited by Eugene H. Lovering Jr. and Jerry L. Sumney, 207-17. Nashville: Abingdon.

Smith, Dwight Moody, Jr. 1965. *The Composition and Order of the Fourth Gospel: Bultmann's Literary Theory.* Yale Publications in Religion 10. New Haven: Yale University Press.

Smith, Joseph Daniel. 1979. "Gaius and the Controversy Over the Johannine Literature." Ph.D. diss., Yale University.

Smith, Morton. 1973. *Clement of Alexandria and a Secret Gospel of Mark.* Cambridge, MA: Harvard University Press.

Swancutt, Diana M. 1997. "Hungers Assuaged by the Bread from Heaven: 'Eating Jesus' as Isaian Call to Belief: The Confluence of Isaiah 55 and Psalm 78 (77) in John 6:22-71." In *Early Christian Interpretation of the Scriptures of Israel: Investigations and Proposals,* edited by Craig A. Evans and James A. Sanders, 218-51. JSNTSup 148. Sheffield: Sheffield Academic Press.

Talbert, Charles H. 1977. *What Is a Gospel? The Genre of the Canonical Gospels.* Philadelphia: Fortress.

Thomas, John Christopher. 1991. *Footwashing in John 13 and the Johannine Community.* JSNTSup 61. Sheffield: Sheffield Academic Press.

Thompson, Marianne Meye. 1993. *The Incarnate Word: Perspectives on Jesus in the Fourth Gospel.* Peabody, MA: Hendrickson. Originally *The Humanity of Jesus in the Fourth Gospel.* Philadelphia: Fortress, 1988.

_____. 1996. "The Historical Jesus and the Johannine Christ." In *EGJ,* 21-42. Louisville: Westminster John Knox.

Thyen, Hartwig. 1971. "Johannes 13 und die 'kirchliche Redaktion' des vierten Evangeliums." In *Tradition und Glaube: Das Frühe Christentum in seiner Umwelt. Festgabe für Karl Georg Kuhn zum 65. Geburtstag,* edited by G. Jeremias, W. H. Kuhn, and H. Stegemann, 343-56. Göttingen: Vandenhoeck & Ruprecht.

Van Belle, Gilbert. 1988. *Johannine Bibliography 1966–1985: A Cumulative Bibliography on the Fourth Gospel.* BETL 82. Leuven: Leuven University Press.

van Tilborg, Sjef. 1993. *Imaginative Love in John.* Biblical Interpretation Series 2. Leiden: E. J. Brill.

_____. 1996. *Reading John in Ephesus.* NovTSup 83. Leiden: E. J. Brill.

Vermes, Geza, ed. 1995. *The Dead Sea Scrolls in English.* 4th ed. New York: Penguin.

Via, Dan O., Jr. 1961. "Darkness, Christ, and the Church in the Fourth Gospel." *SJT* 14: 172-93.

Wahlde, Urban C. von. 1989. *The Earliest Version of John's Gospel: Recovering the Gospel of Signs.* Wilmington, DE: Michael Glazier.

———. 1990. *The Johannine Commandments: 1 John and the Struggle for the Johannine Tradition.* Theological Inquiries: Studies in Contemporary Biblical and Theological Problems. New York: Paulist.

Wuellner, Wilhelm H. 1967. *The Meaning of "Fishers of Men."* NTL. Philadelphia: Westminster.

Yee, Gale A. 1989. *Jewish Feasts and the Gospel of John.* Zacchaeus Studies: New Testament. Wilmington, DE: Michael Glazier.

Young, F. W. 1955. "A Study of the Relation of Isaiah to the Fourth Gospel." *ZNW* 46:215-33.

COMMENTARIES (BOTH CITED AND NOT CITED)

Barrett, C. K. 1978. *The Gospel According to St. John: An Introduction with Commentary and Notes on the Greek Text.* 2nd. ed. Philadelphia: Westminster. — The standard English-language commentary on the Gospel of John. Its lasting value has been underscored by its translation into German for the standard MeyerK series.

Beasley-Murray, George R. 1987. *John.* WBC 36. Waco, TX: Word. — A moderately conservative, well-balanced commentary based on the original Greek text, although discussion of it is confined mostly to the notes and fine print so that English-only readers can use the commentary with profit.

Brodie, Thomas L. 1993. *The Gospel According to John: A Literary and Theological Commentary.* Oxford: Oxford University Press. — Distinguishes itself not only in its insistence on John's literary unity, but also by its emphasis on the Gospel's reflection of aspects and stages of human spirituality.

Brown, Raymond E. 1966, 1970. *The Gospel According to John.* AB. 2 vols. Garden City, NY: Doubleday. — A standard commentary on the English text, in Brown's own translation. Reliable, thorough, and balanced.

Bultmann, Rudolf. 1971. *The Gospel of John: A Commentary.* Translated by G. R. Beasley-Murray, R. W. N. Hoare, and J. K. Riches. Philadelphia: Westminster. — Perhaps the most theologically suggestive of modern commentaries. Despite its rather eccentric literary theory, this commentary is almost always worth consulting. More useful for the reader who does not know Greek than is Barrett (above).

Calvin, [John]. 1959. *The Gospel According to John.* Translated by T. H. L. Parker. 2 vols. Calvin's Commentaries. Grand Rapids, MI: Eerdmans. — Although Calvin draws from the Gospel valuable ammunition against his own theological opponents, he is not unaware of the historical distance involved and offers valuable exegetical and historical insights.

Carson, D. A. 1991. *The Gospel According to John.* Grand Rapids, MI: Eerdmans. — Written from an avowedly conservative point of view, both historically and theologically, this commentary nevertheless contains many valuable and accurate exegetical insights.

Culpepper, R. Alan. 1998. *The Gospel and Letters of John.* Interpreting Biblical Texts. Nashville: Abingdon. An introduction for the student or serious reader, this volume includes an excellent brief commentary on the Gospel of John prefaced by a substantial introduction.

Haenchen, Ernst. 1984. *John 1, John 2.* Translated by Robert W. Funk; edited by Ulrich Busse and Robert W. Funk. Hermeneia. Philadelphia: Fortress. — Because the author died before he could complete his work, this commentary is of uneven quality, but the bibliographies are excellent and the exegesis is sometimes penetrating.

Hoskyns, Edwyn Clement. 1947. *The Fourth Gospel.* Edited by Francis Noel Davey. London: Faber & Faber. — Although now somewhat out of date in light of the progress of historical research, this commentary is still worth consulting because of its profound probing of the theological issues that the text presents.

Kysar, Robert. 1986. *John.* Augsburg Commentary on the New Testament. Minneapolis: Augsburg. — A sound, middle-level commentary that will put the reader in touch with modern perspectives on the Gospel.

Lindars, Barnabas. 1972. *The Gospel of John.* New Century Bible Commentary. Grand Rapids, MI: Eerdmans. — Still a reliable and substantive commentary, although now perhaps being superseded by more recent works.

Malina, Bruce J., and Richard L. Rohrbaugh. 1998. *Social-Science Commentary on the Gospel of John.* Minneapolis: Fortress. — Although providing a fresh and significant perspective on John, this commentary should be supplemented by one of a more conventional approach.

Morris, Leon. 1995. *The Gospel According to John.* Rev. ed. NICNT. Grand Rapids, MI: Eerdmans. — Written from a conservative perspective; full of valuable information, carefully presented.

O'Day, Gail R. 1995. "The Gospel of John: Introduction, Commentary, and Reflections." In *NIB* 9, 494-865. Nashville: Abingdon. — A sound and insightful commentary that regularly suggests lines of connection with the contemporary theological and church scene.

Origen. 1986. "Commentary on John." In ANF. 5th ed. Edited by Allan Menzies. Grand Rapids, MI: Eerdmans. — After more than seventeen centuries Origen's extraordinary exegesis is still worth reading, as, among many other things, he insists on the originality of John and resists efforts to harmonize it with the other Gospels.

Schnackenburg, Rudolf. 1968, 1980, 1982. *The Gospel According to St John.* 3 vols. Translated by Kevin Smyth et al. HTCNT. New York: Herder & Herder; Seabury; Crossroad. — A large, rich, and sound commentary, always worth consulting. A groundbreaking Roman Catholic commentator, Schnackenburg is for the European scene what Raymond Brown has been for the American.

Sloyan, Gerard S. 1988. *John.* Interpretation: A Bible Commentary for Teaching and Preaching. Atlanta: John Knox. — A relatively brief, but reliable and useful commentary, which relates each pericope to its place in modern lectionaries.

Talbert, Charles H. 1992. *Reading John: A Literary and Theological Commentary on the Fourth Gospel and the Johannine Epistles.* New York: Crossroad. — An insightful and provocative commentary that places the Gospel alongside rather than before the Johannine Epistles and often provides excerpts from relevant Johannine and other sources in the text.

Witherington, Ben, III. 1995. *John's Wisdom: A Commentary on the Fourth Gospel.* Louisville: Westminster John Knox. — As the title indicates, a commentary that emphasizes the role of biblical Wisdom, not only in the prologue but throughout the Gospel.

INDEX

Christianity
and Christians, 195, 197, 352
hellenistic, 42
Petrine, 402
See also community, Johannine; Judaism; theology, ecclesiology.
Christology. *See* theology, Christology.
chronology, of Jesus' ministry and death, 250, 258, 362, 364-65
church. *See* community, Johannine; theology, ecclesiology.
Church of the Holy Sepulchre, 355-56, 357, 365
circumcision, 171-72
Clement of Alexandria, and characterization of the Gospel, 29
commands
from the Father, 209, 246
of Jesus, obedience to, 246, 252, 273, 275-76, 278, 281, 284, 285, 287, 308, 321
See also disciple(s); love; theology.
community, Johannine, 57-65, 80-81, 195, 229, 231, 248, 261, 286, 288, 294, 295-98, 307, 317-18, 320, 379, 381, 399, 402, 403
See also Christianity; theology, ecclesiology.
conclusion of the Gospel
first, 385-89
second, 401-6
conflict, of Jesus and his followers,
with chief priests, 166, 173, 176, 228-32, 235, 237, 323, 329, 332-38, 339, 342, 346, 350-51, 357, 363
and desire to kill Jesus, 146, 166, 170, 178, 185, 187, 189, 212, 228-32
and expulsion from synagogue(s), 28, 36-37, 41-42, 134, 161, 180, 194-95, 201, 228, 235, 244, 291
and fear of the Jews, 28, 35, 38, 41, 44, 81, 96, 129-43, 146, 161, 169, 171, 173, 176, 178-90, 190-202, 203-16, 288-89, 299, 308, 310, 333, 336, 341, 343, 346-48, 349-50, 353-54, 359, 363, 365, 367, 379
with Pharisees, 35, 133, 139, 166, 172-73, 176, 190-202, 203-16, 228-29, 231-32, 244, 299, 308, 329, 346
Twelfth Benediction *(birkat ha-minim),* 37-38, 42, 195-96

See also Christ-confessors; demons; disciple(s); dualism; Jamnia; Jesus; Jews, the; Judaism; misunderstanding; opposition; Passion; Pharisees; Roman(s); Sanhedrin; synagogue; world.
Council, the. *See* Sanhedrin.
Counselor, the. *See* Advocate, the.
creation, 49-54, 56, 63, 312, 321
See also word.
criticism
form 22, 325
tradition, 326-27
cross, 238, 320, 352, 354-59, 364, 370
inscription on, 357
crucifixion, the, 34, 39, 56, 90, 184, 252, 259, 287, 305-6, 341, 347, 353-54, 356, 359, 365, 380, 389, 397
dating of, 324
place of, 357, 373
See also flesh; Passion.

darkness at noon, 355
David, 328
See also Messiah.
Dead Sea Scrolls, 34-35, 42, 53, 55, 67, 77, 100, 181, 241, 268, 296, 301
See also Judaism.
death. *See* glorification; Passion.
demon(s), 41, 171, 187-89, 209, 226
See also conflict, of Jesus and his followers; exorcism.
descent. *See* theology, Christology, descent-ascent.
Deuteronomy, 56, 118, 120, 126, 131, 175, 177, 194, 265
See also law; Scripture.
devil, 185-87, 251
See also Satan.
Diatessaron, 24
disciple(s)
actions of, 255
address to, by Jesus, 203, 208, 308-22
call of, 65, 71-80, 390-91
and confession, 178, 370
defection of, 161-63
expulsion of, from synagogue, 36, 194-96, 244, 291
Jesus' continuing presence among, 264, 266-67, 271-73, 275-78, 283-87, 295-96, 299-300
Jesus' friendship and love for, 218, 225, 250, 259, 261-62